SUKARNO: An Autobiography

SUKARNO

An Autobiography

As told to CINDY ADAMS

THE BOBBS-MERRILL COMPANY, INC.

A SUBSIDIARY OF HOWARD W. SAMS & CO., INC.

PUBLISHERS · INDIANAPOLIS · KANSAS CITY · NEW YORK

BS9475A

"Understanding is a wellspring of life unto him that hath it."

PROVERBS 16:22

TO THE UNDERSTANDING OF SUKARNO AND WITH THAT
A BETTER UNDERSTANDING OF MY BELOVED INDONESIA.

Contents

List of Illustrations

❧ I. The Reason for Writing This Book

THE simplest way to describe Sukarno is to say that he is a great lover. He loves his country, he loves his people, he loves women, he loves art, and, best of all, he loves himself.

Sukarno is a man of feeling—an appreciator. He takes a deep breath when he sees a beautiful scene. He waxes lyrical at an Indonesian sunset. He cries when he sings a Negro spiritual.

It has been said of me, "The President of the Republic of Indonesia has too much of the character of a man of the arts." But I thank the Almighty that I was born with sentiment and artistry. How else could I have become The Great Leader of the Revolution, as my 105 million people call me? How else could I have led my nation back to freedom and its own birthright after three and a half centuries of Dutch domination? How else could I have made a revolution in 1945 and created one unified Indonesia out of Java, Bali, Sumatra, Borneo, the Spice Islands, and the rest of the Netherlands East Indies?

The rhythm of a revolution is destruction and construction. Construction calls for the soul of an architect. And in the soul of an architect are the elements of feeling and artistry. The art of guiding a revolution is to find inspiration in everything you see. Can a person find inspiration in anything if he is not a man of feeling and a bit of the artist?

But not everyone agrees with Sukarno's description of Sukarno. They do not all see that the way to approach me is strictly through the heart—that I am like a child. Give me a banana coupled with a little sympathy from a loving heart and I'll kiss you forever. But give me a thousand million dollars and at the same time slap my hand in public, then, though it may mean my life's blood, I say to you, "Go to hell."

Indonesians run on emotion. Ours is the only nation in the world with a special pillow just for hugging. In every Indonesian bed there's one pillow to sleep on plus a long, narrow, round bolster called a *guling*. The *guling*'s sole *raison d'être* is for us to hug during the night.

I become the most lovable person in the world when I feel a wave of friendship, sympathy with my problems, understanding, and affection come out to greet me. Even when it's unspoken I can feel it. And even when dislike is unspoken, I can feel that, too. Either way I react instinctively.

One high-ranking British diplomat still doesn't see that the key to Sukarno turns easily if it is oiled with love. In a recent letter to Ten Downing Street he wrote, "President Sukarno is ungovernable, unpredictable and uncontrollable. He is like a cornered rat."

A nice word for a man who has devoted his entire life to his country; a man who spent over 13 years in prison and exile because he believed in an ideal. Maybe I didn't see eye to eye with him on everything—but a rat? My heart stopped dead when this letter came into my possession. He finished by saying he'd see to it that Sukarno gets "the worst possible press."

I haven't slept in six years. I just can't sleep anymore. Sometimes, late at night, I phone someone close to me, perhaps Subandrio, my First Deputy Prime Minister, and I say, "Bandrio, come and sit with me, keep me company, talk to me of silly things, tell me a joke, say anything as long as it's not political. And if I fall asleep, please forgive me." I read all night, think all night, and I am up at five every morning. For the first time I've begun taking sleeping pills. I'm tired. So tired.

I am not a faultless man. Every human being makes mistakes. On several holy days I publicly asked forgiveness of my people for the mistakes I know I have made plus those I am not aware of. Perhaps one fault is that I'm always pursuing ideals instead of cold facts. I'm constantly trying to subdue or remake circumstances so they can be vehicles to reach what I'm pursuing. The result is that, although I try so hard for my people, I fall victim to vicious attacks.

People ask, "Sukarno, does it bother you when people criticise you?" Of course it does. I hate being scolded. Am I not human like everybody else? If you cut even a Chief of State he will bleed. Sure I want to be liked. I have an ego. I admit it. But nobody without an ego could weld 10,000 islands into a nation. And I am vain. But who is not? Doesn't everyone like to be applauded?

I recall a day when I faced two conflicting reports about myself. Sometimes a chief executive doesn't know what to believe. The first appeared in the pages of *Look* magazine. *Look* had claimed the Indonesian people were all against me. They printed an article quoting a *betjak* driver, the Indonesian equivalent of a taxi driver, as supposedly saying that things were terrible and that even the peasantry were tired of Sukarno now.

I finished the article at five P.M., and was just about to take my usual half-hour walk within the palace compound—that's about my only exercise—when a highly nervous police official was ushered in. I asked him to tell me what was on his mind as we walked.

"Well, Bapak," he began, "it is basically good news." *Bapak* and *Pak* mean "father" and are the affectionate terms my people apply to me.

"What do you mean, basically good news?" I asked.

"Well," he said, "the people are very much for you. They love you. And that goes especially for the lower classes. I know because I have just witnessed a show of their regard for you." Then he stopped.

"Go on," I urged. "Tell me. Where were you and whom did you visit and what did they do?"

"It's like this, Pak," he began. "We have this area where all the prostitutes are. Periodically we spot-check the district because it is our duty to keep them under constant surveillance. Yesterday, a team went in to inspect the conditions and do you know what they found? They found your photo, Pak. Right on the wall."

"Where am I hanging?" I asked him.

"In every single room, Pak. In every room there's, naturally, a bed. Next to every bed there's a table and directly over the table—there's you. You look right down on everything that's happening!"

He peered at me nervously, awaiting orders. "Sir, we are happy our people revere you, but we wonder if it's right for our President to be on the wall looking down on . . . the whole thing. What shall we do? Shall we remove your photos from the walls?"

"Certainly not," I said. "Leave me there. Let my tired old eyes look!"

Nobody today inspires as much conflicting emotion as Sukarno. I am cursed like a villain and worshiped like a god.

It is not uncommon for old men to make pilgrimages to Bapak before they die. One old fisherman who wanted no favors walked 23 days just to prostrate himself before me and kiss my feet. He said he had promised himself that before he dies he would see his President and show his love and devotion to him.

Many believe I am a god with supernatural healing powers. A coconut farmer whose son was desperately ill dreamed he must come to Bapak and ask for water for his son—just plain running tap water from the kitchen. He believed that this water which I personally fetched would contain medicinal properties. I could not argue with him because the Javanese are mystics, and he was convinced his son would die without this gift from my hand. I gave it to him. One week later the boy was completely well.

I constantly make trips to varying parts of my country from Sabang, the northernmost part of Sumatra, to Merauke, which is in West Irian and farthest east. A few years back I visited a tiny village in Central Java. A woman of the village came up to my servant and whispered, "Don't let them take away the President's plate. Please let me have whatever he's left. I'm pregnant and I want a son and I want him to be like Bapak. So, please, just let me eat something that my President has personally touched."

On the island of Bali they believe Sukarno is the reincarnation of Vishnu, the Hindu Rain God, because whenever Bapak comes to the small resthouse I designed and built for myself outside the capital city of Den Pasar, even if it be in the midst of a season-long drought, it means rain. The Balinese are convinced I bring them blessings. The last time I flew to Bali they had been suffering from a dry spell. Just after I arrived, the heavens opened.

Quite frankly, I say a prayer of thanks when it rains during my stay at Tampaksiring because, if ever it didn't, it would hurt my prestige.

But the world reads only about one *betjak* driver. They read only that Sukarno is not an economist. That is true. I am not. But was Kennedy? Is Johnson? Is that a reason for a Western magazine to report that my country is about to suffer economic collapse? Or that it's a "ramshackle nation"? Or to headline one story: "Let's Move on Sukarno"?

If journalists had a bad heart for Japan or the Philippines they could cite certain areas there where whole families—mother, father, and children—commit suicide because of starvation. This is all well known. But no. Only about "The Bad Man of Asia" do they print photographs of people suffering from food shortage due to drought and a plague of rats while in the background they feature my magnificent new hotel. And then the caption: "Sukarno's Indonesia."

But that is NOT Sukarno's Indonesia. Sukarno's Indonesia today can boast a 100 percent literacy rate under the age of 45. When our nation was born 20 years ago we had a six percent literacy rate.

Sukarno's Indonesia is today a nation that is two inches taller than the previous generation. Could children be growing on starvation?

But journalists keep writing that I'm a "Slave of Moscow." Let's get this straight once and for all. I am not, have never been, and could never be a Communist. Me bow down to Moscow? Anybody who ever came near Sukarno knows he has too much ego to be a slave to anybody—except his people. But journalists don't print what's right with Sukarno. They only point up what's wrong with Sukarno.

They like to show my glamorous Indonesia hotel and behind it pictures of slums. The reason "this man who wastes money" built it was to catch the foreign capital we could not otherwise get. We took in two million U.S. dollars its first year of operation. I know we have slums nearby, but rich countries, too, have glittering, lush, million-dollar hotels and around the corner condemned buildings filled with refuse, rot, and decay. I saw the rich in all their pomp driving in shining sedans, but I also saw unfortunates clawing through garbage cans for potato peels. There are slums in all the cities of the world, not just in Sukarno's Djakarta.

The West always accuses me of turning too sweet a face to the Socialist States. "Ooohhhh," they say, "there goes Sukarno playing friendly to the Eastern Bloc again." Well, why not? The Russians never permitted anyone to jeer at me in print. The Chinese always praise Sukarno. They don't embarrass me around the world or treat me like a spoiled child in public by refusing any more candy unless I'm a good boy. People's China always tries to win Sukarno's heart. Khrushchev sent me jams and jellies every two weeks and handpicked apples, corn, and other vegetables from the best of his crop. So am I wrong to be grateful to them? Who can help being nice to those who are nice to him? I have tried to pursue a neutral policy, yes! But down deep in his soul who can blame me for saying, "Thank you, people from the East, for always showing me friendship, for not trying to hurt me. Thank you for telling your citizens Sukarno is at least trying the best he can for his country. Thank you for your gifts." What I am expressing is gratitude—not Communism!

I'm picked on for so many things. Why does he travel so much, my enemies always ask. In June, 1960, following a two-month, four-day tour to India, Hungary, Austria, the United Arab Republic, Guinea, Tunis, Morocco, Portugal, Cuba, Puerto Rico, San Francisco, Hawaii and Japan, I was told a phrase had been coined for me. I did not even know what "Have 707 Will Travel" meant until an American friend explained it. It is true I am the only President who takes so many trips. I have been everywhere except London, although the Queen of England has invited me two times. I hope someday to accept her hospitality.

There is a reason why I travel. I want to make Indonesia known. I want the world to see what Indonesians look like, and to see that we are no longer "a stupid nation of toads," as the Dutch repeatedly told us we were; that no more are we "dumb natives good only to spit on," as they told us over and over; that no more are we second-class citizens who slink around in sarongs with handkerchiefs on our heads perpetually bowing as our former colonial masters demanded.

After the Chinese People's Republic, India, the Soviet Union, and the United States of America, we are fifth in the world in terms of population. Three thousand of our islands are inhabitable. But do you know how many people don't know Indonesia? Or where we're situated? Or whether we're brown, black, yellow, or white? But what they do know is the name of Sukarno. And they know the face of Sukarno.

They don't know we're the world's largest archipelago and that we extend 5,000 kilometers, or across all the nations of Europe from the continent's western shores to its remotest eastern border. They don't know that after Australia we're the sixth largest country in size, with two million square miles of land. They usually aren't aware we lie between two continents, Asia and Australia, and two bodies of water, the Pacific and the Indian oceans; or that we grow the world's best coffee, which is how the expression "a cup of Java" originated; or that Indonesia is the largest oil producer in Southeast Asia and the second largest tin producer in the world, and after the U.S.A. and the U.S.S.R. is the richest country in the universe in terms of natural resources; or that one of every four American automobile tires is manufactured of Indonesian rubber. But what they do know is the name of Sukarno. My Foreign Service tells me one visit of Sukarno to a country is worth 10 years of ambassadors. And that is why I travel and why I always give the facts about my country in every speech I make in every corner of the globe. I want to educate the foreigners and give them their first glimpse of this beloved green land of mine which winds itself around the equator like a girdle of emeralds.

One day my secretary delivered a letter addressed simply "President Sukarno, Indonesia, South East Asia." The writer said he had heard I didn't allow freedom of the press and is that true and if so what a tyrant I am. The man who wrote this crank letter called me a despot. He insulted me, but this I didn't mind. You know what infuriated me? The fact that he didn't think the post office knew where Indonesia was and so he added "South East Asia" to the address!

Public opinion goes in waves. In 1956, when I first visited the United States of America, everybody there loved me. Today it is the fashion to be against Sukarno. However, I have been taken advantage of. Recently I was handed an American girlie magazine. It showed a picture of a half-naked strip-tease girl wearing only panties and standing next to Sukarno in full military dress. It was a combination pasted together to look like a photo of a strip-tease girl undressing herself in front of the President of the Republic of Indonesia. The two photographs are superimposed. This is a filthy thing to do to a Chief of State. Do I have to love America when she does such things to me?

I discussed this kind of tactic with President Kennedy, whom I respected very much. John F. Kennedy and I liked each other at once. He said, "President Sukarno, I admire you greatly. Like myself you have a searching, inquiring mind. You've read everything. You're very well informed." Then he discussed the ideologies I promoted and quoted passages from my speeches. Kennedy had a human approach. We found much in common.

Kennedy was very warm and friendly to me. He took me upstairs to his private bedroom, and there we had our talk.

I said to him, "Look here, are you aware that while you personally might be cementing a friendship, you can often spoil relations with foreign countries by ridiculing, lampooning, or permitting constant criticism of their leaders in your press? Sometimes we may be inclined to act or react more strongly because we are hurt or angered. After all, what is international relations but human relations on a larger scale? This type of continual harpooning ruptures harmony and strains the already difficult relationships between other countries and yours even more than necessary."

"I agree with you, President Sukarno. I, too, have had difficulties with our newspapermen," he sighed. "But, fortunately or unfortunately, freedom of the press is part of the American heritage."

"When Alben Barkley was Vice-President of the United States of America, he visited my country," I said. "And I myself stood right alongside him the day he was being kissed by a swarm of beautiful young girls."

"I'm quite sure Vice-President Barkley must have enjoyed himself immensely," Kennedy chuckled.

"Nonetheless, not one Indonesian paper would print it and

thereby run the risk of embarrassing a statesman around the world. He was a very jolly man and perhaps would not have minded had the picture been released. But that is not the issue. The point is we believe in protecting world leaders in our country."

Kennedy sympathized with this greatly and confided to me, "You are perfectly right, but what can I do? Even I am cursed in my own country."

So I said, "Well, that is your system. If you are cursed at home, I cannot help it. But I don't think I should suffer the same indignities in your country that its own Chief of State must suffer. Your *Time* and *Life* have been particularly nasty to me. Look here, *Time* said, Sukarno can't see a skirt without getting sexy. Always they say bad things. Never the good things I've done."

Although President Kennedy and I had a meeting of the minds, this small circle of agreement never widened to the American press. Still, day after day, they picture me as a Don Juan.

Yes, yes, yes, I love women. Yes. I admit it. But I am not a playboy the way they make me out to be. In Tokyo I have gone with friends to a Geisha House. There's nothing immoral about a Geisha House. You just sit, and have dinner, conversation, and some music. That's all. But it's played up in the Western periodicals as though I were *Le Grand Seducteur*.

Without these little enjoyments, I will die. I love life. Foreigners who visit me claim I run a "happy palace." My ADC's have smiling faces. I joke with them, sing with them. If I don't have fun, songs, and a little entertainment occasionally I will be crushed by this life. I am 64 years old. Being President is an aging job. And when one gets old, it's not particularly good for anybody. So, I must escape once in a while to keep myself alive.

Many simple pleasures are taken from me. For instance, since childhood I've traveled throughout my native Java by bicycle. Now I can't take such a ride without hundreds of thousands following. In Hollywood I was given a tour through the movie studios. Coming off the lot I saw a mailboy pedal by and then park his cycle for the moment. I was feeling gay and jovial so I got on and took off. I wasn't impressing anyone. Just feeling happy. Well, the reverberations and photographs reached all the way around the world. In my own country I can no longer even engage in the most satisfying enjoyment of all: rummaging through art shops looking for treasures and then bargaining for them. Wherever I go mobs congregate.

My doctor has observed that joy is essential for my health. I am then able to get out of myself and my jail for a bit. For that's what my existence is. A prison. The prison of protocol. The prison of decency. The prison of good manners.

Everybody must do something to escape. Ayub Khan goes golfing, Kennedy went sailing, Prince Norodom Sihanouk writes music, the King of Thailand plays the saxophone, Lyndon Johnson has his ranch. I, too, need pleasure. So, whenever I travel, I permit myself the luxury of engaging in the pursuit of happiness. According to the Constitution of the United States of America, everybody is entitled to that.

Being President of necessity makes one lonely. Those qualities that enable one to rise to the Presidency are the same qualities that set him apart. However, to the outsider I am always in high spirits. My personality is such that my extreme unhappiness never shows. Though I may be bleeding inside you can never tell. Isn't Sukarno famous for his "smiling"? No matter what my problems—Malaysia, poverty, another assassination attempt—on the surface Sukarno is always gay.

Many times I sit on my verandah in *Istana Merdeka—Istana* means "palace," *Merdeka* means "freedom"—all by myself. It's not a very magnificent verandah. Semienclosed with awnings to deflect the heat and sun, its sole furnishings are unupholstered, unpainted rattan chairs and tables covered with *batik,* the handpainted cloth of my country. The only concession made to my High Office is one lone chair with a pillow on it. That's called "The President's Chair." And I just sit there. And stare. And look out at the beautiful, restful garden which I planted with my own hands. And I feel very lonely inside.

I like to mix with the people. Essentially that is my nature. And I no longer can. Often I feel I will suffocate, my breathing will stop, if I don't get out and mingle with my own, the common people who gave birth to me.

At times I become like Harun al-Rashid. I drive around the city—alone—with just one aide in civilian clothes behind the wheel. I feel sometimes I just must escape from the problems and feel the rhythm of my country's heartbeat. The problems are always with me like a great, dark shadow looming behind me. I can never get away from them. I can never get beyond their grip. I can never get ahead of them. It's like a big, evil spirit always hounding me.

The uniform and black *pitji* cap are my trademarks. But, occasionally, late at night, I change into open sandals and slacks, and when it's very hot I wear only my underwear top. With the addition of horn-rimmed spectacles I look entirely different. I can and do wander the streets totally unrecognized. It's because I have to see life. I'm a man of the people. I must see them, listen to them, rub against them. I'm happiest when I'm among them. They are the bread of life for me. I feed off the masses.

I listen to their talk. I hear arguments, jokes, romance. And I feel that vitality course through my body.

We go in a tiny, unmarked motorcar. Sometimes I stop and buy *sate* from a sidewalk vendor. *Sate* is barbecued meat served on a stick. I sit on a curb all alone and eat my delicacies from a banana leaf. These are happy hours for me.

My people will recognize me only if they hear my voice. Then they know me immediately. One night I secretly went to Senen, Dja-karta's railroad depot, with my Police Commissioner. I wandered around among the people and nobody even looked up. Finally, to make some conversation, I said to one man, "Where are you taking those bricks and construction materials that you have piled up here?"

Before he could answer, there was a shout. "Hey," cried a woman. "That's Bapak's voice . . . Yes . . . Bapak's voice . . . Hey, every-body, that's Bapak . . . Bapak. . . ." Within seconds a huge crowd gathered. The Commissioner whisked me out of there fast, into our little car, and drove away.

On the whole the Presidency is like solitary confinement. I have a few friends. Not many. Often it is the people's attitude that changes, not yours. They treat you differently. They help to create this island of loneliness around you. So, when I am away from my prison, I try to enjoy myself. In Tokyo I might go to Kokusai Gekijo, where they feature four hundred beautiful girls on stage at one time. In 1963 I discovered my then Ambassador to Japan had never visited there. I twitted him, "Hey, Bambang Sugeng, you are a poor ambassador. A diplomat should taste every kind of life in the country to which he's assigned. Come. . . . Let us go look at the girls."

I also invited a professionally righteous Indonesian who gets shocked when his President discusses women. This man ogled all the beauties, and then stood up, saying, "I can't stand it. I have to leave. It excites me too much." He is a hypocrite. I hate hypocrites.

Of course, now and again my reputation makes me a victim of circumstances. In the Philippines in January, 1964, President

Diosdado Macapagal met me at the airport. He escorted me to the Laurels Mansion, where I was to live. In it were Mr. Laurels, former President of the Philippines, his wife, and their children and grand-children. To make my arrival more festive, they had arranged for their Bayanihan Cultural Ensemble to greet me with The Lenso, an Indonesian dance, in my honor. Two young ladies detached them-selves from the ensemble and requested me to join the dance. One could hardly refuse so I started to dance and . . . BOOM! Flash-bulbs! Snapshots! And the caption: There goes Sukarno the woman-chaser all over again.

I like attractive girls around me because I feel they are like flowers, and I like to gaze at beautiful flowers. In 1946, during those terrible days of the Revolution, the wife of my second secretary was summoned every morning just to crack my breakfast eggs. Oh, I could have cracked them myself, but my wife never got up that early and I have always felt more serene and confident in the face of tensions when I see something smiling around me.

I enjoy young women around my office. When visitors remark about my youthful female adjutants, I joke, "A woman is like a rubber tree. She's not good after thirty years." Let's say I react better to women. They're more understanding—more sympathetic. I find them refreshing. Women just have it for me. Again, I do not mean just physically. I'm drawn to a soft look or something that appears pretty. As an artist, I gravitate naturally toward what pleases the senses.

Late in the day I'm tired. I'm often so exhausted I can barely move a muscle. If some big, unattractive ugly bald male secretary came up with a huge file of documents for me to sign, I would scream at him to go away and leave me alone. Pieces of his skin would actually fall off from the shock waves. I would thunder at him. I would bring down lightning on his head. But when a slim, well-groomed, sweet-smelling girl secretary smiles gently and purrs softly, "Pak, please . . . ," you know what happens? No matter how irritable I am, I get calm. And always I say, "Okay."

In 1961 I was seriously ill. In Vienna they removed a stone from my kidney. This was at the height of our West Irian campaign and among our adversaries there was rejoicing. No need to curse Sukarno or wish him dead anymore, for Sukarno was now at the point of dying. The doctor, therefore, took extra special care of me. He soothed, "Don't worry, President Sukarno, we'll give you the most experienced nurses available." Uggghhh!!! When he said that I was

sicker than when I came in. I knew what to expect. I said nothing because I didn't want to offend the doctor. After all, next day he was
operating on me and I wanted him to like me while he was doing it.
But I thought to myself, "I would recuperate much faster with the
unexperienced nurses because those with the 40 years' experience are
at least 55 years old!"

People say Sukarno likes to look out of the corner of his eye at
beautiful women. Why do they say that? It is not true. Sukarno likes
to look out of his *whole* eye at beautiful women. But this is not a
crime. Even Mohammed admired beauty. And as a devout Moslem I
am a follower of the Prophet Mohammed, who said, "A God who can
make such beautiful creatures as women is a great and good God." I
agree with him.

As the story goes, Mohammed had a slave named Said. Said, the
first convert to Islam, had a very beautiful wife named Zainab. When
Mohammed saw Zainab he uttered the Islamic words usually reserved
for the beginning of a prayer. He said, *"Allahu Akbar."* God is great.

When his disciples asked why he uttered *"Allahu Akbar"* at seeing Zainab, he answered, "I just praised God for making creatures as
beautiful as this woman."

I revere the Prophet. I study his words. Thus, the moral to me is
that it's not sinful or immoral to admire a handsome female. And I'm
not ashamed to do so because when I do I am in reality praising God
and what He has made.

I am simply an outright lover of beauty. I collect bronzes from
Budapest, marble from Italy, paintings from everywhere. For *Istana
Negara*, the State Palace in Djakarta, I personally shopped for the
heavy crystal chandeliers and gold cut-velvet chairs in Europe. I
handpicked rugs in Iraq. I designed my office desk from one uncut
piece of Indonesian *djati* wood. I designed my State dining-room
table from one enormous slab of Indonesian teakwood. I hung every
tapestry, selected every item of bric-a-brac, planned where each vase
or sculpture should stand.

If I spy a scrap of paper on the floor I myself will stoop to pick
it up. Members of my Cabinet laugh about how, in the middle of
important matters, I walk over and straighten their ties. I enjoy food
attractively arranged on a table. I love beauty in every form.

Visiting the State Palace in Bogor, a Texan fell in love with one
of my *objets d'art*. He tried to make a deal with me. "Mr. President,"
he boomed, "I tell you what I'll do for you. I'll give you a Cadillac

for it." I told him . . . well, never mind what I told him. But the point was, "NO!"

I would not give one of my magnificent pieces which I treasure for any Cadillac. If I love someone, I give him a painting or tapestry as a gift! But never ever would I sell it. I'll leave it all to the Indonesian people when I go. Let them put it into a National Museum. Then, if they are restless or disturbed, let them sit in front of a painting and feed on its beauty and stillness until it fills their soul with peace as it has done mine. Yes, I will leave my art to my people. But sell it? Never!

One foreigner who understands me was the American Ambassador to Indonesia, Howard Jones. He had been stationed in Djakarta seven years and was the dean of our diplomatic corps. We engaged in bloody, bitter battles, yet I grew to consider him a dear friend. Howard's description of me is "a cross between Franklin Delano Roosevelt and Clark Gable." Is it any wonder I consider him a dear friend?

One Sunday a few years ago, he and his wife, Marylou, lunched with me and my wife, Hartini, in our little pavilion in Bogor, the cool mountain region outside Djakarta. Contrary to the belief that I have solid gold faucets as befits an Oriental potentate, I do not live in the great State Palace. On the grounds we have a small bungalow (about the size appropriate to a caretaker). It has a couple of small bedrooms, a tiny dining area and a very little living room. It is scarcely lavish. It is very simple. But it is cozy and it is my home.

At the table Howard said, "Mr. President, I think it is time for you to look down the lanes of history. It appears to me the moment is right for you to set down your life story."

As usual, whenever anyone mentioned an autobiography, I answered, "Absolutely not. *Inshallah,* God willing, I have another 10 or 20 years. How do I know what may come of me? Who can tell what my future holds? That's why I have always refused this because I am convinced the balance of life of man can only be made after death."

"Except that the President of the Republic of Indonesia has been Chief of State for 20 years," he answered. "He was elected President for life. He is one of the most debated and criticised men of our times. He. . . ."

". . . has many secrets," I chuckled.

"But he is the only one who can dare tell them and thereby answer the questions of his critics—and friends."

This had been an informal social occasion. I was in sport shirt and bare feet. Hartini had made *nasi goreng* because she knows the Joneses love chicken-fried rice, and the President was eating *puluk*—meaning with his fingers—and we sat across a full table having a pleasant, relaxed time as only old friends can. I sighed, "For a real autobiography, the writer must be in a sad mood as was Rousseau when he wrote his *Confessions,* and such a confessional would prove difficult for me. Many are still alive who would suffer if I told all, and governments with whom I am now on good terms would be seriously offended if I said some of the things I would like to say."

"Nonetheless, Mr. President, foreigners change their attitudes after meeting you and falling under that old Bung Karno magnetic personality. With your personal charm going full speed, even hostile critics leave saying, 'Hey, he doesn't really breathe smoke and fire like a dragon. He's very pleasant.' "

"It's because I am basically friendly," I explained. "I love Easterners, Westerners . . . even Tunku Abdul Rahman and the British. Even those who hate me. I am never vindictive even against those who speak ill of me. Any time they want to be friendly, I'm more than willing. Once I understood De Gaulle disliked me. Even so I met with him in Vienna. After that he liked me."

"That's my point," continued Jones. "You can't meet the world personally, but you can meet them through the pages of a book. You're the greatest orator since William Jennings Bryan. You captivate audiences of a million just across an open lot. Why not reach an even larger audience?"

This discussion lasted on to the dessert, boiled banana, a favorite of mine. "Look here," I finally said. "An autobiography isn't worthy unless the writer feels his life is good for nothing. If he believes he's a great man, the work becomes subjective. Not objective. My autobiography could only be a balance. So much good to ease my own ego and so much bad so that people would buy the book. Put in only good and people will call you egotistical because you praise yourself. Put in only bad and it creates the wrong mental atmosphere for your own people. Only after death can the world honestly weigh, 'Was Sukarno a good man or a bad man?' He can be judged only then."

For years, people have urged me to pen my memoirs. My Press Officer, Mrs. Siel Rachmulyadi, is always the intermediary.

Once I really cursed dear Rocky. In 1960, when Khrushchev was here, 100 foreign newsmen swarmed all over, constantly underfoot.

At one point she said, "Bapak, please don't holler, but not even we know your early background and you've granted very few interviews, so could you please do me a tiny favor and say hello to a nice man from CBS who wants to write your biography?" I turned on her and hollered, "How often must I tell you, 'N-O'! Firstly, I don't know him and, anyway, if I ever wrote my life story I'd do it with a woman. Now, get out of my sight. You're a lackey for foreign newsmen. You're nothing but an *Ouwe Hoer* . . ." That's Dutch for a not very nice term. Rocky stormed out and went home.

Later I was sorry. My aide telephoned and said I wanted to see her. Then I sent my car for her. She walked in expecting to be reprimanded but, instead, her President asked forgiveness.

"Please forgive me, Rocky," I apologized. "I shout and call names sometimes, but that's me. Don't take it personally. When I fly off it means I love you. I holler at all my nearest and dearest. They're my only sounding boards." Then I kissed her on the cheek, which is my normal method of hello and goodbye with my female secretaries—and she left perfectly happy.

That is why Asian problems must be solved in the Asian way. My manner is not exactly the Western style, I think. I cannot see a British Prime Minister hugging his secretary good morning or apologizing after she has stormed out and left him flat.

Little did I know that shortly after this incident I would meet Cindy Adams. Cindy, a newspaperwoman, was in Djakarta in 1961 with her husband, comedian Joey Adams, who was heading President Kennedy's Cultural Exchange Troupe to Southeast Asia. This gay, chic, American lady with her sense of humor fascinated me. Cindy's interview was pleasant and painless. Her story was honest and truthful. She even seemed a little sympathetic to Indonesia and its problems . . . and, anyway, she's the prettiest writer I've ever seen!

We Javanese work on instinct. I'd searched for the right female press officer for a year, but when I met Rocky I knew she was it. I hired her immediately. It was the same with Cindy.

The next time Howard Jones raised the subject of my life story, I surprised him. I grinned, "On one condition. That I collaborate with Cindy Adams."

And what finally decided me to do my autobiography? Well, perhaps it is true the time is approaching when I must realize I am getting old. Now, my poor old eyes tear. I must start looking at the picture with reason. The other morning a niece paid me a visit. I used to bounce her on my lap when she was an infant. Today she weighs 70 kilos. I realized with a shock that no longer could I take her on my knee. She would probably crush my tired old leg. Of course, a beautiful woman still makes me feel young at heart, but when I recognized that this infant was now the mother of several herself, I knew I was getting old.

And so the time has come. If I am ever to set my story down, I must do it now. I may not have the opportunity later. I know people are curious as to whether or not Sukarno was a Japanese collaborator during the Second World War. I suppose only Sukarno can explain that period of his life and so it seems right he should. For years people have asked: Is Sukarno a dictator? Is he a Communist? Why doesn't he allow freedom of the press? How many wives does he have? Why does he build new department stores when his citizens are in rags . . . ?

Only Sukarno himself can answer.

This is a hard job for me. An autobiography is like mental surgery. It's painful. Tearing the adhesive tape off one's memory and opening those wounds—many of which have barely begun to heal—hurts. Also, I shall be doing this in English, a foreign language for me. I make mistakes in my grammar sometimes and often I end up feeling a little frustration.

But perhaps I owe this story to my country, to my nation, to my children, to myself. Therefore, I pray you to remember that better than the language of the written word is the language of the heart. This book is not written to curry favor or beg anybody to like me. I hope only to be able to contribute to a better understanding of Sukarno and with that a better understanding of my beloved Indonesia.

⊰ 2. Child of the Dawn

WHEN I was a small child, maybe two years old, Mother pronounced a benediction on me. She had risen before sunrise and was sitting motionless in the dark on the verandah of our little house, doing nothing, saying nothing, just looking toward the East and patiently watching the break of day.

I, too, got up and came to her. She stretched forth her arms and, gathering me to her bosom, she hugged me silently. Moments later she slowly turned me around so that I, too, faced the East. Then she said softly, "Son, you are looking at the sunrise. And you, my son, will be a man of glory, a great leader of his people, because your mother gave birth to you at dawn. We Javanese believe that one born at the moment of sunrise is predestined. Never, never forget you are a child of the dawn."

With me, it wasn't only the dawn of a new day, but also the dawn of a new century. I was born in 1901.

For Indonesians the nineteenth century was a period of death. But the present era is to live in life, in the rising tide of the revolution of mankind. This is a century of the emergence of new, free nations in Asia and Africa and the emergence of the Socialist States constituting over one thousand million persons. A third phenomenon is the Atomic Age; a fourth the Space Age. Those born in this century are duty bound to do heroic things.

My birthday is double six. June six. It is my supreme good fortune to have been born under Gemini, the sign of twins. And that is me exactly. Two extremes. I can be gentle or exacting; hard as steel, or poetic. My personality is a mixture of reason and emotion. I am forgiving and I am unyielding. I put enemies of the State behind bars, yet I cannot keep a bird in a cage.

Once in Sumatra I was given a monkey. The monkey was chained. I couldn't stand it. I freed him in the forest. When West Irian was returned to us, I was presented with a kangaroo. The animal was caged. I demanded he be returned and given his liberty. I sign death sentences, yet have never raised my hand to slap the

17

breath out of a mosquito. Instead I whisper to it, "Please, mosquito, go away. Please don't bite me." But as Commander-in-Chief I give the orders to kill. Because I am two halves, I can exhibit all shades, understand all sides, lead all people. Perhaps it is mere coincidence. Maybe it is another omen. But those two halves of my nature make me the all-embracing.

There was still another sign when I was born. Mount Kelud, the nearby volcano, erupted. Superstitious folk prophesied, "This is a welcome greeting to baby Sukarno." The Balinese believe their Mount Agung erupts when the people misbehave, so there are some who might say Kelud didn't really welcome me but, rather, expressed anger because such a bad boy was coming to earth.

In contrast to all the symbolism heralding my entrance, the birth itself was most inauspicious. Father could not afford even a midwife. We were too poor. The only person to attend Mother was a friend of our family, a very, very, very old man. It was he and no other who ushered me to my destiny.

In Bogor a pure white marble plaque in relief, depicting the birth of Hercules, hangs in the hallway leading to the State ballroom. It shows infant Hercules in the arms of his mother, while surrounding him are 14 exquisite females—all naked. Can you imagine such great fortune as to be born into the midst of 14 beauties? Sukarno didn't have Hercules' luck. When I was born I had nobody to hug me but a very, very, very old man.

Fifty years later the circumstances of my birth became news. In 1949 our young Republic was in the fourth year of its revolution against the Dutch. This was big all-out war. They hated me like hell in the Netherlands. They talked against me on radio, wrote against me in the papers. One magazine admitted that "Sukarno is energetic, dynamic and not at all the typical slow-moving, slow-thinking Javanese." The writer conceded "Sukarno is not a shy man. Sukarno can speak interchangeably in seven languages. We should face the facts and they are that Sukarno is definitely a leader." All good qualities and characteristics were set forth about me in this article. I shortly realized why. The piece concluded, "Dear reader, do you know why Sukarno has such outstanding features? Because Sukarno is not pure Indonesian, that's why. He is the illegitimate son of a Dutch coffee-planter who made love with a native peasant in the field, then farmed out the baby for adoption."

Unfortunately the only witness to swear to my real father and to testify that I did, indeed, come from my true mother, not some coffee-worker in the field, had long since passed away.

Through generations, Indonesian blood has mixed with the Indian, Arab, some pure Polynesian strains and, of course, Chinese. We are basically the Malay tribe. From the root of *Ma* comes Manila, Madagascar, Malaya, Madura, Maori, Himalaya. Our ancestors migrated across Asia, settled in three thousand islands and became Balinese, Javanese, Atjehnese, Ambonese, Sumatran, and so forth.

I am the child of a Balinese mother of the Brahmin class. My mother, Idaju, is of high caste descent. The last King of Singaradja was the uncle of my mother.

My father was from Java. His full name was Raden Sukemi Sosrodihardjo. *Raden* is a title of nobility meaning "Lord." Father was descended from the Sultan of Kediri.

Again, it is either coincidence or an omen that I was born into the ruling class, but, whatever my birth or destiny, this dedication to my people's freedom was not a sudden decision. I inherited it. Since 1596, when the Dutch first invaded our islands, their efforts to occupy the whole of our territory and our efforts to regain our homeland have darkened the pages of history.

My maternal grandfather and great-grandfather were inspired fighters for freedom. My great-grandfather died in the struggle of Puputan, an area on the north coast of Bali in which the Kingdom of Singaradja is located and in which was fought a historic, bloody battle against the invader. When my great-grandfather saw that everything was lost and his army couldn't conquer the foe, he, with the rest of the Balinese idealists, dressed in white from head to foot and mounted his horse. Each drew his *kris*—that's a short ceremonial dagger—and charged the enemy. They were decimated.

The last King of Singaradja was cheated out of his kingdom, fortune, home, lands, and all his possessions by the Dutch. They invited him onto one of their warships for a talk. Once aboard, they forcibly detained him, and then banished him into exile. After they had occupied his palace and confiscated his property, my mother's family became very poor. Mother's hatred of the Dutch she passed on to me.

In 1946, when Mother was over 70, our infant Republic was engaged in hand-to-hand combat with the enemy. During one battle our troops massed in the backyard of her home in Blitar. My guerrillas told me afterwards, "On this segment of the maneuver it was very quiet. We were all crouched there waiting. It dawned on your mother that she didn't hear anything. There were no gunshots, no screams. With eyes flashing she came at us demanding to know, 'Why are there no gunshots? Why don't you fight? Are you cowards? Why aren't you out shooting the Dutch? Go on, the lot of you, get out and kill those Dutchmen!' "

My father's people were also great patriots. Father's great-great-grandmother was next in rank to a princess, yet she was a cofighter of the great hero of our nation, Diponegoro. She rode right alongside him to his death in the great Java War which lasted from 1825 to 1830.

I was weaned not on television or Wild West sagas but on stories of nationalism and patriotism. I would sit at my mother's feet by the hour and drink in these exciting tales of the freedom fighters in our family.

My beloved mother also told stories of how Father won her. Mother was a Hindu-Buddhist temple maiden whose job was to clean the house of worship every morning and evening. Father, a teacher at the government elementary school in Singaradja, liked coming to the water fountain in front of the temple after class to enjoy the serenity. One day he saw Mother. Another time he sat near the water fountain and again he saw her. Many afternoons later he spoke a little. She answered. Soon he felt attracted to her and she to him.

According to custom, Father called upon her parents to ask decently, "May I please marry your daughter?" They replied, "Oh, no! You are from Java and you are a Moslem. Definitely not. We'll lose our daughter."

As recently as before the Second World War, Balinese women didn't marry strangers. I don't mean foreigners from another country, I mean strangers from another island. The ethnic groups never intermarried. Should such a calamity occur, the newlyweds were barred from their own parents' homes.

One of Sukarno's miracles is that he united his people. The color of our skin may differ, the shape of our noses and foreheads may differ: Irians are black, Sumatrans brown, Javanese are short, inhabitants of the Moluccas taller, people from Lampung have their own features, those from Pasundan have their own features, but no more are we islanders and strangers. Today we are Indonesians and we are one. Our country's motto is *Bhinneka Tunggal Ika*—"Unity in Diversity."

But, back when Father wanted to marry Mother, it was unthinkable. Particularly because, although Father practiced Theosophy, he was legally a Moslem and to marry in a Moslem ceremony meant Mother had to convert to Islam. Their only alternative was to elope.

Balinese elopement follows strict rules. Elopers spend their wedding night in the home of friends while couriers are dispatched to the bride's parents to inform them their daughter is now married. Mother and Father sought refuge with the Javanese Chief of Police, who was a friend of Father's. Mother's family came to take her back, but the Police Chief said, "No, she's under my protection."

It is not our habit to haul a groom into court, but these were unusual circumstances. After all, he was a Javanese Moslem-Theosophist and she a Balinese Hindu-Buddhist. When the case came up, Mother was asked, "Did this man force you against your will?" And Mother replied, "Oh, no. I loved him and eloped because I wanted to."

There was no choice but to allow the marriage. Nonetheless, the court fined mother 25 *seringgits*, the equivalent of 25 dollars. Mother had inherited several gold bracelets and to pay the money she sold her ornaments.

Rightfully feeling unloved in Bali, Father applied to the Department of Education for a transfer to Java. He was sent to Surabaya and there I was born.

❧ 3. Modjokerto: The Pains of Youth

LIKE David Copperfield, I was born amidst poverty and grew up in poverty. I did not own shoes. I did not bathe in water from a tap. I did not know about forks and spoons. Such extreme privation can make a little heart very sad inside.

With my sister Sukarmini, who is two years older, we were a family of four. Father's salary was the Dutch equivalent of 25 rupiahs monthly. Less rent for our house at Djalan Pahlawan 88, the balance was 15 rupiahs, and at our government rate of 45 rupiahs to the dollar you can imagine what a humble household ours was.

When I was six we moved to Modjokerto. Our neighborhood was shabby and the neighbors in like circumstances, yet they always had some money to buy papaya or a sweet. I did not. Never. The big Moslem holiday is Lebaran, the last day of our annual fasting month during which the devout neither eat, drink, nor permit anything to pass their lips from sunup to sundown. Lebaran is like Christmas. It's the signal for feasting and giving of presents. We neither feasted nor gave presents. We had no money.

On Lebaran Eve, it is traditional for children to shoot off fireworks. All the children do now and they did then. All but me.

One Lebaran over half a century ago I lay in my cubicle, which had barely enough room for the bed, blinking mournfully up at the sky through three tiny airholes in the bamboo wall. Each airhole was the size of a brick. I was so miserable. My little heart was breaking. All around me I could hear firecrackers exploding and the high-pitched gleeful voices of my friends. Can anyone know how it feels as a young boy when all your friends may somehow buy a penny's worth of firecrackers—and you not? You feel terrible! You want to die. The only way a small child can fight back is to sob uncontrollably into his bed. I remember crying to Mother, "From year to year always I hope, but never am I able to shoot off even one firecracker." I felt so sorry for myself.

Later that evening a guest came to visit Father. He had in his hand a tiny parcel. "Here," he offered, holding it out to me. I trembled so with the excitement of getting a present that I could barely open it. It contained firecrackers. No treasure or painting or palace has ever given me so much pleasure. Never ever will I forget it.

We were so poor we could barely eat rice once a day. Mostly we had *ubi bolet*, corn chopped with other edibles. Mother could not even buy the regular rice that peasants in the field bought. She could only afford paddy, the unpolished grain. Every morning Mother took a woodblock, a hollowed-out log with a pole in it—something like a mortar and pestle—and she pounded and pounded and pounded this unhusked kernel until it was the kind of rice sold in the market place.

"By doing this," she told me one day as she labored in the broiling hot sun until her hands reddened and blistered, "I save a cent. And one cent can buy you, my son, a vegetable." From that day forth and for years after, every single morning before I went to school I would pound paddy for my mother.

Our kind of poverty makes for closeness. When there was nothing material, when it seemed I had nothing in the whole world but Mama, I clung to her because she was the sole source of my satisfaction; she was the candy I couldn't have and she was all my worldly possessions. Oh, Mama had a heart so big!

Father, however, was a strict schoolmaster. Even after hours he was relentless in teaching me to read and write. "Come now, Karno, learn this by heart: Ha-Na-Tja-Ra-Ka. . . . Come now, Karno, learn the A-B-C-D-E," and on and on until my poor head would ache. Again later, "Come, Karno, recite the alphabet . . . Come, Karno, read this . . . Karno, write that . . ." Father, too, sensed his child of the dawn would be something someday.

The rare times I was naughty he punished me harshly. Like that morning I climbed the *djambu* tree in our yard and knocked down a bird's nest. Father was livid. "I thought I taught you to love animals," he thundered.

I shook with fright, "Yes, Father, you did."

"You will please be so good as to explain the meaning of the phrase: 'Tat Twan Asi, Tat Twam Asi.'"

"It means 'He is I and I am he; you are I and I am you.'"

"And were you not taught this had a special significance?"

"Yes, Father. It means God is in all of us," I said obediently.

He glared at his seven-year-old criminal. "Have you not been instructed to protect all God's living creatures?"

"Yes, Father."

"And do you mind telling me what are birds and eggs?"

"They are God's living creatures." I trembled. "But bringing down that nest was an accident. I didn't mean to do it."

Excuses notwithstanding, Father beat me on my backside with a cane. I was a well-behaved child, but Father demanded rigid discipline and was quick to reprimand when he didn't receive it.

I learned early to perfect games that didn't cost money. Near our house grew a tree with a broad leaf. It started narrow, then fanned out wide and long like an oar. It was a great day for the children when a branch fell off because that meant we had a toy. One would sit on the broad part while another pulled by the long handle and it served as a sled. Sometimes I was the horse, but usually the driver. My nature had taken shape even as a small boy.

And I made the river my friend since it was one place a poor boy could play free. It was also a source of food. I always tried hard to surprise Mama with some small fish for dinner. This once earned me a whipping. It had grown late. When Father realized baby Karno was not home, he was furious. "Why is he out playing so long? Has he no feeling for his mother? Doesn't he realize she will be worried?"

"The village is so tiny nothing could happen without our hearing about it," Mama pointed out.

Nonetheless, Father, who was somewhat stubborn, was infuriated and when I skipped happily home an hour later triumphantly bearing my *cacap* for Mama, Papa grabbed me, fish and all, and caned me soundly.

Mother made up for the disciplinary measures, though. Oh, I loved her dearly. I'd come running to huddle in her lap and she would comfort me.

Despite the choking weeds of poverty, the flowers of love surrounded me. I learned early that affection annihilated all the evils. The desire for love has remained one of the motivating forces of my life. Besides Mother, there was Sarinah, the servant girl who reared me. A servant for us was not like having a servant in the West. On our islands we exist on the principle of *gotong royong*—cooperation, mutual assistance.

Gotong royong is deeply embedded in the Indonesian soil. Paid labor was an unknown concept in the early communities. Whenever heavy work was to be done everybody helped. You need a house built? OK, I'll bring the bricks, my friend will bring the cement. We'll both help you build. That's *gotong royong*. Everybody lending a hand. You have guests drop in at the last moment? OK, don't worry. I will quietly leave a cake at your back door. Or rice. Or *nasi goreng.* That's *gotong royong.* Mutual aid.

Sarinah was part of our household. Unmarried, she was to us a member of the family. She slept with us, lived with us, ate what we ate, but she got no wage whatsoever. She it is who taught me to love. Sarinah taught me to love people. Masses of people. While she cooked in the small shed outside the house, I'd sit with her and she'd preach, "Karno, over and above everybody you must love your mother. But then you must love the small people. You must love humanity." Sarinah is a common name, but this was not a common woman. She was the greatest single influence in my life.

In my young days we shared the same narrow cot. When I had grown up a little, there was no Sarinah anymore. I filled the void by sleeping with Sukarmini in the same bed. Later I slept with our dog Kiar, who was a mixture of fox terrier and something Indonesian—I don't know exactly what. Moslems supposedly don't like dogs, but I adore them.

In his own way, Father gave me much love, too. At the age of 11 I contracted typhus. For two months and a half I lay on the threshold of death. I had only Father's pure faith to sustain me. For the whole two months and a half, Papa slept under my bamboo cot. He lay on the damp cement floor on his pitifully thin straw mat directly under the slats of my bed.

Every single day and every single night for two months and a half Father lay underneath me. It wasn't because he couldn't find any other space to crouch in my tiny quarters. No. It was because of his strong mysticism. Father wanted to pray constantly to save me and he wanted me to receive God's powers, but in order to give me the benefit of his full mystical force pouring straight up from his body to mine, he had to lie under me. In Father's dark, dank, airless, disease-ridden few feet, night and day were alike and there he lay until I was wholly well.

The rent for our house was very low because it was on low land next to a creek. Every rainy season the creek overflowed, flooded the house, and submerged our lot. From December to April we were constantly wet. It was this stagnant, sewage-filled water which contributed to my typhus.

After I recovered we moved to Djalan Residen Pamudji. That house wasn't much better, but at least it was dry. The rooms were off a long dark hall. The smallest, mine, now had a skylight instead of airholes. To raise the additional few pennies rent, we had boarders: three assistant teachers from Father's school and two nephews my age.

My name at birth was Kusno. I started life as an unhealthy child. I had malaria, dysentery, anything and everything. Father thought, "His name is not good. We must give him another so that he may start fresh."

Father was a devotee of *Mahabharata,* the ancient Hindu classics. I had not yet reached puberty when Father said, "We shall name you Karna. Karna is one of the greatest heroes in *Mahabharata.*"

"Then Karna must be a very strong, very great person," I exclaimed excitedly.

"Oh, yes, my son," beamed Father. "Also faithful to his friends and beliefs regardless of the consequences. Known for courage and loyalty, Karna is a fighter for his country and a devoted patriot."

"Doesn't Karna also mean 'ear'?" I asked, somewhat confused.

"Yes. This warrior-hero was so named because of his birth. Once upon a time, as the *Mahabharata* goes, there was a beautiful princess. One day, while playing in her garden, Princess Kunti was seen by the Sun God, Surya. Surya wanted madly to make love to the princess, so he enveloped her and caressed her with the passion and heat of his rays. Through the power of his love rays she became pregnant although still a virgin. Naturally, for the Sun God to have made love to this pure young maiden was a cruel act and now this created a big problem for him. How to deliver the baby without destroying her maidenhood. He could not dare deflower her by bringing forth a child in the normal way. What to do. . . . What to do. . . . Oh, such a big problem for Surya. It was finally solved by taking the baby through the ear of the beautiful princess. Thus, the great *Mahabharata* hero was called Karna or 'ear.'"

Grasping my shoulders tightly, Father looked deep into my eyes. "It has always been my prayer," he declared, "for my son to be a patriot and great hero of his people. You shall be a second Karna." The names Karna and Karno are identical. In Javanese, the "A" sound becomes "O." The "Su" prefix on many of our names means good, best. Thus, Sukarno means the best hero.

Sukarno is, therefore, my real and only name. Some stupid newspaperman once wrote my first name was Achmed. Ridiculous. I am just Sukarno. Having only one name is not unusual in our society.

In school my signature had to be spelled Soekarno—the Dutch

way. In independent Indonesia I have ordered all "OE" spelling back
to "U." The spelling of Soekarno is now SUkarno. However, it is difficult to change one's signature after fifty years so when I myself sign
my name, I still write S-O-E.

Even without baby Kusno-Karno's illnesses, the burden of feeding two children was too heavy for Father. We often had to rely on
our neighbors' inbred sense of collectivism and social justice—namely
gotong royong. The family Munundar shared the same compound
with us. In true Javanese style, if we had no rice we ate theirs. When
we had no clothes we wore theirs.

In kindergarten the mother of my father said to Father, "Give
the baby to me for a while. I shall look after him." And so I went to
live in Tulungagung not far from Modjokerto.

Grandmother and Grandfather were not rich. Who of us was rich
in those days? There were just some who were less poor. Grandmother
had a little *batik* business so at least she was able to give me something to eat.

My grandparents believed I had supernatural powers. When
anyone was sick in the village or had a running sore, Grandmother
would summon me and with my tongue I licked the affected area of
the person. Strangely enough, they were healed. Grandmother also
divined that I had clairvoyance, but my clairvoyant powers disappeared as I began discovering my oratorical gifts. It would seem these
so-called powers were then channeled into another direction. At any
rate, after 17, I never saw mystically again.

My character has not varied one whit in nearly six decades. At
seven I was already a patron of the arts. I worshiped Mary Pickford,
Tom Mix, Eddie Polo, Fatty Arbuckle, Beverly Bayne, and Francis X.
Bushman. Each packet of English Westminster cigarettes contained a
photograph of one star as a premium. I collected the discarded packets and pasted my heroes and heroines on the wall. I guarded this
collection with my life. They were my first real treasures.

At 10 it was already apparent Master Karno had a strong will.
By virtue of my personality I was the dominant figure in every gathering. Even my family would group round me. By my twelfth birthday, I already had a gang. And I led this gang. When Karno wanted
to play cricket in the dust of the square of Modjokerto, everybody
played. If Karno collected stamps, they too collected stamps. They
called me *djago* or champion.

I had a windgun from a friend. We would put this long, narrow hollow reed to our mouths and shoot peas at objects. I was, naturally, the *djago* windgunner. When we climbed trees, I climbed higher than anyone else. I also fell down harder than anyone else. I also cut my head oftener than anyone else. But at least nobody could say I hadn't tried. My destiny even then was to conquer—not be conquered. In the game of spinning tops one friend's top spun faster than mine. I solved that situation with typical Sukarno quick thinking: I threw his in the river.

However, there were areas in which an Indonesian boy of my generation could not excel. The Soccer Club was one. Not only couldn't I become its chairman, I couldn't even retain my membership long. The other participants were Dutch boys who made it plain they didn't like me. Dutch children never played with native children. It just wasn't done. They were the good, the pure, the snow-white Westerners and they looked down on me because I was the native or "inlander."

For me the Soccer Club was a traumatic experience. Towheaded children lined both sides of the entrance shouting, "Hey you —Brownie! . . . Hey, poor stupid brown-skinned boy . . . native . . . inlander . . . peasant. . . . Hey, you forgot your shoes. . . ." Even little blond babies knew enough to spit at us, for this was the first thing their parents taught them when they came out of diapers.

During morning hours I was happy because I attended a native school where we were all equal. We were thirty pupils at the Inlandsche School der Seconde Klass. My father was *Mantri-Guru*, which means leading teacher. Natives were forbidden the title Headmaster.

There was no cohesive Indonesian language yet. Through third grade everybody spoke our regional Javanese dialect. From fourth to fifth the teachers switched to Melayu, the basic Malay language which infiltrated many parts of the Indies and subsequently became the foundation for our national language, *Bahasa Indonesia*. Twice a week we were taught Dutch.

When I reached fifth grade, Father outlined his plans. "My dream is to send you to a Dutch University," he said. "Therefore, our first move is to get you into a Dutch Primary School."

Thinking of the Soccer Club, I asked, "Could I not continue attending a native primary school?"

"Native education only goes to fifth grade. No further provision is made for us. Unless an inlander graduates from a Dutch Primary

School he is automatically barred from a Dutch Secondary School and without this diploma no Dutch University will accept him."

"Does it work on scholastic ability?" I inquired fearfully.

"It works on privilege. Government servants and natives of noble birth are allowed the luxury of educating their children. Nobody else."

Mindful of our circumstances, I asked, "Is it free?"

"No. Inlanders must pay tuition."

"Dutch too?"

"No. For them it is free. But under Colonial rule, nobody can think of a career without a Dutch education, so we must proceed. I shall call upon the Headmaster of the Dutch Primary School to make application."

It was a handsome building of real wood, not rattan like our native school, and the outside was painted light blue. There were seven classrooms, and, unlike tables in the native school, the desks had inkstands and a place for books.

After the examination the Headmaster announced to Father, "Your son is quite clever, but his Dutch is not good enough for the sixth grade of a Dutch-speaking school. We will have to put him one grade behind."

When we left we were very depressed. Father sighed. "A bad blow. However, there is no choice."

"But I am already fourteen," I protested. "Too old for fifth grade. People will imagine I have been left back because of stupidity. It will be embarrassing."

"Very well," decided Father instantaneously. "If it be necessary to tell a lie then we shall. We shall smuggle one year off your age. When you start the new year you will register as thirteen."

There was still the problem of my Dutch. Poor as we were, father hired a teacher who taught Dutch in this Europesche Lagere School to give me special lessons an hour a day. I remember her name exactly. Miss M. P. De La Rieviere. M. P. stood for Maria Paulina. Let us say she was very much less beautiful than any woman has a right to be and she remains in my memory for that reason.

The best way to explain what a Western education meant and how desperately Father would have sacrificed money, principles, anything for it is to tell my very first love affair.

I was 14 and I had lost my heart to Rika Meelhuysen, a Dutch girl. Rika was my first kiss. And I must say I was very nervous with it.

I have since improved. But, oh, I was madly in love with this girl and I surged through the whole gamut of school-boy emotions. I carried her books, I deliberately walked past her house hoping for a glimpse. I always seemed to "accidentally" be where she was. This romance I kept very quiet. I was terrified to utter a word lest my parents find out. I felt sure my father would have thundered at me had he heard I was carrying on with a white girl. Though I yearned to speak to him about it, the fear of his anger froze the words in my throat. So, this burning passion I confided only to my own lovesick soul.

One sultry afternoon I was out bicycle riding with my Rika Meelhuysen when we turned a corner and—banggg!—we bumped right into Father. I began to tremble with fright. He was polite, but I worried terribly about what he would do when I came home. Here was his only son romancing the hated Dutch. I sneaked into the house an hour later still shaking. Father marched directly up to me and said, "Son, don't worry about my feeling concerning your girl friend. It's a very good thing. After all, it can only improve your Dutch!"

When it came time for high school, Father knew what he had to do. He pulled strings to get me into the top academy in East Java, Surabaya's Hogere Burger School. "Son," he said, "I have been planning this move in my mind since the day you came into the world." He had it all arranged for me to lodge in the home of Mr. H. O. S. Tjokroaminoto, the man who changed my whole life.

"Tjokro," he explained to me, "was my friend in Surabaya before you were ever born."

"Oh," I said, surprised, "I thought he was a relation."

"No," answered Father. "Oh maybe . . . somewhere . . . a very far, faraway relationship, but nothing else." Then Papa looked at me a moment. "Do you know who Tjokro is?"

"I only know he travels about making political speeches. I remember he came to our village to make speeches and he slept overnight and you and he talked until dawn."

"Tjokro is the political leader of the Javanese people. Although you will be getting a Dutch education, I do not want your roots to grow in Western soil. That is why I send you to Tjokro, whom the Dutch refer to as 'The Uncrowned King of Java.' I want you never to forget that your heritage is to be a second Karna."

I took nothing with me when I left for Surabaya. I had nothing to take. All that accompanied me was one small bag with a few pieces of clothing. Father appointed one of his teachers to make the six-hour train ride with me. There was no party, no celebration. I remember only that I cried bitterly. I was leaving home. I was leaving my mother. I was just a little scared boy of 15.

The morning I left, Mother had a premonition that I would never again come home to live. In front of our house she ordered, "Get down on the ground, my child. Lie flat out in the dirt." Then Mama stepped over my body. Back and forth three times. This was in accord with the mystic belief that passing over your child with the part of the body from which he came and which contains the magic powers of life transmits to the child the everlasting benedictions of the mother. It's as though each time she says, "This child comes from my womb and I bless him."

Then she bade me arise. Again she turned me toward the East and said solemnly, "Never ever forget, my son, that you are a child of the dawn."

✎ 4. Surabaya: Cookshop of Nationalism

FROM prehistoric animal species unearthed on our archipelago, archeologists have proved that man existed on Java over half a million years ago. Our culture is an ancient one.

Open the book of *Ramayana*. In it, there's reference to "The land of Suarna Dwipa which has seven large kingdoms." Suarna Dwipa, meaning Golden Islands, was the name of our country when immortalized in the Hindu classics two thousand five hundred years ago.

From the ninth century, when we were the Sriwidjaya Empire, through the fourteenth, when we were the Madjapahit Empire, our "prosperous state of renown had reached a scientific level so high that it was the source of knowledge for the entire known world." So is it recorded in the venerable scrolls of Mother China, supposedly the seed of all Asian culture.

We were still internationally prominent when Christopher Columbus came in search of the Spice Islands, that island chain we now call the Moluccas. Had Columbus not sailed after our ginger, nutmeg, pepper, and cloves and, somehow, lost his way, he never would have discovered the American continent.

When the sea route to the Indies was finally discovered, foreign capital thronged to our shores like ants to a sugarpot. From Portugal came Vasco da Gama; from Holland, Cornelius de Houtman. This marked the beginning of Europe's "commercial revolution." Nations not only looked beyond their economic boundaries, but jumped way over them.

This capitalism grew until it had exhausted its possibilities of further growth within its own society. Goods, previously only imported from the East, were now also exported to the East. These Eastern territories thus constituted additional markets for surplus Western commodities and investment opportunities for capital which could no longer find an outlet at home. To control the economy of another country, the country has first to be subjugated. The traders became conquerors; the Asian-African nations became colonized, and greed ushered in the era of imperialism.

Java was taken in the sixteenth century, the Moluccas in the seventeenth century; and slowly Holland subjugated all our islands. Bali was finally mastered in 1906. As the foreign power planted its roots, it sapped our riches, extinguished our individuality, and suppressed the sons and daughters of a great people who had known how to paint, sculpt, write music, and create dances for centuries. We were no longer known to the outside world except by Western exploiters looking for wealth in the Indies.

The effect of imperialism was monstrous. Men were plucked from homes and commandeered to slave in the far-off isles that lacked manpower. Women were forced to work in the *tarum* or indigo garden and, even if giving birth while planting, were not permitted to cease their toil.

Tempe is a cheap, soft cake of fermented soya beans. A *tempe* country means a weakling of a country. That's what we became. We were continuously told we were a nation with brains like cotton wool. We became cowardly—afraid to sit, afraid to stand, because whichever we did was wrong. We became a jellylike people with a small heart. We were weak as *katak* and limp like *kapok*. We became a nation which could only whisper, "Yes, sir."

Indonesians developed an inferiority complex which they retain yet. This cost me some anger recently. The ladies of my Cabinet always serve European desserts. "We have our own delicious confections," I fumed. "Why don't you serve them?" "We are sorry, Pak," they apologized, "but Indonesia is ashamed. We feel Westerners look down their noses at our poor desserts." That's a throwback to the days of the Dutch. It's our centuries-old inferiority coming out again.

The Dutch East Indies Government's continual reference to our insignificance convinced us. To believe you are a stupid, despised race is a weapon in the hands of the conqueror. Imperialism is a collection of visible and invisible powers.

The inevitable reaction to this long-overdue resistance of oppressed elements led to our pioneer revolutionary period. Sun Yat-sen established China's National Movement in 1885. India's National Congress was born in 1887. Aguinaldo and Rizal roused the Philippines in the early 1900's. All Asia was growing up and in the glorious twentieth century, in which isolation could never occur again, even meek, timid Indonesia caught the feeling. In May of 1908 Javanese leaders organized the first national party, called *Budi Utomo,* meaning "Pure Endeavor." In 1912 this gave way to *Sarekat Islam* and a membership of 2½ million under the leadership of my father's friend Mr. H. O. S. Tjokroaminoto.

Indonesia's individual cases of sufferings united and the idea of national unity began to spread. The cradle of redemption was Djakarta, but the infant took her first steps in Surabaya.

In 1916 Surabaya was a bustling, noisy port town, much like New York. It had a good harbor and an active trading center. A key industrial area with fast turnover in sugar, tea, tobacco, and coffee, it had keen competition in commerce from the sharp Chinese plus a large influx of mariners and merchantmen who brought news from all parts of the world. It had a swollen population of young and outspoken dockhands and repair workers. There were rivalries, boycotts, street fights. The town was seething with discontent and revolutionaries. Into this atmosphere stepped a little mama's boy of 15 clutching a small suitcase.

The family of Tjokroaminoto numbered six persons. There were Pak and Bu Tjokro, their sons, Harsono, who was 12 years younger than I, and Anwar, 10 years younger, their daughter Utari, five years younger, and the baby.

Pak Tjokro's sole job was as chairman of *Sarekat Islam* and he was paid meagerly. He lived in a congested *kampong* or neighborhood near the river. Off the street parallel to the river was a *gang* which had houses on either side but was too narrow for cars. Our alley was called "Gang Seven Peneleh," meaning "Gate Number Seven off Peneleh Street." A quarter of the way in stood a shabby house with a semiattached pavilion. Including the attic, it was partitioned off into 10 crackerbox-sized rooms. The family of Pak Tjokro lived in front, we boarders in the rear.

Although all the rooms were poor, students who had boarded there for years had the so-called better ones. My room had no windows at all, and no door. It was so dark that I had to keep the light burning even in daytime. My dark world held one shaky table on which I placed my books, one wooden chair, a peg for my clothes, and a grass mat. No mattress; no pillow.

Surabaya already boasted electricity. Each room had an outlet and each boarder paid extra for his lamp. Only my room didn't have one. I had no money for the bulb. I would study late into the night by candle. I had not even the means to buy a *klambu* to drape over my bamboo stretcher and keep out the mosquitoes. My castle was small as a chickencoop, totally airless, and filled with insects, but at least I had it all to myself.

Including meals it cost 11 guilders or, roughly, four dollars a month. Father managed to send 12½ guilders, which left 50 cents for pocket money. In 1917 father was transferred to Blitar. There he held a better-paying job and became a trifle less poor, so he was able to send $1.50 monthly pocket money.

It was expensive for any inlander to attend Hogere Burger School. Besides 15 guilders for monthly tuition and the uniform caps with HBS on them, we had to pay 75 guilders per term for textbooks. I remember the sum exactly because I counted every guilder and took care not to spend one casually.

Devoted son that I was, I must admit that I wrote home only when I was in great need. Without even opening my letters Father knew Karno was asking for money. My letters always featured that same loving salutation: "Dear Father and Mother, I'm okay and I certainly hope both of you are too." Then, the greetings dispensed with, I'd proceed right to the heart of my problem by the third line. I'd write, "Now, I'm in a great lack of money. Could you please arrange to send some?"

Besides my angel mother, who'd mail a guilder or two secretly whenever she could, I developed another source of income—my sister's husband. They lived within 50 kilometers of Surabaya and Pak Poegoeh always treated me to five guilders return fare. Since it never cost that much, I visited them often.

Pak Poegoeh was six years older than I and profitably employed in the irrigation office of the Department of Public Works. Although we were like brothers, never did I request financial assistance outright. The Javanese way is more indirect. I would ask it of his sister, who then passed it along. And I must say it was carefully thought out. I never asked beyond what I estimated could safely be gotten. As a result of such prudence, I occasionally received more than I asked for. It was a happy holiday when this extra bonus arrived, because I could then treat my friends to a coffee or sweet.

HBS was one kilometer from Gang Peneleh. Everybody except me had a bicycle. I either hitched a ride on the rear of somebody else's or walked.

I saved and saved and when I had amassed eight guilders I

bought a shiny black Fongers—a Dutch cycle. I cared for it like a mother. I shined it, touched it, hugged it. Without asking me, Harsono, who was seven, borrowed it and slammed head-first into a tree. The whole front was broken. Harsono shook with fright. He never had the nerve to tell me and when I finally learned the news I kicked him hard in the rear. Poor Harsono. He cried; he shouted. It took me weeks to get over the shock that my shiny black Fongers was wrecked. Eventually I got eight guilders together again and bought another cycle—but for Harsono.

Once a week I indulged in my sole form of luxury—movies. I dearly love them. However, the way I went to the movies was very different from the way Dutch boys went. I sat in the cheapest seats. The price for my chair was the equivalent of three American pennies. Look here, I was so poor that I could only take those seats that were placed behind the screen. You hear? Behind the screen! We didn't have talking pictures then so I had to read the titles backwards—and in Dutch, yet! I became adept at this and it got so I could read the words very quickly from right to left. I didn't mind because I didn't know any better. I was grateful to be able to go at all. The only time frustration hit me was when they showed a boxing picture. I could never figure out which fist did the punching.

During this period "Yankee Doodle" became a favorite with me (it still is). They played it every intermission and, sitting in the dark behind the screen with nobody else around, I'd sing it softly to myself while they played. I still sing it.

Once a circus came to town. At the performance they unloosed live doves and if one lit on your shoulder you won a prize. We quickly discovered, when the bird landed on a fellow boarder, that the prize was a horse. Well, there we were—Soearli, the lucky winner, a half dozen of us youngsters and this old tired horse. We didn't know what to do with him, but we had to get the beast out of there so we marched him home. The house had a courtyard in back but no entrance other than through the building. We calmly opened the front door of the Great Leader of the Javanese people and paraded our horse through the parlor and into the courtyard, where we anchored him under the *saweh* tree. But nobody had money to feed another mouth even if the mouth belonged to a horse. Two days later Soearli sold him.

Barring one circus and the movies, this was not a gay period for me. I was too serious. I did not engage in fun as other high school boys do. Perhaps the so-called escapades with which I'm credited today are a sort of over-compensation because there were no such lighthearted enjoyments throughout my life until I was 50. Today's search for joy might be my trying to cram in before it's too late all those things which I never got to enjoy in my youth.

I don't really know. I never thought about it before the time came for me to commit this autobiographical self-surgery. However, this is a dialogue between us—between you, the reader, and me. And since I am talking from the overflow of my own emotions, thinking about it all in the light of past miseries, I feel it is maybe true that I am compensating myself.

In any event, I was bitterly unhappy in Surabaya. When I arrived I cried every day. Oh, I missed my mother so much, I can't tell you. Women have always been the great influence in my life. Now, I had no mother, no adoring grandparent to spoil me, no devoted Sarinah to fuss over me. I was all alone.

Bu Tjokro was a lovely lady with a small delicate figure. It was she who personally collected our board every week. It was she who laid down the rules: (1) Dinner at nine P.M. and whoever is late won't get any. (2) Students must be inside their rooms by 10 P.M. (3) Students must rise at four A.M. to study. (4) Flirting is strictly forbidden. I felt close to Bu Tjokro, but she was too busy to mother me. Needing a woman's heart, I turned to Mbok Tambeng, the servant woman, for comfort. She became my mother substitute. She sewed the holes in my trousers. She knew *gado-gado,* a vegetable salad with peanut sauce, was my favorite so she would sneak a little extra for me. Mbok took pity on me and oh! I hungered for it desperately.

Still, Mbok was not sufficient consolation for a sensitive child. My soul cried out for a confidante, even a fatherly heart to whom I could turn. Tjokro wasn't the one. A leader interested only in politics, his wasn't the shoulder you could cry on nor the arm you could snuggle into.

However, Tjokro liked me very much. This affection was expressed particularly the summer of 1918. It was my habit to visit my parents during every school vacation. During this two-month stay in Blitar I'd excitedly looked forward to spending one day with friends in Wlingi, 20 kilometers away. All the plans had been laid and with eager anticipation I waved Papa goodbye, kissed Mama goodbye and set out for my little journey. I had barely arrived at the home of my friends when an ominous rumble filled the air and the earth trembled under foot. Frightened old ladies, squealing children and work-worn laborers spilled out of their huts into the congested *kampong*. Fear and its compatriot, panic, joined the mob as Mount Kelud, the live volcano in Blitar, picked this moment to voice the anger of the gods.

The sky was black with soot and dust for miles and miles. There were lava bursts everywhere. The area was blanketed in smoke and fire and poison. With full force, boiling lava poured down the mountain to a lower spot and massed there halfway between Blitar and Wlingi. Many people died.

I was in great despair because I knew Father and Mother would be worried about me. . . . Is he alive? . . . Is he dead? . . . They were aware their son was directly in the path of the eruption and they could get no news. Meanwhile, I'd heard half our city had been erased so I was paralyzed with worry myself about what might have befallen them.

I had to start back as soon as possible, but no conveyance imaginable could negotiate that sea of bubbling lava. Eventually the only way was on foot. While the lava was still a little hot, I began walking. When I was yet a way off, they spied me and came running to meet me halfway. They hugged me. They kissed me. They stroked my cheeks. "Oh, you're alive," Father cried. "You're alive . . . you're alive." Mother broke into tears. I held onto them with both hands. Oh, we were happy, so happy, to see each other.

Back in Surabaya, Tjokro, too, was worried enough to get in his car and make an all-day drive just to see if I was all right. At first he couldn't locate me or my parents. Our house itself had been saved but it was a mass of lava and mud. He arrived at Djalan Sultan Agung #53 only to find it empty save for a little bird. He was frantic until he saw us.

Tjok loved me in his way; it's just that his way was not enough for a lonely child. He seldom spoke to me. I rarely even saw him. He had no leisure hours. If he came at all, either there'd be callers or he'd meditate in solitude.

Oemar Said Tjokroaminoto was 33 when I came to Surabaya. Tjokro taught me what he was, not what he knew nor what I should be. A person with creativity and high ideals, a fighter who loved his country, Tjok was my idol. I was his student. Consciously and unconsciously he molded me. I sat at his feet and he gave me his books, he gave me his values. He just wasn't capable of giving the man-to-man warmth I craved. With nobody to love me as I yearned to be loved I began to retreat. The only realities in my dark world were nothingness and poverty and so I withdrew into what the English call "the world of the mind." Books became my friends. Surrounded by my own consciousness, I found compensations to neutralize that outside existence of discrimination and hopelessness. In this more eternal, spiritual sphere, I sought my diversions. And there I could live and be a little happy.

All my time was spent reading. While others played, I studied. I pursued knowledge beyond mere lessons. We had a rich library in town run by the Theosophical Society. Father was a Theosophist; therefore I had access to this treasure chest in which there was no limit to a poor boy. I moved wholly into this inner world. There I met with great men. Their thoughts became my thoughts. Their idealism became my intellectual foundation.

Mentally I talked with Thomas Jefferson, with whom I feel friendly and close because he told me all about the Declaration of Independence he wrote in 1776. I discussed George Washington's problems with him. I relived Paul Revere's ride. I deliberately looked for mistakes in the life of Abraham Lincoln so I could argue the points with him.

Nowadays, when people comment, "Hey, Sukarno, why don't you like America?" I say, "You don't know Sukarno or you could never ask such a question." My boyhood was spent worshiping America's founding fathers. I wanted to emulate her heroes. I loved her people. I still do. Even today I read every American magazine from *Vogue* to *Nugget*.

I will always feel friendly toward America. Yes, friendly. I say that publicly. I put myself down on record. I state it in print. A grounding such as mine could not leave me unfriendly to the United States of America.

In the world of my mind, I also communed with Prime Minister Gladstone as well as Sidney and Beatrice Webb; I came face to face with Mazzini, Cavour, and Garibaldi of Italy; Austria's Otto Bauer and Adler; Karl Marx, Friedrich Engels, and Lenin, and I chatted with Jean-Jacques Rousseau, Aristide Briand and Jean Jaurès, the grandest orator in French history. I drank in these stories. I lived their lives. I actually was Voltaire. I was the great fighter of the French Revolution, Danton. A thousand times I, myself, in my black room saved France singlehanded. I became emotionally involved with these statesmen.

In school we heard a lecture about the people's tribunal of the early Greeks. It stayed with me. I visualized angry thinkers making speeches and spouting slogans like "Down with oppression" and "Up with freedom." My emotions became inflamed. That night, when everybody was behind closed doors, my chicken coop became a tribunal and I a young Greek boy fired with enthusiasm. Standing on my shaky table, I got carried away. I started to shout. While I was orating to absolutely nobody, heads popped out of doors, eyes popped out of heads, and teen-aged voices called through the blackness, "Hey, 'No,' are you crazy? . . . What's going on? . . . Hey, are you okay?" . . . And then the shouts turned to, "Oh, it's nothing. Just 'No' saving the world again," and one by one the doors shut and I was left alone in the blackness.

As I grew older, my inner world widened to include the friends of Tjokroaminoto.

Daily, leaders of other parties or branch leaders of *Sarekat Islam* came to visit for several days at a time. While my fellow boarders were out watching a ball game, I would sit at the feet of these men and listen. Sometimes I shared my bed with one of them and talked until the first gray light of dawn.

I loved mealtimes. Food was served family style so I could out-eat everyone and at the same time soak up the political conversation. When the guests were relaxed around the table, I sometimes even dared put questions. These *Mahaputeras*—great sons of the Indonesian people—didn't ignore me because I was a child, either. Once they were discussing capitalism and goods being taken from our islands to make Holland rich. That's when I asked softly, "How much do the Dutch make from Indonesia?"

"This little boy is very inquisitive," said Tjok, and then added, "The Vereeniging Oost Indische Compagnie drains—or steals—about 1,800 million guilders out of our soil annually to nourish The Hague."

"What does our country keep out of it?" I asked, this time a bit louder.

"Our sweating peasants starve on a diet of two and a half cents a day," spat Alimin, the man who introduced me to Marxism.

"We've become a nation of coolies and a coolie among nations," snapped his friend Muso.

"*Sarekat Islam* works to improve conditions by submitting motions to the Government," explained Tjok, pleased to have such an eager pupil. "Tax reductions and labor unions can only be effected by cooperation with the Dutch—no matter how much we hate it."

"But is it right to hate even if it's the Dutch we are hating?"

"We do not hate the people," he corrected. "We hate the system of colonial rule."

"Why are we not better off if our countrymen have fought this system for centuries already?"

"Because always our heroes struggled alone. Each fought with small bands of followers in isolated areas," answered Alimin.

"I see. They lost because they weren't united," I said.

The Indian philosopher, Swami Vivekenanda, had written, "Don't make your head a library. Put your knowledge into action." I started applying what I'd read to what I had been hearing. I drew comparisons between the glorious civilizations of my mind and my own wretched fatherland.

Little by little I became a fierce patriot who realized that no more could a young Indonesian afford the luxury of escaping into the world of imagination. I faced the fact that my country was poor, miserable, and humiliated.

I took endless walks by myself and tried to sort out the thoughts whirling around in my brain. By the hour I stood motionless on the little bridge which spanned the small river and watched the ceaseless parade of humanity. I saw the Indonesian peasant in bare feet shuffling wearily toward his dilapidated hut and I saw the Dutch colonialist riding snappily by in his open landau drawn by two sleek grays. I saw the white families looking so clean while their brown brothers were so dirty, their bodies so smelly, their belongings so ragged, their children so smutchy. I wondered how people could be expected to stay clean when they had no other clothes to change into. I drank in the stench of the rotting garbage and choked sewers and I fixed the stink of my people's poverty firm in my nostrils so that when I'm 10,000 miles away I can still smell it. I looked into the despair of every man and woman I saw. I just drained in the people. My pauper people.

From the bridge I blinked out at the teeming masses and I understood clearly this was our strength and I had a great awareness of their suffering. Even a child cannot remain untouched once he sees signs on swimming pools that scream, "No dogs or inlanders allowed." Dogs were first. Can any human being stay unaffected when he sees the inlander conductor forced to bow to every Dutch passenger who boards his streetcar?

I was a youngster of 15 years slapped in the face by a long-nosed boy for no reason other than that I was a native. Do you not think such actions leave scars? Yes, I had an awareness as a child. My dedication of life started at 16.

My first political club was *Tri Koro Darmo*, which means "Three Holy Objectives" and symbolized the social, economic, and political freedoms we sought. It was a mainly social organization of students my age. Young Java, the next step, had a broader basis.

Even our socializing was on a nationalistic plane. We devoted ourselves to perpetuating indigenous culture such as the teaching of Javanese dances or the instruction of the *gamelan* orchestra. Young Java also did much charity work. We traveled to nearby villages to raise funds for school or to aid victims of the volcano. We staged a show in the needy area and paid our expenses from the admissions.

Now, I must admit that in my youth I was so terribly handsome that I was almost girlish-looking. Because there were few female intellectuals in those days, there weren't many girl members and when Young Java put on a play I was always given the ingenue role. I actually put powder on my face and red on my lips. And I will tell you something, but I don't know what foreigners will think of a President who tells such things. . . . Anyway, I will tell it. I bought two sweet breads. Round breads. Like rolls. And I stuffed them inside my blouse. With this addition to my shapely figure, everybody said I looked absolutely beautiful. Fortunately my part didn't call for kissing any boys on stage. I couldn't waste my money so after the show I pulled the breads out of my blouse and ate them. Watching me on stage, spectators commented that I showed a definite talent for playing to audiences. I concurred wholeheartedly.

Shortly thereafter I seized another opportunity. It was a gathering of the Study Club, an extracurricular group organized for the purpose of arguing about ideals and ideas. It was here I made my first speech. I was 16. The chairman had the floor and I was suddenly overcome with a great urge to talk. Sitting in the audience, I jumped right up on the table. A typically childlike emotional gesture. I haven't changed to this day.

The chairman had said, "It's imperative in this generation that every one of us have a thorough knowledge of the Dutch language."

Everybody agreed. Everybody but me. I was nervous, of course, but, when I had their attention, I said very calmly, "No. I do not agree.

"Our proud ground was once called Nusantara. *Nusa* means island. *Antara* means between. *Nusantara* means these thousands of islands, many of which are larger than the whole of Holland. Her population is but a fraction of ours. Dutch is spoken by only six million persons.

"Why does a tiny land on the other side of the world dominate a nation that was once so powerful we defeated the mighty Kublai Khan?"

In a quiet voice without rush or excitement, I put forth arguments and backed them up with fact. I ended with, "I say we must have first a thorough knowledge of our own language. Let us concentrate now on perpetuating Melayu. Then, in terms of a foreign tongue, let us speak English, which is today the diplomatic language.

"The Dutch are white. We are brown. They have blond, curly hair. Ours is straight and black. They live thousands of miles away. Why then must we speak Dutch?"

Well, there was an awful commotion. They'd never heard this before. I remember the Headmaster of HBS, Mr. Bot, standing there. He didn't do anything, but he looked very unfriendly, as though to say, "Uh-oh, Sukarno is going to make trouble."

Even if I didn't make trouble, I had it. I was a newcomer in the Dutch school and a native besides. HBS had 300 pupils. Only 20 were Indonesian. I was surrounded on all sides by little Dutch boys and little Dutch girls. Except perhaps for a few girls, they did not like me. I walked alone.

School was from seven to one six days a week. Midway there was a recess during which everybody bought snacks or played, but, of course, the Dutch separated from us. They took care to see there was no friendship between us. They also took care to see we had bloody noses. In my freshman term, a smarty in new, starched white shorts, which were regulation the first year, straddled my path and sneered, "Out of my way, native boy." When I stood there, he went BANG-GGGG!!!! Right in the nose! So, I hit him back. Daily I came home with scratches and bruises. I was never a physical person but—although I could stand the insults—I couldn't avoid getting into fist fights. Sometimes I would beat them, but just as often they beat me.

We experienced discrimination scholastically as well. School was so precious to us that if an inlander warranted penalty for any misdemeanor, the Headmaster's punishment was to bar him from classes for two days. We applied ourselves seriously to our studies but, even had we labored day and night, the marks the Dutch children got were automatically higher than what Indonesians could ever earn. Marks went on the basis of numerals. Ten was the highest, six was passing, and that's what most natives received in everything. In fact, we had a joke that 10 was for God, nine for professors, eight for geniuses, seven for the Dutch, and six for us. Ten was never earned by a native child.

I was an exceptional watercolorist. In my second year the teacher instructed us to draw a doghouse. While everybody was still measuring and plotting with pencils, I had already painted a completed house with a dog in it, plus a bone and a chain on the dog. The teacher held up my paper for all to see. She beamed, "This has such life and feeling that it deserves the highest mark possible." But did I get it? No.

It's always that the white man is more clever, more energetic. The white man knows more. The colonial apparatus cannot succeed unless it fosters the supremacy of the white race over the brown-skinned one.

The teachers liked me very much. I was obedient, earnest, and respectful. Only occasionally did I step out of line. I was never really fresh, but once, after my first speech, I was walking along the halls when Professor Egberts saw me and called out, "Well, Sukarno, what's with your Young Java?" and I said, "Well, Professor, what's with your old Holland?"

I was a big favorite with my German teacher, who also chaired our Debating Club. In debating issues back and forth and propounding alien opinions, I developed my rhetoric. Professor Hartagh saw that I could lead youngsters. During one session Hartagh told the 20 pupils collectively and me individually that I would be a great leader some day. This Professor must have had a crystal ball because he told another fellow he'd be a teacher and that's what he became.

One female teacher truly loved me so much that she gave me a Dutch name. Me, the future leader of the Revolution, with a Dutch name! She called me Karl. She even called me "Schat," which is Dutch for darling. If she'd forget her keys or something, she'd single me out and purr, "Schat, will you go up to my room and fetch my keys?" Oh, that was such a great privilege. Some days she invited me to her house for special coaching in French. I was thrilled with these extra favors.

As I grew older I was still thrilled with such extra favors. But for a different reason.

I was very much attracted to Dutch girls. I wanted desperately to make love to them. It was the only way I knew to exert some form of superiority over the white race and make them bend to my will. That's always the aim, isn't it? For a brown-skinned man to over-power the white man? It's some sort of goal to attain. Overpowering a white girl and making her want me became a matter of pride. A handsome boy always has steady girl friends. I had many. They even adored my irregular teeth. But I admit I deliberately went after the white ones.

My first crush was Pauline Gobee, the daughter of one of my teachers. She was beautiful and I was crazy about her. Then there was Laura. Oh, how I adored her. And there was the family Raat. They were Eurasians with several gorgeous daughters. HBS lay in the opposite direction to the house of the family Raat, yet every day for months I circled clear out of my way just to go past and catch a glimpse. There was also the Depot Tiga, an outdoor cafe where some-body occasionally invited me and where we could all sit happily and watch the Dutch girls go by.

Then, like a light shining in the darkness, Mien Hessels came into my life. Gone was Laura, gone was the family Raat, gone even was the excitement of Depot Tiga. Now I had Mien Hessels. She was all mine and I was madly, wildly, insanely in love with this yellow-haired, pink-cheeked tulip. I'd cheerfully have died for her if she'd asked it. I was 18 and wanted nothing more out of life than to possess her body and soul. I craved her passionately and came to the realiza-tion I had to marry her. Nothing else would quench the fire within me. She was the icing on the cake I could never buy. She was creamy-skinned and curly-headed and she represented everything I'd always wanted. To put my arms around Mien Hessels spelled riches to me.

I finally got up the nerve to speak to her father. I dressed in my very best. I wore shoes. Sitting in my dark room I'd rehearsed the words I was going to say, but when I approached the tidy house I quivered with fright. I had never visited a house like this before. The lawn was green velvet with row upon row of flowers standing straight and tall like soldiers. I had no hat to hold in my hand so, instead, I held my heart in my hand.

And there I stood, shaking, in front of the father of my ivory princess, a towering six-footer who stared straight down at me like I was vermin on the ground. "Sir," I said, "if you please, I would like the hand of your daughter in marriage . . . Please."

"You? A dirty native like you?" spat Mr. Hessels. "How dare you even come near my daughter. Out, you filthy animal. Get out!"

Can anyone ever know how whipped I was? Can anyone ever believe such a stain would someday wash off? The pain was such that I thought, "Dear God, never will I get over this," and I was certain down deep in my heart that never could I forget my angel-faced goddess, Mien Hessels.

Twenty-three years later—it's 1942. Wartime. I was gazing at the display in the window of a men's shop on the main street of Djakarta when I heard a voice behind me. "Sukarno?"

I turned to see a strange lady. "Yes, I am Sukarno."

She giggled, "Can you guess who I am?"

I scrutinized her carefully. She was a fat old matron. Ugly, unkempt. And I said, "No, madam, I cannot. Who are you, please?"

"Mien Hessels," she giggled again.

Ugggghhhh! Mien Hessels! My beautiful fairy princess had turned into a witch. You have never seen such a homely, sloppy hag. How she had let herself go. I said goodbye to her quickly and walked along thanking and blessing the good God in Heaven for having spared me. Her father's scolding of me was a blessing in disguise. To think I could have been tied up with this. I thanked God for His divine protection. Ugggghhhh, what a beast!

My career as a teen-aged lover was over when Bu Tjokroaminoto died. The family and boarders moved to another house and my revered leader was thoroughly depressed: his children were young, he was alone, the house was strange. The whole family was terribly unhappy. I could hardly stand it.

We were at the new address only a short while when the brother of Tjok came to me and said, "Sukarno, can you not witness how sad Tjokroaminoto is? Can you not do something to make him feel better?"

My heart was heavy and I answered, "I would happily do anything that might make him smile again, but what can I do? I cannot be a wife to Tjokro."

"No, but perhaps you could be something else to him," he suggested.

"Something else?"

"Yes."

"What?"

"A son-in-law. His daughter, Utari, is now motherless. Tjokro worries much about her future and who will watch over her, give her love. This is a deep concern on his mind. I think, possibly, if you were to ask my niece to marry you it would relieve some little bit of the pressure from Tjokro."

"But she is only 16," I protested.

"Yes, and you not yet 21. There is not such a big age difference. Tell me, Sukarno, do you like my niece a little?"

"Well," I explained slowly, "I owe Tjokro much gratitude and . . . I love Utari . . . But not very much. However, if you think I should ask for her hand because this may make the burden lighter for my idol, then I will do so."

I came to Tjokro and placed my request. He was ecstatic and he immediately moved me, as son-in-law-to-be, to a larger room with more furniture. To the day he died he never learned I proposed this union only out of my great respect and pity for him.

We were married in what we call "a hanging marriage." This is a regular marriage in that it is accepted by law and religion. Indonesians wed *Kawin Gantung* for many reasons. Sometimes it's a prearranged match with the principals not yet ready to fulfill their obligations physically. Or sometimes the bride remains in her father's house until the groom is able to provide financially.

In our case I chose not to take my wife to bed because she was a child. I may be a lover, but I am not a killer of young girls. That is why we were married "hanging" so that, although man and wife formally, the marital rites were also left hanging.

Two very odd things happened moments before I married Utari. The head of the mosque arbitrarily refused to officiate because I was wearing a necktie. He said, "Young man, a necktie is strictly a Christian mannerism and not in keeping with our Islamic custom."

"Sir," I retaliated, "I am aware that formerly a groom wore only our native dress, the sarong. However, that is the old-fashioned way. The law has now become modernized."

"Yes," he snapped, "but our modernization extends only so far as to permit the groom to wear trousers and an open collar."

"It is my preference to be neatly dressed and to wear a necktie," I commented sharply.

"In that case, since you persist in being smart I flatly refuse to perform the ceremony."

Whenever I'm publicly reprimanded or told that I must do thus and so, I become adamant. At this point not even the Prophet himself could have gotten me to remove my tie. I rose from my chair abruptly and retorted loudly, "Perhaps it is better not to go through with this now."

There was a great protest from the mosque clergy, but I thundered, "To hell with you all. I'm a rebel and I'll always be one and I am not about to have anybody dictate to me on my wedding day." Had it not been for one of our guests who was also a holy man capable of performing the service, it is possible Sukarno might never have united with Utari Tjokroaminoto in holy matrimony.

With five minutes left to go as a single man, a second peculiar thing happened. Just before I walked through the door, I reached for a cigarette to have one last puff. I took the box of matches from my pocket, struck one on the side to ignite it and—WHOOSSSHHI!—the whole thing went up in a lick of flame. Every last match in the box caught fire. In the process my finger was burnt. I recognized this as a bad omen and it left me with a dark feeling of foreboding. I took care to say nothing about it to anybody, but I couldn't help having a nagging sensation that . . . well . . . what is this . . .?

Despite my newly married status, my evenings were spent observing Tjokro. I became the tail of Tjokroaminoto. Wherever he went I followed. It was always Sukarno who accompanied him to speaking engagements, never his sons. And I'd just sit there and observe. He had great authority over the people. Nonetheless, as I watched time after time I became aware he never raised or lowered his tone. Never cracked jokes. His speeches were dull.

I never read one of those cheap books on how to be a public speaker nor did I practice in front of a mirror. It isn't that I wasn't vain enough for a mirror, but because I had none. My mirror was Tjokroaminoto. I watched him throw his voice. I saw him gesture, I observed and applied.

I learned to grab my audience's attention at the very beginning. I not only grabbed it, I held it. They listened spellbound. A shiver went through me when I first discerned I embodied the kind of power that could move masses. I made my points simply. My hearers found them easy to grasp because I relied on descriptive terms rather than facts and figures. I appealed to the emotions.

One evening Tjokro couldn't keep an engagement and he asked me to fill in for him. It was a small meeting, but I made the most of it. I started softly. "Our soil is so fertile that if you plant a stick that stick will sprout and become a tree. Yet people in our country lack every necessity and misery is a daily burden. The mountain tops suck the clouds of heaven unto the earth and our ground is blessed with an abundance of rain. Still we are undernourished and our bellies cry out from hunger."

"Yes, that is true," they shouted from their seats.

My voice began to swell. "Do you know why, my friends? Because our colonizers don't care about putting money back to enrich the land they are stripping. They care only about removing what is on the top of it. Oh, they have nourished the ground, yes. But do you know with what? Do you know what they have put back into the soil after 350 years of subjugation? I'll tell you! The emaciated, work-worn, hunger-ridden dead bodies of our people!

"Therefore, I ask you, are you with me? Like me, are you suffering with the obsession to be free? I go to sleep with this thought. I wake up with it. I will die with this ideal in my breast. Are you with me?"

"Yes," they shouted. "Yes . . . we are with you!" They looked up to me as I spoke. They stared at me adoringly, eyes open wide, faces turned up, drinking it all in trustingly, expectantly. It seemed apparent I was becoming a great public speaker. It was in my blood.

I soaked up more and more politics at Tjokro's house, the cookshop of nationalism, and following each speech my comembers began to understand a bit more, then to agree, then to follow me, then to love me. They chose me for secretary of Young Java and in due course I became chairman.

I also wrote for Tjok's periodical, *Utusan Hindia* ("Messenger of the Indies"), but under a *nom de plume,* because you could hardly attend a Dutch School while signing editorials advocating the overthrow of the Dutch Government. I returned to the *Mahabharata* for my alias. I chose the name "Bima," which signifies "Great Warrior," synonymous with bravery and heroism.

I wrote over 500 pieces. All Indonesia talked about them. Mother, who could neither read nor write, and Father never knew it was their little boy who wrote them. True, their greatest dream was for me to be a leader of our people, but not in my teens! Not so young that I could jeopardize my future education. Father might have been so furious he'd have tried in some way to stop me. I never risked telling him that little Karno and brave Bima were one.

That golden prophecy first voiced by Mother at my birth, echoed by my grandmother when I was a small boy, and re-echoed in my teens by Professor Hartagh was uttered again on the threshold of my twentieth year. And by two different people.

Dr. Douwes Dekker Setiabudi was a patriot who had endured many years in exile. When already well over 50, he announced to his National Indies Party, "Gentlemen, I do not wish ever to be called a veteran. Until I enter my grave, I want to remain a fighter for the Republic of Indonesia. However, I have met the youngster Sukarno. I am already growing in years and when the day comes that I will die, I say to you it is my wish that Sukarno and no other be my successor.

"This small boy," he added, "will be the future saviour of the Indonesian people."

The second prediction came from Tjokro. A devout Moslem, he spent many hours in prayer and communion. After a long period of meditation, he turned to the entire family one rainy evening and intoned solemnly, "Follow this boy. He is sent from Allah to be our Great Leader. I am proud to have sheltered him in my house."

June 10, 1921, I graduated. On June 11 the plans I had outlined for myself fell flat. Like my classmates, I intended to go to college in Holland. Mother wouldn't have any of it.

I pleaded with her. "Mother, all the boys who get through HBS automatically go to the Netherlands. That's the normal process. If you want to be educated in a university, you go to Holland."

"No. Absolutely no. My son will not go to the Netherlands," she exclaimed.

"But what's wrong with going abroad?"

"Nothing," she said. "But there is much wrong with going to the Netherlands. What attracts you? The thought of a university degree or the prospect of a white woman?"

"I want to go to a university, Mother."

"In that case you will go to one here. First we must consider the basic fact that governs everything in our lives. Money. It's too expensive to go abroad. Besides, you are a child born with the blood of the Indies. I want you to stay here among your own. Never forget, my son, that your place, your destiny, your heritage, is in these islands."

And so I enrolled in the university at Bandung. It might have been my mother's voice that I heard, but it was the hand of God that was moving me.

⇜ 5. Bandung: Passport to a White World

THE last week of June, 1921, I breezed into Bandung, which is like Princeton or any college town, and I don't mind admitting I was fairly pleased with myself. I even went so far as to affect a cigarette holder, so you can see what a fancy period I went through for a while.

Part of this egotism was due to my success in establishing the *pitji*, that black velveteen cap which is my trademark, as our symbol of nationalism. The unveiling was at a Young Java meeting just before I left Surabaya. Previously there had been much heated discussion on the part of the so-called intelligentsia, who resented the kerchief Javanese men wore with their sarongs, and the *pitji* that *betjak* drivers and other humble people wore. In fact, they scorned all true Indonesian headgear and went uncovered; it was their way of sneering subtly at the lower classes.

They needed to learn that you can't lead the masses unless you're one of them. Although nobody did this among the intellectuals, I deliberately decided to link myself with the common man. At the next meeting I arranged to wear a *pitji*.

I was more than a little excited. Butterflies danced in my stomach. Lurking behind a *sate* seller in the darkened street and watching my snobby compatriots file by all with neat bare heads, all pretending they were white Westerners, I hesitated a second. Then I argued with myself, "Are you a follower or are you a leader?"—"I am a leader," I declared.—"Then prove it," I said to me. "Go ahead. Adjust your *pitji*. Take a deep breath. And walk in . . . NOW!!!"

So I did. Everybody gaped at me wordlessly. It seemed best to pierce the silence by making a speech. "It is important for our cause that political figures never forget they are of the people, not above the people."

Still they stared. I cleared my throat. "We need a symbol of the Indonesian personality. This individualized cap, synonymous with

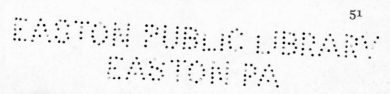

the common worker of the Malay race, is indigenous to our people. The name even devolved from our conquerors. The Dutch word *'pet'* means cap. *'Je'* being the diminutive implying 'little,' the word is actually *'petje.'* I say, let us hold our heads high bearing this cap as a symbol of Free Indonesia."

By the time I strutted off the train at the Bandung Railway Station with my *pitji* at a rakish angle, it was already the nationwide badge of the freedom fighter.

Today it is more like a badge of self-defense for me. After all, I'm getting a little thin on top. Since a Moslem is supposed to wash his hair after he has made love with a woman, friends tease, "Hey, Sukarno, that's probably why you've gotten bald!" Whatever the reason, I'm happy I had the foresight 44 years ago to make this hat so fashionable that our modern society considers it impolite to remove it in public.

Tjokro had a long-time friend in Bandung who had heard often about Tjokro's protégé. When I moved from East Java to this district in Central Java, Tjokro arranged for me to take up lodging in the home of Mr. Hadji Sanusi. I came ahead without Utari to make arrangements and have a look around this town which was to be my home for four years—or so I thought then. I found its climate cool and its women gorgeous. Bandung and I took to each other immediately.

An elderly man introducing himself as Sanusi fetched me personally and escorted me to his house. I knew instantly that my advance scouting trip had not been a waste. Even without examining the room it was clear there were definite advantages to this house. The main advantage was standing in the doorway in the semidarkness framed in a halo of light. She had a petite figure, a luscious red flower in her hair and a dazzling smile. She was Sanusi's wife, Inggit Garnasih.

All the sparks that can shoot out from a callow inexperienced boy of 20 to a matured, experienced woman in her 30's did. The first moment I stepped through that doorway, I thought, "Oh, what an exquisite woman." I knew I'd better stop thinking such thoughts fast so I put my landlady out of my mind—temporarily anyhow—and sent for Utari and concentrated on entering the Technische Hogeschool to graduate with the Degree of Engineer—not adulterer.

Today we have the universities of Indonesia in Djakarta, Gadjah Mada in Jogjakarta, Airlangga in Surabaya, Lambung Mangkurat in Kalimantan, and dozens more filled to capacity. But when I entered

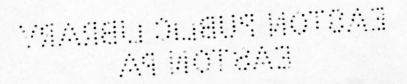

the Technical Institute we were 11 Indonesian students. I was one out of 11 dark faces bobbing around in an ocean of white skin, red hair, freckles, and eyes the color of a cat's. As we expected, the Dutch ignored us on campus. If they did pay attention it was to disparage or sing out, "Hey you, stupid native boy, c'mere." I don't know what magic I possessed. I only know that my presence alone was sufficient to shut up the belittlers and command respect.

We slaved hard at school. Homework was heavy. The six-day-a-week course with quarterly written exams lasting one month was back-breaking.

I had little time for Utari. I also had little in common with her. While I studied math, physics, and mechanics, my wife in name only was in the backyard playing with young girl friends. While I addressed youth groups at night, the baby I had married was romping with a child niece of Mrs. Inggit's. We each went our separate ways. She was very immature. Her shyness was so extreme that she rarely, if ever, even spoke to me.

We lay side by side in the same bed but were physically as brother and sister. In Bandung she took ill. While she lay half dead, I nursed her. Half a dozen times I sponged her feverish body from head to toe with alcohol, yet never once did I touch her. When she was healed there was still no physical intercourse between us. We did not even honestly desire each other in the real bride-and-groom sense. I mean, she was not distasteful to me and I was not distasteful to her, but it was no marriage born of great burning passion.

There wasn't much opportunity to fret about personal happiness because I was soon caught up body and soul in deeper waters. After living in Bandung two months, the papers carried headlines about the latest revolutionary activity, a strike in Garut, West Java. This episode was referred to as the Afdeling Case.

The Colonial Government plainly had been bothered by the steady growth of nationalism. The pesty gnat that once buzzed with harmless political slogans in 1908 was now swollen with the poison of discontent and its bite was deadly. Workers were being organized; they were demanding rights—labor laws guaranteeing a working day shorter than 18 hours; a fair wage and a society which operated with no "*Exploitation de l'homme par l'homme.*"

Indonesia had sprouted labor guilds such as the Union of Sugar Workers and the Amalgamation of Pawnshop Employees. In an age when the West already recognized strikes as the right of trade unions to try to improve their wretched lot, the Government, in an effort to stanch this "radicalism" and "Communism," as they labeled it, passed a new law—Article 161—namely the prohibition to strike. The criminal code now stipulated anyone who even incited anyone to strike was liable to six years' imprisonment.

This affected me personally because the authorities were convinced the strike in Garut was fostered by *Sarekat Islam*. That same day they imprisoned Tjokroaminoto.

His family was destitute. Their agonies were also my own. What to do? Go forward and think of myself and what I hoped to be tomorrow? Or go backward and think of Tjokro and what he did for me yesterday? Before me stretched the highway paved with gold which led to a college diploma. Behind me lay the road back to a dark room and a bleak future. The question was, which is less costly? . . . Which can a native boy afford to lose more easily? His passport to a white world? Or his faith in his principles? For me there was no soul-searching. "I shall leave Bandung tomorrow for Surabaya," I announced firmly to Mrs. Inggit in her kitchen next morning.

"For how long?" she asked.

"I don't know. Perhaps for good. It depends on the length of Tjokro's sentence. Whether six months or 20 years, I must do what I must do."

She was brewing *kopi tubruk,* our strong black Javanese coffee without which I cannot live, and her hands faltered a bit. "By leaving school it is possible you toss away all hopes for a career," was all she said.

"I know that. I also know Tjokro is my father-in-law. I am the eldest son of his family. But it is more than that. Have I not to serve my idol and the Cause?"

"But his new wife hasn't written you for help," she pleaded. "His children haven't sent word they are in need. Nobody has even asked you to come."

"I cannot help that. I feel in my breast it is my duty. . . . No! I feel it is my *privilege* to be able to help this guiding light who showed me the way." I watched the blanket of thick black grounds settle to the bottom of the cup. "I have received word that Tjok's arrest two days ago was totally unexpected. The Dutch suddenly banged on his door late at night and marched him off to prison at the point of a gun. He had no opportunity to make arrangements for his loved ones. There is nobody to look out for them."

"And so it seems clear to you that of all his millions of followers, the obligation is yours?"

"Yes, it is mine. He did not turn his back on me when I needed a home and shelter. I must now do the same for him. To pursue one's own life while one's adopted family are bleeding would not be the Indonesian way."

"You mean," she said softly, "that it would not be the Sukarno way."

I checked out of school the same morning. The President of the Bandung Institute of Technology, Professor Klopper, was troubled by my action. "Is it not your custom for a whole family to deny themselves in order to further the education of one gifted member?" he asked me not unkindly.

"Yes sir. I think, sir, not even starvation would prevent my family from furnishing the funds necessary for my education. As a schoolmaster, Father toils as hard as any laborer. Mother sits hour after hour into the night until her candle and her eyesight grow dim as she handpaints *batik* cloth. To scrape together the precious 300 guilders yearly tuition, they have recently added roomers. My sister and her husband also contribute a certain amount monthly."

"If, in later life," pursued Professor Klopper, "you are fitted only to be a worker in the fields, how will you then pay back those who have subsidized you these years?"

"Such is not our custom," I explained. "They would be angry if I tried. Our way, instead, is to always stand ready to help those who have aided us should they ever need it. That's *gotong royong*. Mutual help. And that is precisely why I must return."

Next day I packed up my wife, my hopes, and my dreams and brought them all back to Surabaya.

To support the household, I signed on as clerk in the railway station. My classification was "Raden Soekarno, B.KL. Der Eerste Klasse, Eerste Categorie." As Bureau Clerk First Class, First Category, I swallowed a diet of fumes and smoke seven hours a day since my airless office fronted the tracks of the dismal platform. My main chore was making up the payroll for the workers. Laboring full time left no opportunity to keep up with studies, but it was good in a way, because this huge, crowded depot was a central hub for trains in and out of the major cities like Madiun, Jogja, Malang, and Bandung, and I came into contact with the masses. Never did I miss a chance to sow the seeds of nationalism.

I earned 165 guilders monthly. I handed over 125 to the family. When they were depressed and unhappy, I took the lot to the movies on whatever of those 40 guilders I had left or I would buy some trifle like a picture postcard. I could afford little, but it meant much to them. I gave them my clothing to wear. I gave them discipline in the form of beatings on the rear with my sandals. I took care of all paternal duties, including seeing to Anwar's circumcision. I personally arranged for the medicine, the Holy Man, and the Selametan feast. Years later, when Anwar had become a political figure, I teased him with, "Now, don't forget I'm the one who circumcised you."

While Tjokro was under political arrest, the Dutch forbade the sons to continue their schooling. So Sukarno coached them. I even taught drawing. There was no money for paper or slates, but the walls at Djalan Plambetan were plain whitewashed cement. Is a white wall not a fine place to draw pictures? So, from memory, I scrawled likenesses and caricatures of my favorite movie heroine, Frances Ford.

After all, future politicians or not, we were purely and simply a household of hungry, frightened children. And me? I was just the tallest, that's all.

Tjokro was released in April, 1922, after seven months. In July, when the next school year officially began, I returned to the Technical Institute . . . and to Mrs. Inggit.

Utari and I no longer shared the same bed—or even the same room. The chasm between us had widened. As a bridegroom my affection toward her had been that of a brother. As head of Tjokroaminoto's household my role had been that of a father. It was now utterly unthinkable to play the part of husband.

I have observed if you open the heart of any man, myself included, it will tell you that happiness in marriage is when the wife is a combination mother, lover, and companion. I want to be mothered by my life partner. If I have a cold I want her to massage me. If I am hungry I wish to eat food she personally prepares. When my shirt has holes I wish my wife to mend it. With Utari the positions were reversed. I was the parent, she the infant.

She was not my beloved because there was no physical attraction and, in fact, we were never lovers. As for a comrade-in-arms, this type could scarcely be a companion to me when I was consumed with saving the world and she with playing catch ball.

It has always been my nature to turn to a woman for comfort. If it is a choice between one with loving arms and one with a sympathetic heart, I will often be drawn to the tender heart. I do not necessarily seek the man-woman relationship, but I require the tender thought and gentle encouragement which only the female heart can give.

Inggit and I were thrown together every night. I have always been one to stay up and read. Inggit also stayed up late preparing for the next day. She was always around. She was the landlady, I the boarder. We lived under the same roof. I saw her in the morning before she wound up her hair. She saw me in pajamas. I took all my meals with her, meals which she prepared, meals like *lodeh*, the vegetable soup with hot coconut milk which I love, or *ontjom*, the soyabean cake I love, or other delicacies she specially geared to my pleasure.

It was she, not my wife, who straightened my room, served me, took care of my clothes and listened to my thoughts. She was the one who mothered me, not Utari.

Mr. Sanusi was an elderly man totally indifferent to his wife. A gambler with a craziness about billiards, every night he was at the club pitting his skill. They were practically divorced though living in the same house. Theirs was not a happy home. All they shared was existence.

Enter into this setting an eager, sensual young boy. He is strongly drawn to her. He sees in her an awakened woman instead of a child like the one playing tag outside. And his passion is aroused. I have always been a very physical man and in those days there wasn't even television . . . just Inggit and me in an empty house. She was lonely. I was lonely. Her marriage wasn't right. My marriage wasn't right. And, as those things will, it grew.

Inggit and I shared a great deal. We both had the same interests. And, maybe, too . . . yes, we both even shared love of Sukarno. Besides being the embodiment of femininity, she also had blind, utter slavish devotion to Sukarno—good or evil, right or wrong. There was nothing in her life but me and what I thought and I hoped and what I dreamed. I talked; she listened. I rhapsodized; she worshiped.

At first we waited. For a few months we waited. I held her in my arms. Yes, that is true. I kissed her. But she kissed me also. Then I kissed her again. Then again . . . and before you knew it, we were caught up in our passion for each other. I was crazy in love with her. I came closer and closer . . . and then one night came the climax. And all the while she was the wife of Mr. Sanusi and I the husband of Utari.

Utari sensed what was happening but she knew her union with

me was never to be a blessed one. Since she had never known me in the true husband-wife sense, there was no jealousy on her part.

Mr. Sanusi, too, knew what was developing, but his marriage had been deteriorating rapidly. I did not have the burden of feeling that I took her away from her husband nor that I broke up a happy home, as the magazines call it. There was nothing to break up. He never even made an effort to recapture her.

Without dramatizing too much, I suppose there were guilt feelings. I don't remember whether I had them or whether I'm bringing them out now in an effort to explain my actions. I also don't know how my people might feel about their President discussing such things. I wouldn't want them to be embarrassed. Let's just say that as our love affair was progressing, I analyzed the guilt. And I have never stopped analyzing it.

I don't mean L'Affaire Inggit. I mean my whole life. It's as though I am eternally analyzing the forces within me. The forces around me. My brain and my soul are always on fire with that ceaseless struggle between good and evil.

After six months in Bandung, I personally escorted Utari home to her father.

"Pak," I said, "I am returning Utari to you."

"Whose decision is this?" Tjokro asked.

"Mine, Pak. It is I who want the divorce."

Then he merely asked, "Has she accepted your decision?"

I answered, "Yes. She is naturally distressed because Javanese girls consider a divorce a drawback somehow. She is perhaps a little embarrassed that after two years it didn't work out. She does not really want the divorce, but she realizes it is best for us both."

Tjokro nodded silently.

"Pak, I waited until you were out of prison and on your feet again to tell you, but this has not been good from the beginning. It just can't be good between us. Out of this cannot grow a happy marriage."

Tjok respected what I said. He asked no personal questions. And, after this happening, Tjok and his family and I were always on good terms. It remained just as it had been before.

All I said officially was, "I divorce you one stage," and our marriage was finished. You see, our methods of divorce are easy. There's no red tape. For Moslems, there are three stages of divorce. Stage one still leaves the way open for a reconciliation within 100 days. Stage two, a stronger step than the first, reiterates your intention to be free of her, but leaves still the slight possibility that maybe you will again become glad with her. The final stage is to say the actual words, "I divorce you." After this third *talak* is pronounced, the union is dissolved officially and the husband cannot remarry this wife without her having an interim marriage to another man.

Islamic laws do not provide for the woman's divorcing the man. Neither can she refuse to get divorced. Of course, if her husband is very naughty and she complains, "My husband beats me," or if she swears, "He never comes to me and, in fact, hasn't touched me in many months," and requests the *Kadi*, the religious judge, to grant her a divorce on these special grounds, he may then do it, for the *Kadi* has the power to say yes in extenuating circumstances.

All this is according to Mohammed and the laws of Islam which were founded in the desert. And where in the sands of the desert should one find lawyers or Letters of Divorcement? That is why we don't have such legal procedures. Thus, in 1922, I just handed my child bride to her father and that was that.

I returned to Surabaya . . . and to my true love. One night, after we were together about a year, I proposed. It was a very simple proposal. We were both alone—as usual—and I murmured, "I love you."

Inggit's "I love you, too," came quickly.

"I would like to marry you," I whispered.

"I would like to be your wife," she whispered back.

"Do you think we'll have difficulty?"

"No," she said softly. "I shall talk to Sanusi tomorrow."

Sanusi was extremely cooperative. Within a very short time she was free. There was no big scene like in the movies. I think he felt this was a very good thing after all. Inggit, he, and I remained on good terms thereafter. In fact, not much later he remarried.

Within a short time, Utari wed Mr. Bachroen Salam, a fellow boarder at Tjokro's. They had eight children and, as of this writing, are still married. So it appeared not much harm had been done on any side.

Inggit and I were married in 1923. My family never voiced one dissenting note when I transferred from a teen-aged wife to another a dozen years older than myself. If they did feel any twinge of shame toward me or of conscience toward Tjokro, I never knew about it.

Inggit with her big eyes and bangle bracelets had no background. She was totally uneducated, but intellectualism was never important to me in a woman. For me, what counts is humanity. This woman loved me dearly. She offered no opinions. Just looked on and watched and supported and adored. She gave me what books never could. She gave me love, warmth, unselfishness—what I needed and hadn't had since I left my mother's home.

Psychiatrists would say it was the mother image. It's possible; who knows? If I did marry her for this reason it was subconscious. She was then and, indeed, still is today a handsome woman. Consciously, anyhow, the feelings she aroused in me were anything but filial.

Inggit in this next period of my life was very good for me. She was my inspiration. She was my encouragement. And I was soon to need all of it.

I was now a sophomore in the university. I was now married to a woman I passionately craved. I was now over 21. My boyhood days were behind me. My life's work stretched before me. The embryonic thought that was nourished by Tjokro and began taking form in Surabaya suddenly burst its cocoon in Bandung and emerged from its chrystalis state a full-fledged political fighter.

With Inggit at my side, I stepped forward to keep my date with destiny.

✒ 6. Marhaenism

I WAS only 20 when a powerful political revelation dawned on me. At first it was but a germ of an idea gnawing away at my brain, but it was soon to become the platform on which our movement stood.

On our islands are laborers poorer even than church rats—too pitiful financially to ever rise socially, politically, or economically—yet each is his own boss, beholden to no one. He is the horse-cart driver who owns his own horse and cart and employs no other manpower. And the self-employed fisherman whose total equipment including the rod, hook, line, and proa is all his. And the farmer who is the sole owner and sole consumer of his product. These constitute the majority of our population. All are possessors of their own means of production so they are not proletarians. They have their own individuality. They fall into no stereotyped slots. Well, then, what are they?

That's what I spent days and nights and months pondering. What is my Indonesian brother? What do you call these workers whom a political economist termed "minimum sufferers"?

One sunny morning I wakened with the desire not to go to school—which wasn't very unusual. I was too full of politics to pay attention to studying.

Pedaling around aimlessly on my cycle—thinking—I found myself in the southern part of Bandung, a compact agricultural area where you see many farmers in their little fields, each of which is less than a third of a hectare. My attention for some reason was captured by a peasant hoeing his property. He was alone. His clothes were shabby. This typical scene struck me as symbolic of my people. I stood there a while contemplating it silently. We Indonesians being a warm, friendly sort, I approached him. In the regional Sundanese, I asked, "Who is the owner of this lot on which you are now working?"

He said to me, "Why, I am, sir."

I said, "Tell me, does anyone own this with you?"

"Oh, no, sir. I own it all by myself."

"Did you buy it?"

61

"No. It was handed down from father to son for generations."

As he continued digging, I also began digging . . . mentally. I thought of my theory. And as I thought more, I asked more. "How about your shovel? It is a little shovel, but is it also yours?"

"Yes, sir."

"And the hoe?"

"Yes, sir."

"Plow?"

"Mine, sir."

"The crop on which you're working, for whom is it?"

"For me, sir."

"Is it sufficient for your needs?"

He shrugged apologetically. "How could a plot so small be sufficient for a wife and four children?"

"Do you sell any of your produce?" I asked.

"There is just barely enough to keep us alive. There is no extra to sell."

"Do you employ anyone else?"

"No, sir. I couldn't afford to."

"Do you ever sell your own labor?"

"No, sir. I must work very hard, but my labors are all for myself."

I pointed to a small cottage. "Who owns that house?"

"That's my house, sir. It is only a small one, but it is mine."

"So then," I said, sifting my own thoughts as we spoke, "would you say that everything is yours?"

"Yes, sir."

I then asked this young farmer his name. And he told me. Marhaen. Marhaen is a common name like Smith or Jones. At that moment the light of inspiration flooded my brain. I would use that name for all Indonesians with the same miserable lot. From then on I would call my people Marhaenists.

The rest of the day I bicycled around working out my new concept. And that night I gave an indoctrination lecture on it to my youth group.

"Our farmers till infinitesimal patches of soil. They are end products of the feudal system under which the first peasant was exploited by the first feudal lord and on down through the centuries. Even those of us who are not farmers are victims of the Dutch trade imperialism, victims whose ancestors were forced into minimal enterprises to eke out an existence. These who constitute nearly the whole Indonesian population are Marhaenists."

I pointed to a cart driver. "You . . . you over there. Do you work in a factory for other people?"

"No," he said.

"Then you are a Marhaenist." I gestured to a *sate* seller. "You . . . you have no partner, no overhead . . . you, too, are a Marhaenist. A Marhaenist is a person with small means; a little man with little ownership, little tools, sufficient to himself. Our tens of millions of impoverished souls work for no person and no person works for them. There is no exploitation of one man by another. Marhaenism is Indonesian Socialism in operation."

The discovery of our national identity under the label of "Marhaenism" was a symbol. So, too, our country's name had to become a symbol. The word "Indonesia" comes from a German ethnologist named Jordan who was a scholar in Holland. His special study was our island chain. Due to the archipelago's proximity to India, he labeled it "The islands of the Indies." *Nesos* being Greek for islands, it came out *Indusnesos*—which eventually became Indonesia.

When we felt the necessity to federate our islands in one comprehensive manner, we fastened on this name and loaded it with political connotations until it, too, became a spearhead of national identity. This was 1922-1923.

These were the years when we were a humiliated race treated like the scum of the earth by our captors. We were permitted nothing. Ground under the Dutch heel at every turn, we were even prevented from mouthing the term "Indonesia." It happened that once, in the heat of a speech, "Indonesia" came out of my mouth. "Stop . . . stop . . . ," the police ordered. They blew their whistles. They beat their sticks. "The use of that word is strictly prohibited . . . halt the meeting. . . ." And the meeting was instantly broken up.

In Surabaya I had been a bird looking for a place to nest. But in Bandung I became mature. My physical appearance ripened accordingly. America's matinee idol of the period was Norman Kerry and in order to look older and more dashing, I grew a moustache like his. Unfortunately, mine wouldn't curl up prettily at the ends the way his did and my wife insisted the only movie star I succeeded in looking like was Charlie Chaplin. Alas, my sole attempt to copy anybody ended in dismal failure and the whole idea was abandoned quickly.

It was in 1922 that I first got into trouble. There had been a huge outdoor mass meeting in Bandung. The whole of the public square was black with people. This was the *Radicale Concentratie*, a monster rally organized by all the nationalist organizations so that representatives of every existent party might come together for a single appearance to protest many things at one time.

Each of the leaders gave speeches. Me, I was just a youngster. I was listening. But suddenly I wanted to say something desperately. I couldn't control myself; they were all speaking nonsense. As usual they were begging. They weren't demanding.

Up shot the eager hand of Sukarno, the guiding star of the Youth Clubs, to request the Chair's permission to address the meeting.

"I want to speak my piece," I yelled.

"Go ahead," the Chairman yelled back.

There were P.I.D., Dutch Secret Police, all over the place. Right in front of me stood one big, scowling red-faced policeman. The supreme power—the white man. He alone could stop me. He, single-handed, could disband the meeting. He, all by himself, with the authority vested in him, could dissolve our assembly and arrest me. But I was young, reckless, and filled with the spirit, so up I jumped and began to shout, "Why does a volcano like Mount Kelud explode? It explodes because the hole in the crater becomes stopped up. There's no way for it to release its inner tensions. Bit by bit the forces inside the volcano accumulate and . . . BUP . . . the whole thing erupts.

"It will be the same with our Nationalist Movement if the Dutch keep stopping our mouths and we are not allowed to give vent to our emotions. *Saudara-Saudara*, brothers and sisters, ladies and gentlemen, one day there will come an explosion with us, too. And when we erupt, The Hague will go sky-high. I hereby challenge the Colonial Government to stop us."

From the corner of my eye I saw the Police Commissioner edging forward to prevent me from speaking further, but I was so fiery that I thundered on.

"What good are tens of thousands of us massing together if all we do is produce petitions? Why are we always 'humbly requesting the esteemed Government' to please, out of the goodness of their hearts, build us a school? Is it not a policy of kneeling before His Excellency, the Governor General of the Netherlands East Indies who, dressed in black tie, receives the delegation which bows and pays respects and submits a petition humbly requesting the reduction of taxes? We humbly request. . . ! That's the phrase our leaders always use.

"Until now we have never been the attackers. Ours is a movement not of pressure but of pleading. Nothing is ever given out of pity. Let us today resort to a policy of self-reliance. Let us stop begging. Instead, let us shout, 'Mr. Imperialist, this is what we DEMAND of you!'"

Well, those omnipotent, all-powerful Dutch policemen who had the power to stop this meeting, did. They stopped it and me. Heyne, the Bandung Police Chief, was furious. Elbowing through the milling mob of standees, he vaulted onto the platform, pulled me off and announced, "Mr. Chairman, now I stop the whole meeting. It's over. Finished. Done. You're all dismissed. Everybody goes home right now. OUT!"

No sooner did Sukarno open his mouth the first time than he came into immediate contact with the law. I became a celebrity overnight and everybody knew the name Sukarno. I had the nucleus of a powerful following but, unfortunately, I also developed a powerful following amongst the Dutch Police. Wherever I went they followed. The word went forth: "There's a troublemaker at the Technical Society. Watch out for him." With one speech the quiet, withdrawn, lovable Karno developed enemies and for the next 20 years I was never to be off their hate list.

My premiere performance created such havoc that I was instantly summoned to the Dean's office. "If you wish to continue at this institute," warned Professor Klopper, "you must devote yourself to schooling. I have no objection to any boy having political ideas, but it must be that first and foremost you are a student. You must promise that, as from today, you won't mix with the political movement again."

I did not lie to him. I put my case honestly. "Professor, what I promise is that I never again shall neglect the lessons you give in college."

"That's not what I asked of you."

"That's all I can give, Professor, but this I give wholeheartedly. I solemnly promise to devote more time to my studies."

He was very nice about it. "Have I your word you will give up addressing mass rallies for the balance of your college days?"

"Yes, sir," I promised. "You have my solemn word."

And I kept my promise. But speaking to the masses was all I lived for, so I did it in fantasy. One night Inggit's boarding house was full of roomers and we had to double up. I shared my bed with a schoolmate. In the middle of the night I was overtaken by an urge to orate passionately as though I were addressing a cheering throng of 10,000. Standing upright, I pretended my bed was a podium.

"Do you know what Indonesia is?" I declaimed to my schoolmate's back. "Indonesia is this beautiful, strong tree. That blue, clear sky. That lazy white cloud. It's this warm air.

"My dear friends, the roaring sea beating upon the shore at dusk is, to me, Indonesia's soul stirring in the thunder of the ocean's waves. When I hear the children laugh, I hear Indonesia. When I inhale our flowers, I breathe in Indonesia. This is what our land means to me."

After a few hours of applauding my heart-tugging phrases, Mr. Djoko Asmo needed sleep more than my oratory. At two A.M. he fell fast asleep despite my ravings. I'd exhausted myself so thoroughly that midway in my impassioned plea, I, too, dropped off. Next morning we discovered we'd forgotten to douse the lamp. Our mosquito netting was badly scorched. The kerosene had burned all the way down and from the steady fumes and smoke both of us were nearly asphyxiated. We were lucky at that. We could've set ourselves on fire. It occurred to me if the future Saviour of Indonesia were going to save his people, first he had to save himself.

I still spent too much time on politics to be a really brilliant student. The fact that I even made the passing grade amazed me. Who studied? Not me. Never. First of all I counted on my photographic memory and, secondly, I was so busy cramming politics that there were no hours left to open a schoolbook.

Mathematics was my nemesis. I am not very strong in mathematics. Architectural drawing I found very attractive, but those engineering calculations and computations were difficult for me. *Kleinste Vierkanten* or what is called Geodetics, a kind of civil engineering where you measure the ground and learn to break it up into square feet, I failed altogether.

For an exam in math, I confess I did cheat just a little. We all cheated in some ways. Take drawing building constructions. I excelled in this. During test periods, the teacher would march up and down the aisles watching everybody. Immediately he was in another part of the classroom with his back to us, one of the boys nearby would hiss, "Ssss, Karno, do my sketch for me, will you?" I'd exchange papers with him, run through a second drawing, and quickly hand it back. My friends returned the favor in *Kleinste Vierkanten* when the Professor would chalk three problems on the blackboard and allot us 45 minutes to work them out. They'd place their papers at an angle on the desk so I could conveniently copy the answers. Naturally, I was smart enough to copy only from students who excelled in mathematics. This is not exactly what you call cheating. In Indonesia, this properly falls under the heading of what we term close cooperation. *Gotong royong.*

The reason I failed and received a mark of three was because once the Professor did a dirty trick. He surprised us all with an oral examination. Each of us took it separately. Just the student and the Professor all alone in the room. I naturally failed.

All the classes were taught in Dutch. It became the language in which I did my thinking. Even today I automatically curse in Dutch. When I pray to God, I pray in Dutch.

Our curriculum was geared to a society of Dutch rule. The science I learned was science of a capitalist technique; for instance, the knowledge about irrigation systems. It was not how to irrigate rice fields in the best manner. It was only about the water supply systems for sugar cane and tobacco. This was irrigation in the interest of imperialism and capitalism, irrigation not to feed the starving masses, but to fatten the plantation owners.

Our instruction in road building could never benefit the population. Roads weren't engineered to be cross-jungle or interisland so our people could ride or walk better. We were taught only to plan byways along the seacoast from harbor to harbor so factories might have maximum transportation of goods and proper communication between sailing vessels.

Take mathematics. No universities anywhere else taught the measure chain. Here it was taught. This is a tape 20 meters long used solely by overseers of slave labor on plantations. In sketching class, when we drafted a model town we also had to indicate the residence of the *Kabupaten*, the District Chief who watches over the slaving peasants.

The week of graduation I discussed this with the Rector Magnificus of the Technical Faculty, Professor Ir. G. Klopper, M.E.

"Why," I asked, "are we stuffed with information geared only to the perpetuation of the colonialists' domination over us?"

"This Technical Institute," he explained, "was established primarily to promote The Hague's policy in the Indies. To keep pace with the rate of expansion and exploitation, my Government feels more engineers and skilled overseers are needed."

"In other words, the reason natives are permitted to attend these classes in the first place is to enable Holland to perpetuate her policy of imperialism here?"

"Yes, Mr. Sukarno, that is correct," he answered.

And so it seemed that although I was to devote my entire life to crushing the colonialists' rule, I had them to thank for my education.

With the two lone Indonesians who stuck it out with me, on May 25, 1926, I was graduated with the Degree of "Ingenieur." My diploma in Civil Engineering stipulated I was a specialist in highways and waterworks. I was now entitled to sign my name: Ir. Dr. Raden Soekarno. When he conferred my Master of Engineering doctorate upon me, the Dean said, "Dr. Sukarno, a diploma may someday crumble and wither away to ashes. It has no immortality. Remember that the only substance which is eternal is a man's character. The memory of it lasts long after he is gone."

I never forgot that.

⤴ 7. "Bahasa Indonesia"

MY promise was fulfilled. My schooling was over. From this moment forth nothing would deter me from the work I was born to do.

Ever since I'd stood on that bridge in Surabaya and heard my people's cry, I knew it was I who must fight for them. The burning desire to set my people free was beyond mere personal ambition. I was consumed with it. It permeated my whole being. It filled my nostrils. It coursed through my veins. It's what a man serves his whole lifetime for. It was more than a duty. More than a calling. For me it was a— religion.

According to my professors, my thesis on harbor construction and waterways plus my theories on city planning had such "a high degree of inventiveness and originality" that I was offered a post of assistant instructor. I turned it down. I was also offered a job with the municipality. I refused that, too.

One of my teachers, Professor Ir. Wolf Schoemaker, was a great man. To him there was no white human being and no brown. No Dutchman or Indonesian. No bond or free. He bowed only to ability. "I appreciate your capabilities," he said, "and I do not want them wasted. You have a creative mind. I urge you to take a job with the Government."

Despite my objections, he recommended me to the director of the Department of Public Works, who proposed me to design a project for the home of the District Chief. Naturally, the head engineer was a Dutchman not at all conversant with Indonesian ways and necessities. Since I didn't want the job anyway, I told him what I thought of his architectural plans: "You'll pardon me, sir, but your conceptions are those of a Dutch grocer. Everything you Dutch design is technically clumsy. The lots in Bandung are only 15 meters wide and 20 deep and the houses are cramped. Bandung is laid out like a chicken coop. Even the roads are narrow because they are conceived according to the narrow Dutch thinking. It is the same with the project you have designed. It has no *schwung*."

Since I'd done such a capital job of refusing this tempting commission, I felt I owed Professor Schoemaker an explanation. "You have said that in a small scope I embody the power to create. Well, I wish to create," I said heavily, "but for my own. I do not believe my future is to be a builder of homes. My destiny is to be an architect of a nation.

"Our nationalist movement's old policy of cooperation with the regime in hopes of begging concessions from them has gained us only broken promises. Through my efforts we recently embarked on a policy of noncooperation. This is based on the desire to be self-reliant and economically independent of foreign help."

My friend heard me out silently; then he said, "My boy, your talents should be put to a maximum use. On your own it may take years to proceed in your profession. Only high-ranking Dutchmen or Government officials can afford an architect's services and these will be loath to commission an untried youngster who also happens to be high on the police list of troublemakers. You would do well to get your start with this offer."

His point was well taken. "Professor, I refuse to cooperate in order to remain free in my thinking and actions. If in any way I am employed by the Dutch I become a silent partner to the oppressive policy of their monopolistic, autocratic regime. The youth of today must break with the tradition of becoming colonial officials immediately after graduation or we will never be free."

"Do not accept a long-term job with the authorities if you feel so strongly," he pleaded, "but just make this one home for the District Chief. Please . . . do it for me."

I did as he asked. It was most successful and I was flooded with offers to perform similar engineering feats for other officials. Although the subsidy from my family ceased after graduation and I had no visible means to support my wife, I refused. I had cooperated with the Government out of my great affection and respect for my Professor. But that was the first and last time I would. Later, when the Department of Public Works offered me a position as a permanent employee, I refused on the basis that I advocated noncooperation.

I badly needed money and a job. I had no prospects for either when I heard of a vacancy in the Ksatrian Institute School, operated by the nationalist leader, Dr. Setiabudi. The position called for an educator to teach two subjects. One subject was history, for which I had a definite leaning. The other? Mathematics! And in all its facets!

Now, as I have already pointed out with painful honesty, if there was one subject in which I definitely did not excel, it was mathematics. But I had no choice. The Professor in charge of interviewing asked, "Dr. Sukarno, you are a certified engineer so, of course, you are well versed in mathematics, is that right?"

"Ohhh, yes sir," I grinned, oozing confidence. "Yes sir. Yes, indeed. Well versed."

"Well then, can you teach mathematics?" he asked.

"Oh, yes indeed, sir," I lied. "I'm very good in mathematics. Excellent, in fact. It's my best subject." Inggit and I had reached bottom. All we could serve guests was one cup of weak tea without sugar. So, what could I have told him? That I absolutely couldn't teach it? That in fact I flunked it? Then I wouldn't get the job.

My friend, Dr. Setiabudi, came to me personally and again inquired, "Sukarno, what do you really think? Can you teach?"

And I repeated in a shocked, hurt voice, "Can I teach! Why, sure I can teach. Of course I can teach. Naturally."

"Mathematics, too?"

"Mathematics positively!"

Oddly enough, the trouble I ran into was with my history lessons. My class numbered 30 pupils, including Anwar Tjokroaminoto. Nobody gave me any pointers in the art of teaching so I inaugurated my own system. Unfortunately, it didn't come anywhere near the official method. In history class I had strictly my own style. I never quite assimilated the theory that children must be instructed factually. My idea was to stir them passionately.

I stuck to a sense of history rather than actual names, dates, and places. I never bothered with what year Columbus discovered America or what date Napoleon met his Waterloo or anything even remotely like what they usually learn in school.

Instead of treating my pupils as boys and girls who could only memorize facts, I philosophized with them. I reasoned why such and such happened. I dramatized episodes theatrically. I didn't impart knowledge coldly and chronologically. Oh no, not me. Not the born orator. I waved my arms and acted it out. When I talked about Sun Yat-sen I actually shouted and thumped the desk.

It was a rule of the Department Van Onderwijs en Eerendienst— The Netherlands East Indies Department of Education—that schools were at given times visited by inspectors. In due process an inspector dropped into my history class. He sat quietly in the back of the room to observe. For two hours I taught in my own individual manner as best I possibly could, knowing all the while he was watching me closely.

It so happened this particular session dealt with imperialism. This being a subject with which I was intimately familiar, I became so emotional that I hopped up and down and cursed the system altogether. Can you imagine? With the Dutch inspector staring at me unbelievingly, I actually called Holland "Those damn colonialists!"

When class and my tirade were both over, the inspector made it quite plain that in his judgment I was not exactly the best educator he'd ever seen and that, needless to say, I did not have a great future in this job. He told me, "Raden Sukarno, you are not a teacher—you are a lecturer!" And that was the end of my brief career as a schoolmaster.

On July 26, 1926, I opened my first engineering office in partnership with a fellow classmate, Ir. Anwari.

I was never again to have the chance to enter the Halls of Science. Life immediately picked me up by the scruff of the neck and cast me onto refuse dumps and into rickety, leaking huts. It threw me into market places and it flung me to the forests, villages, and rice fields. I didn't become a teacher. I became a preacher. My pulpit was a roadside. My congregation? The teeming masses hungering for salvation.

In 1926 I began preaching guided nationalism. Previously I had just left my listeners more conscious of nationalism than they had been before. Now I not only roused them, I directed them. I explained that the time had come when we required a new democratic society to replace the feudalism we'd had for centuries.

I said to my audiences, "No longer should we ally ourselves submissively to a philosophy which has contributed to our destruction. A life divided into classes, castes, and haves and have-nots promotes servility. The phenomenon of modern existence is the elevation of the masses. He who does not heed this will be crushed in the crowd of people and nations fighting for a place.

"We need equality. We've had inequality all our lives. Let us dispense with titles. Although I was born into the ruling class, I never call myself *raden* and I beg you never address me so from this moment forward. Let no one ever refer to me from today as *Tedaking Kusuma Rembesing Madu*—'Descendant of Blue Blood.' No! I am simply the grandson of a farmer. Feudalism belongs to the dead past, not to our Indonesia of the future."

While I was educating my hearers to abolish the system of feudal lords, I went a step further. Language. In the Javanese dialect alone there were 13 grades, depending upon your station, and our archipelago spoke no less than 86 such regional dialects.

"Until now," I said, "the Indonesian language is spoken only by the nobility. Not by the common man. Now, today, this minute, let all of us resolve to learn to speak *Bahasa Indonesia,* the Indonesian language.

"It must be that the Marhaen and the aristocrat may converse in the same tongue. It must be that a man from one island may be able to communicate with his brother on another island. If we who multiply like rabbits are to be one society, one nation, we must have one unified language—the language of the new Indonesia."

Formerly, a Javanese would never ask a higher-grade Javanese, "Have you called me?" He would never dare baldly utter the word "you" to a superior. He would instead use the words "your feet" or "your slippers." Thus he'd inquire, "Have your slippers called me?"

Degrees of servility were also manifest in gestures. I point with my index finger, but a lower-grade person in my presence would point with his thumb. Such humility offered the conquerors a secret weapon which helped breed a nation of "worms" and "frogs," as they called us. We were referred to as "the most timid people on earth."

Many many years later I fell madly in love with a beautiful young princess from one of the four kingdoms of Java, but my advisors decreed that I, as a man associated with the masses, could not marry her. Although I was bleeding, they pointed out how I had led the rebellion against feudalism and thus could not now be a party to it. It ended as a platonic love affair.

In Javanese nobility a wife never loses her high standing. If she marries beneath her, the husband must request her permission for everything. Even to make love to his own wife, the man who might be a *raden* must first ask formally of his bed-mate, the princess, "Madam, may I have your permission to climb upon you?" And then she says, "Yes. Permission granted." So, perhaps it was for the best. I cannot see Sukarno in that position.

In feudal times we had no comprehensive modes of address like Mister or Mistress or Miss that would encompass every stratum of individual. When I proclaimed *Bahasa Indonesia,* we required a whole new set of appellations that could be used interchangeably between the old and young, rich and poor, President and peasant. That's when we developed *Pak* or *Bapak* for father, *Bu* or *Ibu* for mother, and *Bung*, which means brother. It was during this period of our cultural revolution that I became known as Bung Karno.

The year 1926 was my year of three-dimensional maturization. The second facet of the trinity was theism. I thought and spoke much about God. Despite our country's being predominantly Moslem, my concepts were not rooted solely in the Islamic God. Even as I took hesitant steps down the kindergarten path of belief, I did not see The Almighty as a personal God. To my way of thinking freedom for mankind included freedom of religion.

As my theological concepts widened, Tjokro's ideology grew narrower and narrower to me. His vision of independence for our fatherland was viewed strictly through the mircroscopic lens of the Islamic religion.

I no longer went to him for teaching. Neither were his friends considered my tutors any more. Though still a young man, I was no longer a receiver. I was now already a leader. I had followers. I had a reputation. I had become Tjok's political equal. We had no sudden break-up over this. It was more like a slow bit-by-bit estrangement.

Although Tjok and I pulled wide apart politically, we remained close-knit personally. The Asian finds no difficulty in distinguishing between ideology and humanity. When a nationalist named Hadji Misbach attacked Tjok viciously at one congress, I demanded an apology for my old friend. Hadji Misbach stated his regrets.

Opposing someone politically does not mean we cannot cherish him personally. To us, the one has nothing to do with the other. This is unfathomable to the Western mind, but is completely in consonance with the Eastern mentality. I love even those who hate me. For instance, I cite Pak Alimin and Pak Muso. Both often acted as my political instructors when I lived with Tjokro. Later they succumbed to Communism, traveled to Moscow and subsequently, in 1948, after I became President, staged a Communist revolt and an attempted takeover. They plotted my downfall. But we Javanese have a saying: "The one who teaches you must be honored even more than your parent."

When Alimin became a very, very old and ill man, I visited him. Then the papers sneered, "Uh-oh, there goes Sukarno visiting a Communist!"

Yes, Pak Alimin tried to overthrow me. But he was one of my early teachers. I am grateful to him for the good he did teach. I owe him much.

Even harder to forget is the fact that he was one of the leaders of our pioneer struggle. Anyone who fought for the liberation of his country, no matter what he might feel about me later, deserves the gratitude of his people and his President.

It is the same with Tjokro. To my dying day I shall write his name with tenderness.

Politically Bung Karno was a Nationalist. Theologically Bung Karno was a Theist. But Bung Karno had become a tripleheaded believer. Ideologically he was now a Socialist. I repeat that. I became a Socialist. Not a Communist. I did not become a Communist. I did not even become a camouflaged Communist. I have never become a Communist. There are still people who think Socialism is equivalent to Communism. On hearing the word Socialist they cannot sleep. They jump up and yell, "Aha, I knew it! That Sukarno fellow is a Communist!" No, I am not. I am a Socialist. I am a Leftist.

Leftists are those who desire to change the existing capitalistic, imperialistic order. The desire to spread social justice is leftist. It is not necessarily Communistic. A person with such ideals is a leftist. He is not necessarily Communistic. Leftists can even be at odds with the Communists. Leftophobia, the disease of dreading leftist ideas, is a sickness I dread as much as Islamophobia.

Nationalism without social justice is nothingism. How can a miserably poor country such as ours have anything but a Socialist trend?

Hearing me speak on behalf of democracy, a youngster asked if I were a democrat. I said, "Yes, I am most definitely a democrat." Then he said, "But I thought you were a Socialist." "I am," I said. He tied it all up with, "Then you must be a Democratic Socialist."

Perhaps that's one way of labeling me. Indonesians are different from any other people on earth. Our Socialism does not include extreme materialistic concepts since Indonesia is primarily a God-fearing, God-loving nation. Our Socialism is a mixture. We draw political equality from the American Declaration of Independence. We draw spiritual equality from Islam and Christianity. We draw scientific equality from Marx.

To this mixture we add the National identity: Marhaenism. Then we sprinkle in *gotong royong,* which is the spirit, the essence of working together, living together and helping one another. Mix it all up and the result is Indonesian Socialism.

These concepts which I put forward in the '20's and from which I have never deviated don't fall neatly into a box according to the

Western mind but, then, you must remember I do not have a Western mind. Altering our people so that they fall into neat, orderly Western pigeonholes can't be done. Leaders who have tried failed. I always think in terms of the Indonesian mentality.

Since high school I have been a pioneer. I fit into no pattern politically, which is, perhaps, why I am subject to so much misunderstanding. My politics do not correspond to anyone else's. But, then, neither does my background correspond to anyone else's. My grandfather inculcated in me Javanism and mysticism. From Father came Theosophy and Islamism. From Mother, Hinduism and Buddhism. Sarinah gave me humanism. From Tjokro came Socialism. From his friends came Nationalism.

To that I added gleanings of Karl Marxism and Thomas Jeffersonism. I learned economics from Sun Yat-sen, benevolence from Gandhi. I was able to synthesize modern scientific schooling with ancient animistic culture and to translate the end product into living, breathing messages of hope geared to the understanding of a peasant. What came out has been called—in plain terms—Sukarnoism.

I had grown away from *Sarekat Islam*, but had not yet replaced it with any formal party. My so-called political organization in 1926 was the outgrowth of the Bandung Students Club, which had been sponsored by the university so students might play bridge or billiards. It was organized for feasting and fun. Natives were permitted in the club, but after joining I learned we could not be members of the Board. "I cannot accept such a situation," I exclaimed. "I shall leave the club." As in Modjokerto, everybody played follow the leader. When Sukarno quit, the other Indonesians were right behind.

With the five Indonesian members I founded a Study Club. I selected representative literature such as *Handelingen der Tweede Kamer Van de Staten General* ("Actions of the Second Chamber of the State General of Holland") from the library and each of us kept the book one week. At the close of every five-week cycle we held a meeting—usually at my house—and sat up all night long debating the merits of the strategies involved. You could always tell when Bung Karno had had his chance at it. Sentences were underlined. Paragraphs circled. Whoever read it after me could easily see my trend of thought. I left my open criticism in the margins. I marked the pages I agreed with and noted on the bottom those I didn't. Fresh and clean from the library shelves, these treasured volumes were never the same afterwards.

To this Algemeene Studieclub flocked young Indonesian intellectuals, many of whom were freshly returned from Holland with
bright, shiny new academic degrees under their arms. Active ex-
changes of political ideas became our main activity. Branches of the
Study Club sprang up in Solo, Surabaya, and other major cities in
Java. We added a club organ, *Suluh Indonesia Muda*—"Torch of the
Indonesian Youth"—and, as might be expected, Chairman Sukarno
was the prime contributor.

I was so enmeshed politically that I had little thought for anything else, and my engineering office slowed down until it ground to
an absolute standstill. I was so much more concerned with the deep
side of life than the frivolous that even on a sultry, moonlight night
my mind was on isms more than on Inggit. When other young lovers
were rediscovering each other, I was curled up with *Das Kapital*. I
was plunging deeper and deeper.

I thus approached the end of my third *windu*. A *windu* is a period
of eight years. From 1901 to 1909 was the *windu* of childlike thought.
From 1910 to 1918 was the age of development. From 1919 to 1927
was the *windu* of maturization. I was now ready.

ᴈ 8. The Founding of the PNI

THE timing was right for me to start a party of my own. There were two factors.

By 1917 the Hohenzollern Dynasty had crumbled in Germany, Franz Josef had fallen, Czar Alexander was tottering. Splinters from the destroyed thrones of the world flew past the ears of Queen Wilhelmina and the thunder of nearby revolutions rolled over her fields.

The year 1917 brought Lenin's Bolshevik uprising and the birth of the Soviet Union. Béla Kun led a revolt in Hungary. Germany's workers established the Republic of Weimar. To the right of the Motherland and to the left yawned chaos while she herself, after three years of war had raged around her, was materially and spiritually broken.

With contact between the Netherlands and her Indies ruptured because of wartime restrictions and the almost nonexistent sea communication, the largest part of her income—riches from the stepchild, Indonesia—dwindled. Politically Holland was in travail, too. Her great need created a serious vacuum which was soon filled with dissatisfaction and unrest. To complicate her miseries, a Socialist named Dr. Pieter Jelles Troelstra stirred a proletarian revolutionary movement. First the war, then the revolution. Holland was weakened.

Stirred by all this, nationalism was burgeoning in Netherlands India. The Dutch realized they had to soften the hearts of their brown-skinned subjects because they had too much trouble in their own frontyard to risk uprisings in the archipelago. The Indies were the cork on which the Netherlands floated. At all costs they needed to keep their brown "brothers" chained loyally. Since the land of the dikes was too weak to apply force, the climate of world events led to "The November Promises"—and appeasement.

In November, 1918, our Governor General, Count Van Limburg Stirum, promised us wider political rights, greater liberties, freedom to hold mass meetings, a say in Parliament.

We soon learned that Holland had no intention of keeping these short-lived, infamous promises. Within one year she betrayed us by

78

commissioning as governor Dirk Fock, up to that time her most reactionary governor.

Comparatively, our previous regimes had been moderate. Fock was more oppressive and allowed fewer rights than ever. He suppressed, persecuted, and instituted laws minimizing whatever freedom we'd had before. One such stated that even "covered" remarks, if they were reported or repeated, made one liable to arrest. In other words, were you alone in a cave and your solitary ravings were reported to a policeman, you could be sentenced to six years. You could even be jailed for talking in your sleep!

This administration put through the "Exorbitant Law" which sent so many of our brothers and sisters to places of terror. It became lawful to jail or exile a native without trial. As Holland gained strength events worsened. The fearsome Fock was followed by the even more cruel De Graeff.

The time was ripe to press for nationalism. But how?

We had no single powerful party. *Sarekat Islam* had split. Tjok retained the reins of his weakened half while the other faction changed its name to *Sarekat* (meaning union) *Rakjat* (meaning people).

Taking advantage of the dissension, Communism infiltrated *Sarekat Rakjat*. In 1926 they planned and executed their "grand scale physical revolution for liberty and Communism." It failed dismally. Holland crushed it forthwith and over 2,000 leaders were shipped to varying places of exile. Another 10,000 were jailed. The aftermath was chaos.

Sarekat Rakjat was declared illegal. Those who had looked to *Sarekat Rakjat* now had nothing. Those who had grown increasingly dissatisfied with Tjokro also had nothing. There was no solid nationalist nucleus any more.

I, meanwhile, had found my political water-level. Over every cup of *kopi tubruk*, in every corner where men gathered, the name Bung Karno was being discussed. Popular resentment against the Dutch and popularity for Bung Karno gained side by side. On the Fourth of July, 1927, supported by six friends from the Algemeene Studieclub, I founded the PNI, *Partai Nasional Indonesia,* the Indonesian National Party. The people were ready. Bung Karno was ready. Now there was nothing to stop us—but the Dutch.

The PNI's objective was complete independence—NOW. Even my most loyal followers trembled at my radicalism, because former organizations always partially concealed their aims so the Dutch wouldn't persecute them. With me there was to be no concealment.

During debate in a closed room, several friends tried to derail me. "The people are not yet ready," they wailed.

"The people ARE ready," I answered sharply. "And that will be our slogan: Indonesia Free NOW. I say, 'Indonesia *Merdeka* NOW.' "

"This can't be done, Bung," they fretted. "Your ideas are too strong. We will be crushed before we start. The majority who hear you follow blindly, but Indonesia free NOW is too radical. First we must slowly gain national unity."

"We are not united, true. We have too many ideologies, agreed. We must gain national unity, yes. But not slowly any more. Three hundred fifty years has been slowly enough!"

They tried to explain their fearful views. "First we must educate our millions. They must be prepared in order to govern themselves. Second, we must make them healthy so they can stand upright. It is better to have everything complete and final first."

"The only time everything is complete and final is when you're dead," I shouted. "Taking time to slowly educate them can last generations. It is not necessary to write a thesis or knock out malaria before they obtain freedom. Indonesia *Merdeka* NOW. Later we will educate and make healthy our people and our country. Let us now rise up."

"But the Dutch will arrest us!"

"They will also gain a glimmer of respect for us. It's human nature to spit on a weakling of an enemy, but although you fight a stalwart foe, you feel at least he's worth fighting against."

I thought of myself as a rebel. I thought of the PNI as an army of rebels. In 1928 I proposed that all members wear uniforms. This triggered a raging controversy. One loyal constituent from Tegal stood up and declared, "This is not in keeping with the national identity. What we should wear are sarongs without shoes or sandals. Let us look like the revolutionaries we are."

I disagreed. "Many go barefoot who are nonrevolutionary. Many high officials wear sarongs, yet work wholeheartedly for the colonialists. That which characterizes a revolutionary is the fight he puts up. We are an army, my brothers.

"I further suggest we condemn the sarong even in private practice. This old-fashioned native dress has a demeaning effect. The minute an Indonesian dons trousers, he walks erect like any white man. Immediately he wraps that feudal symbol around his middle, he stoops over in a perpetual bow. His shoulders sag. He doesn't stride manfully, he shuffles apologetically. He instantaneously becomes hesitant and servile and subservient."

"Nonetheless," retaliated Dr. Ali Sastroamidjojo, then a branch chairman of PNI and later my first Ambassador to the United States of America, "the sarong is in keeping with Indonesian tradition."

"Indonesian tradition of the past—yes," I exploded. "Not with the new Indonesia of the future. We must be divested of that influence which chains us to the cringing past as nameless, faceless servants and houseboys and peasants. Let us demonstrate we are as progressive as our former masters. We must take our place as upstanding equals. We must put on modern clothing."

Dr. Ali stood up again. "Getting uniforms would cost too much and we don't have any money."

"We will get very cheap uniforms," I suggested. "Just short-sleeved shirts and trousers. Looking crisp and efficient doesn't cost money. We must dress well. We must look like leaders." Some sided with me, some with Ali. I lost.

Nevertheless I retained these sentiments. That is why ever since I took the oath of office in 1945, I have worn a uniform. The foreign press criticizes me for it. They sneer, "Ugggh! President Sukarno's buttons are golden. Uggh! He wears a uniform just to show off."

Look here, I am a mass psychologist. I have other suits. I prefer uniforms for every public appearance because I know downtrodden people delight to see their President crisply tailored. If the Chief Executive appeared in a rumpled, wilted suit like a tourist with his hat brim damp, there would be a groan of disappointment. Our Marhaens can see that every day in every *kampong*. An Indonesian leader must be a commanding figure. He must exude power. For a once-subjugated race, this is imperative.

Our people are so used to seeing the white foreigners in smart uniforms which are symbols of authority and they're so used to seeing themselves in sarongs which are symbols of inferiority. When I became Commander-in-Chief, I knew they wanted a hero figure. I gave that to them. In the beginning I even buckled a gold dagger at my side. The people adored it.

Before someone else says it, I say it first: Yes, I know I personally look well in a uniform. But beyond liking the starched, immaculate image it gives me, when I am cloaked physically in military dress, I am clad mentally in a mantle of confidence. This I transmit to my people. They need it.

The year 1928 was the year for propaganda and speeches. I divided my city into political precincts: North Bandung, South Bandung, East, West, Central, the outskirts, and so on. I addressed each district once a week. They called me "The Lion of the Platform."

We had no microphones so I shouted myself hoarse to a square black with people every afternoon or a meeting hall jammed with standees every evening, or a movie house filled with patriots every morning. We'd use movies for an early rally because at that hour we could rent the theater cheap.

Freedom fighters from every corner of Java converged on Bandung to hear me. One man traveled from South Sumatra to listen to the words of the orator who, he said, "plays on a person's heartstrings like a harpist." This was a tremendous demonstration for him, because he had no money. I had to borrow 2½ cents to buy him rice. We were so poor that even half a cent to us had value. I couldn't afford to be indebted even that much, but the loyalty of this supreme patriot was worth it. After two years I sent him back to take up the work in his home area. Kamar Udin is one of my close associates today.

This period was a hard-working one. It also brought with it the greatest joy I've ever known. To intoxicate the masses until they were heady with the wine of inspiration was all I lived for. To me this was elixir. When I speak about my land I become excited. I become poetic. I wax lyrical. I literally am overcome and this is transmitted to my listeners.

Unfortunately, my listeners were numbering more and more police. They were always hanging around when I spoke and transcribing my remarks carefully. Of course there are ways of putting something over on foreigners so they don't catch every innuendo. You can throw in a regional phrase or express a meaning through gestures. The people understood. And they cheered.

In our day we did not pay off cops. Assuming we could afford to, it was far more satisfying to cheat them. When I came across a new face following me after I left a speech, I was eternally charming. I never raised my voice and yelled, "Now what the hell are you following me for, eh?" Nothing as ill-mannerly as that. Smiling pleasantly, I'd relish leading him a merry chase in the hot sun to one of the ricefields on the edge of town.

Now, rice is planted in little squares. From a plane it looks like a patchwork quilt. Each square is bounded on all sides by a mound of earth. These dikes create a wall so the water in the ricefields stays within the square and keeps the seeds flooded.

I'd lead my tail to the rim of the ricefield, park my cycle on the grass and scamper over the dikes to a friend whom I'd suddenly decided to visit. I'd naturally just happen to pick a friend who lived way back from the road and easily half a mile through the ricefield. I knew full well that those fat, stupid Dutchmen weren't allowed to leave their bicycles unattended and it was their sworn duty to never let the arch fiend, Bung Karno, out of their sight. Well now, what should those damn dumb Dutchmen do? There was no alternative but to waddle as fast as they could after me, either sloshing through the water or teetering on top of those narrow dikes, all the while lugging their huge, heavy bicycles. Watching them sweat and strain and wriggle through the tortures I invented for them gave me enormous pleasure.

Try to imagine the tensions of this period. We were revolutionists, sworn to overthrow the Government. And Sukarno—he was the chief thorn. Every day brought editorials against me and never was there a single hour I wasn't dogged by two detectives and some assorted spies.

I was the prime target for the Dutch. They stalked me like an animal. They reported my every move. It became difficult to escape. When leaders from other cities came in, I had to find some secret place to convene. Often the future President of 105 million conducted his summit meetings crouched in the back of a motorcar. This way the police couldn't hear or see what transpired. Such were the devious methods we had to employ.

I thought up devilish ways to drive policemen insane. Another camouflage for my meetings was a public house of prostitution. Aaahh, it was wonderful. Just absolutely made to order for my needs. Where could a hunted man go that was safe, free from suspicion, and where it wouldn't look like he was going primarily to plot against the Government? Well . . . where else?

We would arrange to congregate at the establishment around eight or nine at night, a respectable hour for such appointments. We'd go singly or in small groups. After we concluded our business, one man would leave by the front, another two by the side door, I by the back door, and so on.

Invariably I was taken into custody next day by the High Commissioner, Albrechts. After interrogating me about my movements, he'd pounce. "Now, look here, Mr. Sukarno, we happen to know for a fact that you were in a certain house of prostitution last night. Do you deny this?"

"No sir," I'd grunt, looking properly guilty as would befit a married man. "I guess I can't lie to you. You've found me out, I guess."

Then he'd lower his jaw right close to mine and bark, "What for? Why did you go there?"

And I'd say, "What do you mean, 'what for'? I'm a man, am I not? I'm over 16, aren't I?"

"Now, look here," he'd smirk, squinting closely at me. "We know everything. What do you think we are, stupid? Come clean. You might as well tell us just why you went there. What was the reason?"

"Well, now, what do you think I went there for?" I'd mutter embarrassedly. "To make love to a girl, that's why."

"I'm going to have to make a full report of this."

"To whom? My wife?"

"No, to the Government," he'd snap.

"Oh," I'd gasp, exhaling a noisy sigh of relief, "that's all right."

Prostitutes are the best spies in the world. I heartily recommend them to every government. My PNI operation in Bandung numbered 670 and I tell you they were the most faithful, most loyal of any party members I've ever known. When it comes to a top-notch spy, give me a good street-walker any time. They're marvelous to work with.

You can't imagine how many good uses they had. First, I could draft them to seduce the Dutch cops. What better way to get a man off guard than by making passionate love with him, eh? When the need arose, I'd point out a particular law-enforcement agent and whisper, "Keep your ears open. I can use whatever secrets you can wheedle from that pig." They'd get them, too. And those dumb officers never knew where our information came from. No upstanding, refined party member of the male sex could have done this for me!

They had still another magnificent quality. They were the only ones of us who always had money. Prostitutes are easy contributors when it comes to dues. Mine were not only cheerful payers, but generous, too. They were great with extra donations. I could have used more of them.

Naturally, I was severely reproached for encouraging prostitutes in the party. Again it was Dr. Ali who spoke up. "It's a fearful shame," he cried, "that we should cheapen our name and our aims by the use of harlots—if you will excuse my using the word. It's disgraceful."

"Why?" I challenged. "They make the best revolutionaries. I do not understand your narrow attitude."

"It is highly immoral!" he charged.

"Did you ever ask the reason why I collected 670 prostitutes?" I asked him. "It's because I know I can never go forward without a force. I need manpower even if it's womanpower. With me it's not a matter of morals. Cold, cold power is all I care about."

"We have sufficient power without recruiting these . . . these . . . ladies," expostulated Dr. Ali. "The PNI has branches throughout the country and all do without such membership. It is only in Bandung that we endure this."

"In this work call girls, strumpets, or whatever you want to call them, are VIP's," I answered. "Other cohorts I can do without. Prostitutes I cannot. Take Mme. Pompadour—she was a courtesan. Look how famous she became in history. Take Théroigne de Méricourt, the great woman leader of France. Take the bread-march on Versailles. Who do you think started it? Whores!"

These ladies of the evening, whose services I took care to partake of only politically, were superb in yet another way. They acted as a magnet. Every Wednesday my branch held a political course and the men came in droves if only to blink at my army of beauties. I personally saw to it they showed up every week, too.

Not only did the enemy frequent my girls professionally, but so did some of our members. A major responsibility was to weed out well-meaning elements—male or female—who talked too much. We also had to weed out cockroaches, Indonesians who were paid to spy on their own. Every side has cockroaches. To ascertain whether our agents were true-blue and could keep their mouths shut, we tested them. For six months to a year my prostitutes held "candidate membership." This means that while we fed them small bits of information and watched them, they remained in the category of postulants. When they ultimately graduated into full-fledged spies, we knew they were trustworthy.

Since their chosen careers often subjected them to seven days' imprisonment or a five-guilder fine, my orders were if they were arrested they must serve the sentence. One time there was a *razzia*, or mass raid, and a whole bunch of Sukarno's rangers were taken in one haul. Loyal and true to their beloved leader, when the bailiff asked them to post their fines, each said in her turn, "No sir, we don't pay."

All 40 paraded to prison. I was delighted. Being behind bars proved a good source of information. Besides, it was smart for the future because they became friendly with the jailers.

I issued a second set of instructions for when they were released. Suppose, afterwards, my fleet was out promenading on their business rounds one evening. Suppose the Chief Warden was walking through the main streets of the town with his wife on his arm at the same moment. As he passed one of my elite, her leader's orders were for her to smile at him gaily and sing out, "Good evening," and call him by name. A few steps farther on he'd undoubtedly meet another of my girls who knew him from the cell and she, too, would address him by name and sing out, "Hello there . . . Good evening to you." His wife went crazy. To me, it was psychological warfare.

Back in those PNI days I was the acknowledged chief, but my poverty was still extreme. Inggit made a little money selling powders and cosmetics, which she concocted in our kitchen, and by taking in boarders. We had only a humble house on Djalan Dewi Sartika 22. We had one boarder named Sahardi, another named Dr. Samsi, whose accounting office took up the front parlor, and my partner, Anwari. The living room was our architecture bureau. Rent for the whole house was 75 guilders per month. Sahardi's board was about 35. I say "about." His rent was 35 but I was always around to borrow a few extra. Even Inggit borrowed a little from boarder Sahardi.

It is truly God's grace that we were provided for in small ways. If friends fell into a few extra cents, they would treat us to coffee and a tapioca cake. Once I promised classmate Sutoto I would treat next since he had invited me so often. The following afternoon he pedaled over to consult his leader. He was hot and weary after a half hour of hard cycling. The head of the whole national movement had to greet him with, "I am sorry, Sutoto, but I cannot play the host to you. I have no money."

And Sutoto sighed, "But you always have no money."

As we pitifully sat on the front step, a journalist cycled by.

"Hey, where are you going?" I called.

"To see about an article for my paper," he called back.

"I'll write it for you."

"For how much?" he asked, slowing down.

"Ten guilders?" The journalist made as though to take up speed again. "OK, five guilders."

There was no answer from the journalist. I lowered my appetite. "Two guilders? I'll tell you what. Just make it enough to treat to coffee and *tapa*. Agreed?"

"Agreed."

My friend propped his bicycle against the house and while he and Sutoto squatted alongside, I wrote a whole editorial. And in pen, too. Never once did I erase, cross out, or rewrite. So much politics was stored in my brain that I always had plenty to say. Fifteen minutes later I handed my friend 1,000 words and with my total paycheck I took Sutoto and Inggit for coffee and *tapa*.

Poverty to us was not a source of shame. We were all idealists. I will tell you how we lived in the late '20's. At the end of a Christmas holiday, Mr. J. A. H. Ondang, a friend, barged in on me late one night. "Bung," he cried, "I am in desperate trouble. Can you help me?"

"Of course, I'll help you, Bung." I smiled. "Unless you need money, in which case do not ask me, because I am in the same need myself."

"You see," he explained, "I went home for this vacation and returned here two days earlier than expected. The landlady of my boarding house has also gone on vacation and she is not yet returned. I can't get into the house."

"Try the hotel," I suggested.

"Impossible. I cannot afford it. The two guilders in my pocket are all I own. I wouldn't have bothered you, Bung, but you're the only person I know in Bandung. Can you give me a bed for the night?"

"I would be glad to, but our small house is already full with people. If you don't mind sharing the bedroom with Inggit and me, we have a carpet there and you are welcome to stay the night." Oh! he was so grateful. He stayed with us three nights. We all helped each other in those days.

Often we had guests. Sympathizers who'd been under surveillance while being educated in Holland were stealthily smuggled back and spirited to my house for consultations. Occasionally we put up carriers of the forbidden *Free Indonesia*, which was printed by our contacts in Holland but wasn't allowed at home. The boys in Amsterdam, therefore, cut pieces out and inserted them into the pages of mailable periodicals. Much information went back and forth across the ocean that way.

On October 28, Sukarno officially proclaimed the solemn pledge: "One Nation, One Flag, One Language." In 1928 we sang our National Anthem for the first time. In 1928 I was denounced on the floor of the

Volksraad—Parliament. The Governor General, expressing serious concern about my activities, warned that he "regrets very much the noncooperation attitude of the PNI," which he said "contains elements antagonistic toward Dutch power."

In December, 1928, I succeeded in obtaining a federation of my own *Partai Nasional Indonesia* with all major nationalist parties. This *Permufakatan Partai-partai Politik Indonesia* (PPPKI) gave our operation a greater unity than ever before. As chairman it put me in greater jeopardy than ever before.

The Government commenced a relentless watch over the PNI and the PPPKI. The great influence my words were able to exercise over the masses presented a living threat to the Dutch. Huge throngs gathered every time Sukarno spoke.

Under my guidance, we conducted joint activity rallies all over the island. They were dominated mainly by PNI speakers, with myself as the attraction most in demand. Dutch rule guaranteed so-called freedom of speech provided the spoken word was "contained inside and could not be heard outside" and provided the assemblage was "contained under one roof and within four walls" and provided all attendees "were over 18."

They also required each visitor to present an invitation. So, we ourselves printed them and sneaked around distributing them as the people were walking in. Money for expenses arrived anonymously. Covertly sympathetic Indonesian officials always managed to slip a little into the right hands.

For outdoor mass rallies, a permit was required one week in advance. You can appreciate the ridiculousness of asking the Government's permission to rail against them one week in advance.

I recall a Sunday in Madiun. As usual when Bung Karno spoke the area was so packed that a few collapsed. In the front, on hard, straight-backed chairs, sat four inspectors. It was my custom for someone to warm up the audience before me. Were I in the mood to speak an hour, my frontrunner would do only five minutes. If I chose to speak a short time, the warmer-upper would do 45 minutes.

Dr. Ali was along. I asked if he would deliver the keynote address. He protested, "Oh, no, Bung. As you know I have just been released from jail. I must watch my step or the police will pick me up again. Let me just sit and listen to you. It will be too dangerous for me to get up and say anything even if it is only a few words."

The crowd was waiting for me. They were tense. Eager. I sat

quietly on the platform praying as I still do just before I speak. The chairman introduced me; I took a sip of water and strode to the podium.

"*Saudara-Saudara*," I said, "beside me sits one of our brothers who was recently in jail because of his beliefs. He says that now he wishes to address you all."

The crowd roared its welcome. Ali nearly died. The sun was scorching, but he was perspiring even more than necessary. I did not want to put him in jeopardy, but it was psychologically important for the audience to see close up one of their leaders who had gone to jail for his convictions and was willing to risk it again.

Ali rose reluctantly. He mumbled a few quick words and sat down hurriedly. The inspectors never took their eyes off him. Then I stood up and took the heat off Ali by inciting to riot.

"Imperialism's most frightening weapon is the system of 'Divide et Impera.' The Dutch have tried to partition us into separate groups all hating the other. We must overcome tribal and regional prejudices by welding the belief that a nation is not one skin-coloring or religious persuasion. Switzerland embraces Germans, French, and Italians, but they're all Swiss. America includes those with dark skin, light skin, red skin, yellow skin. Like Indonesia she is a rainbow of races.

"Throughout eternity the Creator's messengers have known that only in oneness is there might. Perhaps I am a politician with a romantic soul who too often strums the lute of idealism, but when the Israelites revolted against Pharaoh, who set the machinery in motion? Moses. The Great Prophet. He, too, spoke high. And what did he do? He welded all the tribes together into one cohesive force.

"Our Prophet did the same. Mohammed was a great organizer. He herded the faithful into a powerful Islamic society which has militantly withstood wars, persecutions, and the disease of time.

"*Saudara-Saudara*, in any world movement there is first emotion. Then organization. Then revolution! So, let us follow the example of our new countrywide recruiting body, the PPPKI, and let us all be federated into one grand brotherhood with one grand aim: To overthrow the colonial Government. To fight them . . . to stand up together and. . . ."

The inspector with the stick struck it against the floor and yelled, "Stop . . . Stop. . . ." Then all four sprang out of their seats. The excited audience was in an ugly mood because the police had threatened me and they made as though to rush the officers when one vaulted onto the stage and raced out the back whistling for help. Five minutes later a bus bearing 40 armed officers pulled up, dragged me off the stage, down the steps, out to the street, and hustled me to the police station.

I was released after this solemn warning: "Don't push your luck, Mr. Sukarno. If we take you in again, we're going to throw away the key. And you'll rot behind bars for a long while. Now just watch your step. You won't get off so lightly next time."

That night Inggit had a vision. In it she saw uniformed police searching our house. This vision came to her with full force—exactly the same to every detail—for five days straight. The fifth day I had to drive to Solo for a mass meeting.

She walked me to the front door sadly. Her face was drawn and tight. As I left a wave of foreboding swept over her. She called me tenderly by a pet name. "Kus," she said softly, "please . . . please don't go."

ᴆ 9. The Arrest

HANGING over our heads at all times was the threat of arrest. The criminal code stipulated: "Anyone found speaking feelings of hate or hostility—via the written word or the spoken word—or anyone engaging in either direct or indirect activities that lead to incitement to riot or revolt against the government of the Netherlands is liable to up to seven years in jail."

As the PPPKI snowballed, Sukarno became a marked man. I had already received my warning and I well knew the penalty. All revolutionaries did. It was part of the desperate battle we were waging.

Enroute to Solo with one of my PNI lieutenants, Gatot Mangkupradja, I discussed it. "Look here, every agitator in every revolution gets arrested," I warned. "Somewhere, somehow, sometime, in some place, the icy hands of the law will fall on my shoulders. I prepare you in advance."

"Are you afraid?" asked Gatot.

"No, I am not," I answered honestly. "I knew the consequences when I began my work. I also know that it could be any day. It is just a matter of time. We must be ready mentally."

"If you, our leader, are ready then we are, too," he said.

"A person must not engage in a life-and-death battle if he isn't aware beforehand that he will experience reaction. The enemy will gather all his resources again and again in order to retain his stranglehold. But, although down through the ages they put tens of thousands of us in jail and still exile us to unpopulated places far away from the society of man, the day will dawn that they will perish and we will win. Our victory is *historisch notwendig*—it is inevitable."

"Your words lend me courage, Bung Karno," said Gatot.

"In the tumbrel on his way to the guillotine, the leader of the French Revolution said to himself, '*Audace, Danton. Toujours de l'audace.*' He kept repeating, 'Danton, have courage. Don't be afraid,' because he was convinced his labors were historic and the reaction against him of equal moment. He never doubted the ultimate victory. Well, neither do I."

91

"Some of our fighters are in and out of prison steadily," said Gatot wryly. "One small leader in Garut has already been locked up 14 times. Local officials call him 'an offense.' In a half dozen years he spent four months in, two out, six months in, three out, then another eight behind bars. He stayed free one year and a half and his latest sentence is for two years."

We were traveling by taxicab. Our driver was Mr. Suhada, a sympathizer but a very old man who wasn't involved in any of our actual activities. He came along purely to listen and to see. Mr. Suhada had remained quiet so far, but now he asked gently, "Are many of our brothers in exile?"

I didn't have to think of the answer. I knew the number by heart. "More than two thousand have been exiled to Tanah Merah in the jungle of Boven Digul in Stone-Age West New Guinea. And when these bearers of the torch for freedom were driven into the woods they went with smiling faces. When they would not give in one inch, 300 were transferred to an even worse hole, if that can be believed, to the concentration camp at Tanah Tinggi. The ground is full with their graves. Of those 300 only 64 are left.

"Such sacrifices were also made on the islands of Moting and Banda," I said. "But remember, my brothers, no sacrifice is wasted. Do you recall those four leaders who were hanged in Tjiamis?"

They nodded.

"One managed to smuggle out a letter to me the night before undergoing his sentence. It read: 'Bung Karno, tomorrow I am going to be hanged. I leave this earthly world happy, going to the gallows with conviction and spiritual strength knowing that you will continue to carry on this war which was also ours. Fight on, Bung Karno; alter the course of history for all of us who have gone on before you!'"

There was silence in the car. Nobody had anything to say. Dear Suhada drove on mile after mile with tears glistening in his eyes. The only sound was that of our three hearts beating together as one.

In Solo and nearby Jogjakarta we had a series of mass meetings. That night I spoke for the first time about "the forthcoming Pacific war." This was 1929. Everybody thought I was crazy.

With my blood rushing fast from a sense of almost unbearable joy, there broke from my lips the now famous sentence: "Imperialists, look out! When shortly the Pacific war thunders and strikes and splits the skies, when shortly the Pacific Ocean grows red and the earth about it shakes from the explosion of bombs and dynamite, at that point will the Indonesian people cast off their chains and be free."

This utterance was not crystal-ball gazing nor did it reflect hopes based on wishful thinking. I saw Japan becoming too aggressive. To me, this so-called prophecy was merely the product of calculation based on the coming of revolutionary situations.

The conference disbanded at midnight. We had arranged to stay the night at the home of lawyer Sujudi, one of our members in Jogja who lived less than two kilometers away. We were in bed by one A.M.

At five in the morning, when the world was black and still, we were roused by a loud noise. Someone was banging at the door. I was wakened so suddenly that for a second I thought the neighbors were fighting. The banging continued. It got louder and louder, more and more insistent. This was accompanied by harsh voices inside the complex in which Sujudi's home was located.

"Is this the house where the revolutionary leaders are staying?" one voice asked. "Yeah, this is the place," another gruff voice answered. More voices shouted orders, "Surround the building—barricade the gate!" Over it all there was the shattering sound of a club battering at the door . . . harder and harder . . . faster and faster. With a shiver I realized this was it. My number was up.

Gatot Mangkupradja was the first to the door. He opened it and in strode a Dutch Inspector with a half dozen native policemen. We call them *recherche*. All were in uniform. All had pistols drawn. They were the hunters. We were the animals. Ricocheting through the neighborhood could be heard the crackling sound of authority: the clickety-click of boots as they stamped through the house. The white man in charge barked, "Where is the room where Sukarno is asleep?"

My room was back-to-back with Sujudi's. The seven paraded through Sujudi's bedroom and into mine. I got out of bed and stood there in my pajamas. I was calm. Very calm. I knew this was it.

The Inspector faced me squarely and spat, "In the name of the Queen I arrest you."

Always I had been prepared for the worst. When it finally happened, though, it was a rotten feeling. Down deep in your stomach it felt rotten.

"Get all your clothes on," he ordered, "and come with me." He stood in the room and watched as I dressed. I was not allowed to take any belongings. Not even my bag with extra clothing. Just what I was wearing.

Outside, with rifles at the ready, stood 50 policemen blockading the house, the complex, and the street leading to it. Three motorcars were lined up. The middle one was the special vehicle in which we dangerous criminals were escorted to the police station. Into the car were hustled Gatot and the taxi driver, who was totally innocent and whose sole crime was that he loved too much. He loved his country and he loved his leader. Suhada was released subsequently but, meanwhile, they booked him because he, too, looked like a desperado to them.

A few years later he died. His final request was, "Please, I wish to have a photo of Bung Karno placed on my chest." That wish granted, he folded his gnarled hands over my picture and passed away peacefully.

Under heavy guard, flanked by motorcycles and with sirens screaming and bells clanging, Sukarno, Gatot, and the very old man were brought to Margangsan, a prison for the insane.

We were searched one by one, then remanded to a cell. When the iron door clanged shut on us, our whole world closed down. We were totally alone. Everything happened so quickly there hadn't been time to sneak word to our followers. Not one soul knew our whereabouts. They wouldn't even let me contact Inggit.

There was no conversation. We were permitted none. Even so, what was there to say? We knew what this meant and each had his own thoughts. What flashed through my mind was that I hadn't had any premonition. There'd been no omen of danger. I'd gone easily to bed without experiencing any particular sensation that the 29th of December, 1929, was going to be a bad day or THE day. It took me completely by surprise. The whole maneuver had been well planned.

At two in the afternoon they gave us rice. Before and after there was absolutely no contact with anybody. After one whole day and one whole night, the next morning, again at five o'clock, the police came. They told us nothing. Not where we were going. Not what would be done with us.

Two vehicles sped us to the depot. Four policemen with uniforms and pistols sat in each. It was planned to the second. As we pulled in, a train was pulling out. We were ordered aboard. A special car had been set aside for us. Doors on both ends were bolted. Every window was securely locked. We were forbidden to walk around or to get up for any reason. If we had to go to the bathroom a sergeant accompanied us. We weren't allowed to speak on the whole 12-hour trip. We were placed on double benches opposite each other with guards holding down either side. All I could do all day long was gaze at the face of that stupid Dutchman.

At seven P.M. we were ordered to alight in Tjitjalengka, a suburb 30 kilometers out of Bandung, where they had deliberately let us off to avoid undue excitement. There another cordon of brass buttons awaited us. Five commissioners, two helmeted motorcycle men, a half dozen inspectors, and our solemn procession of black sedans raced to Bandung.

The drive was not a long one. We had barely time for a few nervous tremors apiece when we arrived at our new home. The sign read: Bantjeuj Prison.

~ 10. Bantjeuj Prison

BANTJEUJ was a low-class jail. Built in the nineteenth century, it was filthy, rundown, and old. There were two types of cells—one for political prisoners, one for *pepetek* prisoners. *Pepetek,* a low-quality fish eaten by the poorest class, is slang for peasant.

Pepeteks slept on the floor. We upper-strata prisoners luxuriated on soft, downy metal stretchers narrower than the width of one's body and overlaid with straw mats the thickness of a cardboard. The food was *pepetek* food—red rice and chili paste.

Immediately after I entered, my hair was millimetered until I was nearly bald and they put me into the blue prisoners' garb with a number on my back.

My home was Block F. A square of 36 cells facing onto a dirt courtyard; 32 remained empty. Beginning at one corner four consecutive numbers had been reserved. I was in number five, Gatot, seven. The next morning, Maskun and Supriadinata, two other PNI lieutenants, were thrown into nine and eleven respectively.

Our arrest had been no last-minute decision. It was well prepared—even to the cells. Months before we were actually apprehended, friends in Holland had written, "Be careful. The Government in the Netherlands knows more about your activities than you know yourself. You are shortly to be arrested."

As I learned from Maskun and Supriadinata, who had been taken in Bandung at the same hour as I, this Sunday morning there had been a wholesale raid throughout Java. Thousands were captured, including 40 of my top men, on the pretext that the Government had knowledge of an armed revolt allegedly scheduled for the beginning of 1930. This was a lie. This was a ruse to issue an immediate order for the arrest of Sukarno. That night trains were watched, bus stations were surrounded, personal effects were impounded, and mass raids were staged simultaneously in our houses plus our headquarters throughout Java and Sumatra.

An attempt to warn me failed. Police demanding to know "Where's Sukarno?" came to search the house of Ali Sastroamidjojo in

Solo where I'd spent the night previously; Ali immediately passed the word, but when he contacted Jogja he was told, "Thanks for the warning. They took Sukarno 20 minutes ago."

Gatot, Maskun, Supriadinata and I were held incommunicado. No visitors. No letters. We could see nobody, not even other prisoners. After a few days a special prosecutor came and interrogations took place. He interrogated me week after week for three months. I don't know why he bothered. The case was an obvious one. It wasn't a case of robbery in which they needed to uncover the hidden loot. It wasn't a crime for which they had to unearth a motive. They knew what we were doing and why.

My cell was 60 inches wide—half of which was taken up by the cot—and it was exactly as long as a coffin. It had no windows or bars to look through. Three sides of my grave were cement from floor to ceiling. Dutch jails in our day did not resemble those you see in movies where the villain is thrown into a roomy cell with bars and light and air on all sides. Our door was solid black iron with a tiny peephole. The peephole had a cover on the outside. The guard could look in but we could not look out. At exactly eye level there was a grating so you could see straight front. Not down, up or sideways, but straight out. Even had we been able to look around fully, there was nothing to see. Not even other eyes blinking back at you from behind other iron doors. Just cobblestones and dirt.

It was dark, dank, stifling. Sure, I'd faced this silently in the back of my mind a thousand times before . . . but when that heavy door locked me in that first time, I died. It was a shattering experience. I am a sybarite. I am a man who gratifies his senses. I enjoy fine clothes, exciting foods, love-making, and I could not take the isolation, rigidity, filth, the million little humiliations of the lowest form of prison life. I stood on tiptoe to blink through my grating and I whispered hoarsely, "You're trapped, Sukarno. Trapped."

My only real, true friends in Bantjeuj were the *tjitjuks*. *Tjitjuks* are small grayish-to-greenish lizards which change color with their environment. They can be found crawling over the ceilings and walls when darkness settles in. In hot sticky climates they're nature's built-in mosquito repellent. Maybe to some they're not warm or cuddly or lovable, but to me they were the most friendly of all God's creatures when I was in prison.

Food was served in the cell. So, when my *tjitjuks* gathered, I'd feed them, too. I'd hold out a single rice kernel and watch one little lizard friend look down at me from the ceiling. He'd crawl over the ceiling, down the wall, peer at me with his beady eyes, then whip out and grab it and scamper away. I'd sit there quietly, scarcely breathing, and, sure enough, five minutes later he'd come again and I'd feed him another rice kernel. Oh, I welcomed them. I became very attached to them. I was so grateful to have other living creatures share my solitude.

The worst of the whole experience was the isolation. Often, late in the night, I'd feel I was sealed inside this rock-ribbed crypt which was so narrow that by extending my arms I could touch both sides. And I couldn't stand it. I couldn't breathe. I thought I'd die.

When the miseries were the worst, a strange feeling came over me. I would get moments of superphysicality. A mood overtook me which was quite beyond anything normal. I'd lie down on my hard cot and close my eyes. But tight, tight shut. Slowly, because of my imagination, I'd feel my right arm swelling. It became bigger . . . bigger . . . bigger . . . bigger . . . bigger . . . bigger than the whole cell. It grew and grew and grew until it crushed out the walls of the cell. The right arm stands for power, but whether or not this was an omen of my future, I don't know. I know only this came on me in my depths of depression. And then slowly . . . slowly . . . slowly . . . it would go down again and resume its regular size. Sometimes the same night it would happen once more. Then it would recede once more. I never saw it but I felt it.

I experienced still another hallucination. Bantjeuj is in the center of the city, not out in the fields. There are no birds around. And yet, in the late night, when all but my thoughts were still, I heard *perkutut* sparrows right on the top of my cell. I heard them whistling and twittering as clearly as if they were perched on my lap. Nobody else ever heard them, but me. I heard them often.

After 40 days I was allowed my first contact with Inggit. There had been no communications whatsoever until then. We met in a visitors' room. A wire mesh screen separated us. Guards stood around writing down everything we said. We were allowed to speak Indonesian or Dutch, no regional tongue. We did not embrace on this first meeting. It wasn't permitted. Secondly, it is not the Eastern custom. My wife just gazed into my eyes and with all the love she could put into saying "How are you?" she asked, *"Apa kabar?"*

I smiled and said, *"Baik, terima kasih."* Fine, thank you.

What else could you say? There was so much to say that what else could you say? In the five minutes allotted us, we discussed that vision she'd had. Inggit had always been sort of my good-luck charm. Wherever I traveled, she went along. This had been the first time she hadn't accompanied me.

Now, at the prison, she explained, "I stayed in Bandung that weekend because I worried that those police I had 'seen' mentally would really come and ransack the house. And that's what happened. Exactly as it occurred in my vision."

The guards motioned us to speak louder. "Are you being provided for?" I asked.

"The PNI gives me money and your friends also send money and gifts when they drop in to console me. Don't worry about me. How is everything with you?"

How was everything with me? Where would I start to tell her? We loved each other too dearly to share the heaviness in our hearts. I didn't want her to be partner to my hours of torture and she didn't want me to share hers. We talked like two strangers in the street. I wanted to hold her. I wanted to scream that I loved her and that this was all so unfair. But in a dull, lifeless tone I murmured only, "Everything's fine. I don't complain."

The overseers at Bantjeuj were Dutchmen. On the lower level, those who actually carried the locks and keys were Indonesians. Our segregated cell block was specially guarded by one jailer whose sole function was to watch us. Bung Sariko was very nice to me. He recognized this particular prisoner as his political leader. He was my keeper, but he knew I was his saviour.

Secretly all the Indonesian wardens were on my side. They did always special favors for me. It was Sariko who made the first overture by offering cigarettes and books and bringing news that Iskaq, our treasurer, had been arrested. After he proved himself, he whispered one morning, "Bung, if you wish me to smuggle any message in or out, say the word. I'll act as your intermediary. It is my way to serve the cause."

Newspapers were strictly forbidden. I wanted one more than anything in the world at that moment. "A newspaper, Bung," I whispered back. "Get me a newspaper."

Next day I was in the toilet room washing up at the water trough. As I picked up my towel I could feel a newspaper folded into it. The day after, when I lay down on my cot, I heard the crackle of a newspaper. The day after that, when my food was shoved in, a newspaper lay under the plate.

I devised a system so that we might all read it. I managed to sneak in sewing thread and at six P.M., before being locked up for the night, I laid the thin piece along the ground the length of all four cells so it extended clear from my door to Supriadinata's. When I finished my paper, I tied it up with the thread, looked out, hesitated a moment to see nobody was coming, then shouted, "*Vrij*"—"Free." It signified that our block was closed and no sentry stood posted at the moment. Then I called, "Gatot," and that was the signal for Gatot to pull his thread. Tugging it gently brought the paper to his door, whereupon he then slid it underneath. It worked the same for Maskun and Supriadinata. If our guard ever did see the string in the twilight he looked away.

He also warned me when an inspection tour was due. If our cells were unclean when the overseers came by to check, we were subject to penalty. Five-thirty every morning, our first duty was to clean the cell and empty our toilet box. I always worried about Maskun because he was the youngest and inclined toward carelessness. I cautioned him, "Maskun, you must exercise more care because you could almost get punished for nothing in here."

He grinned, "You are so careful about everything and that's because you are an old man. You are 28 already. The reason I am more reckless is because I am only 21. Still young!"

"All right, young trouble-maker," I said back to him, "let's see who gets caught and who doesn't."

On our very next inspection, Maskun was penalized; for three days library and recreation privileges were denied him, and he had to remain confined to quarters. To prevent this happening again, I devised a code. Communications had to be by sounds since we could not see one another. We made use of a system of knocks. Say I'd got word there'd be a surprise inspection the following morning. On the reverberating metal door I'd go tock . . . tock. . . . Two sharp knocks meant "Tomorrow the overseer comes so clean your cell."

Some of the Dutch wardens, who didn't feel we were properly guilty of any crime outside of loving freedom, were sympathetic, too. Besides, they'd have done anything for money. Anything. Not even for very much money. At first I assumed they'd be too afraid of their jobs to accept bribery, but they proved to be the lowliest breed, willing to betray their principles for very little—for the price of a beer.

When I came up against one with a good heart, I'd explain, "Friend, I am working for my people. That's my only crime. Why do you watch me so closely? Please look away a little." Sometimes it worked, sometimes not. Mostly it did. That's how I made friends with the supervisor of the jail, Bos. Mr. Bos was just a plain nice but dumb Dutchman. I never tried to influence his thinking politically. I was just grateful I could utilize him for some comforts occasionally.

One day Bos shuffled up to me in my dark tomb and I could see one eye stuck out like a balloon. "Hey, Bos," I yelled, "what is with your eye? It's all swollen up and discolored."

He stood there rocking on his heels and holding the bad eye. "Ooooohhhh," he moaned, "did you ever see anything so terrible? Ooohhh, I am so sick. I am in such pain."

The poor man was truly suffering very badly. "Tell me, Bos," I asked. "What happened to you?"

He peered at me with the one good eye and groaned, "Oooohhh, oooohhhh, Sukarno, what happened to me!!!! Three days ago I made love with a prostitute. And when it was all over I wiped myself with my handkerchief."

"What has this to do with your eye?"

"Well, naturally, I stuffed the handkerchief back in my pocket when I was finished with . . . when I was finished. Many hours later, without even thinking, I took the handkerchief out again and wiped my eye with it. Well, here's the result. The girl must have been unclean and the infection came into my eye from this girl. And now . . . now . . . will you just look at me!!"

"Oh, you poor man. Poor, poor Bos," I clucked. "I feel so sorry for you." And I did, too. I mean, here he was a Dutch warden. I was his prisoner. He was on the outside having a passionate time cavorting with prostitutes and I was locked in a cold cell without even being able to hold my wife's hand . . . and I felt sorry for him!

As he slunk away moaning and groaning, I was glad Bos hadn't said she was one of my party members. Such a thing could have ruined our friendship.

When I could stomach the loneliness, the darkness and the filth no longer, I played a game with Gatot. I got my hands on a book of *Wayang*. The *Wayang* or "Shadow Play" is the most popular art form in Indonesia. Using leather figures which cast shadows on a screen, the puppeteer depicts stories from the ancient *Mahabharata* and *Ramayana* Hindu classics. It is Indonesian sacred drama.

I made Gatot read this book. I already knew all the stories. From babyhood I've been fascinated by them. I drew *Wayang* figures on my slate in Modjokerto. In Surabaya I'd stay up until six in the morning listening to the *dalang*, the professional narrator, spin the familiar fables, which are a little like European fairy tales. After Gatot obediently studied the book, I ordered him to "Put it down now and recite to me aloud what you have read without looking at the pages."

"In other words you wish me to act out the parts?" shouted Gatot.

"Yes," I shouted back. "Be the *dalang*." Our conversations were at the top of our voices since the cells were four meters apart and each of these four meters was solid stone.

Gatot recited. I waited breathlessly until he arrived at the part about my favorite hero, Gatutkatja. "Gatutkatja has come up against the evil demon," shouted Gatot. "He is losing the battle and he has fallen. Gatutkatja is temporarily defeated."

"Yes," I shouted confidently, "but that is just for a time. He will get up again. He will win once more. You cannot keep a hero down. Just watch."

Gatot continued describing the battle. Finally he came to the inevitable: "Gatutkatja is up again. Gatutkatja is on his feet. He has slain the demon."

Oh! Was I gleeful! I yelled uncontrollably. "Ha! I knew it. What did I tell you. A hero who only wants to do good is never down forever."

Shouting the *Wayang* not only entertained and relaxed me, it comforted and strengthened me. The dark shadows in my thought melted away as mist and I was able to sleep with this reaffirmation of my faith that good will triumph over evil.

✑ II. The Trial

ON the sixteenth of June, 1930, a newspaper report of the Governor General's address opening the *Volksraad* included the announcement that "Sukarno will be brought before the Court straightaway."

A date was set for the trial. Barely three weeks before I met the lawyers I'd personally selected: Mr. Sujudi, chairman of the Central Java branch of PNI and the man at whose home I had been arrested; Mr. Sartono, a comember of the old Algemeene Studieclub who now lived in Djakarta and was vice-chairman in charge of party finances; Mr. Sastromuljono, a friend and patriot who lived in Bandung. No money changed hands. There was none to change. My defenders even paid their own expenses.

At my first meeting with Sartono I said, "I have decided that it is my obligation to prepare my own defense."

"You mean politically?" he asked.

"Yes. Your responsibility is to prepare it judicially."

He appeared worried. "I know," he frowned, "that in your capacity as Chairman of Party Propaganda and Politics, nobody is as able as you to prepare the brief, but do you think this is proper procedure for a courtroom?"

I gazed deep into my friend's troubled eyes. He looked like he needed help more than I did and I put a hand on his shoulder to comfort him. "Sartono," I said, "I do not mean to boast, but when I entered prison I did so with determination. If it's destined that I must endure agony, then let me. Is it not better Sukarno should suffer for a while than Indonesia should suffer forever?"

"I just wonder if this is the smartest way to get you off in the eyes of the law," he fretted.

He knew and I knew I wasn't going to get off. We were allowed to meet alone, in a private room, one hour a week. There was nobody to overhear so I was the first to dare put into words what lay in the back of both our minds. "You know perfectly well," I began softly, "that everybody is just going through the motions. News that I'm already convicted has trickled down from our colleagues in Holland.

103

Had such information not been forwarded to me, still I would know this trial is a farce. You do, too. They have to convict us. Especially me. I am the ringleader."

"Yes," he sighed. "I have read the press notices in the papers."

"Like for instance daily headlines such as 'Sukarno SURE to be sentenced' and 'Impossible to acquit Sukarno say authorities.' I know. I've read them, too."

Sartono removed his glasses, wiped them, and put them on again.

"Since the 29th of December, agitation here and in Holland has not stopped," I declared. "Both countries are looking to me to speak. I cannot look to anybody else. Yes, I have you and our other councillors, but you have your own points of law to look up. It is two weeks to the trial."

"I hurried here as soon as I heard," he apologized, "but the police were making things difficult. It looked for a while as though I, myself, were in danger of arrest."

I looked at him through eyes moist with gratitude. "Sartono, I appreciate all your efforts. Still, lawyers are unswervingly legalistic. They very much adhere to prevailing laws. A revolution rejects today's laws and proceeds on the basis of abandoning them. Thus it is difficult to stage a revolution with solicitors. It is also difficult to stage a defense of a revolutionary with solicitors. We require the human emotion. This I shall provide."

I had secured paper from home. Ink from home. A dictionary from the prison library. Physically it was a backbreaking job. I possessed no table on which to lean. Besides the cot, the single item in my cell was a watercloset. The smelly tin box was a combination one in which you could urinate and also do your big duty. It contained separate sections for two toilet activities. The ugly thing was approximately two feet high by two feet wide. Every morning I was made to slide it out from under the cot, carry it in my arms, cover and all, to the central lavatory and clean it.

Night after night after night, for one month and a half, I lugged this toilet box onto my bed. I sat upright, cross-legged, and placed it in front of me. I spread a thick layer of paper and began to write. In this manner I set down what later became a political history of Indonesia. Called *Indonesia Menggugat*—"Indonesia Accuses"—it was a minute ache-by-ache unveiling of the suffering into which we had been driven as a result of concentrated exploitation during three and a half centuries of Dutch rule. This thesis of colonialism, later published in a dozen languages around the globe and set down in words of fire, was written on the tin top of a combination urinal.

On August 18, 1930, eight months after my arrest, the case came to trial. I was formally accused of breaking Article 169 of the Criminal Code and of infringing Articles 161, 171, and 153. These were the Haatzaai Artikelen—articles against "The Sowing of Hate." I was formally accused with "having participated in an organization which had as its aim the committing of crime as well as . . . the overthrow of the established Netherlands Indies Authority. . . ."

The somber wood panelling of the packed courthouse on Landraad Street darkened even further the already stifling air of gloom that hung over the bench. When I began my speech there wasn't a sound. Not a movement. Not a rustle. Only the gentle whir of the overhead fans could be heard. Standing on the elevated prisoner's dock, I faced the judges' green table and I spoke. For hours and hours I spoke. My bill of particulars against the Netherlands was cited matter-of-factly. Near the end my icy calm melted into frustration. I remember having to pause a moment and grab hold of my thoughts. Then I cleared my throat and plunged on.

"The Court accuses us of committing a crime. Why? What are we guilty of fighting with, Your Honors? With swords? Rifles? Bombs? Our weapons are plans to equalize levies so that the Marhaen who earns a maximum of 60 guilders yearly is not taxed precisely the same as the European who earns a minimum of 9,000.

"Our targets are the exorbitant rights of the Governor General which are nothing short of legalized terror. The only dynamite we ever planted is the voice of our sufferings. Our battlefields are the public meeting halls and public prints.

"Never have we crossed the bounds of the law. Never have we tried building up a formation of secret troops working on the basis of nihilism. Our *modus operandi* is to set our power in motion in ways still legally open to us.

"Yes, we are revolutionaries. However, in our sense 'revolutionary' means 'radical'; wanting to make change quickly. The term should be taken as the inverse of patiently. Even when a worm is hurt, it squirms and turns. So do we. Nothing more.

"We know independence takes a while. We know it can't be achieved in a single breath. Albeit we are accused of allegedly 'plotting an open, bloody revolt that we might seize total independnce in 1930.' Were this true, your mass house searches would have uncovered at least one hidden cache of arms. Yet not even a single knife was found.

"Choppers. Bombs. Dynamite. Ridiculous! As though moral weapons are not sharper and cannot pierce the hearts of a people quicker than thousands of armadas fully equipped. A nation can exist without tanks and guns. A nation cannot exist without faith. Faith! That is what we have. That is our secret weapon.

"All right, somebody may ask, 'But, eventually, will not this independence you seek have someday to be snatched by armed rebellion?'

"I answer: Your Honors, in all sincerity we know not how or if that last step will be taken. Perhaps the Netherlands may understand eventually it is better to end colonialism peacefully. Perhaps Western capitalism will fall.

"Perhaps, as I have been quoted as saying, the Japanese will help us. Imperialism lies in the yellow race as well as the white. It is evident in the lust of the Kingdom of Japan in occupying the Korean Peninsula and in exerting its control over Manchuria and the islands in the Pacific. Someday soon, all Asia will be in danger of the Japanese holocaust. I say only it is my belief that when the tail of this great dragon lashes out, the Colonial Government will not be able to stand.

"Therefore, who can predetermine plans for the independence of our country when we know not what the future portends? What I do know is that PNI leaders are lovers of peace and orderliness. We fight with a knight's honesty. We ask no blood-letting. We ask only an opportunity to build our people's self-respect.

"I am not guilty of plotting an armed revolt. However, if it be the will of Providence that the movement I lead make better progress through my suffering than through my freedom, I surrender my body in utmost willingness to Mother Indonesia and may she acknowledge my fate as a sweet-scented sacrifice laid in her lap. Your Honors, with beating heart I, along with the people of this nation, await your decision."

As I was led back to the House of Detention, the Government Plenipotentiary showed me a kindness by extending his hand. Next day a newspaper recorded the scene with the caption: "Meester Ir. Kievet de Jonge seen shaking hands with that dirty rebel." After each of the 19 long sessions, another daring Dutchman penned articles in his paper, *Het Indische Volk,* about the grave injustice being done.

As his editorials grew warmer, the frowns on his confreres' faces grew deeper. Mr. J. E. Stockvis lost many friends because of me.

The eve of the decision, six of my friends called unannounced on Dr. Sosrokartono, a much-respected mystic in Bandung. As I was later told, they needed comfort, and despite the midnight hour they paid him a visit without a prearranged appointment. An aide who answered the door informed them, "The doctor is expecting you," and ushered them inside, where six chairs stood neatly grouped in a semicircle. My friends were naturally stunned. Without asking their mission, the mystic uttered only three sentences: "Sukarno is Satriya. A warrior like Satriya may fall, but he will rise again. It is not for long."

The next day Gatot Mangkupradja, Maskun, Supriadinata, and Sukarno were found guilty. Sukarno's sentence was the longest. I was condemned to four years of being boxed up in a cell 1½ by 2¼ meters. Four years of not seeing the sun.

My attorneys appealed before the Raad Van Justitie but this Supreme Tribunal upheld the original sentence. Shortly thereafter we were removed to the high stone walls of Sukamiskin prison.

⇜ 12. Sukamiskin Prison

FOR eight months I was in solitary confinement. I saw only my keeper. When other prisoners were not in the yard, he brought me out of my cage for a half hour in the morning and again a half hour in the afternoon. I wasn't even permitted to talk to Gatot. They deliberately kept us apart.

I was never mistreated. In fact, I was always treated too well. With Government officials noting my every move, prison authorities watched carefully to see I'd have nothing to protest about. Extra-special treatment is even more terrible than cruelty because at least the other way there's some contact with humanity.

For fear I'd get friendly with other inmates and contaminate their thoughts, I was put to work near the Director so they could guard me doubly. My duty was in the print shop where I sweated over hundreds of reams of paper which were being readied for notebooks. I hauled the paper, pressed it, loaded and unloaded a huge grease-caked lining and cutting machine, and from sunup to sundown I drew lines on the paper. The whole day, day after day, I would make those lines. Such monotonous work for a brain like mine! All day long drawing lines.

Even at mealtime it was considered too risky for this "dangerous man Sukarno" to mix with Indonesians. I was seated with upper-echelon Dutch criminals like those serving time for fraud or corruption. All I could discuss with those high-class Dutchmen was the food or the weather. The officials saw to it I couldn't get any political talk.

In Sukamiskin I developed the habit of eating fast. Even now when I preside at a State banquet, I finish my food before half my guests are served. See, we were approximately 900 prisoners. The small dining hall accommodated 25 narrow wooden tables of 10 people each. We ate in shifts. Six minutes per shift. We were treated like cattle. At the sound of a gong each man marched in holding his one aluminum plate, aluminum bowl, cup and single spoon. Six minutes later his group marched to the outdoor faucet to rinse their utensils and another 250 were herded in. Six minutes later another 250. It was an assembly line.

We bathed according to the timeclock, too. I was apportioned six minutes to clean my whole body, soiled from head to foot with oil which sticks to hands, feet, and cheeks. Every six minutes another shift. And we'd be a half dozen men fighting for the water under one shower.

Many habits of those long days and nights in jail have stayed with me over these 35 years. I became used to lying on a thin, hard surface so now, even as a Chief of State, I do not sleep on silken sheets and downy mattresses. In fact, many a night I climb out of my soft bed and curl up right on the floor. I sleep better that way.

After the months of solitary, I was permitted cakes and eggs from the outside. These were first examined by the guards carefully. However, before my arrest I'd prearranged a code so that, if the inevitable occurred, and I were arrested, those nearest me would still be able to communicate. In the event of personal bad news, I'd arranged with Inggit to send a salted duck egg. It happened a few times. All I knew was that it was bad news. The terrible part was not knowing what the disaster was. It drove me crazy. It's human nature to steel yourself for the worst. Those were torturous hours for me.

My letters were screened and my wife was granted visiting privileges only twice a month so my biggest channel of information was the religious books which were allowed us from the outside. I had devised a system of tiny needle holes. Say, Inggit sent me a Koran on April 24. I'd turn to the fourth chapter, twenty-fourth page and with gentle fingertips I would feel carefully. There were needle pricks under certain letters. It worked like braille. Under the A there'd be a tiny chit. Under the N a chit and so on. That's how later on I'd learn the bad news that was first heralded by the salted duck egg.

If my wife brought a regular egg, I'd check the shell microscopically before eating it. One pin prick meant "Good news." Two meant "One friend arrested." Three holes meant "Complete *razzia*. All leaders arrested."

Mother and Father never came. They couldn't bear to see their baby boxed into a narrow stable 12 tiles wide by 15 tiles long and let out like an animal on a leash for an airing. My sister Sukarmini, an ardent worker for the PNI, visited twice. With her I'd created a system of visual signals. When she pulled her ear, crossed her fingers or winked her eye, each of these seemingly empty hand and face gestures conveyed special meaning. They spoke whole sentences at the time.

When she saw me, she was taken aback at how I looked. Besides my extreme loss of weight, she was appalled at my color. Both times she made the identical comment: "Karno, you've gotten so black!"

"It is so." I smiled wearily. "I have truly gotten several shades darker than my natural skin color."

"But why?" she exclaimed. "What are they doing to you?"

"It is not what they are doing, but what I am doing," I replied. "The rules require us to remain outside for a few minutes twice a day. Some walk or exercise or play a game like soccer. Others sit under the shade of a tree."

"And you? What do you do?" she asked.

"I lie down, flat out on the ground to soak up the full magnitude of the burning rays of the sun."

"I never knew you to be a sunbather."

"I'm not. In fact, I get dizzy from too much sun. But I must dry out my body. My cell is so cold and dark and so damp that this is the only way I know to warm up the very insides of my bones."

The worst cruelty that can be inflicted on a human being is isolation. How it can twist and warp you for life! I saw terrible things happen. I saw coprisoners go mad sexually. With my own eyes I watched them commit self-satisfaction. I know and have witnessed the frightening effect of isolation on once normal males. In front of me men made love with other men. One intelligent, high-type Dutchman toiled in a menial capacity in the prison laundry. I was nearby when the guard informed him he would be elevated to a position which suited his mental endowments far better than the manual labor to which he had been assigned so long. "We're moving you out tomorrow," said the guard. "From now on, no bending over steam tubs and rubbing your skin raw in scalding water. Because of your good behavior you're being promoted to the dispensary."

The prisoner shrank. His lip began to twitch. "Oh, no," he cried, grabbing the guard's arm. "No . . . no . . . oh, no. Please don't let them do that to me."

The astonished guard figured the prisoner hadn't heard correctly. "You don't understand," repeated the guard. "This is a step up. It's a promotion into easier work."

"Please . . . please," pleaded the prisoner. "I beg of you let me stay in the job in the laundry. I don't mind working hard."

"But why?" asked the guard incredulously.

"Because," he whispered, "it's close quarters here and I'm tightly surrounded all the time. In the laundry I can come in bodily contact with the men around me. In the dispensary I won't have this opportunity. I won't be able to rub up against the men. Please . . . please . . . don't let this happen to me."

This is the effect of isolation on a human being.

There were many cases of homosexuality among the white men. One curlyhaired Dutchman with big broad shoulders and as masculine a look as you'd find anywhere had been sentenced to four years' hard labor. His crime was that he played with boys. How locking him up with nothing but hundreds of boys all around him was supposed to be the cure for his ailment, I don't know.

There is no doubt prison life wreaks havoc with the normal desires of the flesh. Even the Bible states that a man shall cleave unto his wife. I was in the prime of my life, strong, sensual, when the iron gates shut behind me. My body was imprisoned, but my spirit screamed within me. My raw nerve ends cried out in agony in the dead of night. The normal appetites that are a man's God-given right to satisfy do not cease because some justice raps a gavel and says, "Case closed."

Every Christmas time, the Salvation Army prepared parcels of food and delivered them to the prison via carefully screened delivery men and women who wouldn't be the kind to excite us inmates. The last week of 1930 a fat, dirty, ugly old woman who was way over 60 waddled into the jail on her errand of mercy. She was delivering Christmas bread. I knew I was in serious shape when that pig of a fat lady looked gorgeous to me. For one agonizing moment she was the most beautiful female I thought I'd ever seen.

I was deliberately incarcerated in Sukamiskin, which was primarily for Dutch lawbreakers, so that I would not "poison" the atmosphere of Indonesian prison society. But Sukamiskin was the repository for the hardest of criminals. We had three classes of malefactors: those doing up to one year (Gatot, Maskun and Supriadinata belonged in that class); those doing one to 10 such as myself; and the predominant group serving 10 years and over. There was a murderer at my table, but he was serving 20 years instead of life because he had only killed an Indonesian. Another with whom I shared my bread was in for 15 years, along with his brother, for armed robbery and inflicting physical cruelty.

My cell number was 233, up an iron stairway on the second tier off in a corner. The whole block was emptied for me. My nearest neighbor was a homicidal maniac who had robbed a woman, then killed her and her three children.

My best friend was an Indo, the son of a full-blooded European and an Indonesian mother from Priangan. He never approached me without trying to offer some kindness. This "friend," who loved me dearly, was in jail for having murdered his father because the father had tortured his mother.

In Sukamiskin you could get killed for a package of tobacco. Everybody had so little and required so much that you could have an enemy cut down purely by waggling two cigarettes and whispering, "See that fellow over there with the mole on his neck? Kill him for me and these are yours." Further conversation wasn't required. Blithely answering, "OK," the inmate would saunter over and bury a knife in the fellow's gizzard. Sukamiskin numbered lost souls as prisoners. One fellow was serving a 53-year sentence. A man like this has nothing to lose by killing somebody in prison. Especially if he can buy himself some luxuries by doing it. Such was the company in which the child of the dawn found himself.

My lawyers tried to have me serve my sentence outside the walls as had other convicts, including an accused murderer, but the application was denied. The Netherlands East Indies didn't mind letting a Jack the Ripper serve his time outside, but the Lion of the Platform was too dangerous.

However, I might say I grew in jail. I became more determined. My jailroom was my schoolroom.

Because I was forbidden political works, I began to probe Islam. Basically, ours is a religious race. We are a people who know our obligations toward God. You can observe this in Bali, where art and tradition are completely dedicated to the Almighty. Walk in the villages in West Java, hear our people reciting the verses of the Holy Koran in mid-afternoon. In Central Java there still stands a monument to the highly developed spiritual life of our forefathers. It is the Prambanan temple marking the peak of Hindu civilization. Fifty kilometers away stands Borobudur, the largest Buddhist temple in the world. There are mosques and churches in every hamlet. Indonesians are innately dedicated to God. No matter which road of religion we walk, we acknowledge that only the force of Divine Providence could have borne us through our centuries of pain. We are an agrarian nation and what makes things grow? God. We accept that as a fact of life.

So I was inherently God-fearing and God-loving from birth. I never had much organized religion because Father was not deeply involved in it. I discovered Islam myself at 15 when I accompanied the family of Tjokro to a social-religious organization called Moham-madiyah. The meeting hall was directly across from us on Gang Peneleh. Once a month, from eight to midnight, 100 faithful crowded in to hear the lecture, and this was followed by a question-and-an-swer period. Although I listened spellbound, it wasn't until I was put in jail that I really and truly found Islam. It was there I became a real believer.

You can never doubt the presence of the Omnipresent One if you have spent years in blackness. A man is never so close to God as when he gazes through a little hole in his cell and sees the stars, then crouches there for hours in utter stillness to ponder infinity and creation. In solitude is when one can truly kiss the hem. With nothing but solitude I began more and more to believe. At night I would find myself slipping naturally into silent prayer.

I say to you, my brethren, who are reading this book in, I hope, an endeavor to understand Sukarno a little better, five times a day I prostrate myself literally and figuratively in communion with my Maker. Can such a one be communistic? Wherever I am in the world, I turn in the direction of the Kaaba in Mecca at the time of the Subuh prayers, the Lohor prayers, the Ashar prayers, the Magrib prayers and the Isha prayers and—pray to Him.

Everything with me is *"Inshallah"*—if God has willed it. Ask, "Hey, Sukarno, are you going to Bogor this weekend?" I answer, *"Inshallah.* If God has willed it, I go." How can such a person be termed a Communist?

I really began to devour the Koran at 28. That's when I started to read it my every waking hour. Now I understood God is not a person. I realized God is infinity, enveloping the entire universe. Omnipotent. Omnipresent. Not just here or there but everywhere. He is One—God is at the top of the mountain, in the sky, behind the clouds, beyond the stars I gazed at every evening. God is in Venus, within the rings of Saturn. He is not divisible partly in the sun and partly in the moon. No. He is everywhere, in front of me, behind me, guiding me, watching over me. When this realization struck, I knew I need never fear again because God was no farther than my consciousness. I had only to climb down into my own heart to find Him. I knew I was protected for good and always and that He was guiding my every footstep to freedom.

Late one night, down on my knees in my cell, I held a whispered conversation with Him. "God," I prayed, "every human being can be a leader if only of his own family. But I recognize that You are the true Shepherd. I understand that the only voice of man is the Word of God. From this day forward I am prepared to bear the responsibility for all that I do—not only to the Indonesian people, but now also to You."

The Dutch considered us Mohammedans on a par with heathen. In Biblical language, we were "a false and lost generation," they said. Well, heathen or no, I am a Moslem who today holds three of the Vatican's highest orders. Even the President of Ireland complained to me he only has one.

In my dungeon I undertook the study of all religions to see if I were truly one of the "false and lost." If they were better for me then I wanted them. With Pastor Van Lith I commenced the study of Christianity. I particularly cherished "The Sermon on the Mount." Jesus' inspiration imbued the early martyrs so they walked to their deaths singing psalms of praise to Him because they knew "We leave this kingdom, but we will enter the Kingdom of Heaven." I clung to that. I read and reread the Bible. The Old Testament and the New became dear friends to me. I renew their acquaintances often.

Then I read the Koran. And it was only after absorbing the thoughts of Mohammed that I stopped looking to books on sociology for answers to how and why things are. I found all my answers in the words of the Prophet. I felt totally satisfied.

Fortunately, I had already found God and made Him my dearest friend and confidant when I suffered a severe blow. A penitentiary is like a fish net. It has holes all through it. Through one hole word came that the PNI—the child I had sired, nursed, and watched grow into adulthood—had split into two and our unity dissolved. I couldn't stand it. This is what I had gone to prison for, what I had endured solitary confinement for. I had been able to withstand the agonies, humiliations, and the isolation because always I kept before me the high goal. But now . . . it was more than I could bear. I did something I have rarely done in my life. I cried.

I didn't cry when I was arrested. I didn't cry when I was committed. I didn't break down when the massive key turned in the lock and shut me from freedom. Nor even when I felt depressed and sorry for myself in my stone grave. Nor did I weep when I received news that my parents were sick. But when I heard my party had split and the slim chances for my country had thinned out even more, I tell you I couldn't take it. I sobbed like a baby.

But never once did I think of giving up the cause. Never. Defeat never entered my mind. I prayed only, *"Inshallah,* I shall unite them again."

Meanwhile, *Indonesia Menggugat* had been circulated throughout the courts of Europe and many official complaints were lodged from jurists. The Austrian bar averred that since charges were never proven, Sukarno's sentence was inhumanly severe. Sympathetic Dutch jurists spoke out, too. One law professor in Djakarta, struck by the severity, published his opinions in a magazine. He was subsequently summoned by the infuriated Minister of Justice, who censured him for publicly daring to go against Her Majesty's august tribunal. So much legal pressure was applied, both domestically and internationally, that the Governor General commuted my sentence to two years.

Just before my release, there was an article titled "I Begin a New Life" written about me and widely distributed. The morning of the 31st of December, 1931, when I stood in my civilian clothes for the first time in two years, the Director of the prison escorted me to the entrance and asked, "Dr. Sukarno, can you confirm the truth of those words? Are you really beginning a new life?"

With my right hand touching the gateway to liberty, I answered, "A leader does not change because of a sentence. I came into prison to fight for freedom. I leave it the same way."

✑ 13. The Release

MY captors had taken precautions lest my release set off a mass demonstration. Vigilance was stringently maintained everywhere. The route to my house was patrolled, the street around my house purposefully empty. Despite my orders that it was the greater part of wisdom to avoid a mass welcome, still Inggit and a couple of hundred faithful lined the street in an orderly fashion the sunny morning I discharged my debt to Dutch society.

It is Indonesian custom that when a person comes out of jail, there is a *Selametan*. I don't mean it is a custom for Indonesians to be in jail. I mean that all events—weddings, graduations, babies, yes, even coming out of jail, are marked by a feast of peace. My adjustment to society was therefore hardly gradual. From a lonely black closet I plunged directly into Inggit's noisy boarding house.

It was exciting and I was overcome with emotion but, I must say, at that moment the first thing I wanted was not a gay party nor even silk sheets nor a luxurious bath. The first thing I wanted was a woman. However, that had to wait. Second things first. By the hundreds, friends thronged to see me all day and night.

That evening, my friend Thamrin told me, "Your eyes have a new light."

"No," I said. "They stand out because I have lost much weight. When you get slim in the face your features become gaunt."

"No," he insisted. "Your eyes have become very broad. Even when you're heavier they will burn brightly. There is a new fire to them."

"I don't know whether this is so or not," I answered. "I only know that I am truly inspired."

The most famous speech I ever made in my whole life was that very next night. I traveled by express train to Surabaya to personally tell the Greater Indonesia Congress they must take heart because Bung Karno was back ready to fight with them and for them. My eyes filling with tears, I ended by saying, "My love affair with our beloved country is not over. Nor do I intend to be just romantic and

116

hold hands. I intend to fight. *Inshallah,* we shall be united once again."

Sentencing Sukarno had sentenced the entire movement. The Dutch knew that. Upon my entrance into Sukamiskin, the PNI was officially forbidden. My lieutenants subsequently formed *Partai Indonesia,* called *Partindo,* but the movement remained lame. It did scant little but hold a rare meeting and even those were poorly attended for want of a drawing card.

In the absence of strong, decisive leadership, two Netherlands-educated intellectuals, Sjahrir and Hatta, disagreed with the methods of their confreres. A controversy raged between the Hattaists and the Sukarnoists. The result was the inevitable split. I'd ordered Maskun and Gatot, who were freed months before me, to cement the rift. They could not. Maskun sent word, "I am too young. I can't do it." Gatot sent word, "Even together we are not enough. It is better for all to wait another four months and The Bung comes."

When my old members asked me to join Partindo immediately upon my release, I declined. "No," I said firmly. "First I must talk with Hatta. Find out what is in his heart."

They said, "Wherever you go the masses will follow. Is it possible you might join Hatta's party, *Pendidikan Nasional Indonesia?*"

"It is not my thought to join either faction, but rather to weld them together. Two parties are contrary to my beliefs of unity. This is playing right into the hands of the enemy."

I met with the opposition in the home of Gatot shortly after my release. "All right, my brothers, now what is our basic difference?" I asked as we met for the first time.

"With your system the party has no stability," averred Hatta, a man totally opposite to me in nature. Hatta is an economist by trade and disposition. Careful, unemotional, pedantic. A graduate of the Rotterdam Faculty of Economics, he was still walking around mentally with those books under his arms, trying to apply inflexible scientific formulas to a revolution. As usual he dived straight to the heart of the matter without preliminary pleasantries. "When you and three others were jailed, the entire movement fell apart. My idea is to maintain a small nucleus of an organization which will then train cadres infused with our ideology."

"And what will these cadres do? Go to the masses and inspire them as I have done?"

"No," he said. "My concept is based on the practical education of the people rather than one leader's personal magnetism. This way, if our top leaders are removed, the party may carry on with people from the ranks who understand what we are fighting for. In turn they relay this to the next generation so that all along the line we have many who sympathize with us. Currently, without the person of Sukarno there is no party. It is totally dissolved because the people have no confidence in the party itself. There is just confidence in Sukarno."

"Educating people intellectually can take years. Your way can take an eternity," I said.

"Independence may never come about in my lifetime," he agreed. "But at least this way is sure. The movement will continue down through the years."

"And who will be your leader? A textbook? Around what will the millions rally? A phrase? This won't move a single soul. You don't gain power with phrases. The Dutch do not fear phrases. They fear only the real strength made up of the teeming masses. They know that intellectualizing will never endanger them. Intellectualizing may keep us out of jail, but it will also keep us from freedom."

"People will laugh at you if you are again imprisoned," was Hatta's answer. " 'It is his own fault,' they will say. 'Why does Sukarno always make propaganda for an independent Indonesia when he knows the Dutch will stop him? He is a fool.' Independence will take many, many years. The people must be educated to it."

Hatta would not give one inch and so I left that meeting of several hours disheartened. We were worlds apart and he quite inflexible. Still I tried. For many months I tried. At our next session Hatta said, "I wish to keep faith with our army of believers. If the Dutch prevent this generation from moving—and any more moves on the part of nationalist leaders will surely bring such reprisals— then let this generation not move anymore. Let us instead teach the younger intellectuals who will someday replace us to follow our doctrines and later lead us to freedom. This is keeping faith with our country. It is a matter of principle. Honor."

I never quite understood this fancy intellectual hairsplitting. Hatta and Sjahrir never created any might. All they ever did was talk. No action, just conversation. I made one last attempt. "This is war," I said. "A battle for survival. It is not a question of steadfastness with the next generation or honor with the rest of the movement so that the lower echelons can retain diluted principles after their leaders are jailed. Honor doesn't come into such a life-and-death struggle. This is strictly a matter of power. You and Sjahrir go on moralizing and in the meantime you'll end up getting beaten on the head by the enemy.

"Politics is *machtsvorming* and *machtsaanwending*—the formation and utilization of power. With accumulated energies, you can force the enemy into a corner and, if necessary, attack him. Preparing theories and deciding important policy decisions from books is not practical. I am afraid, Hatta, your head is in the revolutionary clouds."

Back in the '20's we had already developed our schism when I was the prime exponent of noncooperation and he of the opinion that cooperation was all right. Hatta and I were never on the same wavelength. The best way to describe Hatta is to relate the afternoon he was enroute somewhere and the only other passenger in the car was a beautiful girl. In a lonely, isolated area the tire went flat. Bachelor Hatta was the type who flushed when he met a girl. He never danced, smiled, or enjoyed life. When the driver returned with help two hours later, he found the girl snuggled into the farthest edge of the motorcar and Hatta in the other corner snoring away. Ugggghh, that man was a hopeless case. We never thought alike on any issues.

The 28th of July, 1932, I joined Partindo and was unanimously elected chairman. The movement was alive again.

As party leader I was paid 70 guilders monthly. And as future Great Leader of the Revolution, I progressed in every way. Even in the movies. Now I sat in front of the screen. Maskun and I also earned a few cents coediting the party organ, *Fikiran Rakjat,* which was published in my house. Then there were boarders. Of course, many like Maskun lived free. How could I take rent from him? He was my friend. I even introduced him to his wife.

I distinctly remember making a political speech at the wedding, too. The newlyweds had no honeymoon unless it was under a tree someplace because they immediately moved in with Inggit and me. It is not the habit of Indonesian girls to scream when love is made to them and since we did not have mattresses in those days there was nothing to squeak. So, although our bedrooms were separated only by a plaited bamboo partition, there was no disturbance.

With Ir. Rooseno I established an architectural bureau again. We had a hard time because contractors preferred Chinese or Dutch architects who would cause them no trouble. Our office rent was 20 guilders. Telephone ½ guilder. We had to earn at least 27½ monthly. Mostly we didn't. Rooseno's major income came from teaching. Because his icebox was always fuller than mine, most of our business was conducted in his kitchen.

Once a month I'd show up for my share of the profits. Helping myself from his icebox, I'd ask, "How much do you owe me?"

He'd say, "Your share is 15 guilders."

I'd say, "Okay." I never checked. Whatever he told me I believed.

It was a reasonably fair division of labor. Rooseno was the engineer-calculator. His job was detail. He computed and calculated and did the hard mathematics. As the architect-artist, I looked after the good appearance of the buildings. Of course, there weren't too many to look after, but I did design a couple of small dwellings which are still standing in Bandung. My designs were beautiful. Not necessarily economic, but beautiful.

I never thought of mundane things like money. Only people who have never breathed the fire of nationalism can concern themselves about such trivia. Liberty was the food I lived on. Ideology. Idealism. The nourishment of the soul. That's what I fed on. I myself lived in rags, but what did it matter? Pulling together my party and my people, that's all I lived for.

But, in keeping with my old PNI sentiments of how an Indonesian leader should look, the members chipped in to provide clothes for me. Instead of cotton or linen, Sukarno was suddenly given Chinese shantung. In place of open-collar sportshirts, Sukarno began to wear fine neckties. The movement believed so passionately in me that they did it voluntarily. I remember my first white silk suit. The donor was named Saddak. Oh, he worshiped me.

It is as the Bible says, "The rich in spirit help the poor in one grand brotherhood." I gave them courage. They gave me clothing— or money. The morning I walked out of prison a free man, a gentleman whom I never saw before thrust 400 guilders into my hand for no reason other than he knew I was without funds. Today this man Dasaad is the richest capitalistic Socialist in the country and my dear friend. But back when he urged that small fortune onto me, he never thought he'd get it back. Come to think of it, he never did get it back. I'm still borrowing from him.

During this year I learned to be cautious in my words. I developed such sway over the people that if I said, "Eat stone," they would. I think it happened because I was only speaking aloud what they themselves were thinking down deep. I formulated my people's hidden feelings into the political and social terms which they would have spoken themselves if they could. I called to the old to remember their sufferings and to see them redeemed. I called to the young to think for themselves and to labor for the future. I became their mouthpiece.

As a boy I first soaked up the written words of the great statesmen of the world, then I drank in the spoken words of the great leaders of our own nation, then I coupled it all with the basic philosophy dug out of the heart of the Marhaen. Sukarno, the Great Ear of the Indonesian people, became Bung Karno, the tongue of the Indonesian people.

I spoke all over—indoors, outdoors, in heat, in rainy season. Once the rain water reached above my ankles and because many spots were impassable, I didn't arrive for a nine A.M. meeting until three. The dispersed crowd swarmed back to stand underneath banana leaves and other improvised covering. At one point it was so bad that I, in my raincoat with torrents from heaven drenching me, suggested, "Well now, to get a bit warmer what if we just start singing together, eh?" From out the thunder, one voice joined mine. Then another. Then a hundred more. Soon 20,000 were raised in harmony and rejoicing. On that simple open lot in Central Java, folk songs of our people bound us together more tightly than chains of iron. When the rain lessened, I finished my message. Not a soul had left.

One follower commented later, "This is something a mere man can't do. This kind of talent is between you and nature."

I told him, "It is because it is not my personal will to strive for freedom. It is Allah's will. I am doing God's work. This is what I was born to do."

Today, anti-Sukarnoists sneer that everything is prearranged for Sukarno when he makes an appearance. I say only, it is true people line both sides of the street when Bapak is to speak. It is also true that you can force a person to stand, but you cannot force him to smile trustingly or gaze admiringly or wave at you happily. I call upon humanity to examine the upturned faces of my people when Bapak speaks. They are smiling at me. Praying for me. Loving me. This no government can force.

They cannot force it any more than the government of the Netherlands East Indies could force them to STOP smiling at me back in the '30's. Overnight, nationalist fever swept the country. Overnight, freedom again became contagious.

I spoke in Solo, where the beautiful princesses of the royal court came out to hear me. These revered, sheltered dainty ladies were so capitivated that the pregnant one repeatedly hit her stomach and chanted, "I want a boy like Sukarno." I suddenly had an inspiration. Handing them *pitjis,* I had them snake around the crowd collecting money for our movement. It was sensational.

I even made inroads on the Dutch. One youth named Paris became a pupil of my teachings and wholly converted to our side. Another time I addressed a gathering in Gresik East Java. The *patih* was present. As a colonial official, it was the sworn duty of this county chief to scrutinize me carefully and report my actions. This good, good man stood genuinely listening to me with his whole heart —and he got carried away. Without thinking he forgot himself and enthusiastically applauded many of my points. The crowd also contained Mr. Fonderplas, Director of the Office of Native Affairs. And that was us. We were the natives. Fonderplas' job was to watch anybody who was watching us—and that included the *patih.*

The *patih* was instantly dismissed. There was quite a hubbub about it in the *Volksraad.* Thamrin tried to defend him. He argued, "What if he did applaud? He is Indonesian after all, isn't he? Why is he not allowed to applaud? Why does he lose his job without having the opportunity to explain?"

Thamrin tried valiantly, but the *patih* was fired nonetheless. This was an important job and he was an important person. This good man had a wife and children to support, too. I felt very bad.

The police started tightening the net. Newspapers were then full of the mutiny aboard the *Seventh Provence,* a battleship with Dutch officers and Indonesian crew. The Dutch, knowing my pattern of playing on anything timely, issued orders forbidding public discussion of the incident lest it incite those on shore to revolt.

My problem was how to capitalize on the situation at my next speech. The police were itching to sweep me off the platform. They were excited and nervous. We were excited and nervous. We arranged things so I was the first speaker. This was to confuse the police, who'd certainly never figure I would dare incite to riot the first five minutes of the meeting. This way, even if they did close us down, I'd already have made my point and the people would have been satisfied to see me. Well, I stood up and went right to work on the

Seventh Provence. The police went right to work on me. The meeting was instantly closed.

I was right back where I was. Number One on their list, as if I'd never been away.

The authorities issued orders that anyone seen reading *Fikiran Rakjat* or wearing the *pitji* was liable to arrest.

I then wrote the pamphlet, *Mentjapai Indonesia Merdeka*—"Toward Indonesian Independence." It was considered so inflammatory that it was confiscated and banned immediately after publication. Copies were seized, houses were searched, any knot of more than three people was encircled. The noose was tightening.

The first of August we held an executive meeting at the home of Thamrin in Djakarta. It broke up after midnight. When I walked out on the street, there, waiting patiently for me in front of the house, stood the Police Commissioner. It was an exact repetition of last time. He said the same words: "Mr. Sukarno, in the name of the Queen I arrest you."

ᲐᲘ 14. Caged

PRECISELY eight months to the day I was again in custody. The rearrest wasn't triggered by anything special. My crime was just that when I came out of prison I didn't shut my big mouth as they had hoped.

The Commissioner barked to me, "Mr. Sukarno, you are irreparable. There is no hope for you to mend your ways. According to our records you were a free citizen only a matter of hours when you took the train to Surabaya and were back making trouble again and you haven't stopped since. It is obvious to Her Majesty's Government that you are all the time going to be a troublemaker."

"Where will you take me?" I asked.

"To prison."

"In Bandung again?"

"Not for the moment. Right now we will detain you in the Police Headquarters in Djakarta."

At headquarters they didn't lock me up. They just directed me to a bench and left me there. I asked the officer in charge, "Sir, may I call my wife?" He didn't answer me.

"May I send word to my attorney?" Still he didn't answer.

"May I see a member of the *Volksraad* or one of the leaders of my party?" No answer.

He just pulled a chair up to his desk and wrote and wrote a document that contained at least one thousand pages of charges against me. Being that I was such a dangerous criminal, they didn't leave me there all alone. Police, armed to the teeth, guarded me on the bench.

I huddled there for hours. And I began to think. During the tensest moments in a man's life, the human mind will often fasten on the most trivial or seemingly unrelated sort of subjects. It's as though this were nature's safety valve to relieve the pressure of fear building within. Here I was a two-time loser. What was to happen to me? Would they just jail me? Exile me? Hang me? What? At the age of 32 my whole life had already come full circle.

Yet all I could picture mentally was a badminton game and a shuttlecock which flies in and out at the whim of the players. Nehru, who had gone back and forth to prison eleven times, once likened himself to a shuttlecock. Sitting there quietly, I said to myself, "No, Karno, you are more like a twig in a pile of burning firewood." "And why is that?" I asked myself. "Because," came the answer, "a twig contributes to the flame of the bonfire, but on the other hand it is consumed by that very bonfire. It is the same with you. You have contributed to the flame of the Revolution, but. . . ."

The soliloquy with myself broke off abruptly. It became apparent that I was, indeed, comparable to a stick because suddenly . . . finally . . . it appeared I was to be consumed by the very lick of flame to which I had contributed.

I put this out of my mind and tried to think of something else. After a while, I was overcome with weariness and I fell asleep on that hard wooden bench. While it was still gray outside, they bundled me onto a train. The next stop was Sukamiskin. They weren't sentimental, though. They didn't put me in my old cell.

They locked me into a special cell set up in the midst of a large hall which had been stripped. There I sat penned in a small cage within a large room. And all alone. For eight months I lived like a dumb hermit.

Then the questions started again. The procedure was to arrest you, put thousands of questions, then send you away—for good. According to that exorbitant rights law, no more technicalities or legalities were required. Simply by invoking his personal decision to exile, the Governor General had ordered thousands of human beings sent far away, never to be heard from again. It was to be the same with Sukarno. With no trial at all, sentence was passed on me. I was to be banished to one of the outermost islands. The length of stay? Until my spirit and my flesh rotted away.

I expected this. After prison the next step was automatic. Their attitude was as though they'd been nice enough to let me out a few months ago and here I repay their kindness by doing the same nasty little things all over again. It was almost as though I wasn't grateful.

Five-thirty one morning I was hurried aboard an express train and locked into a tiny vestibule within one of the railroad cars which had been purposefully emptied. Two uniformed men stood guard. One inside the door. The other outside. Though I saw no sign of anyone, I was told my family was also aboard. My newly enlarged family now included Ibu Amsi, Inggit's mother, and Ratna Djuami, Inggit's baby niece, whom we had adopted. In our custom adoption requires no legalities. It just means someone lives with you and you love him.

At Surabaya they were secluded in a hotel and for the two days and nights I was again incarcerated in a stone cell. It was here Father and Mother saw the baby for whom they'd built such hopes. This was the first time they'd seen me behind bars and I did not look much like Karno, the great hero-warrior of the *Mahabharata*. The experience grieved them so they could hardly stand it. This was over 30 years ago, yet the searing pain of the meeting stays with me still.

"Oh, Karno . . . my dear Karno," sobbed Father, pouring out his grief to me, "what can we do about you? What can we do for you? First you suffer years in prison, a fact which saddened our hearts very much, and now you are to be exiled many, many days from Java."

My cheeks, too, were wet with tears, but I tried to smile a little. "I would give anything, Father, had I become a man with an exalted position who could give pleasure to my parents as befits the education they gave me. However, such is not the will of God."

Tears streaming down her beautiful face, my gentle mother whispered, "To scheme together a movement which will imprison him, then exile him, then free us all, is Sukarno's fate. Karno is no longer the property of his parents. Karno has become the property of the Indonesian people. We must reconcile ourselves to this."

We were permitted three minutes only. I was taken out of the cell long enough to shake hands with Father and kiss Mother. Each feared this was to hold us for eternity; that this hurried farewell might be the last time we'd lay eyes on one another again.

Next day, with tires screeching as we took the corners, I was sped to the harbor, where many had lined the ramp to wave goodbye with little home-made red and white paper flags. Flanked by two detectives, I was marched onto a cargo boat and remanded to a second-class stateroom next to the cattle pens.

Eight days later we arrived at our destination: the remote island of Flores.

❧ 15. Exile

ENDEH, the fishing village selected as my open-air jail for what the Governor General figured would be the rest of my life, had a population of 5,000. They were primitive folk. Fishermen. Coconut-farmers. Peasants.

Even today the nearest town takes eight hours by jeep to reach. The main road is a dirt lane hacked out of the jungle. In rainy season the mud forms fresh patterns and when the scorching tropical sun beats down, those patterns harden and the road has new pits, new ruts. From end to end Endeh can be walked in a couple of hours. It has no telephones, no telegraph system. Our sole contact with the outside was via two packet boats in and out monthly. Twice a month we received mail and newspapers.

Inside Endeh stands an even smaller village of thatch huts, called Ambugaga. Ambugaga's streets were so crude that the clearing on which my house stood had no name. We had no electricity, no running water. My bath was a piece of soap carried to the Wola Wona, a cold running stream with rocks in the middle. Our immediate neighbors were banana trees, coconut trees, and fields of maize. The whole island hadn't one movie, library, or entertainment of any sort.

In every way Endeh, on the remote isle of Flores, was the end of the world for me.

"But why? Why here?" Inggit asked.

"Muting, Banda, or those other dirty places they've thrown our people wouldn't be better." I sighed heavily as we surveyed our dark empty home the night we arrived. "When they conceived the idea of banishment, exiles were originally shipped outside Indonesia. However, they discovered wherever they externed us we conspired against them. Our masters eventually decided to banish troublemakers inside the country where they could watch us."

"But why Flores?" repeated Inggit as she unpacked my crate of books, the only personal possessions we took with us. "Most leaders are banished to Digul."

"That's why," I explained, removing the schoolbooks I'd brought so that each morning and evening I might home-educate Ratna Djuami. "There are 2,600 exiles in Digul. I would have a fine life there. Can you imagine what Sukarno would do with 2,600 ready-made soldiers? I'd change the whole face of Holland right from far-off New Guinea."

Inggit was never a complainer. Her lot in life was to give me a peaceful mind and to offer loving support, not more problems. But I could sense she was unhappy. Not for herself. For me. It is more difficult to watch someone you love being drained than to experience it yourself. It's painful for a wife to witness her husband being stripped of vitality, ambition, zest for life—yes, and even a little manliness. I was an eagle shorn of his wings. Whenever Inggit gazed at me another drop of blood trickled out of her veins.

I never confided my anguish to Inggit. We shared few if any heart-to-heart talks. Though my own heart was black with despair, I tried to buoy her up. Always I worked to discipline my face so it wouldn't betray my insides.

Oh, it was such an unhappy time for me. The detectives handed me over like any other cattle cargo. When their boat left, the only two who spoke to me, outside my family, were gone. Everybody stayed away from me. This was jail again; only the cell was larger.

Not only couldn't I make any friends, but I lost one that came with me. My good and dear mother-in-law, Ibu Amsi, died in my arms. It was I who carried her to her grave. She'd been suffering from arteriosclerosis. One night she went to bed. The next morning she didn't get up. Not the next either. Nor the next. I shook her frantically, but the morning of October 12, 1935, after she had slept for five days, she passed away without regaining consciousness.

I had been very much drawn to this old woman. In those torturous early months in exile when nerves were frayed raw every waking hour, never one cross word passed between my mother-in-law and myself. How we stayed together on top of one another in a tiny box of a house is because we were all good persons. I also a little bit perhaps. Ibu Amsi was even more simple than her daughter. She could neither read nor write. But she was a great woman. I loved her deeply.

With my own hands I built her grave. I myself laid the pedestal of brick. I alone found the boulders and cut them and polished them for her tombstone. In a crude *kampong* cemetery up a narrow lane deep in the heart of the jungle, a handful gathered to pay their last respects. This was my first loss. And it was a hard one.

The only person left to talk to me was Inggit. One evening as we sat in the small frontroom together all alone, as always, Inggit glanced up from her sewing to blurt out, "It can't be they don't know you; they must've read about you or seen your photograph in newspapers; there must be plenty here who recognize you; there must be."

"They know who I am, all right. If they didn't, the Dutch wouldn't take such precautions to keep my arrival secret. None of the townspeople knew Sukarno was coming. And even the officials didn't know when."

I understood what she was getting at—the answer to why everybody avoided me as if I had the plague. "The high people of the town, such as they are, aren't ignoring me because they don't know me but because they do," I said. "These so-called higher classes comprise the Dutch officials, Indonesian officials, and the ruling class like the Radjah. They want nothing to do with me at all. Not even to be seen with me. I might hurt their careers."

"It's such a small town, too," she whispered.

"Yes." I nodded wearily. "It's such a small town."

We both fell mute; I was the first to break the thick silence.

"The upper class are tools. Dutch puppets. They won't come anywhere near except to spy on me. Even their families are ordered not to associate with me. And they're afraid to disobey for fear they'll end up on the Dutch blacklist. Everybody's afraid."

Inggit said, "I heard the Radjah's younger brother was interested in nationalism until the Dutch expelled him from school in Surabaya and shipped him back here so he wouldn't learn any more politics."

"That's what I mean," I said. "How can he be my friend? He's here for the same reason I am—as a punishment."

"But even the lower classes avoid us," said Inggit in a small voice.

"I know."

"It isn't that we're not friendly."

"No. It's not that we're not friendly."

Inggit was fashioning a cotton *kebaya* for herself. That's the low-necked, long-sleeved blouse worn over our national sarong. Laying it aside, she looked at me.

"See," I mused aloud, "in Sukamiskin, my body was imprisoned. In Flores my spirit is in bondage. Here I am exiled from humanity, from people who can discuss my life's work. Those who understand are fearful to talk. Those who will talk don't understand. This is the true concept of exile. Okay! If that's how it is I'll do without the company of these silly intellectuals. I'll make friends with the lowest of the common folk. The ones too simple to care about politics. The ones who can't even read and have nothing to lose. This way, I'll have at least someone to talk to."

I made my own community with a coconut plucker, a motorcar driver, a jobless servant—such were my intimates. I first made the acquaintance of Mr. Kota, a fisherman. Told there was no prohibition against visiting me, he came to my house. Then he brought Darham the tailor. Then I visited them. And so it began.

Besides idleness, loneliness, and friendlessness, I was also suffering acute depression. Flores was utter torture in the early days. I needed something stimulating, or I should kill myself. That's when I began playwriting. From 1934 to 1938 I wrote 12 plays.

My earliest was inspired by *Frankenstein* and called *Dr. Setan*, alias Dr. Devil. My character was an Indonesian Boris Karloff-type who rejuvenated corpses by transplanting the hearts from living people. Like all my works, it had a moral, the underlying message being that the lifeless body of Indonesia would somehow rise and live again.

I organized the Kelimutu Show Club, named after a three-colored lake in Flores. I was the director. Each presentation was rehearsed nightly for two weeks under a tree by the light of the moon. There were no individual scripts so I read every role and my volunteer players memorized by repetition. When you are desperate you can overcome any obstacles. This was my only breath of life. I had to keep it alive. When one couldn't play his role well, I'd coach him far into the night. I even lay on the ground again and again to show Ali Pambe, a motorcar mechanic, how to properly play a dead man.

The difficulties were monumental. Once, Ali Pambe played an interpreter who translated Endenese into Indonesian. But Ali was unlettered. His Indonesian pronunciation wasn't good, so I had first to teach him the language before I could teach him the part.

My club had all male members because the women were afraid of being thought daring. Oddly enough, in backward, antiquated Flores there was a district—*keo* by name—where even now it is allowed for girls to engage in intercourse with any man, and the most outstanding among them—outstanding in satisfying men—are in great demand for marriage.

Geography notwithstanding, no Flores ladies would play a role on stage. In the first place, the custom was for Moslem ladies to be in the shadows. Secondly, they were afraid of me. So I solved the problem by writing almost no female parts and, if I did, men played them.

I personally rented a barn from the church and converted it into a theater. I myself sold the tickets. Each presentation ran three days and we played to 500 per performance. This was a major social event. Even the Dutch bought tickets. The proceeds paid our rent.

I made the wardrobe. I painted the back wall of our makeshift stage so it looked like a forest or palace or whatever we wanted to portray. I fashioned streamers and banners from paper and sheets and hung them in public places like the bazaar. I built our sets and furniture. I rehearsed two men and two women to sing *Kerontjongs*—happy songs—during intermission. And I was grateful for all this work. It gave me something to do. It filled those dismal hours.

After every performance, I even brought each member of the cast back to my house for supper. Oh, how hard I slaved not only to produce the plays but to keep the players happy. It meant so much to me.

I stopped at nothing. I am a skillful, very famous smuggler, and I even got us a curtain. In the interisland shipping company, the common seamen were Indonesians and all of them were sympathizers. When word was passed Bung Karno needed a curtain, one sailor personally bootlegged one in for me on the next shipment.

From off a Surabaya-bound ship one gray morning, a strong, strapping stoker eased up to me at the dock which was crowded with every such exciting event as a ship's arrival. Surreptitiously he hissed, "Bung, say the word and we smuggle you out. No one will ever know."

"No thank you, friend," I blinked gratefully. "I've had many chances and often thought that it would be nice to sneak out and work again for my people."

"Then why not?" he persisted. "We'll hide you out and take you to friends. You'll be perfectly safe."

"If I escape it will be only to fight again for freedom. Immediately I do that I will be caught and sent back. It would serve no purpose."

"Can't you work in secret?"

"That is not for Bung Karno. My value is as an ensign on high. While I remain here, our Marhaens can point to how their leader, too, suffers for the cause. I have thought temptingly of escape and I have weighed the good against the bad. It seems best for Sukarno to remain a symbol of martyrdom."

"If ever you change your mind, Bung, just send the word."

I hugged my friend to my breast and without embarrassment kissed him on both cheeks. "Thank you, but one day all of us will be free and then I, too, shall be free."

"Are you really convinced?" asked the stoker.

My answer was pure Javanese. This means I took the roundabout way of getting to the point: "If there's smoke in the rear of this ship I conclude there's a fire. Conviction based on logic. *Ilmu Jakin*. However, if I walk behind and see the flames with my own eyes, it is conviction based on vision. *Ainul Jakin*. But maybe my eyesight is faulty. If I then plunge my hands into the flames and scorch myself, that is deep conviction based on unshakable truth. *Hakul Jakin*. It is with *Hakul Jakin* that I know we will be free.

"The Dutch are marching side by side with cheese and butter while we march together with the sun of history. Some day, somehow we will win. In that dawn, my brother, I shall not escape from Flores under cover, but shall parade out head high."

Less tax, my Government exile allotment was under 10 dollars a week. The cupboard was bare much of the time. I earned extra money by selling materials from a textile shop in Bandung. They paid 10 percent commission on everything I sold. Peddling house to house with my sample case, I'd say, "Ma'am, I'm cheaper than the stores here. Would you please like to order something from me?"

I then sent a money order to this shop and after the space of several ships the cloth came. It took months, but one thing I had was time. For what should I hurry? I even had a side deal with an associate salesman. We made a secret price between us. Whatever extra he charged he kept. This way he made a little living and I made a little living.

Let none of my friends in Java boast they kept me supplied with parcels of food and clothing during these years. Oh, there might have been one or two, but seldom. When such a rarity occurred, I immediately forwarded the majority of its contents to the unfortunates in Digul. I did the same with whatever guilders came into my possession.

Although we had precious little money, we managed. My needs are simple. For instance, I do not drink exotic beverages nor eat meat from a four-footed animal. My table consists of plain rice, vegetables, fruits, sometimes chicken or eggs and a little dried salt fish. Vegetables came from the garden I planted alongside our house, the fish from my fishermen friends.

In Endeh, restrictions were placed even on these small pleasures. I was allowed down to the seacoast to watch my fishermen friends, but I couldn't step in the boat to talk with them. A boat could mean escape. I was also permitted to roam within five kilometers of my house, but one step more subjected me to penalty.

There were eight policemen in the town so despite civilian dress I knew them. Besides, they alone rode special black bicycles with the marking "Hima" on them. Another dead giveaway was their precise distance. If a mysterious Dutchman always hung 60 meters in back of me, then I knew for sure.

I remember an afternoon when a "civilian" followed me down the main road which we shared with geese, goats, water buffaloes, and oxen. I cycled past the houses on stilts and out toward the river. The road leading up was short and so he puffed right along almost neck and neck with me. As he halted there spying, two dogs leaped out at him barking and growling. This ferocious pillar of law enforcement was so terrified he scrambled onto his bicycle and stood straight up on the seat clutching a tree with both arms. Hot and dirty though I was, this spectacle refreshed me more than the river.

Later I complained to the chief, "I don't mind your fat slob 'secretly' shadowing me, but I don't like him being so close."

The official apologized. "Sorry, Dr. Sukarno. We'd instructed him to remain 60 meters away."

I was under steady surveillance. One afternoon I taught a group of youngsters *"Indonesia Raya,"* our National Anthem. Since this was prohibited, I took the extreme caution of teaching them in a place other than my home. Not that I had anything to lose, but I wanted to protect them. We went on a little picnic. Still somebody reported this grave crime.

The brother of the Radjah was instructed to ascertain what harm had been done by my treacherous treasonous act of corrupting sub-teen-aged boys. He obediently investigated the psychological effect on the citizenry. The answer was, "None." They didn't get inflamed. They didn't even know what *"Indonesia Raya"* was.

Nonetheless, I was summoned to headquarters, severely censured and fined five guilders—two dollars.

Flores will eternally remain in my memory for several reasons. It was here I heard Tjokro had passed away. Near the end, when he was badly ill, I had written him, "You, the great patriot who gathered our people together in the fight for freedom, will never be forgotten. I pray you recover soon." Weeks later when the packetboat came in bearing our newspapers, a big story about Tjokro told how even on his deathbed he had shown Sukarno's letter to everyone. I wept for my dear friend.

In Flores it happened, too, that I stripped myself of superstition. Always I had believed in good days and bad days, blessed charms and evil charms. In Bandung somebody gave me a ring with a stone. Inside this stone was a hole with a black liquid which never spilled out, but was always contained there. Something like a small seed floated inside and it always rose to the top. An admirer gave this strange phenomenon to me with, "Sukarno, may you always be on top like this floating seed." It was steeped in black magic, but I believed it. I believed anything in those days because I needed all the help I could get.

"Don't forget, Sukarno," he said, "this stone is a special one. It is a luck bringer."

Okay. I believed him. Immediately afterwards I got deported to Flores. I didn't believe him so much any more. That's when I told myself this foolishness had got to stop. And I said to myself, "You have seen the evils of superstition, yet isn't it so you do not eat from a saucer with a crack in it because you believe all manner of dire things will befall you if you do?"

I had to admit this was true. One day I deliberately requested a cracked saucer. I trembled a little because I had enough troubles without adding more by breaking a potent law, but I set the saucer on a table and stared it down. Then I made a speech to this silly plate which held such authority over me. I said, "You . . . you dead, lifeless, stupid thing. You can have no power over my destiny. I face you. I am free of you. Now I eat out of you."

That has become my pattern for any fear which threatens me. I face it and then I am no longer afraid.

Aaahh, but still I held the stone. I yearned to have the courage to part with this great luck-bringer. As I thought greatly about my stone, it happened that I needed money. It is the history of Sukarno that he never has money and what's more he always needs it; even now it is the same. I made the acquaintance of a prosperous copra merchant in town. I decided to sell him this great luck-bringer. And being a good salesman I laid it on thick.

"Look here," I plunged, "I have in my possession a rare treasure. You will always make a great profit with a stone like this because it is one of its kind. There's no other like it in the universe." It happens it was true and I wasn't lying, but it also happens I needed funds badly and wanted the most from him.

Then I poured on the last bit of steam. "Tell you what I'll do with you. You're such a nice fellow that I'll let you in on a very exceptional deal. If you give me a measly, paltry 150 guilders I'll give you the stone."

"Agreed," he shouted and consummated the transaction. My salesmanship was so superior that he actually feared I'd change my mind.

And so I parted with my last bonafide, guaranteed luck piece. For such proof of my freedom from superstition, have I not to be grateful to Flores?

In isolated, dull Endeh I had much time to think. In front of my house grew a *klavih* tree. By the hour I sat against it and hoped and wished. Under its branches I prayed and I thought about some day . . . some day. . . . It was the same feeling MacArthur had later. With every nervecell throbbing in my whole body, I kept knowing that somehow—somewhere—sometime—I shall return. Only this fiery patriotism still burning hot within my breast kept me alive.

Inggit forever told me she felt in her bones I would be something some day. But I never discussed it. I never talked about the future. I only thought about it. Every waking hour I thought about it.

I thought that only once in our three and a half centuries of subjugation did the outside world hear about us. In 1883 Krakatoa, our famous volcano, erupted. It rocketed stones, gravel, and dust into an orbit which circled the earth for years. Long after, whenever the sky in Europe was colored red, people attributed it to Krakatoa. That was like me. I had made a big noise and now I was silenced.

When a pack of cats made their home near my *klavih* and it was no longer peaceful, I took to walking in the woods. I searched for a quiet spot where the wind stirred the leaves of the trees because these whispers of God sounded like a lullaby to me—a song of my beloved Java.

A favorite lonely retreat was beneath the *sukun* tree facing the ocean. *Sukun*, a fruit that looks like an avocado, is a sort of monkey bread which, when peeled, sliced long like a cucumber and fried, tastes like sweet potato. I'd sit and look at the tree. And I'd see the Hindu Trinity in operation. I'd see Brahma the Creator in the buds sprouting along the grayish bark. I'd see Vishnu the Preserver in the oval green fruit and widespread leaves. I would see Shiva the Destroyer in the dead branches falling from the thick trunk. This was what was transpiring in my body. I felt my old cells rotting and dying within.

I was suffering headaches and was not feeling healthy at all. Still I'd crawl out of bed every morning to sit under the *sukun* far from my home. The *sukun* stood on a grassy knoll overlooking the inlet. There, with an unobstructed view of infinity and boundless blue sky and puffy white clouds and an occasional stray goat wandering past, I would daydream hour upon hour.

Sometimes it turned cold at the seacoast and I would take a chill. Many times I suffered chills when it wasn't cold. But I sat still. An unseen force dragged me there day after day.

I would gaze at the ocean rushing up in great slapping waves hitting rhythmically against the shore. And I thought how the ocean will never come to a standstill. It will have high tides and low tides, but it will roll on eternally. It is the same with our Revolution, I thought. Our Revolution can never come to a halt. Our Revolution, like the ocean, was the product of God, the only Cause and Creator. And I knew . . . I had to know . . . that all creations of the Infinite One, including myself and my country, were under the law of the Supreme Being.

One day I didn't have the strength to sit under my tree as usual. I couldn't even get up from my bed.

That was the day the doctor told me I was very close to dying of malaria.

⇟ 16. Bengkulu

WHEN news of my serious illness reached Djakarta, Thamrin protested in the *Volksraad*, "We make you responsible for Sukarno's well-being. He must get to a larger place where it's healthier and he may receive better attention."

"We must find first another locality which is also nonpolitical," hedged the chairman.

"Yes, yes, and primitive and backward, too, so that it will present no challenge. Yes, I know all that. But I serve notice on you now that if Sukarno dies, Indonesia, the world will hold you personally responsible for his murder. Flores is malaria-infested. Sukarno is very sick. His life lies in the hands of the Dutch Government. He must be removed. And quickly."

The Hague took immediate action. The first I knew about it was one evening a week later. I was resting quietly in my house when tailor Darham burst in. He was out of breath from running.

"I have just come from Toko de Leeuw," he panted.

"That grocery store is well over a kilometer away. Have you run all this distance?" I asked.

"Yes," he gasped. "As you know it is owned by the Chinese Lie Siang-tek who is a copra merchant and is very rich."

"Yes, yes," I blurted impatiently, "but what has this to do with why you ran here so fast?"

"He is rich enough to have a radio," continued Darham, unperturbed by my outburst. "While shopping I heard a bulletin come over the air at 1930 hours. It said Engineer Sukarno and his family are to be removed to another place of exile."

I accepted the news calmly. In fact, I fell silent a moment in order to thank God for His mercy. Then I asked quietly, "Did they say where?"

"Bengkulu."

"In South Sumatra?"

"Yes."

"Did the radio say when?"

"No. It said only what I have told you."

This was February, 1938. I had been nearly five years in Flores.

Many came down to the dock to see me off. Some to wish me well. Some to wish me ill. Some just to stare. A few even to beg to be taken along. One such was our servant. On the voyage I was kept in isolation, but always Riwu slept on the floor near my bed and stayed at my feet like a faithful dog. Darham was another who wouldn't remain behind. He tailored a suit and a pair of cream-colored pajamas as my bon voyage gift, then sailed right along with me.

The Dutch took considerable pains to blur my moment of arrival for fear of a demonstration. News broadcasts publicized my coming as four P.M., when in reality it was early that morning. Surabaya, usually a busy harbor, was still as the dead of night when we docked. Police had blocked off the pier so people weren't allowed anywhere in the vicinity. As I reached the bottom rung of the gangway and took my first deep breath in my beloved birthplace, the door of the waiting car opened and whisked me in. I was sped by night train to Merak, the end tip of West Java. There, in hurried stealth and elaborate secrecy, I was bundled aboard a trading vessel for Bengkulu.

Isolated by the Bukit Barisan Range, mountainous Bengkulu is a town of small traders and planters. Besides its giant flower, the *Rafflesia Arnoldi,* which grows three feet in diameter, it is outstanding in absolutely no regard. Not even in friendship.

This Moslem stronghold was bigotedly orthodox. Women were heavily veiled. They rarely accompanied their men. At the first social gathering I attended, I asked, "Why is there a screen separating men from women?" Nobody had an answer so I removed the barrier. Shortly another sprang up between the townsfolk and myself.

Our mosque was filthy, rundown, and old. I designed one with handsome pillars, simple carving, and uncluttered white stone fencing and I persuaded the town fathers to build it. They at first resented anyone who wanted change. Bad words passed between us and right off I made enemies. It was agonizing for me, particularly since I needed companionship so badly.

Security police kept my house under surveillance day and night. Any visitor had his name written down, was summoned next day for questioning, then shadowed by plainclothesmen. It took nerve to extend kindness to Sukarno. My lone friend was the headmaster of the Indonesian school who, although he knew he'd been marked, came often and brought with him a tiny girl whom I cuddled on my lap.

I never forgot his kindness. When I became President, I asked, "What can I now do for you? Say your wish." My friend was dying. He answered only, "Please help my family when I go. Guide my daughter." I did. I even found the daughter a husband.

So many of the babies I bounced on my knee have grown into beautiful women and their parents have come pleading, "Please, Bapak, find my daughter a husband." I now have a list of 300 such maidens. I think I am the only Chief of State who is also a marriage arranger.

It happened that during these years my own marriage was in need of some arranging. Perhaps my anxiety stemmed from Indonesia's way of life. Even among monogamists Indonesians breed many children. Over two million yearly. Maybe there's little else for our poor to do. Maybe we're a passionate, warmblooded race whose hot nights are made for love-making. General Romulo once observed, "I think of all Asians, we Filipinos are the handsomest." I said, "Possibly, but we Indonesians are the sexiest!"

We have families with 11, 13, 18 children. The sister of my father had 23. Everybody had babies. Everybody but Sukarno. Inggit could not bear children so a part of me and a part of my life remained barren. I was missing fulfillment. We had been married nearly 20 years. Still no son. I felt so much had been taken from me. . . . Why this, too?

When the depression became almost unbearable I arranged to be close to youngsters in every way. In Flores I'd adopted two more —Sukarti, the daughter of a Javanese civil servant, and Jumir, another distant relative of Inggit's who today has six offspring of her own. In Bengkulu I pretended everybody else's were mine. My neighbors, the Soerjomihardjos, had a boy of 10. Ahmad and I spent hours together. When a Dutch child spit on him, it was I who dried his tears and squared his shoulders with, "This is our country, Ahmad. Someday we'll be important in our own land. Someday we'll do what we want, not what we're told. Don't worry."

Then I became an educator of children. The head of the local Mohammadiyah, Pak Hassan Din, dropped in one morning unannounced as is our custom. "Here," he began, "Mohammadiyah operates a religious elementary school and we are short of teachers. In Endeh you were in close contact with Bandung's Islamic Association, 'Persatuan Islam,' and we hear you correspond with the learned teacher, Achmad Hassan. Would you honor us by serving as an instructor?"

"I would consider it a privilege," I answered.

"But . . . remember . . . no talking politics."

"Absolutely not." I grinned. "Except I might just mention Mohammed always preached love for his country."

In my class was Fatmawati, the young daughter of Hassan Din. *Fatma* means "Lotus." *Wati* means "in the possession of." Silky hair parted in the center hung down her back in two long braids. Fatmawati came from a humble home in Tjurup, a small hamlet some kilometers away. She was a year younger than my first adopted daughter, Ratna Djuami, and when she joined Ratna Djuami in attending a home economics class in Bengkulu—the only so-called higher education in the area—she needed somewhere to live. I happily welcomed her as part of our family.

I enjoyed Fatmawati. I taught her to play badminton. She walked with me along the sandy shore and with whitecaps slapping at our feet we'd discuss life or God and Islam. On such an outing she asked, "Why are Mohammedans allowed more than one wife?"

"In 650 Mohammed expanded Islam, then had to defend it against the Arabs, the clan of Mecca, even against his own family," I answered. "The slogan in those days was: 'The sword in one hand and the Koran in the other.' There were many casualties amongst the men."

"That means many widows," Fatmawati murmured.

"Exactly," I said. "But the prophet received the revelation from God that to ease the situation Moslems might be allowed up to four wives. In Bali, however, they practice unlimited polygamy. One 76-year-old Balinese prince recently married his 36th wife. She's 16."

"A good age to be a bride," offered 15-and-a-half-year-old Fatmawati.

At Bante Panjang the undertow was terrific and the sharks plentiful. Swimming wasn't permitted, but there was a three-sided coral reef which formed a natural pool. As we waded there, she asked, "Aren't Islamic laws unfair to women?"

"On the contrary, the Prophet's teaching raised the female standard. Before, their status was abysmal. Parents buried daughters alive because they were so unimportant. Men would merely offer a father bride money and buy his daughter as a wife. Today women are no longer paid for, as when you sell a goat. Women are equal partners in the marriage contract.

"Asian marriage laws are adaptable to local conditions. Here girls outnumber boys by several percent. These surplus women are still entitled to a married life; thus Islam provides for them to be legal wives with standing in the community. But in Tibet, where men outnumber women, they practice polyandry. This proves the adaptability of religious and social laws in the East."

"How do Westerners manage?"

"Western men often have mistresses. The disadvantage is that their babies must be cast aside or covered up or called a filthy name all their lives. In our society they are honored and respected."

Fatmawati walked along the seacoast silently, then asked, "Need a Moslem husband get the first wife's consent before marrying a second wife?"

"It is not obligatory. It is nowhere mentioned in the Koran. This was later on added in the Fiqh, the. . . ."

". . . man-made laws added in 700 or 800 which, along with common sense, are based on the Koran and the Hadith, the sayings of the Prophet."

"Right," I said, smiling at my bright little pupil.

At this stage in my Bengkulu period I occupied the position of village wise man. I was called on to solve everybody's problems—for instance, that of the official who laid claim to a buffalo belonging to a Marhaen in the area. The Marhaen was frantic. This buffalo constituted great riches to him. So he came to me, his "Spiritual Advisor." I advised him, "Take the matter to court and I will pray for you." Three days later the buffalo was returned.

My neighbor, a dairy farmer, needed money desperately. He believed by laying his problem at my feet it somehow would be solved. He was right, too. I went out and pawned my only suit to give him the three guilders 60 cents he needed.

So, to the humble villagers I slowly became a kind of god. What Fatmawati felt for me was hero worship. I was over 20 years older than she and she called me Bapak even then. To me she was just a pretty child, one of the many with whom I'd surrounded myself to stop the aching loneliness. What I felt for her was fatherly affection.

Inggit didn't see it that way. We had a radio in our back room. One night friends were listening to it with us. Fatmawati also came in to listen. There was a space on the divan next to me so she sat down. Later that night Inggit announced, "I feel there is a romance glowing in this house. Do not try to hide it. One cannot lie about the way the eyes sparkle when another comes near."

"Don't be ridiculous," I answered hotly. "She is like a daughter to me."

"It is not our custom for women to be so intimate with men. Daughters are close to mothers, not fathers. Take care, Mr. Sukarno, to see this relationship in the proper light."

It developed if there were an argument between Fatmawati and Sukarti or Ratna Djuami, Inggit always sided with whoever opposed Fatmawati. I, therefore, had to take her part. An invisible wall was springing up, with me being forcibly thrown toward Fatma.

After two years she moved to board with her grandmother who lived nearby. Still we were thrown together because her aunt married my nephew and there were Selametans, subsequent holiday get-togethers and so on.

The years rolled along and Fatmawati was no longer a child but a beautiful woman. She turned 17 and there was talk a marriage would be arranged for her. My wife was nearly 53. I was still young, vital, in the prime of life. I wanted children. My wife couldn't give them to me. I wanted gaiety. Inggit didn't think along those lines any more. I woke one morning in a cold sweat. I realized Fatmawati could soon be lost to me and that I needed her.

Then I realized I was right back where I'd been 20 years earlier. Back in the midst of that same struggle between good and evil. I thought about Ardjuna, the *Mahabharata* hero, who asked Krishna, the Deity, "Where are you?" And Krishna answered, "I am in the winds. I am present in the water. I am the moon. I am in the rays of the moon. I am even in the smile of the girl who fascinates you."

Then, I argued with myself, if in that beautiful smile of the beautiful girl is God, should my enjoying that smile make me feel guilty? No. Then if I love the beautiful smile of the beautiful girl and if that smile is God's reflection and He created this beautiful girl and I but appreciate His handiwork, then why is it a sin to want to take her?

Again, it was the constant warfare between good and evil trying to eat away at the small happiness I had found in the midst of the nothingness I'd known all my life.

Out walking of an afternoon, Fatmawati asked me, "What is your type of woman?"

I gazed at this simple country girl in her ankle-length, loose-fitting red Sumatran robe and her modest yellow veil. "I like the unsophisticated type. Not the modern ladies with short skirts, tight blouses and much bright lipstick. I prefer old-fashioned women who tend their husband and fetch his slippers. I do not like the new generation of American women who I have heard make their husbands do the dishes."

"I agree," she whispered, peering shyly at me through downcast lashes.

"And I would like a woman who is happy with many children. I love children very much."

"So do I," she said.

The weeks ripened into months and our tentative feelings blossomed into love. Nevertheless I tried to quell my boyish heart out of my great affection for Inggit. I had no wish to hurt her.

"This is all my fault," she repeated over and over when she opened the subject one unhappy evening. "This is what happens when you shelter a strange girl in your house. But I never figured it would happen like this. She is like my own child."

"I am very grateful for our life together," I explained. "You have been my backbone and right arm for half my existence on earth. However, I wish to experience the joy of children. I pray especially to someday have a boy child."

"And I cannot bear you a son, is that it?"

"Yes," I admitted.

"I do not accept a second wife. I want a divorce."

We both knew the choice was not hers to make, but I felt bad. "I have no wish to divorce you," I said.

"I do not want your pity," she snapped.

"I have no wish to cast you aside," I continued. "It is my desire to consider you in the topmost position and for you to remain the first wife, thus retaining all the honor associated with this while I exercise my religious and civil rights and take a second wife to continue my name."

"No."

"To marry again is a necessity for me, but I make you a proposition. Although I love Fatmawati, I will forget her if you find another whom you deem better suited for me. Pick one who hasn't been like a daughter and therefore will leave you free of the resentment you now feel."

Tears filled my eyes as I pleaded with her. "Perhaps had I known a normal life with normal pleasures I could accept the emptiness of no sons. But I have never had anything but poverty and travail. I am now 40. At 28 I was put away. Twelve of the best years of a man's youth I have spent in isolation. Somewhere . . . somehow . . . there should be some compensation. I feel I can't bear being deprived of this, too."

Ratna Djuami left to attend school in Java. Inggit and I were practically alone. The relationship was strained, but we carried on. I didn't know what to do so I threw myself into work. I designed houses for people. I lectured to the instructors at the Mohammadiyah. I organized the first and only Sumatra-Java Inter-Island Seminar of all religious leaders and successfully laid before them plans to modernize Islam.

I even took the son-in-law-to-be of the Resident as a private pupil in Javanese lessons because he was a field assistant on a tea plantation and his workers were Javanese and in Bengkulu only Sukarno knew that dialect. This Dutch boy and I became fast friends. When Jimmy finally got married he appointed me to stand up for him, but the Resident apologetically refused, saying, "It is impossible for the country's star prisoner to be best man at my daughter's wedding." He did, however, invite me to the ceremony.

After a year during which time I accepted no payment, Jimmy gave me two dachshunds. Ohhh, did I love those dogs. I slept with them. I shouted for them by clucking with my tongue, "Tuktuktuktuk," and, since I never got around to naming them, they became known as "Tuktuk One" and "Tuktuk Two."

I tried taking my mind off personal problems by cultivating other pets. I acquired 50 rice sparrows very cheaply. Then I bought an enormous birdcage and added a boy *barau-barau* bird and a girl *barau-barau* so he wouldn't be lonely. But it was not good. I had to let them all go. I couldn't bear seeing anything caged up.

When the menagerie didn't satisfy me, I flung myself into beautifying our backyard. The road leading to the street was pitted with rocks. I hired two coolies to cart them out. The chairman of a local youth organization heard what I was doing and one Sunday he showed up with a dozen buddies and in two hours they finished everything. When that project was over and the ache in my heart was still there, I launched a Saturday night debating club. We'd discuss Darwin's Theory of Evolution or "Which is better, rice or maize—and why?" or a subject like "What is the influence of the moon on the female behavior?" I made up my opinions as I went along. Sometimes I believed what I said, sometimes not. Sometimes I just tried to light a fire under my own spirit.

I also oiled my brains by writing articles. Since this wasn't allowed, I used the aliases Guntur and Abdurrachman. One trouble was that I do not type and my very clear, very legible penmanship was well known. A person's handwriting is a dead giveaway to his character. Any slight attempt to defy detection still reveals the same characteristics so I changed the formation of my letters totally by either printing big block letters or writing with my left hand.

In May, 1940, Hitler invaded Holland. The Government immediately summoned me to headquarters at Fort Marlborough, a stone and iron fortress overlooking a steep cliff. Their faces were glum. "Engineer Sukarno," they said, "we wish to commemorate this terrible event. As the only artist in Bengkulu, you are commissioned to build a monument in memoriam."

"You mean, after harassing me because I wanted freedom for my people, you now suddenly request that I, your prisoner, build you a monument because another people took your freedom away from you?"

"Yes."

Much as I desired to satisfy my artistic tastes, what I did was pile three stones on top of each other. And that's all I did. They were horrified to say the least. But I did not exactly feel like making a thing of beauty for them.

Regarding the war, I'd foreseen the tensions in Europe and the burgeonings of Hitlerism back in my Bandung days. In the mid-'30's I predicted Japan would join Hitler to make a stand against Britain and America in the Pacific and that under this cover Indonesia would gain her freedom. Since then I'd computed when the Asian war would hit and how long it would last and I concluded the weak link in Japan's imperialist chain would be Indonesia. Our spread-out country was the most likely to break them. Thus, in Flores in 1938 I prophesied Indonesia would surge forward and burst her shackles by 1945. I even wrote a play about my beliefs titled, "Indonesia '45." As I waited, biding my time patiently, I was both excited and fearful.

I became a steady contributor to Anwar Tjokroaminoto's newspaper. Now I wrote under my own name because, temporarily anyhow, my sentiments put Holland and me on the same side. In July, 1941, I wrote the following words in *Pemandangan Daily:*

Patriotism must not be based on that narrow kind of "national" nationalism which, like Italy or Germany, places the glory of a nation above those inside it. I pray God to spare us the stupidity of believing such fascism is our road to freedom.

Bombarding homes, killing women and children, attacking weak countries, arresting innocents, executing millions of Jews, is the ISM that wants to rule by itself. Fascism does not allow parliament. Fascism is the last effort to save capitalism.

All humanity must hate the Hitlers and Mussolinis of the world. Anti-Nazism, Antifascism must be Indonesia's ideological banner. I lift my pen today to vomit my hatred for this disease which inevitably leads to war and catastrophe.

This moral evil is not of the whites alone. Japan, too, has this lust for power which needs petroleum, coal, and oil concessions for her armada and which makes her people forget their knightliness in order to dig their claws into their brothers.

Japan, a disaster-bearing dragon of grasping covetousness, will soon join in a savage struggle endangering the peace and safety of the Asian nations in her race against the West. Like three great lion kings facing each other ready to spring, Britain is at the ready in Singapore, Japan prepares her weapons inside her own borders as well as the Marianas, America has fortresses in Hawaii, Guam, Manila, Pearl Harbor.

My friends, the time is nigh when the blue waters of the Pacific will become a bloody holocaust without equal in the history of the world!

But this war which I'd calculated would bring my hopes and dreams full circle was still a ways off so, for the present, I shelved it mentally to arm myself physically for the battle raging inside me.

The fall of 1941 I cabled Ratna Djuami and her fiancé, Asmara Hadi, who was also my long-time follower, to visit Bengkulu that we might discuss my personal life. We three took a solemn stroll along the Bante Panjang. "I beg you to understand," I pleaded. "I'm only a human being. I would like to marry again. Please, what is the opinion of you both?"

Asmara Hadi said, "I am in sympathy with you personally. I liken you to Napoleon and other great leaders of history who I have read were very physical men. However, from the political point of view this is not good. Although you've been away since 1934, you have remained our symbol. The people pray you will soon stand up and lead them again. And they know from your writings the time is not far distant. What will people say if you divorce Inggit now when she is old and has stood loyally by your side through years of prison and exile? How will it look?"

"Please, Oemi," I said earnestly to Ratna Djuami, calling her by her pet name. "Do you understand my pain?"

"I agree with Asmara Hadi. Although my heart goes out to you personally, I feel this will doom you politically."

"But you are young. You must understand more than your mother," I pleaded. "And do not worry for yourself. Even should I marry Fatmawati, I shall still love you. The white-capped waves in front of us will be my witness."

Before any decision could be made, the Japanese invaded Sumatra. The date was February 12, 1942.

✑ 17. The Escape

THE point of entry for the Japanese troops was Palembang, East Sumatra. The Dutch military withdrew. They didn't fight. They fled. The only thing they stopped for was Sukarno.

The Dutch were fearful of leaving me behind lest the Japanese make use of my talents to turn all sentiment against Holland and, therefore, against the Allied Forces. They admittedly worried about the postwar period, too. Sukarno loose to play on the heartstrings of an emotional people wasn't going to make it easy to reclaim the Indies.

They knew even better than I that in Java and elsewhere the people still talked of Sukarno, still placed him at the head of their dreams. Perhaps it's because there was no other to take Sukarno's place. Since my exile the movement had fallen apart. All chiefs had been jailed or exiled. In '36 a diluted party, Gerindo, had resumed but there was no fiery leader. All the masses could do was remember. And they did. During those years I was tucked away they remembered their few moments of hope and glory under the Lion of the Platform. It has happened before in religious and political history that in trying to suppress a leader, the opposition succeeds in perpetuating his name. It was the same with Sukarno. My popularity was as great as though I'd never been away.

Word came that the Japanese were marching to Bengkulu. A day ahead of their arrival, two Dutch policemen paid me a hurried visit. "Pack your things," they commanded. "You're moving out."

"When?"

"Tonight. And don't ask questions. Just follow orders. You and your family will be moved at midnight. Secretly and quietly. You may take two small bags of clothing. No personal possessions. You will be heavily guarded between now and then so do not try to escape."

Eight-year-old Sukarti somehow sensed the rising tensions. Frightened, she clung to me with both arms. "Hold me, Oom," she whispered. *Oom* is Dutch for uncle. As the policemen barked orders

I stroked her head to comfort her. "May I please know where we are being taken?" I asked.

"To the West Sumatran seaport of Padang, where you will be safe because our army is stationed there in large numbers to aid in the evacuation. Thousands of civilian refugees and military personnel are escaping from Padang, our port of embarkation for Australia, and it has been arranged to put you aboard the last boatload of evacuees."

"How long will we be in Padang?"

"Overnight. A convoy of seven ships is prepared to leave the day after you arrive. Now hurry. We are racing against time."

We had only a few hours to pull ourselves together. There was no opportunity to be frightened or confused. I didn't know whether it was good that I was being lifted out of the hands of the Japanese or whether it was bad that I was still to remain in the hands of the Dutch. I had mixed emotions. Fleeing Bengkulu meant leaving my place of exile. This made me happy. But Australia meant going to another place of exile. This made me unhappy. Now, of all times, I didn't wish to leave my beloved homeland. How could I fight for freedom thousands of miles away?

Events moved too quickly to waste time in thinking. I managed only to sneak five minutes alone. Bengkulu is a small town and in those stolen moments I made it to the house of Fatmawati's uncle where her family were huddled together under one roof steeling themselves against the invader. I knocked lightly on their door and whispered, "It is Sukarno. Let me in. I have come to say goodbye."

I had one fleeting second with Fatmawati. We held each other's hands tightly and I said simply, "Only Allah knows what will happen to us. Perhaps we may never come through this alive. Perhaps we may end up on opposite sides of the world. But wherever our paths lead, whatever happens to you and me, wherever we may be, I know that God will bless us and the love we hold for each other. *Inshallah,* someday . . . somewhere . . . we shall meet again."

At 11 P.M. we heard that the enemy was already at Lubuklinggau, the railway junction between Palembang and Bengkulu. At midnight, the police chief crept stealthily into my house. Down the road, behind a row of bushes, he'd hidden a pickup truck. Four policemen sat inside. Within 15 minutes Inggit, Sukarti, myself, Riwu (our 23-year-old servant from Flores who would not remain behind without me), and our luggage were all packed tight in the pickup truck.

Near my house stood two gasoline dumps—one located at Fort

Marlborough, a short distance away; the other right in my yard, which was also Government property, under a clump of coconut trees. The Dutch practiced the scorched-earth policy. Exactly as we left our front door, the huge reservoir of petrol and oil at Fort Marlborough erupted in flames. This signaled our captors to set fire to the drums at my house. That served two purposes. Besides preventing it from falling into enemy hands, it created a diversion. The explosion could be heard for miles and the whole town as far as the eye could see was on fire. Under cover of this, they spirited me out of Bengkulu.

To throw bloodhounds off the track, the police set a southerly direction. When it was apparent nobody followed us, they swung north and headed for Muko Muko, a distance of approximately 240 kilometers, where we were to spend the night. There were thirteen wide, muddy, alligator-infested rivers to cross. And none had bridges. We floated across on rafts and home-made barges. At five P.M. the next afternoon our weary band of travelers arrived at Muko Muko.

We stayed in a house heavily guarded by police. Three o'clock the next morning they roused us. "Okay, get a move on," growled the one in charge. "We're pulling out."

"Why so early?" I asked.

"We have a hard trip ahead and have to make it as far as we can before that scorching sun comes up full or we'll never live through it."

On the street we discovered our escort of four from Bengkulu had been replaced by six leathery-faced guards from Muko Muko. They stood armed with rifles and pistols, and carried water canteens. There was another change, too. The motorcar had changed into a bullock cart. On the bottom lay packets of food—tins of rice—more than just for a day's outing; enough for a week's supply.

"We're scheduled to go the whole rest of the way on foot," said the one with the canteen slung over his shoulder.

My wife looked up in horror. "All the way to Padang?"

"That's right."

"Three hundred kilometers?" she gasped.

"That's right," he snapped. "Let's move."

"Why can't we go by car?" I asked as we piled Sukarti and the luggage in the cart.

"What's ahead is solid, dense, barely passable jungle. The only way through is by a twisting, turning footpath which in spots is scarcely wide enough for a single file."

I was better off than the others because walking has always been my prime exercise, but I worried about Inggit. "Don't be too panicky about the walk," I soothed. "After all, these dumb policemen aren't marathon hikers any more than you are."

In any event we had no choice. Behind us was the Japanese army, in front the Dutch army. Alongside at all times, flanking us every moment of the day and night, trudged six policemen with rifles. So we walked. And we walked. And walked. Our path wound through the dense jungle along the west coast of South Sumatra. I had shoes on. My wife owned only the open-toed slippers Indonesian ladies wear, which are hardly support for a walk of several days through miles of forests of rattan trees and scratchy, dried weeds as high as your knee. Her feet were bruised and swollen. Part of the time she rode in the oxcart, but the footpath was steep and not only was the bull no help but I had to help the bull. I pushed him and pulled him and many times he just stood and watched while I hauled the cart myself.

In such jungles there are occasional isolated huts belonging to a hunter or woodsman. In one we made camp at six P.M. We were in the middle of nowhere, but physically none of us could go on. We were too tired. We were puffy from insect bites. Sukarti wore no hat and was badly flushed from the sun.

The hut was built on stilts to keep animals away, yet you could sense the presence of uninvited guests. A snake wriggled across your foot. A lizard whipped across the ceiling. On the floor lay a rough-hewn scratchy mat. That mat was our bed. The night-time noises of the wild beasts alongside our sanctuary were chilling. Our neighbors were tigers, bears, civet cats, deer, boars, and lots of monkeys. The sound of monkeys chattering in the trees never stopped. "Wild animals won't attack unless they're hungry," the policeman with the canteen had told us, so we prayed they wouldn't be hungry. I took most of my courage from our honor guard, who never wandered more than a few feet away.

In the middle of the night Sukarti peered over the edge of the hut, which had no door. "I'm frightened, Oom." She shivered. "Aren't you?"

"Yes, Karti," I whispered, comforting her. "I am. But those policemen give me strength." I crawled to the edge with her and looked down. "See the six of them there? Even in the dead of night they take turns standing watch with their guns. They're more afraid of NOT delivering us than we are of the animals. It's their sworn duty to deliver Sukarno alive to the authorities in Padang. So, come, let's go to sleep and let them worry, OK?"

Fruits from the jungle, rice our protectors brought along, and a little tapioca left over in the hut constituted breakfast. It was still black when we set out again on foot. Toward noon we came across a running stream. We all bathed fully clothed in the clean, cool water and drank our fill. Farther into the bush surrounded by a cornfield stood an empty cottage. Midday we stopped in for a nap.

The rustle of wild beasts in the dense foliage could be heard and we passed innumerable tiger tracks, but the only animals that actually barred our way were monkeys. We saw black monkeys nearly as big as chimpanzees standing erect like any human being. On their hind legs they lumbered up close as we plodded by, but although our hearts skipped a beat, we were never harmed.

Using matches the police carried, we cooked rice in a tin that vegetables came in and added a fish we caught in the river. This was parceled out among the ten of us. It wasn't fancy but neither did we starve. Inggit was so worn out that once she ate standing up. "I'm too tired," she whimpered, leaning against the high earthen wall of a ravine we were passing through. "If I sit down I won't be able to get up."

The third day one of the Dutchmen broke down from frustration and weariness. We had only ourselves to worry about, but in addition to the sun, thirst, exhaustion and animals, they had us to watch out for. There was no cruelty directed toward us. Though we were prisoners and jailers we all pulled together. But there wasn't too much conversation. There were no passersby and we ourselves didn't feel very joyous. I alone engaged in a little banter. It is my nature to try to be merry no matter what. "It took an invasion, but I want to thank you fellows for showing me the countryside," I quipped.

The short balding one smiled. "In your four years in Bengkulu, didn't you ever step outside the tight boundary imposed on you?"

"Once. I'd written a play which was being performed at a charity affair outside limits. This was right after a new Resident had replaced the one I knew well. He was the type who adhered rigidly to regulations so I asked him, 'Will you allow me please to go to this place which is a little over the bounds?'

"To make this terribly important decision on his own was not possible. He called all the way to the Governor General in Java. The Governor General cabled back he was very glad about the whole thing. He said 'It delights me to learn Engineer Sukarno is out of politics and concentrating on show business.' Isn't that ridiculous?"

The policeman laughed appreciatively. As Riwu shimmied down a tree and cracked a coconut so we might partake of the cool refreshing milk, I related the tale of Manap Sofiano, the prima donna artiste of my company.

"One day he bought a piano at auction and told the auctioneer, 'Sukarno will be my personal guarantee to pay this debt.' 'Ohh, okay,' agreed the auctioneer, 'if you're a friend of Sukarno it's all right.' Three months later Sofiano packed his belongings and his upright and moved away. Before he left I said, 'Hey, give me a letter of agreement before the village chief stating you intend to pay. This way, in case you happen to forget, I have legal rights.'

"When months passed without word from Sofiano, I wrote him, 'The time is come. Pay now or I take you to court.' Sofiano wrote back, 'I do not mind for myself, but I have five small children. If I'm in jail they will suffer.'

"Naturally I didn't want to hurt innocent children, so what else could I do? I paid the 60 guilders myself. Besides"—I grinned—"he was such a good actor that I forgave him anything."

With such light conversation I tried to raise the spirits of my bedraggled troupe. The fourth day we emerged from the woods and caught a bus into the town. Coincidentally with my arrival, the ship scheduled to transport us was blown to bits near the island of Enggano, right off the coast. The Japanese army was a few days behind us, the Japanese navy a few leagues away from us.

Padang itself was in chaos and confusion. The only thing sure was that the mighty Dutch conquerors were in a state of panic. Merchants had abandoned their shops. There was looting, robbing, hysteria. "See," sneered a six-foot-two-inch Dutchman as he fled leaving us defenseless, "we're barely gone and already you natives are having trouble governing yourselves."

The military tried to put me on a plane, but all were either in use or out of commission. Holland's problem now was not how to save Sukarno, but how to save herself. Like the coward she was, she ran like hell. She left the island and the Indonesians totally undefended. Undefended, that is, except for Sukarno. She left me behind. That was her big mistake.

At the hotel I directed Inggit, "You and Riwu and Sukarti remain here."

All around people were running and screaming and making last-minute hurried preparations. "Where are you going?" asked Inggit, trembling.

"My friend from Bengkulu, Waworunto, lives here. I must find him and make arrangements to stay."

Waworunto greeted me with open arms. He fell on me. "Sukarno, my brother," he cried, tears streaming down his face. "I have here a fine house with many rooms but I am all alone. My wife and children were evacuated and there is no one to live with me. Please . . . please bring your family and consider this your home." That wonderful man moved out of his master bedroom, a large room in the front right off the parlor, and left it for Inggit and me.

It was a matter of days at the most before the Imperial Nipponese Army would take Padang. As I walked the streets I realized my poor, weak, subservient, undefended brothers needed to be rallied. There was nobody in charge. Nobody but Sukarno. Right actions are simply efforts to fulfill the service of God. I knew the time had come once more to go forth and answer the Call. I assumed leadership immediately.

There was a local organization of traders in the area. I saw its chief and he set to work rounding up his people. Then I sent Waworunto in one direction and Riwu in another to marshal the rest. A mass rally was held in the market place. There I organized a People's Command to function as an interim government and to maintain order. "Friends," I boomed, in my first speech in nine years, "I call upon you to obey the invaders. The Japanese are very strong. We are very weak. Your job is not to fight them. Remember, we do not have weapons. We do not have training. We will all be annihilated if we attempt open opposition.

"An unarmed man cannot oppose a large number of warriors, but all the armies of all the states on earth combined have no power to enslave a single soul that has determined to stay free. *Saudara-Saudara*, I ask you: Who can chain a people if their spirit will not be chained?

"We have to win the utmost from this enemy. Therefore we must be careful. Our countrymen must be warned not to resist. At all costs avoid clashes in the beginning. Do not panic. I repeat: Do not panic. The first rule your leader gives you is to obey the Japanese. And trust. Trust in Allah to deliver us."

The rally ended with public prayers led by myself as Imam.

Moslems can't sermonize or ad lib the gist of a prayer. It must be exact. Word for word. At one point, because I was overly excited, I forgot the words of the following *Ajat* and with thousands watching I had to hiss to a Hadji sitting crosslegged on the ground near by, "Hey—what comes next?"

The prayers ended, the people dispersed, I retired to the home of Waworunto and waited. It didn't take long. One week later they came. It was four in the morning. Maybe five. I was lying in bed but I wasn't sleeping. I was tense. Wide awake. It was a very still night. No unusual noises. In fact, not even the usual noises. My family was sleeping peacefully. They were suddenly awakened by a growing noise. At first it sounded like thunder. Big rolls of noise getting louder and louder and louder. The fearsome, curdling sound was the thunder of armored cars and tanks and foot soldiers marching into Padang.

The Japanese had arrived.

⊰ 18. The Japanese Arrive

THE night was hot, but I lay there shivering. I realized this thunderous noise was the drumroll to action. It signified the end of an era.

Next morning I rose early and took a quiet stroll throughout the town. The Japanese had forced the stores open without placing anyone in charge. This invited the Indonesians to plunder. It being their first opportunity to treat themselves to luxuries, they did. The Japanese cleverly sent the Dutch police through the streets to restore order, thereby furthering the concentration of hatred on Western authority.

On every street the Japanese were welcomed with friendly shouts and cheers of enthusiasm. "Why is this?" asked Waworunto.

"Because our people hate the Dutch. They hate them even more now that they have fled like rats and left us totally alone. Not one attempted to protect us or this land. They swore to fight to their last drop of blood and then ran scared.

"Look here," I said as we walked slowly. "The first factor in the emotions of an invaded people is the attitude they held toward their previous bosses whom the new invaders vanquished. If you hate somebody you then love those who kick them out. Besides, humiliating defeat was inflicted on our superior and almighty white masters by an Asian race. It's no wonder our people hail them as liberators."

Waworunto, my good and true friend who is now dead, looked quietly at me. "And do you hail them as liberators, too?"

"No! I know what they are. I have watched their past performances. I know they are Fascists. But I also know this is the end of Dutch Imperialism. Exactly as I predicted, we will suffer through a period of Japanese occupation to be followed by freedom from all foreign domination forever."

Across the street we witnessed a Japanese soldier slam an Indonesian across the head with the butt of his rifle.

"Then it is your intention to use the Japanese?" Waworunto quickly asked me.

We walked on. There was nothing we could do. "Of course,"

156

A PHOTO TAKEN IN 1916 WHEN I WAS A STUDENT IN A DUTCH-ADMINISTERED HIGH SCHOOL IN SURABAYA. (*Photo Deppen*)

HERE I AM (EXTREME LEFT, SECOND ROW) WITH OTHER MEMBERS OF MY
GRADUATING CLASS FROM HIGH SCHOOL IN SURABAYA.

IN 1928 (I WAS THEN ALREADY CALLED BUNG KARNO) WITH MY ADOPTED
DAUGHTER, RATNA DJUAMI. THE MOUSTACHE LASTED ONLY A SHORT WHILE.
(*Photo Djapenpro Djabar*)

MY FIRST APPEARANCE AFTER RELEASE FROM PRISON BEFORE THE PNI (PARTAI NASIONAL INDONESIA) CONGRESS, 1932.

SIPPING KOPI TUBRUK, THE STRONG BLACK JAVANESE COFFEE I CANNOT LIVE WITHOUT, DURING COLLEGE DAYS IN BANDUNG, 1925.

THE PRISONERS AND THEIR ATTORNEYS IN THE BANDUNG COURT CASE OF 1931. FROM LEFT TO RIGHT, PRISONER MASKUN, PRISONER GATOT MANGKUPRADJA, MYSELF, LAWYER SUJUDI, LAWYER SARTONO, LAWYER SASTROMULJONO, PRISONER SUPRIADINATA. (*Photo Deppen*)

DURING EXILE AT BENGKULU IN 1939, SUKARNO (TOP ROW, CENTER) WITH
MME. INGGIT SUKARNO (CENTER ROW, SECOND FROM RIGHT), FATMAWATI
(FIRST ROW, LEFT) AND RATNA DJUAMI (FIRST ROW, RIGHT).

HERE I AM WITH MY CABINET AT OUR FIRST PRESS CONFERENCE FOLLOWING
THE AMERICAN AND BRITISH LANDINGS IN INDONESIA, 1945. VICE-PRESIDENT
HATTA IS ON MY RIGHT; ON MY LEFT, ACHMAD SUBARDJO. (*Photo Deppen*)

AUGUST 17, 1945. FLANKED BY VICE-PRESIDENT HATTA AND CAPTAIN LATIEF,
I READ THE PROCLAMATION OF INDONESIA'S INDEPENDENCE. (*Photo Deppen*)

ON THE SAME AUGUST 17, THE RED-AND-WHITE FLAG IS HOISTED FOR THE
FIRST TIME. LEFT TO RIGHT: SUKARNO, VICE-PRESIDENT HATTA, CAPTAIN
LATIEF. (*Photo Deppen*)

FOLLOWED BY GENERAL SUDIRMAN, COLONEL NASUTION AND COLONEL
SUDIRO, I INSPECT THE PEOPLE'S SECURITY FORCE ON THE DJAKARTA-BEKASI
BORDER, JULY, 1946. (*Photo Deppen*)

THAT DARK DAY IN DECEMBER, 1948, WHEN THE DUTCH ARRESTED ME AND SENT ME INTO EXILE ON BERASTAGI. HATTA CAN BE SEEN IN THE BACKGROUND.

WITH MRS. ROOSEVELT DURING HER VISIT TO INDONESIA IN 1952 AS A MEMBER OF THE UNITED NATIONS ECONOMIC AND SOCIAL COUNCIL. (*Photo Deppen*)

DECEMBER 19, 1949. I AM MADE PRESIDENT OF INDONESIA.

MME. FATMAWATI SUKARNO AND I CELEBRATE THE FIRST BIRTHDAY OF OUR SON, GUNTUR SUKARNOPUTRA. (*Photo Deppen*)

IN MY ROBES AS A HADJI DURING MY PILGRIMAGE TO MECCA IN 1955, RESTING IN A CAMP AT AROPAH, SAUDI ARABIA. (*Photo Deppen*)

LINING UP WITH OTHER CITIZENS BEFORE A BALLOT BOX DURING A 1956 ELECTION FOR MEMBERS OF THE HOUSE OF REPRESENTATIVES. I'M THE ONE IN DARK GLASSES. (*Photo Deppen*)

THIS SHOWS A PORTION OF A TYPICAL AUDIENCE FOR ONE OF MY PUB-LIC SPEECHES. (*Photo Deppen*)

DURING MY AMERICAN TOUR MY SON GUNTUR TOOK SPECIAL PLEASURE IN OUR VISIT TO DISNEYLAND. (*Photo Deppen*)

A GROUP CELEBRATING INDEPENDENCE DAY CARRIES A COPY OF THE
TEXT OF THE PROCLAMATION WHICH READS:
  WE THE PEOPLE OF INDONESIA HEREBY DECLARE INDONESIA'S IN-
DEPENDENCE. MATTERS CONCERNING THE TRANSFER OF POWER
AND OTHER MATTERS WILL BE EXECUTED IN AN ORDERLY MANNER
AND IN THE SHORTEST POSSIBLE TIME.
                    ON BEHALF OF THE INDONESIAN PEOPLE
                              (SIGNED) SOEKARNO   HATTA
                                        (Photo Deppen)

CHATTING WITH PRESIDENT KENNEDY AND VICE-PRESIDENT JOHNSON JUST BEFORE I LEFT WASHINGTON AFTER MY ONE-DAY INFORMAL VISIT IN 1961. (*Wide World Photos*)

WITH PREMIER MAO TSE-TUNG DURING MY VISIT TO THE CHINESE PEOPLE'S REPUBLIC. (*Photo Deppen*)

CAMBODIAN PREMIER, PRINCE NORODOM SIHANOUK, WITH HIS WIFE AND MME. HARTINI SUKARNO (FAR RIGHT), 1964. (*Photo Deppen*)

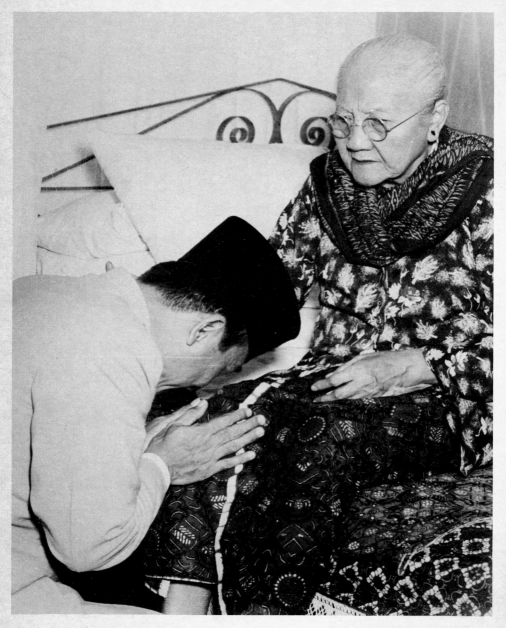

KNEELING BEFORE MY LATE MOTHER, WHO RESIDED IN BLITAR, EAST JAVA.
(*Photo Deppen*)

I answered in an undertone. "I know all about their brutality. I know of Nipponese behavior in occupied territory—but okay. I am fully prepared for a few years of this. I must rationally consider what they can do for my people. We must be grateful to the Japanese. We can use them. If human beings stay in the groove of colonialism without anything radical to stir them or their colonizers, it is difficult to ever make a revolution."

Waworunto stared at me, his eyes open wide. The truth of what I was saying was dawning on him.

"Look here, Bung," I said, "this chaos, confusion, inflamed feelings—or even just the change itself—will of necessity bring the result for which I have sacrificed my whole life."

We walked along in silence, each busy with his own thoughts. Then my friend commented, "Perhaps our citizens will always consider them liberators and ever remain strongly pro-Japanese, thereby making it difficult someday to rid our land of them, too."

"This is not possible," I explained. "It is folly for an invader to imagine he will long be loved or that a colonized society will remain content while undergoing his domination. No matter how weak, degenerate, or barbaric the old colonizers and no matter how civilized the new in their manners or intelligence, a once-colonized people will always regard the disappearance of foreign domination as a liberation. Such will happen here, too."

"And when will that be?"

"When we are ready," I said simply. "When we are ready."

I made no moves. I just waited. One day later Captain Sakaguchi, Division Commander of the Padang Area, came to the house of Waworunto and introduced himself. Speaking in French, he said, *"Est-ce que vous pouvez parler Français?"*

"Oui," I answered. *"Je sais Français."*

"Je suis Sakaguchi," he said.

"Bon," I said.

There was silence a moment, then, *"Vous êtes Ingenieur Sukarno, n'est-ce pas?"*

"Oui. Vous avez raison."

The official identifications over, he explained, "I am a member of *Sendenbu*, the Department of Propaganda."

"What do you wish of me?" I asked warily.

"Nothing. I know you are the man to get acquainted with and so I do. That is all. I do not come to give you orders."

Sakaguchi smiled broadly. It seemed unnecessary for a conqueror to be so ingratiating so I asked, "Why do you specifically call on me?"

"Meeting the famous Sukarno is my first order of business. We know all about you. We know you are the Indonesian leader and an influential person."

"Is that why you visit me here instead of requesting me to come to your office?"

"Exactly," he bowed. "It is our great honor to treat you with respect. Mr. Sukarno is already very famous throughout this continent."

"May I ask where your information comes from?"

"You forget, Mr. Sukarno, many Japanese lived here in former times and many have returned in the Japanese army."

"I see."

"We have a most efficient spy system. We know everything about everybody including their whereabouts. Immediately upon taking Bengkulu we ascertained your present position. Our first act was to look you up."

"And your second act?"

"To look after you."

When the Japanese arrived, Padang unfurled its red-and-white Indonesian flag. The citizens thought they were "freed." After centuries of being forbidden our own banner, what a thrill to see that sacred *Merah-Putih* flown. Instantly bulletins were posted on trees and store fronts to the effect that only the Rising Sun would be hoisted. Coincident with this blow, the conquerors seized our newspapers. The "liberation" of Padang was short-lived.

I went to Sakaguchi's office and requested a postponement of the flag order.

"This is very heavy for us and it's going to be a difficult situation," I said. "If not met as diplomatically as possible it might cause serious repercussions—for both sides."

Sakaguchi indicated he understood the problem, but cautioned, "Perhaps, Mr. Sukarno, you should not take TOO LONG about it."

This was a black day for my people and for me. I went first to the mosque and prayed. Then, at a mass meeting I instructed my brothers to lower their flags until "such time as we may fly our colors free of all foreign domination."

Every flag came down. I abhorred Hitler, but this outcome unconsciously reminded me of one phrase of his: *Gross sein heissat Massen bewegen können*—Greatness is the ability to move the masses into action. Had it not been Sukarno speaking they'd have rebelled, realizing all too abruptly the sons of Nippon were not the heroes they imagined. And I was fearful of any uprising. We were too untrained a people to rout a force as militaristic as the Japanese—yet.

Three days later Sakaguchi called again. Again we conversed in French. It wasn't until months later I learned Sakaguchi spoke Indonesian. "Monsieur Sukarno," he said, "I bring a message. Your presence is requested by Le Commandant de Bukittinggi."

"Requested?" I repeated.

"Oui, Monsieur. Requested."

"Not ordered?" I asked.

"No, Monsieur. Requested."

From Captain Sakaguchi's obsequious manner, it was obvious Holland's fears were to be realized. The Japanese were going to suggest I work with them. The commander of that mighty division which had marched in during the night was the Military Commandant of Bukittinggi, Colonel Fujiyama. It was he who sent word personally "requesting" Mr. Sukarno to please come.

Mr. Sukarno came.

We traveled by train and word spread Sukarno was on board. Those in our car told passengers in adjacent cars. At one stop, Padangpandjang, everybody on the platform began shouting for Sukarno. Our car was so mobbed I had to stick my head out the window and make a short speech to appease the people. None of this was lost on Sakaguchi.

It's an hour and a half inland to this cool mountain city. In the heart of the Minangkabau tribe, the city is known for its gay horse carts which are used as transport in the hilly streets and for its colorful three-pointed roofs, symbolic of Minangkabau architecture.

Bukittinggi was a very important city. Strategically located, it has access on only three sides and is so situated in the mountains that its inhabitants control all passage in and out. Colonel Fujiyama's headquarters, a mansion that once belonged to a wealthy Dutchman, was also strategically placed. It towered atop Lembah Ngarai, a deep gorge with tall mountains on either side making a bare, rocky wall high in the sky. Below a ribbon of river wended its way lazily. Around stood trees and grandiose greenery. Looking out and down thousands and thousands of feet from Fujiyama's window was a most impressive sight.

It was there I had my little known but enormously important meeting. My famous meeting. The meeting which determined my strategy for the rest of the war. The meeting which up until now has pinned on me the label "Japanese collaborator."

Commandant Fujiyama spoke in his native tongue. In the room was an American interpreter captured in Singapore. "Mr. Sukarno," said Fujiyama, motioning me to sit, "this war is to free Asia from the yoke of Western colonialism."

I knew I was being sounded out and I chose my words carefully. Each syllable of mine would be sifted, weighed, and examined. I knew it. "You Japanese have a slogan which says, 'Free Asia.' Is that right?" I asked after a few moments.

"Yes, Mr. Sukarno," he said, offering me a cigarette. "That is so."

I puffed the cigarette lazily, then said casually, "And do you intend to abide by that slogan?"

"Yes, Mr. Sukarno, we do," he said, watching me carefully.

"Well, then, would you say Indonesia is a part of Asia?"

"Of course, Mr. Sukarno."

I took a deep breath. "So then I am to assume your aim is also to free Indonesia, is that correct?"

The pause was no longer than a heartbeat. "Yes, Mr. Sukarno. Perfectly correct."

During this high-level conversation, a little shuffling Japanese soldier served tea. My nerves were strung tight and I picked at my fingernails, a habit of mine when I'm nervous. We waited for the rattling of the tea cups to subside. Even after he pattered away the noise was still there. At least, inside me. My teeth and my bones were all rattling. The life or death of my country depended on the successful outcome of this talk.

After the soldier exited, Fujiyama resumed. "In the light of this understanding, we wish to know if you are interested in helping the Japanese army."

"In what way?"

"In keeping peace."

"May I ask how I alone can keep peace for the Japanese army?"

The Supreme Commander of the Imperial Japanese 25th Army smiled. On his level they did a lot of that. "We understand Sukarno alone commands the masses. Therefore, the simplest way to get to the people is to get to Sukarno. Our job is not to reach millions of Indonesians. Our job is to win one Indonesian. Namely, you. It is then hoped you will reach the millions for us."

His manner made it apparent he had to win me. Out in the

streets my people weren't hailing his people quite so loudly any more. The first flush had already faded. He knew if he turned against me and harmed me in any way, if he tried to force me to do anything against my will, the whole population would rise against him. The Japanese needed me and I knew it. But I also needed them to make my country ready for revolution.

This was like a game of volleyball. Except that the stakes were freedom. Colonel Fujiyama had first serve. Now it was my turn. Allah, I prayed silently, show me the way.

"Well," I said, "now that I know what you want, I presume you know what I want."

"No, Mr. Sukarno, I do not. What would the Indonesians really like?"

"To be free."

"As a patriot who loves his people and longs for their liberty, you must realize independent Indonesia can be established only in cooperation with Japan," he retaliated.

"Yes," I nodded. "It has become clear and bright to me that our lifeline lies in Japan. . . . Will your government help me to liberate Indonesia?"

"If you promise total cooperation during our occupation, we will grant our unconditional promise to establish the freedom of your homeland."

"Can I be guaranteed that during the whole period I work for you, it will also be permissible for me to work for my people in the full knowledge that my ultimate aim is someday . . . somehow . . . to release them from the yoke of both Dutch—and Japanese—domination?"

"It is guaranteed. The Japanese government will put no obstacles in your way."

I looked at him. We both looked at each other. Measured one another.

"You see, Mr. Sukarno," he continued, making his point carefully, "I am an administrator. You are a nation with layers of Javanese, Balinese, Hindu, Moslem, Buddhist, Dutch, Malaysian, Polynesian, Chinese, Filipino, Arabic, and other cultures, breeds, religions, and heterogeneous customs. You are spread out. Communications are difficult. My assignment is to marshal this area into good running order quickly. The most efficient method is to keep the populace quiet and functioning harmoniously. To accomplish that I am told I must do business with Sukarno. In return I promise official and active cooperation politically."

I had to trust this little man because I saw in him the key. "Very well," I said. "If this is your promise, okay. I pledge my full cooperation. I will make propaganda for you. But only as it continues along the line of emancipating Indonesia and only so it is understood that while I conspire with you I will also try at the same time to gain sovereignty for my people."

"Agreed," he said.

"It is also understood that the proviso whereby I remain unhampered in my ceaseless labors for nationalism is not to be known just to you, but to the entire High Command."

"My government will be so apprised. It is on this basis we pledge our mutual support to one another."

Following this two-hour historic meeting, they served me sukiyaki. It was the first time I'd ever tasted it and it was quite good, I thought.

Their desire to be gracious didn't end there. Instead of dismissing me they asked when I wished to return home. Indicating my readiness, I was escorted outside. There Sakaguchi beamed, "Allow us to take care of your transportation," and pointed to a shiny black Buick. Buicks weren't plentiful in Bukittinggi, so this car had undoubtedly been captured from some well-to-do trader and whereever he was languishing at the moment he wasn't about to take a motor trip.

"This Buick is all for you," Sakaguchi bowed. "It is at your disposal as long as you wish it."

I tell you, I was really so proud. There I was fresh from exile and a beautiful Buick awaited me. Of course, it had no gasoline. Just barely enough to squeak into Padang. They had given me courtesy, they had given me lunch and they had given me a car—but no fuel.

My friends—and those of you who are not my friends but who I hope will understand Sukarno better after you finish his book—this is the first time I have told my story of how, when, where, and why I decided to throw my lot in with the Japanese. Puppet . . . quisling . . . I know all the words. However, without the condition that the Japanese work with me toward making my country free, I would never have done it. Until this very moment it's never been properly explained. The outside world does not understand. They think Sukarno was a collaborator. For me to squeeze more and more political concessions out of the victors, I was forced into many things that ripped me apart. But I had to do them. If I didn't keep my bargain they wouldn't keep theirs.

One morning Sakaguchi came to me. He was pleasant but firm. "We face a serious rice problem," he said crisply. "It seems rice in Padang is very scarce. In fact, there is almost none. I warn you, if the Japanese get no rice the Indonesians will have none. It is not our desire to force it out of those who control its output because that will create havoc and go against the nice way we are trying to do things. At least, the nice way we are so far trying. Nonetheless, there are alternatives, Mr. Sukarno, as I'm sure you understand. I suggest you urge your stubborn countrymen to be sensible."

I immediately called on the rice merchants. I explained I needed so many tons—and fast! Well, as long as it was me asking, I got it. As much as I wanted and as soon as I wanted it. Sending it to me solved everyone's problem. The Japanese were saved from starvation. The Indonesians were saved from torture.

Another crisis was the sex life of the soldier. Seems they hadn't had any for some while. That would be strictly their problem, except for the fact they were in my country. The women they were eager to ravage were my Indonesian women. Now the Minangkabau tribes are very religious. Their women are reared scrupulously. I cautioned Fujiyama, "If your boys attempt anything with my girls, the people will revolt. You'll have a full-scale uprising in Sumatra."

I knew I couldn't let the army play around with the Minangkabau girls and I knew that if this problem weren't solved I'd have an even bigger one on my hands.

I consulted with a religious leader. "According to Islam," I began, "a man must not make love with a girl if he does not intend to marry her. This is a sin."

"That is correct," he said.

I wasn't one hundred percent certain how to phrase what I was driving at so I thought a moment, then said, "Is it possible this ruling could be set aside in certain cases?"

"No. It is impossible. Not even for Bung Karno is this possible," protested the shocked *ulama*.

I then unfolded a plan. "Purely as an emergency measure, for the good of our girls and our country, I would like to utilize the services of prostitutes in the area. This way the foreigners will be satisfied and will not ravage our maidens."

"Under these circumstances," said the *ulama* kindly, "even if one had to kill it would not be considered a sin."

Bolstered by the guarantee that my idea would not be construed a mortal sin, I approached the prostitutes. "I would not suggest you to do something against your nature," I pointed out, "but this plan is in conformity with your chosen trade."

"I hear the Japs are rich and quite free with their money," chortled one, obviously pleased with the arrangement.

"True," I concurred. "They also have wristwatches and other trinkets and ornaments."

"I consider this mutually beneficial all around," announced the spokeswoman. "Not only will we be great patriots, but it's a sound business proposition."

I gathered 120 into a segregated district and penned them in a camp surrounded by high fences. Each man was handed a card permitting him one visit per week. At each visit his card was punched. Possibly it isn't such a good story to tell. I mean, perhaps it doesn't seem right for a leader of a nation to be procuring girls. In fact, I am aware there's a word to describe this type of person. But this was a serious difficulty which could have created terrible unhappiness, so I healed it the best way I knew how. It worked out very well, too, I'm pleased to add. Everybody was very happy with my plan.

Because they needed me to solve every administrative problem, the Japanese were anxious to keep me content. Fujiyama offered every facility. I steadfastly refused all. I accepted only what was essential. My liaison mission necessitated touring distant communities. During these travels I, naturally, sparked the local chiefs and the people with hope and revitalized their nationalistic consciousness for the future. For these trips I needed fuel.

Fujiyama periodically provided two hundred liters in a drum. He also provided a long paper in Japanese explaining if I went to such and such a place on such and such a road they'd supply me. Nonetheless I took care to ask for no more than I required. Often my boys sneaked 25 kilometers into the jungle to find those gasoline dumps the Dutch had hidden. I tried anything and everything so as not to be more beholden than necessary to the Japanese.

Always Fujiyama asked, "Does Mr. Sukarno feel in need of money?"

And I'd say, "No, thank you. My people provide everything. When I was sick recently, word went out. Up and down the streets you could hear Marhaens passing the news, 'Hey, Bung Karno's calcium tablets are finished. He needs more. Get it.' In an hour a new bottle was there."

"Where did it come from?" he would ask casually.

"I do not know," I'd answer just as casually. What I didn't tell him was Padang numbered many Chinese shopkeepers who could get anything if they wanted to. And when it came to me they wanted to.

"Well then, does Mr. Sukarno need another place to stay?"

And I'd say, "No, thank you. I stay in the house of Waworunto rent-free. It is sufficient for me. I do not need special privileges."

"May we supply you with aides?"

"No, thank you. Other races cannot understand our system of voluntary help, but that is our way. I have more than enough assistance." A local journalist became my driver. His name is Suska. Suska, at this writing, is my Ambassador to India. Another, who had been chairman of the neighborhood Partindo, offered gratefully to serve the cause without pay. Gunadi, a man from Bengkulu, labored as my full-time secretary without salary.

When he couldn't oblige me beyond gasoline, Fujiyama asked others what I needed. Always they were instructed to reply, "Thank you, but Bung Karno needs nothing. His people supply all he needs."

I requested so little that when I demanded something, I usually got it. It wasn't very long before I had to start demanding. On March 1 Japan invaded Djakarta. Within one week they took Java on the same principle as they took Sumatra: the Dutch fled. They were now in supreme command of the archipelago. Their arrogance was felt immediately.

In retaliation there began underground activity of violently anti-Japanese nationalists. Several, indulging in sabotage and open hostility, were arrested by the dreaded Secret Police. One unfortunate I knew intimately. His name was Anwar. Anwar had been tortured. The *Kempeitai*, the Japanese Secret Police, were eager to make an example of him since he was the first subversive caught. They pulled his fingernails out.

I raced to Bukittinggi, deposited my belongings at the home of a friend, Munadji, and drove off to consult with officials. Meanwhile a thief crept into Munadji's house and robbed my personal belongings, which weren't much because I never owned much. But gone was the bag in which Inggit had a gold necklace with a charm studded with brilliants.

In Bukittinggi, if Sukarno admired something, shopkeepers forced it on him without accepting money. In Bukittinggi, they wanted only to give me, not to take from me. Thus the police correctly assumed the robber was a stranger passing through. News was circulated that Bung Karno was the victim and two days later the property was mysteriously returned. To avoid arrest, the thief, a Chinese named Lian, arranged with a religious leader to secrete the things in a corner of a certain rice field, whereupon the religious leader was to go there to pray and behold! he would find Bung Karno's belongings. And so it happened.

Two days running I returned to plead for Anwar. I said, "I know him well. While you honor your vow of cooperation with Indonesia's nationalist aspirations, he and the other nationalists will not plot against you. He merely misconstrued the removal of our flag and other events that happened as a symbol of your breaking faith. He didn't mean anything against you personally. If you let him out I'm sure I can make of him a good worker. I personally vouch for his patriotism."

Two hours after this second visit they released him.

❧ 19. The Japanese Occupation

MEANWHILE General Imamura, Commander-in-Chief of the army of occupation with headquarters in Djakarta, had ordered the top Indonesian leaders to form a civilian governing board, but they demurred, saying, "No, we don't sit in any cabinet without Sukarno."

Imamura dispatched a letter to Colonel Fujiyama which stated, "The bulk of the occupied forces plus the governing head of these forces is in Java. The real administrative task is here and civilian affairs are not proceeding well. We badly need the help of the most influential man." The letter concluded, "This is a military order to release Sukarno."

When Fujiyama instructed me to leave immediately for Palembang, where a ship would take me to Djakarta, my heart leapt for joy. To return to my beloved Java was what I'd prayed for since the invasion four months before, but I hadn't known the best way to implement it. Now, to think God had heard my prayers and was ordering me back!

Near Palembang we were involved in an accident. Two Japanese vehicles careening along at high speed crashed in front of us. One was a jeep, the first I'd ever seen in my life. The other was a heavy van. The two officers in the van were shaken but, barring minor bruises, unhurt. Pulling themselves together they hurried on their way. The jeep was totally demolished. The passenger, a captain, was critically wounded. His aide had been thrown to the side of the road and merely lay under a tree dazed. When he came to, he said, "It is urgent we proceed to Palembang immediately. We take your Buick."

"But," I sputtered, "this is my property. The Commandant of this area gave me special permission." I flashed my ownership letter. "This will prove what I say."

Portions of this "conversation" were conducted in sign language. Letter notwithstanding, the aide bowed stiffly, uttered something like "We high priority business. So sorry," and drove off, leaving me stranded on the road. Military police who rushed to the scene acknowledged the validity of my credentials. The next vehicle which happened along was a truck. They confiscated it promptly and now we drove off, leaving the previous owners stranded on the road.

We added two extra passengers. The first was an Indonesian who was thrown from the van and had been lying in the bushes, face down, in a pool of blood. He was dead. I could not leave this poor man in a forest surrounded by unfriendly faces. Lifting the bloodied corpse into the truck, I took him along for proper burial. Our second addition was the soldier who had been detailed to drive us. Inggit was placed next to him. The rest of us sat in back. The only trouble was that Inggit would not sit next to a Japanese. I ultimately unraveled this knot by stuffing Tuktuk One and Tuktuk Two on the seat between them.

In Palembang I ran into more trouble. The authorities wouldn't let me proceed to Djakarta as per my instructions. The man in charge dismissed me curtly with, "Travel between Sumatra and Java is forbidden."

"There's a misunderstanding somewhere," I argued. "Those are my orders forwarded by your own High Command."

"There is no civilian travel between Sumatra and Java now," he reiterated, standing up to dismiss me. When I persisted he jabbed a button and I was hauled off to the headquarters of the dreaded *Kempeitai.*

The *Kempeitai* decided to investigate me. "We need more information on you, Mr. Sukarno," hissed a fat-bellied officer toying with a Samurai sword. "We are given to understand through our channels that you are a bad man who doesn't have our best interests at heart."

"Ridiculous," I snorted. "And I can prove it." I whipped out the good-conduct courtesy card Fujiyama had given me for just such emergencies. He read it slowly. Then he reread it. And it was this tiny white piece of pasteboard which saved my life. It did not, however, expedite my transportation problem. He now demanded my assistance locally before signing the exit permit.

Smiled Fatbelly, who had since replaced his Samurai sword, "If you really are a good man with good intentions, then I expect you will delay your departure to help us iron out several difficulties caused by your stupid countrymen."

He sat on the edge of his desk, I on a chair. We were nose to nose and at close range his face was an interesting study. The mouth was smiling, but the eyes were not. "We would prefer not to have to detain you forcibly, Mr. Sukarno," he hissed.

"I'll give you whatever assistance I can," I said, considering there was nothing else to say under the circumstances.

The Japanese in Palembang and I didn't get along well. I did one thing they did not like at all. But, then, they did many things I didn't like, either. I'd witnessed brutalities that turned my stomach and I spoke up about them. As I told Fatbelly, "On numerous occasions I have noticed your men are too quick with their hands. With my own eyes I've seen them repeatedly slap Indonesians."

I held my breath and paused, but he just stared at me, idly swinging his foot back and forth—each time barely grazing my leg —and waited for me to reach a conclusion. "These beatings of my people must stop. That's hardly the way to inspire comradeship and get people to trust you," I pointed out. "If you wish my cooperation you will have to give me cooperation."

"There is some mistake," he grunted. "Those guilty of misconduct are soldiers from Korea. Our own pure Japanese boys are much better behaved. They would never commit such acts."

"Commander," I said, "it doesn't make much difference to the slapped Indonesian who is doing it. The point is, it should be stopped. By everybody."

"Very well, Mr. Sukarno. You have my word. The Battalion Commanders will be instructed to have this stopped instantly." It didn't happen again.

One month later they freed me to leave, but the military in Palembang had only one available boat, a motorboat with a caterpillar motor. This whole seagoing craft was eight meters long and the passenger list was to include a captain, two soldiers, Inggit, myself, Sukarti, our luggage, Riwu and, of course, Tuktuk One and Tuktuk Two. I tried for a bigger boat but they told me I'd have to wait. I'd waited in occupied Sumatra five and a half months. That was enough. Although scarcely my idea of an ocean-going liner, this was the first opportunity offered me to make for home and I grabbed it.

It took four days and four nights. We slept sitting up in our seats with the wind and spray biting our faces twenty-four hours a day. It was not a pleasurable trip. As we navigated the Strait of Bangka, a storm broke and we had to ride it out with no covering. Then, the boat nearly capsized altogether because we hit some lowlying coral islands. In addition, I was nervous because I'd never learned to swim. My water sports heretofore had centered around a blownup inner tube in which I sat and splashed.

We'd brought cooked vegetables, dried fish, and other provisions in jars plus a packet of rice, but I could eat nothing. All I had in my stomach was a little orange juice. I was so seasick I thought I'd die. Our tiny float bobbed and pitched and rocked and rolled and I was pale green the whole four days.

I was sick, I was nauseated, I was dizzy, my head ached, the sun burned me raw, the seaspray had cracked my lips, I was hungry and weak—but what did I care? I was back in Java. I was so grateful to return alive and safe that I donated all our possessions—everything —to the captain. This was a new beginning for me. A new life for my country. I wanted to start out fresh.

My first glimpse of my beloved native land was through the inlet from the Java Sea. It was a sunny hot noon as we chugged past lines of smelly fishing scows and rowboats, beyond the aquarium built onto the dock and into the harbor of Pasar Ikan, which is so narrow that two barges can barely pass each other. It was crowded with stalls selling sea products. The water was filthy. Leaves, fishheads, and garbage floated by. The stink of dead fish filled the air. But, as I was helped up the stone steps leading to the ground, I thought, "This is the most beautiful sight I've ever seen in my life."

There was nobody to meet the boat. I requested a passing fisherman to contact my ex-brother-in-law, Anwar Tjokroaminoto, and the lawyer who defended me in Bandung, Sartono, and Hatta, who was also in Djakarta. At the pier edge stood a lean-to office. The soldiers motioned me into the shack and told me to sit. I sat. And waited.

Anwar was the first to arrive. God bless him. He ran in with tears in his eyes. We embraced and kissed each other unashamed. There was no loud backslapping. The atmosphere was rather one of silent gratitude. Tears streamed down both our cheeks. As I recall we did not say much. We could not. The words would not come out of our throats. Instead they welled up in our eyes.

"How is your brother Harsono?" I asked, my voice cracking with emotion.

"Fine."

"Utari?"

"Everybody is fine. It is more important I ask how you are."

"I, too, am fine."

We pulled apart and surveyed one another from arm's length. He saw a tired, thin man in an ill-fitting white jacket and shapeless trousers. My clothes were very old-fashioned. They were either home-made by my tailor boarder from Flores, Mr. Darham, or of pre-exile vintage.

Anwar wore a double-breasted cream-colored jacket. After I dried my cheeks and kissed the ground beneath me and rubbed my eyes to make positive it was truly Anwar, not a vision, I then settled down to realities. I felt the material of his jacket. "Your clothing is beautifully tailored," I commented.

"It was made by De Koning," he boasted.

"But he was Djakarta's most famous tailor in Dutch time. How can you afford him?"

He cupped his hands and talked directly into my ear. "I came in through the back door. I cannot pay his prices, but I have a friend who works as an apprentice tailor in Mr. De Koning's shop."

"You suppose he could do the same for me?"

"Of course. As soon as you get settled I'll take you."

Ofttimes future generations harken back to the immortal death-less phrases spoken at a great moment in history. I would like to be able to herewith record inspiring, moving prose to set down in words of fire for immortality, but the truth is after I asked after Anwar and his family, the item I asked after next was his tailor. That same week I went down for my first professional suit in many years.

A half hour later Sartono and Hatta rushed in. Hatta and I had not corresponded in all the years and although there was much to say and much to ask, each had but one question for the other. Hatta whispered, "What is your opinion on the outcome of the occupation?"

I whispered back, "The Japanese will not stay here long. They will lose the war and we will destroy them. That is, provided we do not oppose them openly."

Then I asked, "Tell me, Bung Hatta, how is the spirit of nation-alism in our people?"

"It has not been hurt by the war. Our people have already grown suspicious of the 'liberators' and eagerly they await the return of Bung Karno."

The Japanese had arranged for a fine-looking, two-story house on the main avenue of Djakarta. It had a lawn, porch, and garage, and it was furnished except for dishes, glassware, and the other breakables which the Dutch had methodically smashed before they left. There was, of course, no welcome-home party because nobody knew when I'd arrive and, too, there were rigorous regulations against gatherings. Inside the house, however, I met several members of "The Reception Committee for Bung Karno." Their faces shone with quiet happiness and they fell to their knees and kissed my hands. I held theirs tightly in mine. I was quite overcome. These dear people had been assigned the task of finding me suitable living quarters.

"The Dutch have been thrown into concentration camps," said Achmad Subardjo, "so if you go walking you will see the city is full of beautiful empty mansions. My wife took one side of the street, Mrs. Sartono the other. In a matter of days they found this."

"It is quite a large house," I said, examining the interior.

"We felt our leader would need much room for visitors. Ever since it was rumored you would soon be coming, the excitement of people from the villages, mountains, seasides, and far-off provinces has mounted. Despite privation they're willing to make any sacrifice to come see The Bung in the flesh. They cannot believe you are truly here and free and ready to take your place as their hero once again."

That night Inggit and I walked around our new home on the wide, tree-lined "rich man's row" of Djakarta. It had taken a long time. Nearly 13 years. It had taken prison and exile. And it had taken a war. But I was back where I belonged. Once again I was the leader of my people. I was home.

⮑ 20. Collaborator or Hero . . . ?

THAT night I went to the home of Hatta and we had our first tactical meeting. "You and I have gone through a deep quarrel period," I said. "Although there was a time we may not have loved each other, we now have a job far bigger than either of us. Differences in terms of party or strategy no longer exist. Today we are one. United in the common struggle."

"Agreed," declared Hatta.

We shook hands solemnly. "This," I pledged, "is our symbol of *Dwi Tunggal*—two-in-one. Our solemn oath to work side-by-side, never to be separated until our country is wholly free."

Along with Sjahrir, the only other person present, plans for future operations were laid swiftly. It was agreed we'd function on two levels. On the surface openly and underground secretly. Each level to accomplish tasks the other could not.

"To gain political concessions in terms of military training and administrative jobs for our people, we must make an appearance of collaboration," I said.

"Obviously your power is with the masses," outlined Hatta, "so you will have to work on the surface."

"Correct. You will assist me since you are too well-known a nationalist to work underground."

"That leaves me," suggested Sjahrir, "to work underground and organize radio monitoring and other secret operations."

Our short one-hour discussion evolved such a simple formula that, when re-examined two decades later, it almost seems profound. In reality our strategy was the only possible one. We had no alternatives. "This is the chance we have waited for," I exulted. "Of this I am certain. The occupation will prove a magnificent opportunity to educate and ready our people. With all Dutch personnel imprisoned and without enough Japanese to administer the entire archipelago, they'll need us desperately. Indonesia will soon see her masters are not so bright on their own."

I paced up and down as I thought aloud. "But first our people must be brought to suffering because only then can they be awakened. Ours is a peaceful, easygoing, forgiving race. Although we were nearly seventy million governed by 500,000, our masses would never rile up enough to fight under Dutch rule. The Dutch tempered their mastery with fake benevolence. The Japs do not.

"We know they cut off people's heads with one stroke of their swords. We know their trick of forcing victims to drink quarts of water, then jumping on their stomachs. We're familiar with those agonized shrieks coming from *Kempeitai* headquarters late at night. We've heard *Kempeitai* guards are kept deliberately drunk so as to dull their sensibilities. Japanese are hard. Cruel. Quick to inflict brutalities. They will make our people have to fight."

"They will also give us confidence," commented Hatta. "No more is an Asian inferior."

"These conditions will create determination. When our people are really pressed the mental revolution will come. After that, the physical revolution."

I sat down. Through the sandals I picked at my toenails, a sure sign I was excited. I unconsciously picked so deep my big toe began to bleed. "We must get a nationalist movement going," I murmured.

"Impossible," retorted Hatta. "Mass gatherings or politicking of any sort is forbidden."

"You cannot rouse the people without a people's movement," I stated flatly. "I cannot sit by passively. Just giving advice is not sufficient for me. There must be activity. We cannot let our men fight even covertly without guidance. If I cannot form a movement of my own I shall infiltrate a Japanese-sponsored one. What about The Three A's?"

The Three A's was a psychologically wrong organization based on the irritating slogan: Japan the Leader of Asia, Japan the Protector of Asia, Japan the Light of Asia.

"It is doing poorly," snorted Sjahrir. "Its original purpose was to get as much foodstuffs, natural resources, and even manpower out of us as possible."

"But without giving anything in return," added Hatta. "That plus its pompous propaganda, the fact there's no Indonesian leader at its helm and the growing antagonism of Indonesians has caused it to retrograde rapidly. Better you stay outside The Three A's."

"No. I think I will join it."

"Why?"

"To change it."

My first night in Djakarta I went to bed dizzy with excitement. The next morning would complete the circle. I was to meet Lt. General Imamura.

He received me in his sitting room in the big white palace which heretofore had housed the Governor General. That sitting room is now my study. General Imamura was a true Samurai. Lean, above average height, gentlemanly, respectful, and noble. After he bade me be seated, he too sat down. His posture was ramrod straight.

I spoke Indonesian. He Japanese. We had an interpreter. I went alone without a second. The General, of course, had an aide. Generals always do. He opened the conversation: "I called you to Java with good intentions. You will be forced into nothing against your will. The outcome of our talks—whether you wish to cooperate with us or remain a looker-on—depends fully on yourself."

"May I ask what plans has the Dai Nippon Teikoku Government for Indonesia?"

Answered Imamura, "I am only the Chief Commander of an expedition army. His Excellency The Emperor alone decides whether your country will be granted autonomy on a high degree under the aegis of His government or whether it will gain freedom as a constituent state in a federation with Japan or whether it becomes a totally independent, sovereign state. I can issue no promise of precisely what form your liberty will take. Such decisions will not come to the foreground before the end of the war. However, we are conversant with your aims and your terms and they coincide with our own."

My next sentence was, "Thank you, General. Thank you for being the man who kicked out the hated Dutch. I tried for years. My country tried for centuries. But it was Imamura who did it."

"May I tell you, Dr. Sukarno, how I conquered the mighty white man on your shores? With bluff, that's what. Pure bluff."

My face undoubtedly mirrored my confusion because the General permitted a smile and gaily related the steps of his victory. "When my army landed in Java I had only a few battalions left and I had to divide them. Some were dropped in West Java, Central Java, a few in Djakarta, a few in Banten. Those under my personal command landed in Kalidjati. And they were in rags. My men had rifles but no uniforms. Way in advance of my arrival, the Dutch Governor General fled to Bandung."

"It's surrounded by mountains so he figured it's an easily defended city."

"Correct," nodded Imamura. "I called Bandung and ordered him to Kalidjati for peace talks. He came. And fast, too. I was headquartered in a tiny room. With a lot of noise but no troops to back up my bravado, I demanded, 'Well, are you going to surrender? If not I shall bomb you off the face of the world.' So he and his men quickly surrendered."

"With a torn, bedraggled remnant of an army," I said to the conqueror facing me, "you kicked out those who will always be considered the real tyrants of Indonesia. I am eternally grateful to you."

This drama I was playing reminded me of the Philippines' hero, General Aguinaldo. He fought the Spaniards for years and when the Americans conquered the ex-conquerors, Aguinaldo first said to the Americans, "Thank you." Later, when the U.S. wanted to stay in the Philippines, he tried hard to kick them out.

"How long do you estimate the military will function in an administrative capacity here?" I asked.

"I do not honestly know. I have no plan as yet."

Well, I had. And I made my first move. "To lead my people in accordance with the military government, I must have people to lead. Civilian affairs can only be expedited when my countrymen are placed in administrative capacities. Only Indonesians know the region, idioms, the ways of their brothers."

"If that is how best to promote prosperity and welfare, Indonesians will be permitted to participate in solving the State's affairs on an escalating scale. Government positions will be released to them immediately."

In terms of political concessions I had the upper hand. He was a military leader. He knew about arms. I was a political leader. I knew about nation-building. In my hands he would be a baby.

I outlined my plan to Hatta that night. "At Japanese government expense we will teach our people to be executives. To give orders, not just take them. To prepare them to be chiefs and administrators. To put the reins of government in their hands for that someday when we take over and proclaim independence. How can you staff a government if you don't have personnel?"

Without pausing for an answer, I continued, "Formerly every administrator was Dutch . . . Dutch . . . Dutch . . . every single one was a Dutchman!"

"And our people either letter carriers or order takers," added Hatta. "Always in some menial capacity. Always subservient."

"Now those poor, downtrodden, stupid natives will become officials. They'll learn how to make decisions, run businesses, command. I have planted the seed and the Japanese are nourishing it."

I spat on the ground. "That's why anybody with intelligence hates the Dutch. They requested our cooperation, too, but without offering us any incentive to gain from it. When I think of the hypocrisy of the Netherlands I could vomit. What did they ever do for us? Nothing! I know there'll be people against me because I'm working with the Japanese. But why not? Utilizing what's placed in front of me is a brilliant tactic on my part and that's how I intend to look at it."

In November The Three A's was abandoned. In March I took my first official job with the new organization, Putera. Tokyo recognized this "Center of People's Manpower" as the means whereby I'd rally native support behind their war effort. Sukarno recognized it as the second-best instrument to an out-and-out political machine.

As chairman my duty was to alleviate domestic difficulties. Take the serious textile problem. Marhaens were wearing ricebags made of jute or shirts fashioned from curtains. Newborn babes were wrapped in tablecloths. I journeyed about telling the villagers, "We have a wild native bush called rosella. Its fibers can be woven. Grow it. Weave it." It was as I thought. When my people were forced to be ingenious they were. But while I was at it I'd handpick a devoted patriot and instruct the suburban authorities, "You'll get more accomplished with an Indonesian in charge. Here, make this man head of the program. I personally vouch for his loyalties."

We had no soap. I told my neighbors to create soap from oil and burnt coconut leaves. Ashes of burnt coconut leaves yield a chemical which sudses when mixed with oil. Then I'd select one of my trusted followers and tell the particular official, "I have a friend here who knows how to do this. Put him in charge of your problem."

We had no electric light. My orders went out to "Plant castor. It grows easily like hedges and its seeds make a lubricant called castor oil which burns brightly." And how do I know this? Because I am Javanese. Because my family had to make do lots of times. Because most of my life I burned the seeds of castor since I could not afford light bulbs.

That's why conquerors need the leaders of the occupied territory. Only a native knows how to solve a native matter. An enemy cannot—ever—anywhere—at any time—occupy a country without the assistance of the leaders of that country.

We had no medicines. "Cure with the natural roots our ancestors used," I instructed. "For malaria use the herb *ketepeng*. For fever brew tea made from the long grass *alangalang*." Indonesia is still utilizing these discoveries today.

Food was a major hurdle. The army confiscated every grain of rice. Nonessential people were forbidden even one single kilo. In Bali they were dying of starvation. I managed to secure a huge pile of papaya seeds and apportioned two per person. The tasty fruit sprang up in every corner of the island.

To combat hunger the military erected a massive radio network with speakers in each village so everyone who had previously just heard the name of Sukarno could now hear the voice of Sukarno. "Ladies," blared their speakers, "in your spare time do what Ibu Inggit and I do. Plant maize. In your own front yard you can plant enough to feed your family." Well, Sukarno told them so they planted. Each compound sprouted a maize crop. It helped.

Of course, I had to turn the hatred off the Japanese for the food shortage so I made speeches like, "Enemy spies whisper in your ears that Dai Nippon causes your difficulties. This is false. Months ago the world learned India is ravaged by famine. Allied countries, too, suffer misery and queue daily for a crust of bread. If they say, 'No,' they tell lies as big as an elephant. If you believe these lies you are like a frog under a nutshell. Years ago Winston Churchill already complained the British were short of rations. War entails difficulties everywhere.

"Previously rice was brought in from Burma, from Thailand. But ships are being torpedoed. Shortages are a natural outcome of war. And whose fault is it that we import food? Holland, not Japan! She commandeered our best rice lands for sugar, tobacco, or anything which could be exported to earn money. Therefore, until that day we stand on our own free of imperialist exploitation we are dependent on rice import."

My orders were to "Attack the Allies, laud the Axis, drum up hatred for our enemies the British, the Americans and the Dutch and enlist support for Dai Nippon." However, despite my speeches microscopically prechecked by the Department of Propaganda, a careful study will reveal 75 percent of them were pure nationalism.

For instance, pointing to a sentinel holding a rifle and bayonet I'd say, "He does this because he loves his homeland. He is fighting for his nation. He's ready to die for his country. So . . . must . . . we!!!"

Then I would indoctrinate my brothers to their precolonial greatness. "The Madjapahit Empire triumphed only after being tempered by hardship in the wars with Kublai Khan. Sultan Agoeng Hanjokrokoesoemo made the state of Mataram powerful after trials in the Senapati war. Not until the Crusades did Moslems in the golden age of Islam wax strong. Says God Almighty in the Koran: 'There are moments when your difficulties are useful and necessary!' "

I'm a master at choosing words so foreigners who speak the language cannot catch the regional idiom. I'd play on *Mahabharata* stories because 80 percent of all Indonesians were weaned on them. They know Ardjuna is the hero of five brothers whose kingdoms were falsely taken in a great war. Those five represent good. The invaders represent evil.

Each name brings to our minds a human character. Ardjuna signifies a figure of self-control. His brother, Werkoodoro, means one who is truthful. Mention Gatutkatja and everybody thinks of Sukarno. Refer to Buto Chakil and they know it's the demon. In *Wayang* good figures always sit on the right, evil on the left. Gold, white, or black faces mean the good men, red mean the villains. It was easy to convey my real thoughts.

Another method was animal symbolism. From my prewar writings my people knew I considered Japan the modern imperialist of Asia. So, during this period I coined my famous metaphor: "Under the blanket of the Rising Sun the Chinese dragon cooperates with the white elephant of Thailand, the caribou of the Philippines, the peacock of Burma, the Nandi cow of India, the hydra snake of Vietnam and, now, with the Banteng buffalo of Indonesia, in ridding our continent of Imperialism."

To the Indonesian mind this was clear. It meant the occupied territories were united in the desire to exterminate aggression. I did not say we were cooperating with the Rising Sun. I said we were cooperating UNDER the Rising Sun.

Imamura was pleased with my oratory, which he considered purely a vehicle to keep the vanquished in line. When I requested permission "To write and travel in order to alleviate complexities in areas I cannot reach," he placed newspapers and planes at my disposal. He allowed me mass rallies. I addressed 50,000 at one meeting, 100,000 at another. Sukarno's face, not just his name, penetrated the archipelago. I have the Japanese to thank for that.

Once more I electrified. I inspired. I thrilled. More and more Nippon needed my cooperation.

Nonetheless, let nobody think because of my position I had it soft or rich during the war. When everybody was hungry, Sukarno was hungry. When there was no food, Sukarno had no food. I had to look myself for rice to feed my family. The leader of a nation had to go to the countryside to scrape together five kilos just like the poorest peasant.

And there was the time I was slow in switching off a lamp during the blackout. A small shaft of light shone for a second in the dark. Immediately I flicked it off there was a battering at our door. Inggit quickly answered it and faced a surly group of Military Police.

"What can I do for you?" she quaked.

The Captain snarled, "Who is the owner of this house?"

"I am," she replied.

"No," he snapped, "we mean the man of the house. Where is your husband?"

I was way inside but I came out. The Captain growled at me about the light; then with the flat of his hand he whipped out and went bang . . . bang . . . bang . . . bang . . . back and forth across my face.

Inggit fell to her knees screaming, "Please . . . please . . . don't beat him. It was I who was responsible, not he. It was not his fault. Please forgive him. I did it!"

They paid no attention. They were bent on taking it out on me. My face was cut. My lip and nose bled profusely. But I uttered not one word. I didn't plead for myself. I just stood it calmly saying to myself all the while, "The pain of any individual is merely gravel on the path to independence. Step over it. If you fall down, pick yourself up and walk right on."

I reported the incident to Colonel Nakayama, the Chief Administrator, and, of course, he apologized and said "The Captain didn't know who you were" and that "measures would be taken against him at once," but they were watching me at all times.

On certain occasions Imamura would make a speech. The response was mild. I would give the translation with great vigor and a few typically Sukarnoesque twists. The people went wild. After every phrase they shouted and clapped. The *Kempeitai* would grow suspicious. They marched me to headquarters, where I was shouted at and threatened. I was sure I would be hanged. An interpreter whom they employed but whose loyalties were with me was brought in to face me. He vouched for my words. Many frightening hours later I was freed.

Wherever I went officers accompanied me or scrutinized me secretly. The *Kempeitai* visited me often at unspecified intervals. I had to watch myself at every moment. The Japanese were not stupid. They never completely trusted me. Underground agents sent word plans had been laid to behead all Indonesian leaders. Rumors were they just needed me to win the hearts of my people for them and once this task was finished, so would I be. I was always in danger.

Risky or not, I kept in secret communication with the underground. Sometimes I'd meet a contact late in the night in the clinic of my friend, Dr. Suharto, when every light was off and every person behind closed doors. Sometimes I'd meet a contact out in the open socially, exchange seemingly pleasant words, and the next day whispers would go forth to his subordinates, "This we may do. . . . This we may not." Those orders came from me. I alone possessed certain facts. I was a funnel for information going both ways. But the Japanese had ways of discouraging one's spirit.

Men caught speaking Dutch were subject to beatings. Women were pulled from their homes and shipped to "nurseries," only the nurseries were brothels. Men or women who passed a sentry in the street and didn't bow would get slapped. With such punishments for minor infractions, the measures taken against those in the underground forced one to be careful.

Spies were everywhere. Disguised as *sate* sellers they'd walk the streets, all the while listening for that telltale tick . . . tick of a wireless which meant somebody was sending or receiving. Suharto's nephew was captured in the criminal act of listening to a clandestine radio. He was sentenced to death. My good and true associate, Dr. Suharto, did not request me to get him out because he considered the charges were too grave and pleading his case would place me in great jeopardy.

I, however, had my eyes and ears in the Military Police. They always knew in advance when trouble was brewing and their duty was to channel information up to me. Word was passed verbally. You couldn't dare put anything in writing. The information went to an agent in the Sendenbu, Department of Propaganda, who then contacted his counterpart in Putera. Eventually, news reached me that there'd been a raid and this Dr. Darmasetyawan had been arrested and tortured. One day after I heard the date for execution was officially set, Suharto found his nephew sitting in his front room. It was all done very quickly. There had been no fanfare.

Indonesians have big families with hundreds of relatives and word can travel from village to village across a whole island in a matter of days. They're better than phones. In this mouth-to-mouth way came another message: "Lawyer Sujudi's been arrested. Get word to Sukarno." This fine patriot had risked his reputation for me. It was in his house that I was arrested in December, '29. Contacting the authorities in question, I pledged my skin as security for Sujudi. "He couldn't be guilty of conspiring against Japan," I pleaded. "The charges must be a mistake. Sujudi is a devoted nationalist and would never go against the honorable Japanese who are helping to give us our freedom." They released him.

Reports reached me that for weeks the *Kempeitai* had Amir Sjarifuddin, one of our captured underground leaders, hanging upside down by his feet. He was drinking his own urine. He couldn't last much longer. I negotiated his release by ordering the officials in charge, "Free him or you no longer have my cooperation." It took iron guts to make such a statement. But it took even more guts to look at him when they let him out. He was thin as a finger. It is unbelievable that man can suffer like that and still live.

I have accomplished many such works. Until now they have lain buried deep in my soul. I do not shout my good deeds from the housetops, much as it may seem. Throughout my life I have done good to all mankind whenever I was able to so do. I know it. And God knows it. That's all that's important.

↝ 21. My First-Born

PHYSICALLY and emotionally I was not doing well in 1943. The tensions took a heavy toll. As a chronic malaria patient I was hospitalized weeks at a spell.

In addition, I suffered kidney trouble. Often I'd double up with agonizing attacks. Sometimes I'd be in a cold sweat and I would even weave a little on the podium. More than once when I finished a speech I'd have to crawl to the car on all fours.

My personal life was not good either. Emotionally I was in knots. My life was a mass of jangled nerve ends. Inggit and I were not getting on well. One night, to try for a little soft conversation and peace, I accompanied a friend to a Geisha House. When I came home Inggit went on a rampage. She screamed at me. She threw things. One of them, a cup, caught me on the side of the head.

The matter of Fatmawati still lay between us although all this while Fatmawati and I were not in contact. Mail delivery had been curtailed and so our total exchange had been the one letter which I'd written just to say I was safe in Djakarta. This I sent by the hand of a trusted messenger who put it in the keeping of a goldsmith enroute to Sumatra.

By this time we'd moved because I never liked a two-story house. In this second home our daughter and her husband, Asmara Hadi, lived with us. Even they concurred, finally, that the situation between Inggit and myself could continue no longer. "Bu," cried Ratna Djuami to Inggit one night, "Bapak has become ill at ease, nervous. He's unstrung. His health is poor."

"And we agree it is because of his personal life," said Asmara Hadi reluctantly. "Perhaps if he were not torn in other directions things would be different, but this unhappiness heaped onto all his other problems is sapping his strength."

I appealed to Inggit. "I shall personally find you a house. And I shall see you have everything you need always. But as you know our arguments are getting frequent and they are no good for you, either."

"This is the only way, Bu," sighed Asmara Hadi. "Our whole

country needs Bapak. Not just you or me or Ratna Djuami. He belongs to us all. The people need him and no other as their leader. And what will happen to Indonesia if he collapses?"

After the divorce it was arranged for Inggit to return to her home town. That morning she had first to go to the dentist. My heart had always been close to my wife and I did not wish her to go alone so I accompanied her. We arrived home late, tired, neither of us feeling well, and were confronted by a gathering of women come to pay their respects to Inggit. They remained an hour during which nobody did much talking. I remember fidgeting considerably. It was a very trying time. Then I personally escorted Inggit to Bandung, unpacked her, made certain she was comfortable and bade her farewell.

In June, 1943, Fatma and I were married by proxy. It took much arranging to transport her and her parents to Java, nor could I immediately get to Sumatra, and I did not wish to wait any longer. I suddenly wanted very much to be married. Acording to Islam the ceremony is perfectly allowable provided there is a bride and something to represent the groom. I had more than something. I had someone. I sent a telegram to a close male friend requesting him to personally represent me. He showed this to the parents of Fatma and it was okay. The bride and my stand-in went before the *kadi* and, although she was temporarily in Bengkulu and I in Djakarta, we were now man and wife. In a few weeks, she was able to join me.

The following year Fatmawati bore me a son. I cannot tell you the joy this gave me. I was 43 years old and at long last Allah had granted me a child.

At news of Fatma's pregnancy, Mother, Father, and my sister hurried from Blitar. They were so excited. Both sets of parents lived with us in the pavilion adjacent to our house until the baby came. It was my father who supervised the entire proceeding. He it was who sat by the hour instructing Fatma how to prepare herself. Always you would see them huddled together and always you could hear Father saying something like, "Now, don't forget to add to our list baby powder, a small knife to cut the cord and a corset for yourself."

The night she gave birth we entertained important visitors— Japanese and Indonesian. Fatmawati was busy hostessing, but later in the evening she began to feel pain. I personally carried her to the room and summoned the doctor. From that moment I never left her side nor did I shut my eyes until she delivered my precious son. I sat next to her on the bed, holding her hand all the while she gave birth.

I am not a man who can stand the sight of blood, but this moment of creation was the most exquisite of my entire life. At five A.M., as the cry went out from the mosque calling people to prayer, my first child, Guntur Sukarnoputra—Sukarnoputra meaning son of Sukarno—was born.

The good God in His infinite mercy and wisdom spared my father long enough to greet my flesh into the world. Afterward he fell ill. Fatma nursed him faithfully many months until the end.

I was reminded of *The Gardener,* a book I'd read at age 13. I didn't then understand its significance. It talked about how the withered brown leaves of a tree must fall off to make room for the new green shoots.

Three decades later I understood.

✑ 22. What Price Freedom

LATE '43 saw the implementation of the second part of my program, military preparedness for my people, which took the form of a volunteer army called Peta.

Throughout occupied territories, the Japanese had suffered staggering losses and they were spread thin. They were anxious to bolster their ranks with the youth of Indonesia who had never experienced any schooling under the Dutch and thus had no pro-Western sympathies. In theory the simple, uneducated, childlike Indonesians would be putty in Japanese hands. They were to be indoctrinated to hate the West and trained how to kill. The High Command acceded to the formation of Peta in order to ready a native force to fight the Allies if and when the invasion came. Far better, thought the Generals, to spill Indonesian blood than Japanese.

As for me, I recognized this as an opportunity for our ragged flock to become proficient in soldiering. For the first time Indonesians would learn to handle guns, to defend themselves. They were taught army discipline, guerrilla training, how to ambush, how to fire a rifle from a crawling position, how to fashion home-made grenades from a coconut shell filled with petrol. They learned how to fight the enemy —whoever the enemy might be.

The High Command requested Sukarno's help in attracting the proper candidates for officers. I capitalized on this immediately. "Sirs," I pointed out, "a human being will not voluntarily defend his homeland unless he is a strong patriot. The feelings of hate toward the Allies which you preach must be reinforced by the positive energies of love for one's country which I teach. A man who will lead his men in battle must have something to fight for."

"Then, Mr. Sukarno," they ordered, "you will furnish us the names of men whose loyalty to their country you personally vouch for."

I handpicked leaders like Gatot Mangkupradja, the PNI rebel with whom I'd been arrested in '29. He was made head of Peta. I looked for young men whom I could control and who could eventually become the heroes of our Revolution. I singlehandedly proposed the future colonels and generals of our Republican Army back in the fall of 1943.

Before I tapped a man, I found out everything about him. These green youths knew full well they weren't undergoing military training to turn their cannon on the Americans and British, but because soon they would command regiments in the service of their country. You want to know how they knew it? Because I damn well told it to each and every one personally. That's how! It was no secret to them exactly why they were selected and for what.

They understood. And I understood. And Hatta and our other trusted leaders understood. But a hard core of youngsters in the underground did not understand. They were solidly against Peta. They fought me on it. They took every opportunity to make sure I knew they were opposed.

I expected there'd be those who would not comprehend what I was trying to do, yet I could not run around begging everybody, "Oh, please believe me, I am not a collaborator!" Occasionally I took time to account for my logic to a few who held contradictory views. At the hospital my doctor broached the subject. "In the eyes of many, supporting a Japanese military institution can only help Japan," he said.

I rebuked him sharply. "This is a shallow policy. Anybody who thinks this cannot see the long view. The ultimate purpose is to be equipped to fight for freedom. There is no other purpose."

"But the Japs are conquerors. Enemies. To promise to fight alongside them is to help Fascism!"

"That attitude is stupid," I snapped wearily. "All right, so the Japanese are conquerors and must be kicked out. But they're conquerors whom we can use. I am helping to form Peta—yes! But not for them! Can't you understand that? For us! For you! For me! For our country! Would you rather remain a colony the rest of eternity?"

"But," he persisted, "if the Japanese are for Peta and we are anti-Japanese, isn't it logical to be anti-Peta?"

Between the malaria and my frustration, I was shaking all over. "Of course they're for Peta. They founded it so we'd fight with them against the Allies. But we will use this as a tool to fight Holland, Japan, or anybody who opposes our independence. Peta troops are not anti-Allies. They're pro-Indonesia!"

"But the people are saying about you that. . . ."

"They're saying nothing," I interrupted. "If they believed I

wasn't doing what's best for us they wouldn't follow me, would they?
. . . Well, would they?"

"No."

"And they do, don't they?"

"Yes. Completely."

"So my people aren't saying anything. It's just a few young hotheads who are saying whatever it is."

"That you are cooperating with the enemy," he finished.

"Well, get this straight," I said coldly. "I will cooperate with the
damn devil in hell if it will help my country."

It was heartbreaking. Sometimes embarrassing, anonymous notes
found their way under my door. One such said, "Because we are led
by a weak leader with the spirit of a mouse we dare not struggle. But
if we were led by a strong leader with the spirit of a *banten* then we
would fight."

Oh, that was a sad day. My face filled with the sort of pain opiates
cannot relieve. Fatmawati gazed at me pityingly, unable to share my
burden. When I found my voice my only comment was pure Javanese: "Ducks go together, but eagles fly alone."

When troubled I often consulted a *kiayi*, a religious leader, but
this night I sat alone to think. And pray. To try to look to my inner self.
I have never been one to confide my problems. Everything I keep
within.

Fatmawati sat at my feet, her tiny shape silhouetted in the darkness, a prayer shawl wound around her head. She spoke softly, "In the
Koran, Mohammed says, 'I am a prophet, but even I make mistakes.'"

"I have made mistakes in my life," I admitted heavily. "In the
past I acknowledged them and there is strength in the acknowledging,
too. But the courage of a man lies in the belief that he's right. I could
not live if I didn't strongly and surely believe that what I'm doing at
the time I'm doing it is right. Otherwise I would become weak. I
firmly believe my stand on Peta is correct . . . I must believe. . . ."

Hatta assisted me well in those days. He is too dry a man to work
magic over the masses, but at least he could understand my tactics,
and work alongside me. He helped me in making propaganda for
Peta. We both donned the green uniforms and took two days' worth
of marching and shooting exercises ourselves.

The night of the anonymous note, Gatot Mangkupradja visited
me. He put his hand on my shoulder and reminisced, "Bung, remember Bantjeuj? Remember we'd occasionally wrestle in the dusty

courtyard surrounding our cellblock when they took us out for our airing?"

I nodded, wondering what he was driving at.

"Remember you always lost until the morning you figured out in a struggle between two powers it's not physical bulk that wins, but tactic and strategy?"

"I remember," I said, smiling at him gratefully.

"You were right then and you're right now."

"Thank you, my friend," I muttered huskily.

In November, 1943, Hatta and I were "invited" to Tokyo to "Thank the Emperor for his beneficence." Friends were edgy about the journey. "Bung," they whispered confidentially, "we have heard frightening stories about their taking other leaders in other countries to visit the Emperor and somehow these leaders never came back."

"What happened?" I asked.

"We do not know, but it is said they were thrown out of the plane from very high up."

With such gay bon voyage tales to cheer us, Hatta and I left.

High-ranking civilian authorities met our plane and went out of their way to please us. The Minister of Overseas Territory took us sightseeing in Kyoto. Somebody else arranged a 15-course dinner in our honor. We were taken to a chrysanthemum exhibit with the largest flowers you've ever seen. We were given a tour of the rural districts to see how industrious Japanese subjects were and how every corner of ground had food planted on it. Prime Minister Tojo arranged a reception in his home. Starting with Japanese food served on the floor Japanese-style, we then removed to a European-furnished room with Western cuisine followed by dancing girls and entertainment.

During the seventeen-day trip, they laid it on thick. They showed us steel factories, munitions plants, and shipyards in full production for the war effort. I marveled to Hatta, "Their industry is overwhelming. If the aim was to impress me they've succeeded."

"This is your first time outside Indonesia," countered Hatta. "When viewed in that relation the difference is monumental. And they know it. That's why you're invited here. But I spent eleven years in Europe where I have seen even bigger factories."

Hatta and I sat and stared at one another in a luxurious suite in the Imperial Hotel. We stared at the flowers, the fruit, and we wondered why. What for? "Granted they're trying to impress us they're strong militarily and they'll positively win the war," I conceded, "but they also know our political future compels us to keep saying this publicly anyhow, so why the display? It can only be the war is going worse than they expected and it must be they need our cooperation more than we realize."

When we were received by the Emperor my hunch crystallized. For three days protocol men briefed us on how to act. So many paces forward, then a deep bow. So many more paces forward, then another bow. Donning the striped trousers and black jackets we'd had made specially for this audience, we practiced our obeisances in front of a mirror.

When the aide marched us from the anteroom to the throne room of the Imperial Palace, Hatta and I adjusted our morning coats, took a deep breath and walked in. I was just set to prostrate myself when the Emperor stuck out his hand for me to shake.

Everybody was shocked. Later the stunned officials clucked, "This is a rare happening. The Emperor doesn't do this unless foreigners are of high station. It has never before occurred that such a high hand has touched such a low hand. What can be the meaning?"

Everybody began to interpret this, trying to grasp the inner subtleties of such a world-shattering event. In Djakarta, Shimitsu of the Sendenbu, the Propaganda Ministry, translated it. "There is only one explanation. He has done this as a friend. It is a good sign signifying you will soon be free."

"Considering he has not announced any exact date for our day of liberation, how did you arrive at this decision?" I asked.

"If Tenno Heika considered you a colonial power, you would be a servant. He would never shake your hand. Touching you means he accepts you on a high political level. Furthermore, he decorated you with a medallion, the highest decoration he could award you. It carries with it his personal blessing."

I was soon to need it, too. The year 1944 was the year of mounting difficulties for the land of the Rising Sun—the year of the Great Nipponese retreat. The Allies were launching massive and successful counteroffensives against the Japanese strongholds in the Pacific. Our people sensed a break in the invincible Japanese armor. While the peasants in Java were dying of starvation, brutality, and ruthless exploitation at the hands of the military, and while the intellectuals in Borneo were being methodically exterminated to quell thoughts of uprising, thousands more seethed with revolt. Open defiance of the Japanese began. In February armed revolt broke out in the Peta garrison at Blitar.

They instigated a surprise raid on the telephone exchange, the police headquarters, the munitions depots. This largest single attack on Japanese authority during the occupation was speedily crushed. Their retaliatory massacre of the participants sickened all of Indonesia. The populace looked to me. But I had to look away. I was powerless. There was nothing I could do.

What is not known until now is that Sukarno himself was involved in this rebellion. This Peta revolt might have been a surprise to Dai Nippon, but not to Sukarno. I knew about it well in advance. Do not forget my home is in Blitar. My parents lived in Blitar.

During a visit with my parents, a group of the Peta officers called on me. They talked to me of a revolt. "We have only begun to plan," they confided, "but we wish to know your opinion."

"Consider the consequences," I said heavily. "I hope you realize such an endeavor will be resisted."

"We will succeed," said Suprijadi, leader of the insurrection.

"My opinion is that you are too weak to risk such a maneuver now."

"We will succeed," repeated Suprijadi.

I peered into their eager, young faces and realized nothing would dissuade them. I said only, "Should you fail you must be prepared to face the worst. The Japanese will execute you."

"Will you be able to protect us?" asked Suprijadi.

"No. You are soldiers, not civilians. Under the military code your penalty is automatic. Besides, I must explain this clearly to you. If you insist on carrying this out, I am for it. I will help you plan it. However, I will have to be extremely careful to cover my tracks. Do not think the Japanese will consider it a coincidence that this happened in my hometown. Under no circumstances will I reveal myself. I will be forced to disclaim any knowledge of the affair in order to defend Peta's future.

"Peta is the vital tool in our forthcoming Revolution. I cannot sacrifice my whole army for the sake of a few. If you are caught it will be my duty to try to do something to salvage the rest of Peta."

And that was what I did. When the Japanese condemned the revolt and sentenced my boys to death, I did not protect them. I could not.

In the first chapter of this book I admitted several memories would be painful to set down. These pages are difficult for me. I cannot discuss this period without experiencing great emotion. Even twenty years later, the wounds are not totally healed. The deeds I had to do and the suffering I endured at the hands of a small segment who would not understand are scars I will carry to the grave.

While we are probing such painful subjects, let us discuss the *romushas*. The Japanese needed laborers in their work projects in occupied territories outside Indonesia. The *romushas* were male laborers the military picked up at random from roadsides and villages. In many a district which had not a single male left between the ages of 16 and 60, women did the plowing, shoveling, and other back-breaking work. Since conscripting hundreds of thousands would have caused wholesale rebellions, Dai Nippon preferred to lure *romushas* with promises of enticing wages and the title, "Heroes of Labor." In reality they were slaves and I was the one assigned the task of enlisting them.

Thousands never came back. They died in foreign lands. Often they were treated as inhumanly as the prisoners of war with whom they were shackled side-by-side to build the notorious Burma Road. Yes, I knew about them. Yes, yes, yes, I knew they'd travel in airless boxcars packed in thousands at a time. I knew they were down to skin and bone. And I couldn't help them.

In fact, it was I—Sukarno—who sent them to work. Yes, it was I. I shipped them to their deaths. Yes, yes, yes, yes, I am the one. I made statements supporting the recruitment of *romushas*. I had pictures taken near Bogor with a tropical helmet on my head and a shovel in my hand showing how easy and glorious it was to be a *romusha*. With reporters, photographers, the Gunseikan—Commander-in-Chief—and Civil Authorities I made trips to Banten, the western tip of Java, to inspect the pitiable skeletons slaving on the home front down deep in the coal and gold mines. It was horrible. Hopeless.

And it was I who gave them to the Japanese. Sounds terrible, doesn't it? They tell me the people won't like to read this—is that right? Well, I do not blame them. Nobody likes the ugly truth.

The afternoon hundreds of pictures were circulated showing me with the *romushas* as though I were bestowing approval on the whole plan, five medical students marched into my office. I knew each by name. They were youngsters, not diplomats, and they carried their distrust on their faces. They closed the heavy, dark wood doors, silently walked the length of the barnlike room with the high ceiling and stood at my desk, which was way over against the left wall near the windows.

"It is getting so you will no longer be trusted by our people," blurted out one. "How can you answer the *romusha* question?"

I answered dully. Of what consolation were words? "There are two ways to work. One is the revolutionary way, which brings bloodshed and death, as witness the Peta revolt. It came too soon. We were not ready. We are still not ready. The second way is to work with Japan, consolidate your strength and bide your time until her downfall. I follow the second way."

"But why do you sell us out?" flared another. "Why do you give our people to them? Is it because you feel if you don't do this dirty job that another will?"

I banged my fist on the table angrily. "No! Definitely not! Never have I fooled myself into feeling that I'm only doing what another would do in my place. This is negative thinking. I do not try to give myself an 'out.' I think positively. To me, giving the Japanese what they want in return for more concessions that I need is the positive way to freedom.

"There are casualties in every war. A Commander-in-Chief's job is to win the war even if it means losing a few battles on the way. If I must sacrifice thousands to save millions, I will. We are in a struggle for survival. As leader of this country I cannot afford the luxury of sensitivity."

I looked into the eyes of each one of them. "Sit down," I sighed. "Put your questions straight."

One said, "Why do you not oppose the Japanese? Why do you help them? Why do you make speeches against the Allies? Why do you concoct slogans like '*Inggris kita linggis Amerika kita setrika*'— Chop the British and iron the Americans?"

"My lot is to keep the Japanese believing I am swaying the masses to their aid. Otherwise they will remove me, and we are now on the brink of what we've been fighting for all our lives. At all costs I must stay in this position. Only I can keep the pressure on Japan and only I can keep the lid on Indonesia—until the time is right.

"You must know down deep in your hearts . . . all of you . . . one by one . . . individually . . . must know and believe and trust me. I know there are so many who die. But all of you, too, would without Sukarno. Worse things would be happening. You like all the rest of our countrymen would be used as bullets for their cannons were anybody but Sukarno here."

"Why could you not save Muchtar?" the little one asked.

"Muchtar headed the laboratory which injected trainsful of

romushas with anti-tetanus serum prior to being shipped out. The vaccine was faulty. Within three days tens of thousands died. The enormity of this was beyond what I could offer the Japanese in return."

The medical students had given me much difficulty. Many were Sjahrir's pupils. The prime result of his so-called underground work was that he'd inspired a small band of impatient, dissatisfied young men who nearly succeeded in getting themselves killed. When the Japanese began controlling their curriculum, they rebelled. To instigate punishment, the Japanese shaved the tops of the students' heads and beat their bald spots with the full force of a heavy ruler. The students went out on strike. They were immediately jailed. For three months they were tortured, then sentenced to death. It was Sukarno who pleaded they were just youngsters, not political brains, and it was Sukarno who freed them.

I gazed into the eyes of my passionate young jurors. "Who dares deny Sukarno has put his neck on the line every day for his people?"

The five darted quick looks at each other, then the spokesman said softly, "We are sorry, Bung. We apologize. It's just that Allied counter-propaganda coming over the radio is very strong. Sometimes we forget. Many of us have you to thank for our lives. Saving us took iron nerve."

"This whole occupation is a war of nerves. In the case of you students the price was my increased cooperation. In the case of the *romushas* the price was my increased benefits. Forced labor for freedom. That was the bargain.

"We have just been granted permission to sing our National Anthem, '*Indonesia Raya*,' at all gatherings. We have just been granted permission to fly our sacred *Merah Putih* side-by-side with the Japanese flag. We have just been granted permission to formulate the Chuo Sangi In, an Indonesian civilian body which will act as advisors to the Japanese Military Government.

"With every hair on my body I care only for my country. And there is no need for me to unburden my heart to every youngster who walks in here. I have sacrificed my life for this soil. No matter who calls me collaborator I don't have to prove to them or to the world what I've done. The pages of Indonesia's Revolution will be written with the blood of Sukarno. History will vindicate me."

❧ 23. The Beginning of the End

IN July, 1944, the strategic island of Saipan fell to the Americans. This meant the collapse of the defense line of the Marianas. Island by island the searoute between Japan and Indonesia was picked off.

No longer could Japan suck vital raw materials from the country someone once labeled "The Big Loot of Asia." Additionally, it became obvious Indonesia's Army of Occupation would have to defend itself without appreciable help from Tokyo or the mainland. The Military realized that at all costs it now desperately needed a cooperative native population. To fight a war on two fronts—against enemy invaders and hostile inhabitants—would prove suicidal.

Concessions to nationalism were accelerated. On September 7, Tokyo announced that the propitious date for the immediate establishment of free Indonesia was being decided upon. Under my Chairmanship a new organization, Java Hokokai, was readied to swing into operation as our first apparatus of government.

In February, 1945, Dai Nippon surrendered the Philippines. Each additional loss fertilized the blooms of liberty.

In March, Hatta and I flew to Makassar. The secret mission was for high-level talks to determine the actual form our State would take. Japan was pushing for a monarchy. "As you have seen on your recent visit, the Balinese lean toward a kingdom," pointed out the officials. "They insist Sukarno be King of Indonesia."

"I have had a duty to my followers since 1926," I answered firmly. "In the very beginning when freedom was only a far-off dream, I made a pledge that we would not be a monarchy. I have talked always against anything but a republic."

Hatta, who had seconded me well throughout the occupation, now smelled approaching victory and so, once again, he reverted to type and disagreed with Sukarno. Hatta was a Federalist. Sukarno wanted one State. Hatta wanted several states. I realized this was the end of our *Dwi-Tunggal* handshake. No more were we two-in-one.

During my five days in Makassar, we were bombed 22 times. Air raid signals came at 15-minute intervals. For the entire five days I was secreted in an underground cave infested with bugs and mosquitoes. There a mosquito bit me and I developed a brand-new malaria condition—of a recurring type. I would feel good half a year, then I would be ill again. I suffered from this Malaria Tertian on and off for eight years.

The city was under constant bombardment because the Allies somehow learned Sukarno was in Makassar. There wasn't any doubt but they were after me personally. I can't really blame them. They thought me a war criminal. The return trip was very unpleasant. A convoy of two small fighters flanked us but the Allied aircraft followed along every minute. Six American planes hugged the sky right over us all the way back and as our navy craft flew over Java the six intercepted us.

We dropped to a very low altitude. It was frightening. We flew so low we barely skimmed the coconut trees and yet they stayed right on our tail to Djakarta. The air raid sirens were still going when we landed.

The first of April the Americans invaded Okinawa. The 29th of April the Emperor sponsored a committee for the preparation of Indonesian independence. The seventh of May Germany capitulated. The 28th of May our committee for the preparation of independence convened. Clearly, nothing could stop us now.

Meetings of this preparatory committee were held at the building which had housed the old *Volksraad*. It's heavy, typically overdone Dutch architecture. Dark wooden walls, stained glass ceilings, solid marble floors. The enormous room was apportioned into 10 rows. Six desks and chairs in each row. The only thing orderly about the meeting was the room. The proceedings were pure chaos.

Nationalists from throughout the archipelago, chosen by me and approved by the Japanese, attended the sittings with their own plans, rules, and painfully hairsplitting suggestions worked out in advance. No one coordinated with the other. The sophisticates of Java, the traders of Sumatra, the peasants from the outer islands found no common ground. During siesta time from one to five, the Islamist group met separately, the Nationalist group met separately, the Federalists and Unitarians met separately. Those who claimed our territory constituted exactly the boundaries of the former Netherlands East Indies formed one group. Others who claimed more or were satisfied with less formed another group. Orthodox Moslems pushed for a State on an Islamic-Theocratic basis. There were moderates who decided we

were too immature to govern ourselves at all. There was a great twisting and turning and lack of cohesion. For three days there was solid
disagreement concerning the basic principles of Indonesia *Merdeka.*

I sat through the hubbub letting everybody say his piece. My
hair stood on end listening to them expounding plans worked out to
the smallest detail. They brought forth far too many ifs and con-
jectural problems. At this rate none of us would know *Merdeka* until
we were in our graves. If the Japanese had liberated us that day we'd
have had to say, "Wait a while . . . hold it a minute. We're not ready
yet."

I'd had 16 years to prepare what I wanted to say. In my black
tomb in Bantjeuj, the principles upon which our republic would
someday be based had begun knocking at the door of my thought. I
knew we couldn't found our nation on the Constitution of the United
States of America. Nor on the Communist Manifesto. We couldn't
borrow anybody's way of life, including Japan's Tenno Koodoo
Seishim, Divinity of the Emperor. Marhaenist Indonesia corresponds
to no other concept. Year after year I'd turned this over in my brain.

In friendless Flores, spending incalculable hours under my private tree pondering, the actual formation of this God-sent inspiration
which has since been termed *Pantja Sila*—five principles—came to
me. I do not say I created the *Pantja Sila.* What I did was to dig way
down deep into the soil of our own traditions and I came up with
five beautiful pearls.

The night before I was to speak I walked out in my garden. Alone.
And I gazed up at the stars. And I marveled at the perfection of crea-
tion. And I cried softly. I said to God, "I am crying because tomorrow
I shall experience a historic moment in my life. And I need Your help.

"I know the thoughts I shall speak are not mine. You unfolded
them to me. Yours is the only Creative Mind. You have guided every
breath of my life.

"Please . . . please give me again Your guidance and inspiration
tomorrow."

At nine A.M., as usual, we convened at our desks. Each desk had a
name plate. We were called to order with a prayer, then I rose and
walked to the raised marble platform. There, between the two huge
pillars where once the Governor General stood to officially open the
Volksraad, I unwrapped my five precious pearls: Nationalism, Internationalism, Democracy, Social Justice, and Belief in One God.

I explained our future must be rooted in Nationalism because

"Men cannot be separated from place. It is impossible to separate people from the earth under their feet."

Then I outlined the bounds of our Nationalism. "God Almighty made the map of the world. Even if a child looks at it he can see we are the only island unity between the Pacific and Indian Oceans and between the Asian and Australian continents. Our nation, therefore, comprises all human beings throughout this entire archipelago from the northern tip of Sumatra to Irian."

This led to my second pearl. Internationalism. "It must not be *Indonesia uber Alles*," I cautioned. "Indonesia is only a small part of the world. To quote Gandhi, 'I am a Nationalist but my Nationalism is humanity.'"

Speaking without notes, I warned against the corn-haired, blue-eyed Aryan brand of isolation and told the assembly "Nationalism cannot flourish if it does not grow in the garden of Internationalism."

The third pearl was Democracy. For centuries our land has lived by the tribal custom of *Musjawarah* and *Mufakat:* deliberation and agreement. This is democratic consultation Asian-style. As someone who is convinced strength lies in representative government, I said, "We shall not be a State for one individual or one group" but "All for all, one for all, all for one.

"Let Moslems work hard so most seats in our People's Representative Body are occupied by Moslems. If Christians desire every regulation of the State to conform with the Bible, let them work themselves just as hard so that the greater part of the delegates be Christians. That is just.

"Like the pounding and husking of paddy to obtain rice, let our minds constantly rub against one another."

There wasn't a sound in the chamber. Even the overhead fans whirred noiselessly. Tears glistened in the eyes of my brothers.

Pearl number four was Social Justice. "Do we want capitalists to do their unscrupulous worst or do we want the entire people to prosper because they feel cherished by their Motherland which gives them the basic necessities?" I asked.

I reminded them our generations have long hoped for the manifestation of Ratu Adil, our Goddess of Justice who stands for Social Equality. "We do not want political democracy alone," I thundered. "We want Social Democracy. Economic Democracy. A new world in which there will be common prosperity."

Last was the Belief in One God: "Let us build *Merdeka* in awe of The One Supreme God" but "Let every Indonesian believe in his own God. Let each worship as he chooses. Let us declare the fifth principle as the civilized way: Belief in one God with mutual respect for one another."

Being steeped in symbolism, I summed up my feelings accordingly, "The fundamental obligations of Islam are five in number. Our fingers are five on each hand. We have five senses. Even the heroes of the *Mahabharata* are five. Thus the principles on which we found our State are five."

My hour-long speech concluded with "*Pantja Sila* can be unraveled to be 10 parts, 20, 50, 1,000 parts. And if I compress them all into one genuine Indonesian term then I get—*gotong royong*. This means toiling hard together, sweating hard together. Acts of service by all for the interest of all.

"The principle of *gotong royong* is between the rich and poor, the Moslem and Christian, between Indonesian and non-Indonesian. This, *Saudara-Saudara*, is what I propose to you."

The applause was deafening. The representatives jumped out of their seats and accepted my State philosophy by acclamation.

One area of the room was not jumping with joy. The Japanese. From the corner of my eye I spied the small gallery along the side wall. Here, where enrapt spectators once sat during the Dutch time, angry Japanese now fumed. Not once did I advocate devotion to their "God," the Emperor. Not once did my words praise Dai Nippon. I had not bowed to their government's suggestions at all. In fact, my speech even stated I was antimonarchy since "I am a Moslem. And, as a Moslem, I am a Democrat. Does not Islam say that heads of State, both Caliphs and Emirs, should be chosen by the people?"

No, the Japanese definitely weren't happy about *Pantja Sila*. But I did not care. I went on record publicly anyhow.

The time had come to assure the world I was not a Japanese puppet. Despite the secret police with guns at their sides, I did what I had to do. From this moment forth the broad lines of the Indonesian State were determined and Sukarno became the Father of Independence.

⊰ 24. A Meeting in Saigon

YOU could feel the momentum of the Revolution building.

One sunny July morning, about 80 representatives assembled in the old *Volksraad*. As chairman, I was on the rostrum. After we'd been two hours hammering out points, the senior Japanese present, an officer named Saito, announced, "The final decision as to whether you will be a republic, a monarchy, or whatever lies exclusively in the hands of the Emperor."

This triggered a free-for-all. A knot of young men—we call them *pemudas*—became enraged that Japan was dictating their terms of freedom. Shouts of "We are tired of cautious tactics" and "Indonesians will no longer await orders from Tokyo" crowded the air.

I rapped the gavel. I was aware our foreign "guests" were armed and could have put us down forcibly if we made too many disrespectful moves, but I also had to make the *pemudas* understand I was with them wholly. As prudently as possible, I soothed, "We all are of one mind, but much progress has come to us at the hands of Dai Nippon. We owe them the courtesy of considering their proposals."

Inflammatory statements such as "Efforts to dictate to us in future will be sabotaged by the youth" were screamed at the top of the lungs. The *pemudas* gave free vent to their emotions. I had to discipline mine. The secret police lining the room stood tensely at attention. They watched me carefully. Very carefully.

Backed by a dozen *pemudas*, Chairul Saleh, one of the leaders of the underground, spat, "The accent today is on youth. And before we youths accept anything interpreted by the Japanese we will declare war on you." His gang applauded.

Chairul stormed out followed by his cohorts. They immediately dispersed and disappeared. I ordered the meeting postponed.

That afternoon a delegation visited my home. I understood the outburst had not been directed at me, but at the enemy. I recognized this was a tactic and that we were all on the same side. "Hi there, revolutionaries," I called gaily. "Come on in."

"Bung," they said, "the situation is deteriorating rapidly for the Japanese. Allied ships are moving up. At any moment this whole thing can collapse. We must seize independence by ourselves. Now. Forcibly. We cannot wait for Japan to hand it to us as a present, because the Allies will take back the present once Japan surrenders. They will only honor an all-Indonesian Proclamation."

"Besides," added another, "if independence is a product of the Japs, they'll direct it on their terms. This is already happening. We don't want our *Merdeka* subject to their control."

I said nothing. I just listened.

"They're calculating independence in terms of September, but they may not last that long. They're already beaten," fretted B. M. Diah, a young newspaperman. "We must proclaim sovereignty before they capitulate or we will never get it because the Allies will open the door for Holland all over again."

"Then there's the war criminal threat," cried a third *pemuda*. "If we don't proclaim immediately, you stand the chance of being arrested as a collaborator and then we'll have no leader. Everything can go down the drain."

"Bung," said Chairul Saleh, "we get our news by monitoring broadcasts beamed from Australia. We are also tuned in to the United States. Besides the official radio in our homes which is sealed so the knobs twist to no other than the government station, in our closets, hidden, we have clandestine sets. Djakarta may broadcast daily victories for the Imperial fleet, but we know better."

Another 20-year-old intellectual urged, "Bung, the moment Japan surrenders, we're trapped. We will never be able to gain freedom again. The Allies will never give it. Although Dai Nippon liberated Burma and the Philippines, the timing is now wrong for us. They waited too long. It's too late. And the end is near, Bung. The end is near."

I was angered by their shortsightedness and impetuosity. "We cannot force our will at this instant without being massacred by the Japanese. They have all the weapons. We have none. And the Japanese are finished. Why should we now provoke a full-scale battle with them? You hot-blooded young men will end up with civil war and we do not have sufficient cadres marshaled to prevent the Japanese measures which will surely be taken. They will kill us all in one bloodbath."

Baby Guntur cried softly in the back of the house. Fatmawati got up to tend him. "If you wish to bring down bloodshed unnecessarily you'll do it without me."

They could resent my cautiousness all they liked and they could lay plans to fight for independence all they liked, but they knew as well as I that without Sukarno they didn't stand a chance. They couldn't do it alone.

"Oh, no, Bung," cried Diah. "You are our leader. We need you to do it. Among ourselves we argued who could proclaim independence but we concluded only Sukarno is loved nationwide. A small group may follow us, but the whole country will follow you. Only you can sway the masses. Nobody else will do."

Commented Chairul, "We can't move without Sukarno. That's why we keep after you. By ourselves we cannot give birth to our idea."

"It's just that perhaps being a little older, you think more conservatively than we," suggested another quietly.

"Everybody's hopes are pinned on you, Bung," they pleaded. "The whole country rallies around you. You are our great orator. Hatta is a theoretician. A systematical dry brain who does not speak to the spirit of our Revolution. Only Bung Karno burns us with fire."

"All of us in this room have the same ends in sight," I sighed wearily. "But your childlike passions will cut us to bits. My legal maneuvering will accomplish our aims. You are too emotional. You do not bear the grave responsibility I do. I must function solely with a cold, calculating brain because as Sukarno goes so go seventy million people."

I unbuttoned my shirt and sat in my underwear top. I was hot. The evening was hot. We were all under great stress. "Everything you are saying I already know," I stated quietly. "But we are within reach of our goal. Be patient. Trust. I don't want independence, for which I've sweated all my life, to be donated to me like alms to a beggar. *Merdeka* must be the fruit of our own efforts.

"But if we can gain ground in conjunction with the Japanese and if we can use them as a shield, I will not sacrifice lives just so you can be heroic. Let us spend the next weeks in preparation. It is better we spill much sweat now while waiting than that we should spill much blood fighting."

From then on there was frenzy. If an underground cell numbered only 25 *pemudas,* those 25 each had their own individual circles so the over-all contact numbered 250. Then, again, each of the 250 had their own circles. All of these were out rounding up high-school students, laborers, Barisan Pelopor members—that was the civilian youth army. What they were being readied for was not clear, but each was told to "be ready."

To the boys in the political sections of the underground fell the task of making preparations for how the news of our Revolution would reach the outside world when we finally began it. They saw to it that a transmitter from a Japanese radio station was brought home because it "needed repair." They "borrowed" tape recorders. They stole a microphone.

The boys in the sabotage divisions were reassigned to stealing armaments and secreting them for the Day. Non-Peta members made deals with the police and navy, pleading, "We cannot fight at your side if we have no weapons." They got weapons. The Japanese got money.

One underground chapter raised the necessary funds by means of a relative with a weaving factory. The Japanese controlled the output, but the Japanese were also highly corrupt. Via two hidden handlooms the relative produced extra bolts of *batik* which were peddled on the black market. Less payoffs to the right Japanese, all proceeds went for *Merdeka*.

On August 8, General Terauchi, Supreme Commander of all Nipponese forces in Southeast Asia, summoned me without explanation to his headquarters outside Saigon. The plane was full. Twenty military big shots accompanied my party.

We left at five A.M., secretly. Orders were to say not a word even to our families. The sky along our route was full of Allied aircraft. So, for the salvation of us all nobody was to know I was aboard.

I was nervous. I sensed something important was afoot, but I didn't know what. I pleaded illness so my personal physician could come along. I needed Suharto because I trusted him implicitly and he spoke a little Japanese. My orders were, "Tell jokes, sing those silly Japanese songs you picked up from your patients, dance, get Miyoshi, your interpreter acquaintance, drunk. Act the fool. Use your silliness as a cloud to dig up whatever you can about why we're here."

Before we emplaned one Colonel noticed Suharto buddying up to the Japanese brass and accosted him in the aisle. "You are not among the top Indonesian leaders. This is an important mission. Just why are you on this flight?"

I held my breath and Suharto parried, "I'm Bung Karno's doctor."

The Colonel retorted, "We have doctors enough for this trip."

Suharto began clowning with him and the Colonel returned to his seat and told his superior, "No need of suspicion. He is just a clown."

It was seven P.M. when we arrived and visibility was poor. It was rainy and a heavy fog blanketed the area. Saigon countryside is all flat grassland and the pilot couldn't distinguish the landing strip. Nonetheless it was growing late and the light was fading so there was no choice but to set down somehow. After circling over an hour we crashlanded onto a field and barely missed bumping a buffalo. Luggage was thrown around. Everybody was cut and bruised. We were all badly shaken. A dozen soldiers came running toward the plane. "Where are we?" asked one of us.

"One hundred kilometers from Saigon," replied one of them.

Ordered to call for transportation, they rang up and reported, "Someone from Djakarta just landed here."

"No, not SOMEONE," I hollered. "Tell them Sukarno landed here!"

We spent several nerve-wracking hours waiting for cars to fetch us. Suharto hadn't yet learned the purpose of our visit, but we knew why Terauchi personally summoned us. With travel to Tokyo now impossible, he was the nearest accessible representative of the Imperial Government.

We arrived at the palace in Saigon after midnight. I was aware we were being closely guarded.

Next morning in Dalath, outside Saigon, General Terauchi announced, "It is up to you now. The Imperial Government now puts the process of independence totally in your hands."

I didn't understand. Neither did Hatta. We just mumbled, "Thank you. Thank you very much." We couldn't understand what was happening.

Terauchi, tall, slim, European in appearance, continued, "The big question is how exactly do YOU wish to proceed?"

Hatta and I exchanged looks. We thought it was just a gesture. We'd had several such. It seemed likely that this was merely another. We didn't understand what had happened. Not until we returned to Saigon did we accidentally hear about Hiroshima and the bomb. I knew then the war would be over in a matter of moments. Then I first comprehended Terauchi's words. I reconstructed exactly what he'd said and it suddenly had meaning.

Although they knew about the bomb and we knew about the bomb, and they knew they were finished and we knew they were finished, not by hint or twitch of the eyebrow did any of them let drop one solitary word about it. From my old Young Java training I was still a good actor so I never let on either. There were still banquets to attend, ceremonies to observe, and everybody pretended the war was going wonderfully. They were putting it on. We were putting it on. The whole thing was a farce.

Enroute to Djakarta I spoke my thoughts aloud to Hatta. "International law stipulates only four conditions for a country to be considered independent. First there's the existence of a country. Second there's the existence of a people and third the existence of a government. We have the initial two and we can set up a government. The fourth requirement is another nation willing to accord you recognition, right?"

"Yes," he replied, "and Japan will do that for us."

I took a deep breath and exhaled slowly. "Well, I guess there's nothing to stop us. We have everything we need. All we have to do—is do it!"

There was no luxurious passenger plane or military escort any more. Homeward bound we had a pilot, copilot, and a brokendown, worn-out bomber riddled with bulletholes. It wasn't equipped for passengers. There were no seats. We either had to stand the whole time or lie down. And we were freezing. There was no temperature control or heating system. There was also no lavatory.

I whispered to Suharto, "I have to pass water. What should I do?"

He peered around and shrugged, "There isn't any place else so you have no choice. You'll just have to do it here."

"OK," I said. I stepped unobtrusively to the rear and relieved myself. Well, just as I did a strong gust of wind whipped in through a bunch of bulletholes and swept the whole thing right through the plane. My poor comrades got a very bad shower.

In this semi-wet condition the Great Leader of the Revolution arrived in Djakarta. It was the 14th of August.

Pemudas swarmed my house upon my return to Djakarta. "What is the word of Sukarno?" they asked each other. "What are your orders?" they asked me. "Command us, Bung . . . what . . . when . . . how. . . ."

A famous twelfth-century Javanese ruler had prophesied "One day the white man will come and occupy our land for three centuries."

This, he predicted, would be followed by "The reign of yellow men with short legs from the land of the sun in the north." The prophecy added these would remain just "The length of the lifetime of an ear of maize." The life of maize is about three and a half months. Throughout the occupation we clung to this and now the yellow man had been in our land three and a half years.

My message to my people was, "Say no more that we will be free when the *djagung* or maize is ripe, but now—right now—because the *djagung* has blossomed!"

On the 15th of August, Japan surrendered. About ten o'clock that night I was busily planning every detail of the strategy of the Proclamation with my friends Sayuti Melik and his wife Trimoorti, who was my secretary, when I was told I had callers who wished to see me privately and urgently.

A delegation of *pemudas* awaited me on the verandah. "Now, Bung. Now. Tonight," commanded Chairul Saleh. "Let us make a large-scale revolution tonight. We have Peta troops, *pemudas*, Barisan Pelopor men, even the Hei Ho auxiliary soldiers are all prepared. At your signal Djakarta will be in flames. Thousands and thousands of armed and ready troops will surround the city and carry out a successful armed revolt and topple the whole Japanese army."

I sat down. "A leader of a country has a thousand eyes and ears," I said slowly. "I knew you were holding secret talks all over. I knew there were secret passwords flying fast. I can see for myself you're acting mysteriously and that you each have three or four aliases and that high-level decisions regarding our country are being made in the gardens behind the zoo, in the hallways of the medical laboratory, and on bicycles. Some of you have even taken to wearing low slouch hats on your heads like make-believe revolutionaries.

"But you have no cohesion. There isn't unity among you. There are leftist groups, Sjahrir groups, intellectual groups all making decisions independently of the other. In fear of the *Kempeitai* you sleep in different houses every night. Your couriers cycle between points parceling out hurried instructions. But from whom?"

I needed the support of these youngsters. They constituted a vital force for the moment I was ready to strike. I also had to control them lest they make a move too soon. "The trouble with you," I chastised, "is that you won't allow time for rational unfoldment."

Sukarni, one of the ringleaders, spoke up. "We must quickly take matters in our own hands because the Japanese can't decide how to handle us. They don't know whether to squash us or let us run wild because they're finished anyhow. Before they formulate any concrete plans we must surprise them."

"All right," I conceded. "You say you have *pemuda* strength. All right. Prove it to me. I'm not sure of your backing."

"We are ready to fight with our lives," they all shouted.

"Yes, I know," I retorted exasperatedly, "but your handful is not enough against the armed might and total preparedness of the Japanese army. What can you show me? What is your actual strength? What are your security measures for our women and children? How do you propose to defend this freedom once you claim it? We will not have the help of the Japanese or the Allies. We shall have to rely solely on our own might."

In tense times like these I am extremely calm. Everybody was excited and overwrought. But I felt my whole body and soul to be controlled by some Supreme Power at this moment. I was icily calm.

"Let's assume you can make a revolution in Djakarta," I continued. "Okay. But what do you hotheads plan to do about the other places far from here? . . . Hmmm? You don't know, is that right? Nobody even thought of that, am I correct? Well, that's what I'm doing. Covering every possibility so there won't be the chilling after-effects from an uprising that's sloppy and badly timed.

"A revolt against Dutch Imperialism is not a *coup d'état*. It's not like tossing one ruler out of his palace. This is more than that. Indonesia comprises more territory than the compound of a palace or the city of Djakarta. Do you not all realize this?"

Oh, this was a difficult period. It was a time of fighting against the people in our own ranks.

"Do you think I am not totally prepared with a plan without your telling me how or what to do? But my tactics call *first* for a proclamation to be read simultaneously in every area, second a fiery, rousing speech, and then lastly the Revolution. My business is to know human emotions. I know you need a symbol behind which to rally the people. They will then be primed. They'll be prepared. Eager. By the time we fire the opening gun, Marhaens in every corner of our country will be so ready they'll be screaming for revolution. Right now, nobody anywhere is prepared or has any orders.

"Our brothers in far-off Atjeh and Lombok can't wrest arms from our conquerors in one concerted effort if they don't know about it, can they? To swing the masses behind a rebellion you must first arouse their sentiments. With his senses inflamed, every potential revolutionary will be straining to answer the call to act."

The house and surroundings were dark. Way inside my living room one lone light shone. In the darkness I caught a glint of something shiny. It looked like a piece of steel. I looked again and saw it was a knife. A long knife tucked into the belt of one of the *pemudas*. Then I noticed each of them had bulges in his pockets. My visitors were armed to the teeth with guns, knives, even machetes.

Behind the door leading to the verandah I could make out the shadowy silhouettes of Fatmawati, Sayuti Melik, and Trimoorti. They, too, must have seen what I saw because they huddled together frightened.

"I have worked at this business of freedom longer than you children so do not think you can pressure me," I said coldly.

Despite our hot and heavy argument, nobody pounded tables or shouted. Our voices were controlled. There were open gardens surrounding the house and we talked so that we couldn't be overheard.

One of the *pemudas* taunted me in a low voice: "Perhaps our great Bung is scared. Perhaps he sees ghosts in the dark. Perhaps he still awaits orders from the Emperor."

Wikana, another of the leaders, followed this taunt with a sudden surprise move. He tried to bluff me. "We don't want to threaten you, Bung," he rasped, taking a menacing step toward me, an outstretched knife in his hand. "But the Revolution is now in our hands and we COMMAND you. If you do not make the Revolution tonight, then...."

"Then *what?*" I cried, leaping out of my chair in blazing fury. "Don't you threaten me. Don't you dare command me. You will do what I want. I will never be forced into YOUR will!"

I sprang into the center of those standing with weapons in their hands, bent my head down, stuck my neck way out and made the gesture of cutting my throat. "HERE," I sneered. "Here is my neck. Chop it off . . . go on, cut my head off . . . you can kill me . . . but I will never risk unnecessary bloodshed because you want to do things your way."

There was stunned silence. Nobody knew what to do. Nobody made a move. They were frightened. Embarrassed. Angry. Frustrated. I raised my head and, with deliberation, stared them down. I gazed right into their faces until one by one each dropped his eyes.

I sat down again. Beads of sweat stood out on my top lip. Nobody would ever call Sukarno cowardly again. I caught Fatmawati's eye on the other side of the doorjamb. Her face was drawn and tight. She was watching intently. In a low tone I picked up the conversation, "What is very important in war and revolution is exact timing. In Saigon I already planned this whole operation toward the 17th."

"Why is the 17th better than today or the 16th?" asked Sukarni.

"I'm a mystic. I cannot rationalize logically why 17 feels hopeful to me. But I feel in my inner self that two days from now is the right time. Seventeen is holy. Seventeen is a sacred number. First of all this is our holy month of Ramadan, during which we fast until Lebaran, is that right?"

"Yes."

"That makes this the holiest of periods, is that right?"

"Yes."

"Friday is Djumat Legi. Sweet Friday. Holy Friday. And Friday is the 17th. The Koran came on earth the 17th. Moslems perform 17 *rakaats* daily. Why did Mohammed decree 17 bows instead of 10 or 20? Because the holiness of number 17 is not of man's making.

"When I first heard the surrender news, I thought we should proclaim immediately. Then I realized it was God's will for this to fall on His holy day. The proclamation will be the 17th. The Revolution will follow."

I rose to dismiss them. "Everything is directed at me. I am the eye of the storm. Everybody comes to me, tears at me. Nobody comes to Hatta. Or Sjahrir. Or you. But they come to me.

"I have *pemudas* on one side, older leaders on another side, religious leaders on another side. Hatta pulls me in one direction. Sjahrir in another. I must follow my own heart. It is the only quiet, unemotional voice around. Everybody is ready to offer advice, but when it is time to act you all courageously back away and point the finger at me.

" 'Sure, you do it,' everybody says. 'Nobody can lead us. Hey you, Sukarno, you are the one to put your neck on the line,' everybody says. Well, if you cannot do it yourself and if you have no able leaders and if I'm the only one to do it—then it'll be done MY way!"

ᵔᵍ 25. *Kidnapped*

SJAHRIR was the one stirring up the *pemudas*. Never to my face but, secretly, always he sneered, "Sukarno is crazy . . . Sukarno is Japanese-minded . . . Sukarno is a coward."

He was vicious. And what actually did Sjahrir do for the Republic? Nothing except criticize me. While I was taking hammer blows on the head, his entire underground effort can be summed up by saying he sat quietly and safely away somewhere listening to a clandestine radio. He was the one issuing bulletins about the surrender in those last urgent days.

Sjahrir never took it on the chin like I did. He never permitted himself to be in the line of fire. All his fighting was done behind my back. He was responsible for steaming up the youth against me and for what happened later that night.

When the *pemudas* left my home around midnight, they'd warned, "The situation may be very bad tomorrow. Our followers are excited. If you don't come through with what we have promised them they will go wild. And you'll be responsible for whatever happens."

At three A.M. I was still up. I could not sleep. I sat in the dining room all alone taking my *sahur*. *Sahur* is the last food we may eat before sundown during the fasting month. The house was still. Everybody was asleep. Our dining room opened onto the garden and the doors were ajar. I heard sounds from the bushes, and a band of uniformed *pemudas* walked in stealthily.

Sukarni had a long-handled knife as well as a pistol. With the true flair of an adventurer, he pulled his knife and barked, "Get dressed. . . . The time has come."

"Yes," I flashed, my eyes bright with anger. "For me to get killed. If I lead your revolt and it fails my head will roll on the ground. So will yours . . . and theirs. But men can be replaced, leaders not. If I'm killed who will then lead the people when the proper moment does arrive?"

Countered another of the *pemudas*, brandishing a Japanese

saber, "That's why we're spiriting you out of town in the dead of night. It has been decided to remove you to safety."

"Ohhhhh," I gasped, "this is the wrong, wrong way to act. Can you not understand your toy mutiny is hopelessly doomed? I understand your love for your country. I appreciate your spirit. But that's all you have. You also need wise tactics and a cool head."

I was speaking with heat. I wasn't fearful. I knew they wouldn't harm me. But I was frustrated. Infuriated. Particularly because they wouldn't listen to logic. This was a great patriotic adventure to them. This was high drama.

"The moment is now," they chanted feverishly. "Now. Now is when Japanese morale is low and their spirit crushed. Now they are already broken. Now is when we must take up arms!"

I spoke my heart out nearly the whole night, but it made no difference. Their minds were made up.

From the conversation I pieced together what had transpired after they left me. They'd been disgusted to the point of frustration. Sitting on the floor of the students' dorm, nursing stale coffee and a borrowed cigarette, one great revolutionary spirit idly commented, "If we could show Sukarno that thousands were really ready to rise and fight, I bet he'd believe we could win."

"Probably if he were free of the clutches of the *Kempeitai* he'd see things our way," complained another. "They're always watching him."

"Maybe we ought to get him out of here and take him where our own can surround him," threw in a third.

"Good idea," shouted another with great imagination. "Let's spirit him out of his surroundings."

A Peta officer from Rengasdenklok had a brainstorm. "How about removing him to my territory? It's relatively free of Japanese. Only one commandant and two civilian officials. We can protect him there while the Revolution rages in Djakarta."

"And if he's out of this area we can speed ahead with our plans without being interfered with," shouted another.

"Yes . . . yes . . . snatch Sukarno. . . ." Everybody agreed. It hadn't been a long-term plan. Just one born of the inspiration of the moment.

The result of their passion was that in the blackness just before dawn I walked inside to get Fatma. She was sitting in bed, clutching baby Guntur in her arms. She had waked earlier at the sound of angry voices. I told her to dress and quickly pack a bag. She asked no questions. Calmly she did as she was told. We both went quietly. There was nothing more to be gained by argument.

"The Japanese are liable to shoot any civilians seen driving in the dead of night," said one of the boys, handing me a uniform complete with hat and shoes. "Put this on."

"What about Ibu Fatmawati?" I asked.

"It is not unusual for a military party to travel with members of their family," he answered.

I put my uniform on. I looked ridiculous. It was too small, but there was little point in explaining their plan was not well thought out. They acted and thought as swashbuckling adventurers. I guess if they had ever stopped to think what was really happening they'd have died from fright and wouldn't have been able to fight for their country at all. Anyway, I buttoned the uniform on over my pajamas.

Two cars stood at the curb. In the lead car sat their other captive, Hatta, a disgusted look on his face. In the second were more soldiers and enough tins of food for several days' supply.

As we passed Bogor I speculated on our ultimate destination, but nobody would admit where we were headed. With the first chink of dawn baby Guntur began crying. He was hungry. For ten months, Indonesian ladies breast-feed. Nine-and-a-half-month-old Guntur's diet was half mother's milk, half regular milk. Fatmawati had remembered to remove his formula from the stove, but we raced out so fast she had neglected to take it with us. The pan was still sitting in the kitchen.

So, the whole historic kidnapping of Bung Karno was held up while the Fiat pulled off to a side and Fatmawati breast-fed baby Guntur.

In a prearranged area free of Japanese sentries, we changed into a truck commandeered from the Djakarta garrison. The truck resembled a gigantic iron skeleton. There was no canvas covering across the top or sides. Neither were there seats. Fatma and Guntur sat with the driver and we squatted on the floor in the back with another 20 soldiers.

"Only a military van could transport us to our final destination," Sukarni volunteered. "Along this road another vehicle might attract attention. This way we look like a troop movement. If we're stopped we can say we're enroute to another post."

"Why didn't you start out in this?" I asked.

"To drive a troop truck up to a private house in the center of the city, particularly Sukarno's house, would look suspicious. And we must exercise great care to avoid patrols. Rumors are flying that the Japs received orders to pick up our leaders."

Near nine in the morning, our strange band pulled into the remote town of Rengasdenklok and we were deposited smack in the center of a ricefield. Patrols dotted the vicinity so we all walked quietly. On the ricefield stood a little bamboo hut on stilts of the type probably used by the farmer of the field. We were ordered to climb up.

Half our escort stood guard at the base while the others reconnoitered. At noontime they decided our hideout was unsafe so they moved us to a nearby mosque temporarily. When the all-clear signal came, they paraded us along a riverbed toward the edge of the Peta compound where stood a not very attractive house set back from the road in a garden filled with pigs. The house belonged to a Chinese peasant. The lieutenant in charge strode inside. Within minutes the owner and his family of seven which included tiny babies obediently marched out with their bedrolls.

"Where will they go?" I asked.

"To the home of his eldest son down the road. Early this morning I approached his second son, whom I know," explained the lieutenant, "and requested the loan of his house for three or four days. I said important guests were coming from Djakarta and needed a place to stay. I did not mention your name."

I walked through the big, ugly house. It certainly wasn't anything special so I asked, "Why this house in particular?"

"It's the only one near the garrison that's large enough to house all of you plus . . ." with his head he indicated the outdoors. Following his gaze I saw a dozen *pemudas* standing watch. All carried rifles and fixed bayonets. Another dozen blocked the road.

The tiny area was under martial law.

By way of explanation, Lt. Umar told me, "The 14th I received word from Djakarta that the insurrection would begin today so I approached the chief of our youth movement. I told him on the 15th night we'd have a big job to do and that I needed his volunteers to support the Peta. The result is the entire town is mobilized. And ready."

"For what?" I cracked drily. There were no big forces. No bombs. Even in the distance there was no burning of Japanese property. No nothing. Everything looked sleepily calm. "If this is your revolution you'd better put a little more life in it."

We waited there all day. They treated us well. They even sent for special milk for baby Guntur. There was no rough stuff. In fact, nothing happened. Not even in Djakarta. Periodically couriers arrived and departed. Whenever one returned I'd ask, "Well? Huh? Has the big revolt started yet?"

Each time they'd shake their heads sadly and mumble, "There's no news yet from Djakarta."

After we had waited hours and hours for some sign, I again inquired of the lieutenant, "Well? How about this revolution with which everybody threatened me and from which my family and I were 'spirited to safety'? Has it started yet?"

"No. Not yet."

At six that evening, as we finished our *buka,* the meal with which you break the day-long Ramadan fast, Ahmad Subardjo, the man who had welcomed me to my new home when I returned from Bengkulu, chugged up in a rickety, wheezing Czechoslovakian Skoda. I was surprised to see him. "I have come to fetch you back," he called.

"Really? How come? What's happening?"

"Nothing. That's precisely the point," he retorted peevishly. "The *pemudas'* big act did not take place. Not one thing has come off. There is no revolution. There is nothing going on but an enormous yell from everybody, 'Where's Bung Karno? . . . Get Bung Karno.' Nobody but that handful of teen-aged warriors will move without Sukarno."

His face showed plainly what a whole lot of nonsense the *pemudas* had put everybody to. "Maybe the subconscious idea in hiding you away was to try and force you into doing things their way. I don't know. Nobody knows. I guess it's just the excitement of the period, which is quite unlike anything we've ever experienced before."

Within 15 minutes we were a procession of three cars starting back. Subardjo filled me in on what had transpired since my absence. At 10 A.M. there was to have been a meeting of the Independence Preparatory Committee to discuss the actual wording of the Proclamation which I planned to deliver shortly. Subardjo was on this committee.

When the members began gathering and Sukarno could not be located, news of the abduction spread like wildfire. Questions were asked. Wikana, one of the *pemudas* in on the kidnap plans, confided my whereabouts to Subardjo. Since it had become apparent to the foolish young rebels that their plan was rashly conceived and totally fruitless and nothing would happen without Sukarno's presence, it was agreed to bring me back. Subardjo was the likeliest go-between because he had contact with the *pemudas* and he was a friend of mine.

Further, he was liaison man for the Imperial Navy, and his superior, Admiral Mayeda, was sympathetic to our cause. Through Subardjo, Admiral Mayeda offered his house as the sanctuary where I could safely make the long-awaited Proclamation of Independence for the Republic of Indonesia. "And we desperately need his protection," fretted Subardjo. "The military threatens anyone who mentions openly that Japan has capitulated and that we're taking matters into our own hands. The *Kempeitai* are arresting people right and left. The Japanese are totally demoralized. Discipline is slack. Everybody's scared."

On the way home, as we passed the town of Klender, we noticed a fire burning from afar. Patriot Sukarni, who was already nervous and highly agitated and had been toying with a revolver, jumped up and down in his seat. "Ha!" he screeched. "You see. It is already starting. The revolution is underway just as we promised. Djakarta is in flames. Let us hasten back to Rengasdenklok."

"No, go nearer and investigate," I instructed.

We drove abreast of the flames. We even got out to take a good look. Close inspection revealed it was one skinny, ragged little peasant burning hay.

I turned to Sukarni and laughed right in his face. "Is this your revolution?" I taunted him. "This is no fire. No large-scale uprising. This is no hundreds of thousands waiting for a signal. This is just one small Marhaenist burning his straw."

"And stop playing hero," ordered Subardjo. "Put that revolver away."

A crowd of *pemudas* were standing out in front of Pegangsaan Timur 56. My wife and baby went into our house. There I learned the *Kempeitai* had come that morning and over and over they demanded of my in-laws, "Where is Sukarno? . . . It is impossible you shouldn't know where your son-in-law and daughter are. . . ." And Father-in-law kept repeating, "But I don't know. I don't know anything. I was asleep when they left." At bayonet point they had marched him off to headquarters.

It was now midnight. One more minute to go until Sweet Friday. The Holy Seventeenth of August.

✑ 26. The Proclamation

ADMIRAL MAYEDA was a broadminded, deeply religious idealist. A well-traveled man who had visited Indonesia before the war, he was able to sympathize with us. Particularly in these last hours. He came downstairs to reaffirm personally his guarantee of protection, but also to explain that beyond his walls he could not be responsible. That was the province of the military.

I rushed immediately to the big white palace to secure the neutrality—if not the overt approval—of the *Gunseikan*. Colonel Nishimura, aide to the *Gunseikan*, informed me, "The Japanese have no power any more. As of this moment our only function is to act as the police detail of the Allied Forces. We are sorry. We regret our promises of independence, but the fact remains we are forbidden to alter the status quo. The military is powerless to help you."

I made one last desperate attempt. "Colonel," I said, "let me make it clear we plan to take our independence by force—if necessary. BUT if the General would just look away and allow us to continue without the active interference of the military, it would prove better for everybody. Your troops are tired of fighting and there's little point in starting a fresh war over something that doesn't mean much to them. Yet, on the other hand, we have no wish to be turned over to the Allies as so much inventory. We intend to proceed—with deliberation—to take what the Emperor promised us right along."

I pleaded, "Allow us this opportunity to make our proclamation. After all, we have no wish to fight you. We wish only to fight for our freedom."

Replied Colonel Nishimura, "We are bound by the surrender terms to turn this country over to the Allies in a condition of status quo. The *Gunseikan's* orders are that Indonesians are forbidden to change their civil servants or make any adjustments in government whatsoever. Further, if the youngsters start trouble we have no alternative but to shoot to kill."

Now it was do or die.

The proclamation was short. By the very nature of the word it is an impersonal announcement. It is not a rehearsal of pain and poverty. How can one ever find phrases exquisite enough to commemorate the sweet sacrifice of thousands whose bodies lie in the unmarked graves of Boven Digul? The answer is: you don't even try. The terse unemotional statement with which we finally demanded our place in the sun after 350 years read simply:

> We the people of Indonesia hereby declare Indonesia's independence. Matters concerning the transfer of power and other matters will be executed in an orderly manner and in the shortest possible time.
>
> On behalf of the Indonesian people
> (Signed) Soekarno   Hatta

Nor was this inscribed on a parchment of gold. The actual words were scribbled on a torn piece of paper. Somebody located a pad with blue lines on it such as are in children's lesson books. I ripped out a sheet and with my own hand wrote lengthwise across the blue lines.

Nor did we search for a special quill steeped in tradition. Who thought about such things? We didn't even preserve the historic plume which scrawled the immortal words. I know Presidents of the United States distribute pens with which they sign important bills, but me, with a great moment of history staring me in the face—I don't even remember where the pen came from. I think I borrowed it from somebody.

After all these years of praying, planning, and hoping, this was not what I imagined the Supreme Occasion would be. This was hardly the moment of glory my mother envisioned when she faced toward the East. It was not what I pictured in my black tomb at Bantjeuj. There were no trumpets blowing. There was no choir of angels. No elaborate ritual. No uniformed equerry. It was not marked by reporters, photographers, speeches. It was not attended by dignitaries in striped trousers or glamorously clad ladies in satins and jewels. Nor was the setting the throne room of Queen Juliana's palace, but a little anteroom off the foyer of a Japanese admiral's house.

Did we even propose a toast? To the best of my memory, if there was any refreshment served, it was a glass of warm soda and then only to revivify our ragged handful who hadn't slept in days.

The great final act of triumph for which I'd dedicated my whole being was now over. And it had been nothing. I felt no elation. I was just tired. Sick tired. It was four A.M.

I not only hadn't slept for two days, but I had a bad attack of malaria. I was quivering from head to foot. I ran a temperature of 104. Despite the seriousness of my condition, I could not go to bed when I arrived home. I went directly to my writing table and remained there for hours. Fatmawati knew enough to let me alone. What burned inside me was brighter than the fever. I started right away issuing directives to the leaders of the country. To one I wrote detailed instructions on how to mobilize his troops for defense. To another I forwarded orders on the takeover of government on a village level. To another I wrote, "Tomorrow you will hear through the radio the news that we are now a free people. As soon as you hear it form local committees for independence in every city in your area."

I wrote dozens and dozens of notes until I finally keeled over. "I feel very ill," I complained to Fatmawati, and then I had to go to bed. I yearned to stay up and work, but I was physically unable. I was very nauseated. By orders of Suharto nobody was allowed in the bedroom. I shut the door and passed out cold.

Meanwhile, everybody was running around wildly. There was no organization, but everyone was busy spreading the word by telephone, on bicycles, knocking at doors, and shouting to passersby. At seven A.M. a hundred or more were already assembled under my window. They came in crowds carrying bamboo *runtjing* spears, rocks, shovels, sticks, cleavers, or what we call *golok,* and anything else they could wield. Word was sent out that Bung Karno will make the Proclamation. We must protect Bung Karno. Farmers, vendors, fishermen, civil servants, the young, the old, everybody began marching toward Pegangsaan Timur 56.

The nearby Peta garrison, which had been in turmoil for a week, went on instant alert. In case the Japanese surrounded Pegangsaan with tanks, a unit of 170 soldiers and five officers, with an arsenal of weapons smuggled in preparation for The Day, were deployed to attack from the rear. The surrounding streets, *kampongs,* houses, and roads leading to Number 56 were sealed off with troops. An armed guard patrolled each corner of my little garden.

Barisan Pelopor, the civilian youth army of which I was chairman, was called to arms. Five top judo experts were dispatched to surround me bodily at all times. When my first official bodyguards arrived at nine A.M. they had to shoulder their way past hundreds already massed. The news of the Proclamation had traveled from mouth to mouth. One group of students borrowed mimeographs from the Japanese offices where they worked and stayed up all night printing crude handbills. In the morning they stole pickup trucks to drive around and stick them on fenceposts, toss them in train windows and leave them on doorsteps.

From all corners the streets leading to Bung Karno were black with people. One car disgorged twenty students. They were in the car, on the car, in the luggage compartment, everywhere. But things were orderly. There was no noise. They had been told I was not well. Then, too, everybody was nervous and tense.

Somehow they sensed there had to be a crowd gathered to hear Bung Karno announce their freedom. You cannot make a Proclamation alone. A Proclamation requires an audience. At nine some 500 stood in front of my verandah. Fatmawati, who had been sitting on the bed as I slept, woke me. I was pale and shaken. I'd had only a few minutes' sleep.

"Now, Bung, now. . . ." the people were clamoring. "Make the Proclamation now. . . ." Everybody was calling out to me. "Now, Bung . . . speak the words of freedom now . . . please, Bung, it is late . . . the sun is getting hot . . . the people are excited. They are restless. They are herded together out in the frontyard. Speak the Proclamation." I still had fever, but I kept my wits about me. In the light of all the pressures on me, it is amazing I could still function clearly.

"Hatta is not present," I said. "I will not read the Proclamation without Hatta."

At this crucial moment in history, Sukarno and Indonesia waited for Hatta to show up.

He was eventually ushered into the bedroom where I still lay quite alone except for Fatmawati. I got dressed. All in white. No great words that should be recorded in the archives passed between us. Neither of us had any fire. We were both worn. And, yes, perhaps even a little frightened, I think.

There wasn't any protocol. Nobody was in charge. Nothing proceeded according to plan because there wasn't any. The senior Peta officer present, Captain Latief, came in and asked, "Are you ready?" We nodded mutely. I walked out. Behind me came Hatta and Fatmawati.

As I went out a Peta man stationed himself at the phone in my office which fronted the proceedings. The Peta garrison, primed to respond to the signal should any Japanese show up, hung at the other end.

The ceremony was simple. But what we lacked in pomp we made up in hope. I walked to the microphone stolen from the Japanese radio station and tersely delivered our Proclamation. My wife had made a flag out of two pieces of cloth. A length of white material and one of red. She sewed them together by hand. This was the first official banner of the Republic. Our mast was a length of bamboo stuck into the ground only moments before. It was crude. Not even very high.

There was no one instructed to hoist our sacred *Merah-Putih*. There had been no preparations. Nobody had thought that far ahead. Captain Latief, one of the few present in uniform, was near the pole. Everybody waited tensely while he took our flag, attached it to the skinny, raveled strings and flew it . . . alone . . . proudly . . . for the first time in three and a half centuries.

There was no music, no band. After the flag went up we all sang "*Indonesia Raya.*"

With that I heard the Peta man in my office say into the phone, "Okay. All clear."

Then he hung up and I walked inside and went back to my room. It was 10 o'clock. The Revolution had begun.

⅋ 27. The Revolution Begins

"ALLAH be praised, the colors of the Republic are now raised," I prayed silently. "If ever they are lowered again, it will be over the dead bodies of our seventy-two million brothers. Let it be that we never forget the slogan of the Revolution:

Sekali Merdeka Tetap Merdeka—Once Free
Forever Free!"

Sudiro, my personal secretary, knocked on my bedroom door. I was slumped in the chair, my head in my hands.

"Five *Kempeitai* officers have shouldered their way into the living room," he reported. "They ask to speak to you. Our boys are just awaiting the word. What should we do?"

I came out and was confronted by an irate Chief of Police. "What have you done, Mr. Sukarno?" he demanded.

"Proclaimed our independence," I replied softly.

"But you cannot do that," he stormed. "The Allies instructed us to continue our administrative role until they arrive. The *Gunseikan* ordered me to tell you it is absolutely forbidden to speak the Proclamation."

"But it is already spoken. I have just now done it."

His hand involuntarily went to his hip and he made a half menacing step toward me, but a quick look around revealed hundreds of grim-faced guards armed with hatchets, sickles, and those sharp pointed bamboo *runtjing* spears which, with one thrust, can chop a large hole clean through a man's guts. Death by bamboo *runtjing* is slow and torturous. The Japanese left quietly.

I put out an order for a "Prepared to Die" corps of volunteers to defend the flag. The scene was unforgettable. The elderly who were clustered under the shade of the trees, the women carrying infants in their arms, all surged forward. Fatmawati set up a soup kitchen to feed the first wave of hundreds who formed a human hedge around Pegangsaan Timur 56.

I was sick. I was tired. I was so busy working for the country

and keeping alive that I was not aware of all the events that transpired next. Early the following morning there was a meeting of
leaders representing the most important religious, social, tribal, economic, and civic groups in Indonesia. It was at this meeting they
elected me President by acclamation. I don't even recall such details
as who actually proposed me. I remember only somebody uttering
something uninspirational like, "Well, we're a State as of yesterday.
And a State needs a President. How about Sukarno?"

It was as simple as that. And can you imagine what The Great
Mouthpiece of the Indonesian people then said in grateful apprecia-
tion? My momentous words of acceptance which will now be recorded for posterity were, "Okay." That was it. That's all I said.
"Okay." I didn't make any fuss. Nobody made any fuss. There was
too much to do.

Having been elected to the highest office in the land, the new
President walked home. On the street I passed a sidewalk vendor
selling the barbecued bits of skewered meat which is our favorite
national dish. His Excellency the President of the Republic of Indonesia hailed the barefoot, bareback restaurateur and issued his first
executive order: "Please make for me 50 sticks of chicken *sate*." I
squatted right there in the gutter and the muck and we ate them and
that was the whole celebration feast in my honor.

We had been through so much and there was so much more to go
through that we were wrung dry of emotion. At home I picked the
glamorous surroundings of the kitchen to make this world-shattering
pronouncement to my wife with the exciting comment, "They made
me President today. The people elected me President."

Fatmawati expressed no joy. She remarked only, "One late night
before your father died, just we two were sitting together. I was
massaging him, trying to ease his pain, when suddenly he said, 'I have
a mystic premonition that soon . . . very soon . . . my son will sit in
the big white palace.' So this comes as no surprise. Three months ago
your father predicted it."

One trouble with being President was that we had no such word
in our language. That's an English term. Since this was the title they
saw fit to bestow on me, we had to "Indonesia it up." The "T" was
dropped. From that day forth I was Presiden Sukarno.

My devoted followers decided a "Presiden" had to have a limousine so they "arranged" for one. Sudiro knew of a seven-passenger
Buick which is "The biggest, most beautiful in Djakarta and has cur-

tains in the back window." Unfortunately this Presidential limousine happened to belong to the Japanese Chief of Railways. Such a minor detail did not trouble Sudiro. Unknown to me he went hunting for the car and found it parked in a garage.

It happens that Sudiro knew the driver and said to him, "Look, I want you to give me the keys to the car."

"Why?" asked the boy, terrified.

"What do you mean, 'Why?'," repeated Sudiro, shocked by such stupidity. "Because it is my intention to steal it for our President."

"Oh, okay," grinned the patriot, climbing happily out of the front seat and handing the keys over.

"Quick," ordered Sudiro, "head back for your village in Central Java before anyone knows what happened. And hide yourself well because it will be dangerous for you to be around here once this is discovered."

Sudiro had the keys and a beautiful, big, black seven-passenger limousine with curtains in the rear window—but he couldn't drive. Few of us could. Where should we learn? Natives had no cars during Dutch time and only officials were permitted them in Japanese time. Another friend of Sudiro's, who also drove for the Japanese, piloted it to its new home in my backyard.

The establishment of our government fell into three parts. Part one was the executive end. We adopted the constitution, arranged for copies of the Proclamation to penetrate every corner of every jungle in the archipelago, planned our civilian defense, inaugurated our government departments, and elected ministers from among our top administrators.

Part two was to send word to the world. This fell primarily to Adam Malik, one of the chiefs of our underground who worked for Domei, the Japanese News Agency. When the Japanese stopped for lunch on the 17th he operated their shortwave transmitter to put our message of freedom on the air. He was out, gone and in hiding before they finished their sukiyaki. He'd already spent considerable time as a "guest" of the *Kempeitai* and had no wish to do so again.

The Japanese knew instantly what Malik had done because the shortwave was beamed to Domei branches in other cities. But it was also picked up by our underground who were monitoring the air-waves. Malik's morsecast was received by a group operating out of a mosque. They flashed it through Central Java within an hour. Another group, with mobile equipment temporarily set up in a university, beamed the message to Medan, the central relay in Sumatra, and so it went. It reached the Philippines, Ceylon, Australia, and Saigon and within a week the outside world learned it from the Allies.

The third facet of our job was taking over from the Japanese. Peta, Barisan Pelopor, and Hei Ho raided munitions factories, disarmed entire Japanese units, clashed with sentries guarding radio stations, telegraph stations, harbors, railways. They dragged high officials from their beds, ousted their functionaries from government buildings. Our boys acquired strategic real estate and seized control of much of the communications media.

The techniques learned by our professionals gradually spread to the masses by the system of "He who knows passes it on to another." Japan offered more than token resistance in some situtations, but their demoralization, poor discipline, and lack of will were no match for the zeal of newly trained youths fired by the red-and-white insignia pinned to their breasts.

These colors were not decided upon arbitrarily for the Revolution. They began with the first seeds of creation. A female's blood is red. A man's sperm is white. The sun is red. The moon is white. The tincture of our soil is red. The juice of a plant is white. Before there was organized religion, creatures worshiped the basic things. So it traveled down the ages to our current civilization. Red stands for courage. White for purity. The mystical offering of the Javanese comprises red porridge and white porridge. Our colors are over 6,000 years old.

My people are great ones for symbols. So, I ordered 10 million red-and-white little paper flags distributed by courier to remote parts of the country. It helped those in the outlying islands feel they were part of the fight. As the Prophet invented the Salam to unify his followers, so the inspiration descended from God Almighty to proclaim one national greeting for the Indonesian people. The first of September I decreed every citizen of the Republic should greet another by raising his hand, spreading fingers wide in token of our five principles and shouting, *"MERDEKA."*

My people clamored to hear their President. I announced that the 19th of September, in the huge open square fronting the big, white palace, President Sukarno would make his first State of the Union address. The Japanese simultaneously announced that the meeting was prohibited. The atmosphere was fraught with tension.

The day before the 19th our men were sent to check the field for mines. Early that morning fully armed Japanese were posted with rifles at the ready and bayonets drawn, yet the citizens of the Republic never wavered. They came and they came and they never stopped coming. One million Indonesians crowded onto this field. Our people were not afraid to die. Better to die for freedom than live in death.

For hours and hours they stood calmly until "The Presiden" showed up. There was no motorcycle escort. Just me in my limousine insulated with *pemudas* lying across the roof and hood. When I stepped to the grandstand they blanketed me with their bodies and formed a protective armor of flesh and blood. Anybody who wanted to get me would have had to pierce several layers of people first. The crowd went wild when they saw me. Despite machineguns and tanks, the Japanese quailed at what might have happened if they had forbidden me to speak.

"*Saudara-Saudara,*" I said, "we will continue to defend our Proclamation. Not one word is withdrawn."

That was my whole State of the Union Address. Everybody was nervous. This was not a moment for long speech-making. One wrong motion on anybody's part could have precipitated a massacre. I said simply:

I know you came here to see your President and to hear his orders. Well, if you still have faith and confidence in your President, follow his first command. Go home quietly. Leave this gathering now in an orderly fashion and wait to hear from your district leaders. Now . . . disband . . . go home . . . quietly.

That was all I said. And that was all it took. The one million souls instantly dispersed at this directive from their Chief. The Japanese couldn't help but have respect.

The Allied Forces arrived in September. The first landing were British troops and they brought with them the foreign press. Our first press conference was held on the porch of Pegangsaan Timur 56. The reporters were very aggressive. Some stood. Some sat. But all directed questions with their hands on their hips and cigarettes dangling from their mouths. In the group was one Dutchman who pretended to be an American with *The New York Times*. My "Press Officer" was a schoolboy who suddenly found himself in charge of war correspondents. He never checked credentials. What did he know about such things? He later perfected a foolproof method of discovering Dutchmen. If you trample hard enough on his toes, the Dutchman hollers, "OW!'" The American or Englishman hollers, "OUCH!"

The newspapermen didn't ask me much. What they did was accuse. As I suspected, their chief accusation was, "You were a Japanese collaborator, is that right?" The Englishman from Singapore wanted to know, "How come your speeches, which we've heard on radio, repeatedly stated you would smash the Allied Forces from the shores of Java?"

We served tea. Despite their rudeness I was a good host. Patiently I explained, "In '42 we were untrained and I felt the smart tactic was to have the Japanese fight our battle for us. Now it is '45 and we are trained and ready to fight our own battle. Check the gains on both sides and you will find Sukarno got much more out of the Japanese than the Japanese got out of Sukarno."

I was not at all at a loss for words and I tried hard to be pleasant, but as is the story of my life with Western journalists, most of their dispatches were unflattering.

After tea they requested permits to go into the field and see what was what. We didn't know about permits. What permits? We waved them on cheerily with, "Sure. Go ahead," but they insisted on official permission. My "Press Officer" made up some type of card and stamped it with some sort of seal which meant nothing since nobody'd ever seen it before. How could it be honored if nobody knew what it meant? But this was our first attempt at officialdom and the reporters went away satisfied.

Immediately on their heels and under cover of the British came the Dutch, reinforced by soldiers who'd been prisoners of war during the occupation. As soon as they were let loose, they prowled the cities shooting at anything or anybody who looked suspicious. To prevent trouble, I ordered all Indonesians off the streets after eight P.M. They complied to a man. Still the Dutch patrols went looking for trouble. They forced open our homes, looted them, and dragged off any or all of the inhabitants. When we retaliated, the Dutch burned our buildings to the ground.

Day by day the situation worsened. Street clashes between Dutch and Indonesians increased. *Pemudas* were kidnapped on the roads, shanghaied to work camps in other Dutch territories and never heard of again. Women and children were shot as they walked the streets. NICA (Netherlands Indies Civil Administration) troops were bloodthirsty. They set up machine guns and rained open fire on funeral processions. Youngsters riding their cycles were shot in the legs for no reason whatsoever.

In a body NICA bandits would descend on a *kampong* hunting for *pemudas*. In one narrow lane the NICA opened fire right inside a *pemuda's* house. The youth, shot in the neck, died instantly. His old mother's arm was ripped open by bullets while a two-year-old baby in her arms was shot in the cheek.

NICA drove the streets of Djakarta shooting indiscriminately at civilians just to break the spirit of opposition. At gunpoint they robbed aged passengers on trains. They set fire to homes and tommy-gunned those who tried to extinguish the flames. Records on file show 8,000 innocent civilians in the city of Djakarta were killed between September and December.

If it's wondered why I hold little love for the British, one reason is that all this systematic terrorism was perpetrated under their eyes. They were responsible for maintaining "Law and Order" in the Islands. The Allied command placed our welfare in the hands of the British whose job was to oversee the repatriation of the Japanese and to free the Dutch internees. When they protected the Dutch landings and unleashed this terrorism as a result, they didn't want to be "in the middle." They wanted to complete their assignments and get out. So their way of handling the wholesale butchering of Indonesians was to look away. We now had NICA against us, Japanese against us and the British, whose ranks were swelled by Australians, Paks, Gurkhas, and Indians. In key cities throughout Java, Sumatra and Bali, fighting was heavy. Clearly, we had to marshal our resources.

On October 5, the People's Army of the Republic was born. Its vital statistics were five men to every gun. If one volunteer came in leading 10 recruits, he became a corporal. Another leading 20 recruits became a sergeant. But any fellow who brought rifles and a handful of smuggled grenades automatically became an officer.

Some commandeered Dutch uniforms. Some wore the floppy hats and short-sleeved shirts of the Australian army. Others stripped the Japanese and wore boots, sabers, and Japanese rank insignias. Such a snappily attired enlisted man often marched beside an officer wearing nothing but a *pitji* and ragged shorts. Some wore all white regalia. Others fell heir to vats of dye and sported uniforms either as green as grass or as black as pitch. We had men without weapons, without uniforms, and without wages, but our army was on its way.

And none too soon. That infamous, savage, never-to-be-forgotten Battle of Surabaya, the first battle of the Republic, exploded the last days of October. The British provoked it by demanding all Indonesians lay down their arms and surrender unconditionally within 24 hours or else. . . . The Indonesians retaliated by massacring the British troops who attempted to wrest control of the port in a revolution that had nothing to do with them in the first place. The British were hacked to pieces with knives, literally torn limb from limb, brutally slain. It was a vicious, bloody fight. True, ours is a basically weak and tame and quiet race. But even the Dutch said there is the soul of a tiger in the Indonesian. And when we are pressed we are capable of great deeds. We did not start the battle of Surabaya, but when it looked like we might finish it, the British put in a hurried call to Sukarno to save them.

At two A.M. my bodyguard, asleep on a chair in the office, was roused from his slumbers by the insistent ringing of the phone. It was Surabaya. Tukimin tapped gingerly at the bedroom door and then waited, his ear pressed to the panel for fully five minutes. There was no sound. Gingerly he tapped again.

"Yes," I called sleepily. "What is it?"

Faithful, loyal Tukimin whispered, "It's the ADC to the British Commander, Pak. He says it's extremely urgent. I told him you were asleep, but he demanded I wake you."

I was on the phone for thirty minutes. Afterward I shared none of my inner turmoil with Fatmawati or Tukimin. I said only, "I leave for Surabaya in a British army plane tomorrow," then I went back into the bedroom and noiselessly shut the door.

The British had occupied several buildings and in the center of Surabaya they maintained headquarters. The city itself was pandemonium. There was bloody hand-to-hand combat on every street corner. Bodies were strewn everywhere. Decapitated, dismembered trunks lay piled one on top of the other. The dead were just accumulating in the streets. Indonesians were shooting and stabbing and murdering wildly. Everybody was fighting. With whatever they had they fought—young men with clubs, old men with prayers.

In the middle of the gutter, right in front of headquarters, a blood-spattered old Javanese stood stark still. His gnarled hands, drawn up to chest level, clutched a ceremonial dagger with a short blade. He didn't look right or left. Just held tightly to his *kris,* the blade pointed downward, praying, believing unequivocally in its supernatural power and transfusing the strength from the *kris* to his body. This was his method of fighting.

For two hours Hatta, who had been elected Vice-President, and I talked with the British. They treated us adequately. It wasn't lavish. There was no attitude even remotely like that accorded Chiefs of State. But they sent for me because they needed me, since it was clear nothing could stop this mayhem except, maybe, Sukarno, so they were at least respectful. Our agreement was a Cease Fire. They provided me a jeep and I went forth to do what I'd been brought to do. I drove wherever my young warriors were and I talked to them face to face. Each held a gun. Each gun was cocked and loaded. It was the first time many had ever seen firearms, let alone shot them. It was also the first time they'd ever seen their President, let alone spoken to him. They were nervous, excited, and itchy-fingered. One boy of maybe 16 years was standing next to me holding his rifle upright and hanging on my every word. At something I said he became uncontrollably excited and . . . BOOOMMMMMMMM! that damn rifle went off. And right behind my ear, too.

I drove around all day and night shouting, "Stop fighting. The terms of agreement are to cease fire and stand fast. Don't shoot. Those are my orders. Stop fighting instantly."

Although there was panic on the streets, the moment they saw me and heard my voice they obeyed. With rifles cocked and knives set to plunge, they froze dead in their tracks. I stopped the fighting cold on the third of November.

I stayed our people from killing the British in the hopes that the rest of our battles could be fought at the conference table. I should have known better. A few days later the commander of the British forces in Surabaya, General Mallaby, was killed. He was not a well-liked officer among his own men. It was therefore never proved which side did it. The only reason anybody cared who killed Mallaby was that the British used this incident to demand an "Immediate Unconditional Surrender."

My troops, who'd been religiously abiding by the Cease Fire agreement, were suddenly commanded to "Come out with your arms in the air." This precipitated the bloodiest battle our land has ever seen. The British Air Force bombed Surabaya. British battleships pounded us from the sea. Under this barrage they landed additional divisions who used my civilians as shields. The British saved themselves from slaughter by negotiating a Cease Fire, but while my men respected the orders to "stand fast" the British turned around and attacked us from land, sea, and air. Have I to love the British for that?

On November 10 we launched our counterattack. The fighting was fierce. If one of our men was machinegunned, two came up to replace him. If two were killed, four rushed up to replace them. Only the frontline had weapons. When they were weary, they dropped their guns and retreated empty-handed. The next line then moved along and picked up the same weapons. Broadcasts to our Chinese citizens to erect a Chinese Defense Army helped. Surabaya began evacuating. On the road, women and children were bombed, old people strafed. The roads out were clogged with the bodies of our dead and they couldn't be removed because the shelling continued for days.

This was a terrible time. I was nervous. Very nervous. It was one of the few occasions that I was, although I never showed it. The only tell-tale signs were my fingers drumming. "Oh, what should I do . . . what should I do," I thought.

I appealed to the world. I spoke in English for a tape-recorded broadcast to London. I protested to the U.N. I cabled President Truman asking his good offices because the soldiers killing us were carrying water canteens and driving trucks with U.S.A. signs, thereby creating "natural suspicion on the part of Indonesians who had nothing against America." Nobody helped. Fired with an undying will for freedom, Surabayans resisted valiantly until November 30. From this bloodbath in which so many of my brothers were wiped out, the one point that emerged was that Indonesia would never give up. We would never succumb to colonialism again—NEVER!!

Meanwhile, the situation in Djakarta was also fraught with peril, for me particularly. The Allies were screaming, "Execute Sukarno as a collaborator." I worried considerably that this might happen. Friends thought at the very least I'd wind up in jail for a dozen years. The British were making repeated attempts to arrest me so they could force me to stand trial as a war criminal and the Dutch were making repeated efforts to just assassinate me outright.

They hated me. They tried to blow up my car. They shot and nearly killed my driver. Their forces were well organized. Ours were not. We had no discipline, no staff. Not even food! I didn't get paid.

By whom? Who should pay me? One night my ministers were at Pegangsaan late for emergency conferences and I had neither coffee nor a crust of bread to serve. Tukimin left in my motorcar to borrow groceries for his President. The NICA were gunning for me that night. Their orders were "Kill Sukarno on sight." Thinking I was in "the Sukarno car," the NICA deliberately rammed a huge truck into it. They jumped free at the last moment, but the truck crashed head-on into the car. It was totally demolished. Tukimin would have been too, had *pemudas* not gotten him to a hospital.

The afternoon following this attempt on my life, Red Cross planes dropped food and supplies to a Dutch camp close by Pegangsaan. They overshot their mark and the cases, containing tins of sardines, cans of soda, and medical equipment, fell and broke open only inches from my verandah. From such a height the impact sounded like a bomb. My guards came running.

"Clear this stuff off the ground and take it to the Dutch under a white flag. Tell them this was intended for them and make sure they get it!!"

The youngsters looked stunned. Here they were, sworn to kill the Dutch and their President orders them to bring supplies to the enemy camp. "We do not hate the Dutch people," I explained. "We hate only the Colonial Government. But if any human beings are hungry or in pain then we shall personally share our food and give our blood to ease their agonies. Politics is politics, but humanity is humanity."

So many attempts were made to pick me off that I began sleeping in a different house every night. NICA troops repeatedly set traps to kill me. Despite my wall of human protection, it was unsafe. We devised a plan. We selected several friends who could be trusted implicitly and nightly we alternated. Sometimes guards took Fatmawati and Guntur to one house and me to another. Sometimes we went together. As darkness fell we made our selection. Not even these dearly trusted friends knew when we'd come to them.

After six P.M. the streets were no longer safe. One of our guards first made the trip to the selected house to see if all was clear. Then I disguised myself as a motorcar driver or a coolie complete with sarong and Javanese head kerchief. Often I effected a limp or other physical manifestation to throw NICA off the track. We crept stealthily through little-used paths in the bushes. We never took an open street. For fear NICA would hear, we'd rap on the selected house very quietly. Occasionally nobody would answer because they were terrified at who it might be. When a familiar face appeared cautiously at the peephole in the upper part of the door, I'd stand on tiptoe, crane my neck and hiss, "It's me . . . Sukarno . . . the President."

Sometimes I feared to utter a sound at all. I just pointed to my face and made desperate motions. Sometimes the gate was locked and I had to climb over it. A couple of times there wasn't sleeping space. My guard camped outside on the ground while the President and The First Lady rolled up on the carpet. Early in the morning we reversed the process and made it back to Pegangsaan while it was still dark.

After a few weeks of this I moved my wife, baby, and in-laws into a suburb a couple of hours' drive away. They hid in a primitive shack occupied by a village mystic whom I knew and trusted well. Twice a week, around eleven at night, I made the drive through the wooded area to visit them. I'd stay the night and, again, back to Pegangsaan before sunrise.

There were so many crises and I had to be everywhere. Everybody wanted to see their leader, touch him, hear him, kiss his feet, his knees. Many cried when they came face to face with me. When I first came to the Batak tribes, I met with an old chieftain who was chewing betel nut. His mouth was red with the juice. When he saw me he hugged me and cried on my chest and the red juice came dripping down my shirt. In many cases their love caused as much difficulty as the enemy's hatred.

Take the problem of rice. The grain which fed Djakarta came from the outside area of Bekasi. The Marhaens there were deliberately delaying our trucks or refusing to send them back laden. They were just doing it so they'd be noticed and I'd come there personally to lecture them. I agreed to come. When they arrived to escort me to Bekasi, a sudden emergency took me to East Java. I left a handwritten note explaining, but they were frantic. How could they convince their neighborhood this was truly a letter from the hand of President Sukarno?

They lifted one painting of baby Guntur and one of Fatmawati off my wall to prove they were actually in my house. With my letter and the State Secretary himself to guarantee its authenticity, they departed satisfied. No more rice trouble.

Another problem was our newly liberated youngsters. With their hatred of anything that wasn't brown-skinned, some had turned into bandits and were causing great trouble. They delayed and derailed trains carrying innocent Dutch internees. They pillaged. They terrified. They agreed to stop only on one condition. "Have Bapak come to us personally" was the condition.

My advisors were panicky. "Bung," they fretted, "what if this is a trick? Suppose they ignore you and your prestige is hurt? Worse, suppose they do you bodily harm? With the baser instincts of all nationalities prevailing these days, nobody can tell what will happen. You mustn't go!" I prayed silently and in the middle of the discussion I stood up and announced, "I am going."

At the rendezvous point a crowd of angry young bandits with cutlasses, sabers, and axes swarmed my car. Immediately they saw it really was Bapak they became calm. And respectful. I did not rebuke them. Instead I enlisted their patriotism. In a warm, fatherly tone, I said, "We have sacrificed much to govern ourselves. But we have finally done it. We have a State of our own. The whites never thought we could accomplish anything on our own. As you know the slogan of the Republican Government is, 'All is running well.' It is the one item with which we can impress the Allies so that they'll see we are capable of self-rule. Therefore, interfering with trains and throwing them off schedule is also throwing our chances of freedom off the track. We must show the outside world that if a train is due from Surabaya at seven, under the new administration it WILL arrive at seven."

The lecture was over. They got the point. From then on all was OK. No more incidents.

In a revolution you can't stop too long to think about anything. You have to work on nerve. I was so busy living each hour that I never realized until years later what risks I took. Take the morning I negotiated an area cease fire in a tiny, dark, dirty little cubbyhole of a telephone booth in British-occupied Magelang. The news of the cease fire had not yet begun to travel to the soldiers on either side when a lady who looked like my mother raced up sobbing hysterically that her baby son had been captured. She pointed toward where they took him. I walked in. Slowly but steadily. I said not a word. I held no white flag. Just kept walking directly into the enemy camp. All alone. Nobody went with me.

I was within close range of a machine gun nest trained right at my heart when an Indonesian voice from somewhere yelled in English, "Hey, everybody . . . hold your fire . . . that's Sukarno going in there . . . don't shoot. . . !"

Just as though I had every right in the world to be there, I walked into the bushes and with all the authority at my command I demanded to see the commander, ordered the release of the child and walked out with him. The British were all so stunned that they complied.

And why didn't I wait another hour until news of the cease fire filtered through the lines? And how did I dare penetrate enemy territory knowing there was a price on my head? I don't know. One trigger-happy hero and I could have been stone dead. Where any of us got the courage and strength to do half the things we did, only God knows. I don't know.

Meanwhile, the situation in Djakarta had become so critical that I could no longer remain. Without a solid police force, we were no match for the NICA. It wasn't the life of the leader of the State, but the life of the entire State that was in jeopardy. The afternoon of the third of January, I announced to my ministers, guards, and loyal aides, "The seat of the government must be removed to an area free of Dutch that we may establish a Republican stronghold."

Jogjakarta fitted the need. Jogjakarta is also the center of Java. The decision was made. "We will shift the capital tomorrow night. None of you will take any belongings whatsoever," I cautioned. "Nor will I. There will be no time to crate furnishings or move treasured possessions. Besides, you are all close to me so you are all being watched."

Our house was right in front of the railroad tracks, so at six o'clock the following evening a darkened string of coaches slid to a noiseless stop behind Pegangsaan. Silently, without even breathing aloud, we sneaked out the rear and climbed aboard one. NICA were searching all trains as they moved in or out. Ours wasn't connected to any others. And it was kept dark. We had a faithful engineer in the cab. It looked like a lone boxcar such as the unattached ones often found at a railroad siding before they're coupled onto another. The NICA thought we were only an empty car being shunted onto another track.

Had we been discovered, the whole State could have been wiped out with one grenade. But you actually don't stop to think if what you're doing is safe. Of course it was not. But the Republic was born in risks. Any revolutionary movement asks courage. And so, on the black moonless night of the fourth of January, 1946, we shifted the cradle of the infant Republic of Indonesia to Jogjakarta.

✌ 28. At War with the Dutch

"THE City of Pilgrimage," as Jogja became known, numbered 170,000 inhabitants. In the next few weeks, the entire government moved inland and the population swelled to 600,000. Our ministers were billeted in homes with Jogjanese families. Our ministries were the front parlors. Our flags which ran the whole length of a bamboo pole flew in every yard.

We operated more like a band of thieves than a government. We had nothing. No typewriters, stationery, airplanes; the only salvageable radio equipment was of 1935 vintage. We also had no money. Indonesia's Japanese currency had depreciated. In the first minutes after independence, Dr. Suharto acted as our treasurer. And his was a one-man business. He had no time to count out devalued bills so he'd weigh up a pile and parcel it out to us by the kilo. By the time we removed to Central Java we had our own money. That is, the Republic was grinding out currency on a hand printing press, so in theory we had our own money, but it wasn't good anywhere. Nobody would accept it. We had nothing to back it up but our printing press.

The only way to get what we desperately needed was to smuggle. And everybody smuggled for the Republic. My current Ambassador to Japan ran sugar. My former Ambassador to America ran opium. Singapore, Bangkok, Hong Kong, and Manila were four excellent smugglers' towns. My men worked all four.

Singapore was a goldmine. We robbed their warehouses for textiles until we discovered the British were easily corrupted and could be bribed with contraband we'd smuggle elsewhere in return for ready-made army uniforms from military stores. Singapore suddenly suffered a big rash of fires of army supply stores. Our contacts couldn't dare tell their superiors they were being bribed so one by one each burned his emporium down to "legitimately" account for the losses.

You could always tell where my men made a killing. One week a military unit sported Canadian hats. The following month another blossomed forth in English blouses. Following a good run of luck, our top smuggler presented me with a package. "It's a skirt from the Australian Women's Army Corps," he beamed happily. "The material's very good quality and never been worn." I wasn't the sort who looked trim in brown wool skirts but I badly needed something so I remade it into a pair of military shorts and had a perfectly good outfit for a long while.

A high official in my Cabinet smuggled nine kilograms of gold and 300 kilograms of silver from Sumatra as a down payment for 20,000 uniforms. Our men were judged differently depending on whose side you were on. The man who arranged the gold and silver trade and also spirited out 8,000 tons of rubber was Pak Gani. The Netherlands called him a top swindler. The Indonesians knew him as the Minister of Economics.

Besides those foreign soldiers of fortune who'd hijack anybody for money, we were also helped by idealists. One dear boy just showed up from nowhere one day and introduced himself. "My name's Bob Freberg. I'm an American. I'm a pilot and I sympathize with your struggle. How can I help?"

After the war Hong Kong had a sale on used airplanes. I mean, what can't you buy in Hong Kong, right? Everything's for sale there if you've got the price. And by hook or crook, by gold or opium, we managed to get the price. We bought two second-hand Dakotas and Bob Freberg flew me everywhere. He crashed in '47 when I sent him to Palembang with money to aid the Sumatran guerrillas. Never will I forget my American friend, Bob Freberg.

The Indians were helpful, too. During the Battle of Surabaya, 600 deserted to us. We got many good things out of the Indians. They're born smugglers. India was starving. In return for tons of rice, friends there smuggled us an airplane. Always altering its course, this plane ferried back and forth to Manila. It loaded at two A.M. with a cargo of coffee or quinine and returned immediately with the spare parts, medicines, supplies, and munitions they had ready for me. The Dutch finally shot it down in Jogja.

There was little coordination in our piracy. Everybody worked his own way through individual connections with money handed personally to the Republic's agents in each country. If one area had oil, it shipped oil independently of anybody else. Another secretly unloaded its vanilla beans in Bangkok. One group of my boys had a hot sugar operation going. They chartered a six-hundred-ton ship from Singapore, sailed it up around the northernmost tip of Sumatra and down the southern coast of Java. They smuggled the sugar across 100 kilometers of bad road to the harbor. There they'd work all night to carry it bag by bag into 40 sampans and send them off to the ship which was anchored at least 30 miles off shore. Ten times that beautiful ship ran the Dutch blockade for us.

The one commodity we had was raw materials. Our Minister of Economics arranged to export goods to Britain, and Britain guaranteed the shipments safety from Dutch buccaneering on the high seas because they then had a scheme to double-Dutch the Dutch. Holland needed our tin and rubber desperately. Britain acted as the middleman, bought the products, then resold them to the Dutch for a higher price.

We even smuggled within our own borders. The Sultan of Jogja was a major liaison between the Dutch-held capital of Djakarta and the Republican-held capital of Jogjakarta. Whenever he took the 12-hour train trip to West Java, he swapped crates of Jogja-made cigars for automobile tires. At one point the total capital of the Republic of Indonesia was transferred into gold bricks, stuffed in shoe boxes and soap dishes and hidden in the back room of the Sultan's office.

Meanwhile, the British were anxious to discard the uncomfortable role they had assumed. They served notice on Holland they were pulling out and placed great pressure on The Hague to come to terms with the Republic. The Dutch by now occupied the tin islands of Bangka and Belitung off the east coast of Sumatra. Next they took Bali. They also held key cities in Java and Sumatra. Some cities belonged to both sides. Bandung was half Republican, half Dutch. However, with the withdrawal of British muscle, Holland could not muster sufficient strength to overthrow the Republic. They were also losing control of their vast economic interests in Indonesia. Additionally, our struggle had reached the outside world. Public sentiment was reacting unfavorably to Holland.

We, too, were eager for respite since the daily fighting throughout localized areas of the archipelago was draining us steadily. Thanks to colonialism, we were never on an equal footing with the rest of the world to begin with. The Revolution was badly handicapping us still further. Illiteracy mounted. Health, business, and progress dropped. We were isolated. Our capital was surrounded by enemy territory. We could not trade. The isolation had worked ruin with our pitiable attempts at economic stability.

Things were stalemated. The Dutch did not have sufficient might to overthrow the Republic and the Republic lacked the strength to overthrow the Dutch. The spring of 1946 we met for talks in the Netherlands.

The talks failed. It was a hopeless deadlock.

Negotiations were subsequently resumed in Linggadjati in northeastern Java. It was near the harbor of Tjirebon so if things went wrong we wouldn't be walled in. Too, we didn't want those high-class Dutchmen to get sick from the heat so we picked a cool region.

The Linggadjati agreement comprised 17 articles. The principal provisions were:

1. Dutch recognition of our authority in the islands of Java, Madura, and Sumatra, which was based largely on the fact that our armies were already well entrenched there.

2. Cooperation between our governments in establishing one democratic federal state to be called the United States of Indonesia and that this USI would consist of three member states. The first member state was to be the Republic of Indonesia, embracing only the three islands of Java, Sumatra, and Madura. The second member was to be the State of Borneo, the largest of all our islands, and the third, the Great Eastern State, was to embody what lies east of Java and east of Borneo and which is in reality all the rest of the former Netherlands East Indies territory.

3. The USI and the Kingdom of the Netherlands (inclusive of Curaçao and Surinam, its Latin American possessions) cooperate toward forming an equal political partnership, the Netherlands-Indonesian Union, to be inaugurated by January 1, 1949.

The agreement called for gradual evacuation of Dutch troops, which was a major victory for us, and it called for guaranteed protection of Holland's economic interests, which was a major victory for her. The bone in the Republic's throat was that the over-all head of the Netherlands-Indonesian Union would be Queen Juliana.

Linggadjati was a shower of ice water on the fire of revolution. Sjahrir, then Prime Minister, was its architect, not I. He hated Japan maniacally and consequently was lenient in dealing with Holland. Holland-educated, he'd worked in a Dutch labor organization in his youth. Whereas I constantly attacked them, Sjahrir said constantly kind things regarding them. We disagreed as usual.

However difficult our domestic problems, the immediate need was for a united front against the common enemy: colonialism. Linggadjati was by far not the best solution but at the moment, after months of wrangling, it was the only one. Although our delegation was never happy about it we reluctantly accepted it.

I must take a moment to discuss our delegation. They were villagers, traders, humble folk. Take Minister Lemeina—a country doctor. We'd met fleetingly during wartime when he had healed me of a headache and, again, fleetingly, when I visited his town following independence. Shortly thereafter an aide summoned him to Djakarta. A Christian from Molucca, he embodied two minorities I wanted in my Cabinet to demonstrate our motto: Unity In Diversity. More important, in his presence I received a sixth-sense instant reaction and when such violent intuitive waves of human judgment come over me I'm never wrong. I sensed he was one of the most intensely honest men I'd ever met.

I said to him, "Look here, I want you to be a minister." Over these 20 years I've been proved right. He's as honest a type as Jesus of Nazareth. Today he's my Second Deputy Prime Minister and takes over as "Acting President ex-officio" when I leave the country.

But then he was no professional diplomat, just a rural doctor. For two years during the occupation he'd owned only a pair of undershorts. Now, suddenly, he was representing his beloved nation in a diplomatic delegation. He had but two shirts to his name. One he wore. One he washed. For every official reception, he borrowed a necktie from a friend. When asked to become an Instant Diplomat he said, "Fortunately I room with a colleague who's almost as tall as I and he has a suit I can borrow. It doesn't fit too well, but I'll only have to wear it for a couple of hours at a time. I'm sure I can get away with it. Don't worry. I won't shame our country."

Villagers in borrowed rags were now suddenly in politics, sitting in conferences with Queen Juliana's august representatives who carried sleek briefcases and black diplomats' homburgs, entering into negotiations with the "impartial" British, each of whom was a Sir or a Lord. Several of my delegates had even to borrow shoes, and the British and Dutch were calling them "Your Excellency." My ministers' greatest difficulty was trying not to giggle at the ridiculousness of it all.

The Dutch were tricky. They slipped many hitches into the Linggadjati agreement. I acquiesced to terms provided we would be a free nation. But, for us, "free" and "independent" are identical. Holland interpreted "free" as a grade lower than "independent." The core of Linggadjati was a word incorporated in the text of several articles: cooperation. Without cooperation between both parties, many of the clauses could never be implemented. They used so many tricks that I did not trust them nor the Linggadjati agreement nor the military truce which was signed the 14th of October, 1946.

This was the eye of the hurricane. Although storm warnings were still posted in everyone's heart, we desperately needed breathing space and thus I accepted the United States of Indonesia as a temporary tactic. I knew someday future bargaining sessions would demolish this and return us to our basic concept of one sovereign, independent, unitary republic. Armed hostilities ceased. The hate-twisted faces of the NICA killers gave way to the empty, meaningless smiles of the professional diplomats. The truce was on.

We used this calm to establish ourselves. On the international scene we commenced diplomatic relations with the Arab League, India, Burma, Afghanistan, China, the United States, Britain, Czechoslovakia. The salary of our first emissary to the Philippines was six dollars per week. His "embassy" was the home of a barber wherein he and his wife boarded. For an appointment with the President of the Philippines, he borrowed the barber's jacket. Once the "Ambassador's" total capital was 20 cents. He and his wife bought three apples. With that and water they lived for two days. Such was the beginning of our Foreign Service.

Domestically we weren't much better off. Government guests were put up at a house and three times daily a presidential aide loaded the presidential Cadillac with food for the VIPs. That's how we operated in those days. We knew nothing about protocol. Along with the way everything was being run, the officer in charge of protocol seemed the logical individual to serve in this post because of his background. Mutahar was an ex-sailor. When India and China opened their consular offices in Jogja, I wished to entertain them in the Executive Mansion. A white palace behind high walls, it had previously housed the Governor General during Dutch occupancy and the Japanese High Command, but during the Revolution it was only a shell. "What will we do about dishes?" I asked Mutahar. "The *istana* here is not equipped. The Japanese looted everything before they left. I have only one set of cheap green plastic cups and saucers which were smuggled from a hardware store in Manila."

"There is no difficulty at all," smiled Mutahar calmly. Mutahar was always calm. "I will go to Oen, the Chinese restaurant in town, and borrow their dishes and silver."

Mutahar then dashed around to all the neighbors and rang their bells collecting tablecloths. When Fatmawati asked did he know what kind to get, he said, "We will use only white ones."

"How clever of you to know so much about table decorating," she praised. "What made you decide on only white?"

"White is *sutji,*" he explained. "Sacred. It stands for purity. Cleanliness. Holiness. Besides, that's the only color we can get a lot of."

Our first important guest was General Romulo of the Philippines. We wanted to serve him with great elegance. But we couldn't. We had no wine. So he drank water. That's all we had.

At this dinner other foreign statesmen comprised the remainder of the guest list. "How will we seat everybody?" fretted the major-domo of the *istana.*

Said my "Protocol Officer" coolly, "The President will grace the head of the table facing the front porch. Opposite will be the chairman of parliament. The military sits on his left. On his right we put the Cabinet."

"And where will be the honored diplomats?"

"In between," said Mutahar, making it up as he went along. Mutahar arbitrarily decided all regulations himself, taking great consolation from the fact that nobody knew any more than he did anyhow. When he was seriously stuck he went to the *kraton* (the Sultan's palace) and with few revisions we nationalists, who'd fought all our lives against feudalism, borrowed high Javanese protocol as our guide. What couldn't be stolen totally from their system was bent, twisted, and renovated until it fit the Republic.

This first big diplomatic dinner was to be in the Great Hall of the *istana.* On both sides of the Great Hall glass and curtained doors lead to a foyer. "Bung," instructed Mutahar, "your back will be to the wall and you will clearly be able to see me behind that first door on your right. I'll stand at an angle so that I'll be partially obscured and only from your vantage point can I be seen.

"With regard to the festivities, I have it all arranged. I will waggle with my finger. That means you stand up. I will blink with my eyes. That means you introduce the honored guests. I will nod with my head. This means you should make a toast."

Throughout the entire evening, Mutahar gave signals. I was so deep in political talk and so taken up with trying to solve the grave problems before us all that I never even realized I was blindly following an etiquette expert who didn't know a 21-gun salute from an oyster fork.

We had so many silly protocol problems. A civilian fighter had developed into my aide. It was decided to give him a rank and make him official. "I hereby dub you a lieutenant," I said. "Thank you very much, Pak," he beamed gratefully, obviously highly pleased with his individual promotion from a nothing to an officer.

Immediately we had trouble. One of my advisors hissed, "You can't do that. Queen Juliana of the Netherlands rules over only 10 million subjects and her private adjutant is a colonel. How will it look for Sukarno, President of the Republic of Indonesia, who rules over 70 million, to have only a lieutenant?"

"Quite right," I agreed and summoned my newly commissioned aide-de-camp. "How long have you been a lieutenant?" I asked when he arrived.

"An hour and a half, Pak," he saluted crisply.

"Well, we're a young country and growing fast. As of this afternoon you are a major."

During this truce we tried to build ourselves up domestically. We encouraged the Boy Scout and Girl Scout movements. We started an association of youngsters called the Youth Congress of the Republic and our delegation was admitted to the World Federation of Democratic Youth in 1947. Plans for agricultural progress were outlined. Labor organizations were founded. Physical reconstruction work was begun. Football, high-jumping, javelin-throwing contests were held. We inaugurated a Sports Week and a nationwide Sports Association. We organized English-speaking students for weekly foreign broadcasts. We decreed English as our second language. I established schools from simple elementary village institutions to the first university, which we founded within the walls of the Sultan's *kraton*.

In those days I was accessible to everyone. I had no enemies in Jogja. I walked around freely without guards. I'd play ball with children on my daily afternoon walks. I'd stop into homes and have hot cooked vegetables. I'd make homey conversation with the farmers like "How's your health . . . how many children do you have . . . have you enough food?" Simple questions for simple folk. And for me—simple pleasures.

Nobody called me Mr. President or Your Excellency. At most they combined my official title with my affectionate one. What came out was "President Bung Karno." I was not their Chief of State. I was their Big Brother. Because I was so much one of them they came to me for everything. A new minister charged that his predecessor's automobile went with the ministerial post and should, therefore, be passed on to him. The predecessor countered the automobile was given him originally when he was a Japanese official and therefore was now his personal possession. Who do you think had to arbitrate this crisis? The President.

In 1946 and 1947 people didn't understand what a President's duties were. They also didn't understand exactly what independence meant. Following our declaration that everybody was free we had difficulty making the Marhaens pay passage in the tram cars. "Why?" they'd cry with a hurt and bewildered look. "We're free, aren't we?"

In the months immediately succeeding Linggadjati, the battlefront of the Revolution had moved to the conference table. During this period of truce our representatives were supposedly cooperating to implement the points in the agreement. But the threat of war hung heavily over us. The mighty giants of the West had no respect for their lilliputian brothers. Our voices were raised, but our opinions were not heard. I realized an Asian nation which did not possess military preparedness would never be respected. We had no wish to be warlike, but we had no wish to be humiliated any more either. The Republic had no alternative but to bolster its armed forces.

Our air force began with one pilot and a handful of junked Dutch planes. Volunteers were put through a rigorous examination. The sole question asked was, "Would you dare go up in our planes?" If they answered, "Yes," they were inducted into the air force. We began the navy with a few wooden vessels. When the first anniversary of our armed forces actually came around it was a thrilling day for us. To give it the full pomp and pageantry due the occasion, it was decided I should review the troops on horseback. The only trouble was—I didn't know how to ride a horse.

"What will you do?" fretted Fatmawati.

"I will first face the fact that I am a vain man," I answered. "I will, therefore, do what a vain man would do. I will take riding lessons."

"But the parade is tomorrow," she gasped.

"Then I shall have to learn all in one day," I answered.

After my lesson I instructed the cavalry man in charge to "Give me a very meek, old, tame, nearly dead horse for the parade."

But the officer said, "Oh, no, Bapak. Not for you. Your horse must be young and snorting. He must exhibit a fighting spirit and be the best looking of the whole group."

I was, frankly, considerably nervous. I'd never controlled a horse before. My previous contact had been limited to petting one's neck. I also learned the particular animal they selected had never ridden to the sound of music before. They intended giving him a one-day con-centrated course on how not to get excited.

Well, the bugles blew, the drums rolled, the troops stiffened and I mounted up. The horse got carried away with the music. He went wild. But suddenly I saw the hordes lined up to see me and my vanity took over. The cheers and screams of the millions at the parade ground were like elixir. With a flick of my wrist I mastered him with precision. I bent him so perfectly to my will that he moved in slow, measured steps just as I wanted him to. That nice horse never knew that I was more scared than he was.

Along with my troops I, too, was in uniform. I'd personally designed one that looked well and authoritative, yet cost nothing. It was a long-sleeved, open-collar white shirt with military pockets. The shirt was worn outside the trousers. It was cheaper than a jacket, looked trim for evening ceremonies and served well as a functional work uniform. Everybody adopted this "Bung Karno Style" and it was quite a rage throughout the Revolution. It became a national suit. People even had it made out of bedsheets.

The Dutch were slowly beginning what they termed "Pacifica-tion Exercises." They had to "pacify" those nationalists in territories which, under the USI agreement, fell under Netherlands jurisdiction. In this regard Indonesia will never forget the "Westerling Affair," in which Holland's notorious Captain Westerling "pacified" 40,000 ci-vilians and soldiers in one area of Celebes. His method was butchery, beheading, and methodical annihilation by means of firing squads.

Nor will we forget Lieutenant Governor General Van Mook ordering NICA soldiers to ransack a civilian mission hospital belong-ing to us. Van Mook thought it was used by guerrillas. He made up for his error by murdering all the women and children anyhow. Even an aged man who lay in bed with his hands up was shot dead.

On the heels of this mayhem, word came that Van Mook had captured General Imamura and was bringing him to Djakarta to stand trial as a war criminal. There was talk of hanging him without bringing him to court. Imamura had many talks with me over the years. He was a true military gentleman who fought for his country honorably. He was no butcher. Secretly I sent my men to Imamura's cell with this message, "If you wish to be liberated, say the word. Our President's orders are to break you out and take you to safety."

Answered Imamura, "I am a true Samurai. I am not guilty of the killing of unarmed Dutch nationals. I have committed no atrocities. Unflinchingly I shall face whatever it is as a noble officer. Thank your President, but send word I remain where I am."

This Japanese knight had kicked hell out of the Dutch, who were at this moment committing the atrocities with which they were charging him. I wanted to save him. I sent a warning to Van Mook: "Execute Imamura and I go on an international radio hookup and publicly accuse you of stabbing, raping, and bludgeoning innocent women. I tell you straight out I will prove to the world the war crimes you yourself have committed."

Imamura was sentenced to 10 years. It was Sukarno who saved his life.

Diplomatically, my country was doing poorly. Linggadjati had established broad principles of agreement with specific details to be worked out subsequently, but Holland was hungry. Her appetite for second helpings of territory increased daily. Discussions became heated. Pros and cons of Linggadjati flared up. On Holland's side all points became "flexible" subject to "individual interpretation."

Hope for a settlement grew feebler. Internal pressure was applied by a handful of enlightened Dutch liberals to Holland's emisseries, who could not see that what had transpired in India, Burma, the Philippines, Pakistan, Ceylon, and all around Asia was happening to them. The death knell of colonialism was tolling in The Hague. But the reactionary Dutch wouldn't listen.

Fresh atrocities were committed daily. Puppet states in our outlying regions were set up. Repeated border clashes were provoked. Patrols were gunned down. Houses were burned to the ground for "hiding guerrillas." Then began what the Netherlands termed "Mopping Up Operations." They shelled Palembang and Medan in Sumatra and cities like Modjokerto in East Java. Thousands fell victim. A thousand and one reasons were forwarded by Van Mook to justify this genocide. The excuse for attacking Sumatra was "starvation." Indonesians were suffering hunger and the Dutch wanted to come in and feed them, he said, but their humane efforts were being misunderstood, he said. Yes, our people were hungry, but it was due to Van

Mook's tight blockade which permitted no supplies to get through. The excuse for invading Java was "the Republican government couldn't control its dissident extremist elements." Yes, we had dissidents, but it was because of too great concessions at Linggadjati.

Indications reached me that a full-scale invasion was brewing. I wired Van Mook in Djakarta: "This is our holy month of fasting. I warn you that to start war against Moslems during Ramadan will cause you great destruction. You must lose. When freedom is threatened and opposition waged in retaliation, Islam considers war holy and defense tactics purifying. We will, therefore, be blessed. Against this you cannot stand."

Van Mook paid no attention. Early on the morning of July 21, 1947, tanks, soldiers, ships, and bombers unleashed attacks against Java, Madura, and Sumatra. It was well planned. To marshal such might required long-range planning, before and even during Linggadjati. This was no spur-of-the-moment toy invasion. Armored columns and powerful air and sea support launched all-out death to the Republic. They called it by the cute term "a police action."

The work of police is to maintain security, keep away bandits, arrest thieves. But to rain down bullets, bombs, and dynamite and to make use of modern weapons, mortars, and cannon on an infant nation that has no armed strength is NOT a police action. It's war. An all-out war. They named it a "police action" because they claimed it was not to crush the Republic, but merely "to arrest some guilty persons."

By bombing our millions? That's arresting some guilty persons?

To justify themselves, the Netherlands charged we'd acted in direct violation of Linggadjati by seeking diplomatic recognition from foreign governments. Had we not done so, we wouldn't have survived. It was the outside world that sprang to our defense.

Tank-tipped mechanized columns cut deep into Republican arteries. Within five days they penetrated hundreds of miles into our strongholds. Within two weeks they took most of our cities, major towns, communications media, and harbors. Against such formidable strength, the weak, unprepared Republican forces could not stand.

A few days later Pak Ichsan, my palace secretary, said, "The action is all around us. Any day it will strike Jogja. You must flee immediately to the hills of Madiun. Friends there have found us a coffee plantation set back in the slope of the mountain where we may hide out and be safe. Madiun is far enough away to be free of harm, yet close enough in case of emergency."

Leaving our home was difficult because we now had two babies. In January my daughter was born. We had wanted a girl so badly. Before Fatmawati even became pregnant she dreamt my father gave her a red *kembang sepatu* flower. This meant clearly she'd soon bear a daughter. Never will I forget the night of January 23. It was thundering. My wife lay in the bedroom which had been outfitted specially as a hospital. Suddenly the lights went out, the roof caved in, the dark, swollen clouds opened and water rained in like a river.

The doctor and the Sisters carried Fatmawati into her own sleeping room. She was soaked, as were the instruments, bedclothes, everything. In the darkness, by the light of a candle, our daughter was born. We named her Megawati. Mega means clouds.

I now looked at my sleeping daughter. She was following in the path of her brother. It seemed my babies were always to spend their first year on earth in running and hiding.

Guards still surrounded the *istana,* so it looked as though I were officially in residence. Those few who accompanied us were not allowed to tell their families they were going away. For the first month they were permitted no communication and none of their loved ones knew their whereabouts. It was the only way to maintain top security. None balked. None asked questions. Not one asked where we were going or for how long. There was nothing—no wife, no child—more important to any of them than the success of the Revolution. They obeyed blindly.

We took no servants. The larger the company you travel with, the greater your chances of detection. The First Lady of the land nursed the children and cooked and cleaned herself. The 80-mile drive up steep slopes was too far from the city of Madiun for newspaper or radio reports. Nor could I go for walks since not even the neighbors knew I was there. I didn't have a dog to pet either because it was too cold for animals.

Via an elaborate system we maintained the appearance that I was still in Jogja. Every day at one o'clock, we had a standing radio telephone hookup between the *istana* and the plantation. When urgent appointments had to be kept, we'd leave the plantation at sundown, board a special train complete with bed and shower and arrive at Jogja before sunup. Late that night it was back to Madiun until another important engagement had to be kept. Occasionally, Fatma made the trip so she, too, could be seen in Jogja. Also, we periodically changed aides lest certain faces be permanently missing from the *istana*. We maintained this arrangement for several months.

In this all-out act of Dutch aggression our casualties were surprisingly low. The reason was that our armies avoided frontal combat with the heavily mechanized Dutch troops. Instead they withdrew from the flat terrain on which tanks navigate and melted back into the mountains and hills. Westerners had never fought in bushes. Their setup was roads and streets. We were too ill-equipped to fight their way so we forced them into fighting our way.

Our forces couldn't destroy tanks and mortars, so they destroyed the target at which these tanks and mortars were pointed. Heavy artillery is aimed at large objects. Our tactic was to never permit large objects such as a large detachment of troops. Only little handfuls of marauders. Three men would blow up a bridge. Two men would destroy an oil drum. You can't shoot an object you can't see so always they remained hidden behind trees, in bushes, lying flat. Once my men disappeared from the cities and took to the jungles they had nothing to fear from tanks or aircraft. Holland's expensive equipment was useless.

One of the five principles of war is surprise. The best way to defend is to attack. By watching the Dutch *modus operandi,* my generals ascertained that when the enemy headed for a maneuver they were physically and mentally prepared. Rule one was never attack full scale when they're in this state of readiness, but launch a token frontal assault which is just enough to make them feel cocky. My men observed that after the opposition felt they'd been successful, they'd be relaxed and whistling and off guard on the way home. That's when my boys would kill.

Holland could never win an all-out war because she was fighting Indonesia. And Indonesia consists of villages. And our villagers live on *gotong royong.* Guerrillas did not live in camps. They lived right with the families they were protecting. They worked on their fields, slept in their huts, ate their food, integrated with them. When the people are with you it's impossible for the enemy to win.

Let me show how our guerrillas worked. A soldier only has calluses inside his index finger and inside his thumb. That's where he holds his gun. Even when standing at attention, those two fingers are in use holding the gun at his side. A soldier's left hand is always clean. The feet are another give-away. A soldier's toes are close together because he wears shoes. But after a raid our guerrillas disappeared into the villages and labored in the fields with the peasants. The Indonesian system of rice planting is the wet system. From planting and seeding and wading nearly to their knees in water, the guerrillas had spread toes and all of their hands were callused, not just the two fingers. No Dutch spies could tell our soldiers apart from our field workers.

Ten guerrillas to one village constituted a squad. Three neighboring villages constituted a platoon. In the center of a company of 150 was set the battalion commander, who periodically toured his area. Each tour took a week. Every inch of terrain had to be crossed on foot. The platoons were connected by couriers who issued warnings by means of the village chief's *ketongan*. Two blasts on this hollow wood pipe meant there was an ambush. A rising tone meant a troop was coming. When the signal came, villagers ran to the valleys and guerrillas manned the houses and fields. They had no uniforms. Nothing about them looked military.

Women fought, too. Our Revolution created freedom for the sexes as well. No more shrinking Moslem women. They were not second-class citizens in the new world. A female in Indonesia can even become President of the Republic. During the Sriwidjaja and Madjapahit empires we had Commanders-in-Chief who were women. A few hundred years later our little girls from the village were just as tough.

They fought with braids and slacks and tommyguns. Our women walked around wearing ammunition belts, their only jewelry being a gleaming rifle. I had a secretary from Pulau Tello Island. A beautiful girl. One day she came to me carrying a bag. "What's in the bag?" I inquired.

"Would you really like to see?" she asked.

"Of course."

She opened it and dumped it out at my feet. It was the bloody head of a Dutchman. "This is my first trophy, Bapak," she squealed gleefully. "And it's all for you."

"Get out of here with that," I screamed at the top of my lungs. "Get out."

I think she was a little hurt that I didn't appreciate her present.

The Dutch aggression had created a stir throughout the world. There was much sympathy for our cause. Egypt and Australia boycotted Dutch ships. India's response was prompt. "What has become of the United Nations charter?" asked Nehru of the world. "No European country has any business to set its army in Asia against our people. When it does so the spirit of new Asia will not tolerate such things."

The United States denounced the aggression vocally, but it took

India and Australia to formally lay our pain before the Security Council. The Security Council ordered a Cease Fire. The Republic obeyed by ordering its troops to cease fire. The Netherlands obeyed by ordering its troops to cease fire. The only ones who didn't obey were the Netherlands troops who steadfastly penetrated deeper into Republican territory. When it comes to cease-fire terminology I guess I don't understand English. Or Dutch. To me it means "stand fast." But the British interpretation in Surabaya was a surrender order. And the Dutch interpretation everywhere was "fire when ready."

The Security Council dispatched a Committee of Good Offices, comprised of delegates from Belgium, Australia, and France, to negotiate another truce. This was a painful period for our new country. We were in the position of begging for the good will of all nations in the world. We always walked around with our hand out. Only the alms we pleaded for were understanding and acceptance. The kind of charity we wanted was the kind Jesus preached.

On the eighth of December, 1947, the Good Offices Committee opened negotiations aboard neutral territory, the unarmed U.S. naval transport *Renville,* which had been anchored in Philippine waters. Holland refused all three of the Committee's compromise proposals and submitted her own 12-point program providing the same shackles that had bound us at Linggadjati but adding several more. Among our new losses were the territorial gains the Dutch had made since the aggression; they would now remain permanently theirs. The three islands of Sumatra, Java, and Madura, constituting our entire Republic, were eaten into so that Holland annexed West Java, East Sumatra, and Madura to her territories.

At this rate it wouldn't take long before we'd be back where we were in 1942, several wars and much bloodshed ago. We were further informed "liberty of action would be resumed" were these points "not accepted unconditionally by the Republic."

That meant war. Dutch troops were already moving. I was violently opposed. So was our whole Cabinet. It was a thoroughly unacceptable, unpalatable, and unfair proposal. However, my commanders informed me of their critical shortage of ammunition and supplies. We couldn't hold out under another attack. There was no choice but to negotiate. And fast. The Hague gave us only a matter of hours.

We wrangled, haggled, and prayed. Finally we submitted a counterproposal of six points calling for the continuance of the U.N.

role in Indonesian affairs, which, at least, guaranteed recognition of the Republic by the world, plus a future plebiscite, conducted under the Good Offices Committee's scrutiny, to determine whether the Dutch-held areas of the Republic chose to remain under Dutch jurisdiction or return to the Motherland. We were taking our fight from the bullet to the ballot.

And so the *Renville* agreement was signed. It won us no freedom. It gave us only a reprieve.

◅ 29. Bangka

IN December, 1948, the Dutch dropped a package of Christmas cheer down my chimney. At 5:30 in the morning of Sunday, the 19th, they bombed Jogjakarta.

Barring a pitiful handful, our entire army was outside the town on maneuvers. At first, when dozens of bombers darkened the skies, our people thought, "Oh, how nice that we have so many airplanes we can get together for a routine drill."

One hour of heavy bombing interlaced with rocket-firing P-51's and the Dutch had captured the airport. Low-flying Spitfires strafed the streets lengthwise and crosswise. The heavens were black with airplanes. One thousand paratroopers took the post office and radio station, and set fire to the automobiles. The Republic's skeleton army was taken prisoner. The Dutch had a cute trick of transporting people to places of detention in hermetically sealed boxcars so that all arrived dead. By noon Jogja was surrounded.

Two hours before the landing, our army Commander-in-Chief, Sudirman, who was still in his 20's, woke me up. Revealing his advance information, he pleaded, "I urge you to escape. My plan is to flee the city into the jungles. Come with us."

Hurriedly dressing myself, I said, "You are a soldier. Your place is in the field with your men. It is not my place to escape. I must remain here that I may be in a position to bargain for us and to lead us."

"There is probably a price on your head. If you stay they may kill you."

"And if I run they may shoot me. Either way I face death, but don't worry; I have no fear."

"Our men bury the Dutch dead. Our way has been to fight civilized, but . . ." Sudirman clenched his fists ". . . we will send word if anybody harms Sukarno there will be no mercy. It will be mass murder."

My sitting room opened out onto a verandah. Sudirman darted out and looked anxiously at the sky. There was still no sign. "Have you any last-minute instructions before I leave?" he asked.

"Yes. Put up no fight on the streets of Jogja. We haven't a chance. But get your army outside the cities, General, and fight to the death. I order you to spread them through the villages. Infect the country-side with them. Put them behind every bush. This is 100 percent total guerrilla warfare. Though we return to amputations without anesthesia and sterilized banana leaves for bandages, let the world never say independence was awarded us out of a diplomat's brief-case. Let them know we bought it and paid dearly with our blood and sweat and determination.

"And don't come out of the hills until your President orders you to. Remember, even if your leaders are taken, the next man, be he soldier or civilian, must take over. Let it be agreed Indonesia will NEVER NEVER EVER SURRENDER."

I did not even think to send out my family. When the first bombs dropped, I quickly took Fatmawati and my two babies into the back room of the palace because the military barracks in front of the *istana* was hit repeatedly. Poor Guntur. My poor child. He kept shivering. All I could do was cover him with a straw matting and protect him with my body.

Hurrying from their homes, the Cabinet assembled in varying stages of disarray in the little room behind the Great Hall for what-ever last-minute frantic preparations could be made. Plans were hastily drawn for a war cabinet embodying those ministers who were outside Jogja that day. "We shall go ahead with preparations for moving the seat of the government," I announced to Hatta, Sjahrir, Lemeina, Air Marshal Suryadarma, and the others assembled. "As per our plan in just such a case of emergency as this, the provisional government of the Republic will be transferred to Sumatra."

We fashioned a quick draft of an announcement for broadcast. It was only a couple of lines, but knowing we were already encircled and this was our final opportunity, we dispatched a courier, and our last communication, before Radio Republic Indonesia went off the air, was a message to the world.

The telegraph office was in the home of a man who lived nearby. Before it was seized we managed to send two cables, one to Sumatra giving it full powers to form an interim government, the other to New Delhi, our nearest embassy, with instructions to make contact with the new government in Sumatra.

I ordered our important papers burned to prevent their falling into Dutch hands. There was no time to select which documents to salvage so all the records we had amassed from the time of the Japanese occupation straight up through the Revolution were destroyed. By accident the *Pantja Sila* and a copy of the Constitution were saved.

My last act was to call Mutahar to my private chambers. "Whatever may happen to me I don't know," I said simply. "But I hereby give you an order. No matter what, I commission you to safeguard our holy flag with your life. It must not fall into enemy hands. Some day, *Inshallah,* you must return it to me personally and into the hands of no other unless he be the leader who replaces me. If you die saving this flag, another must be entrusted with the obligation and he must then give it into my hands personally as you would have done."

From the day we made our proclamation the sacred *Merah Putih* had flown day in and night out, through rain and gunfire, until we moved to Jogja. On the train I'd carried it folded inside my own personal case. Here it was kept in the safe and flown only on August 17. The red part was faded pink, but in our hearts it was as crimson as the blood that was spilled to save it.

Mutahar fell silent. He closed his eyes and prayed. All around us was bombardment. The Dutch were pouring in through every street. His was a heavy responsibility. He finally resolved the situation by plucking out the threads by hand and separating the two halves. The white part he hid inside his clothing, the red part in his suitcase.

It was a very tense morning. And yet I was icy calm. God gives me total lack of feeling in times of great emotional stress. At 1:30 the Colonial Army lined up with machineguns across from the *istana*. My small palace guard, less than one platoon, resisted valiantly, but in the face of overwhelming odds I ordered them to lay down their arms. Mid-afternoon I dispatched a guard with a white flag. For good measure, the Dutch machinegunned the front hall and strafed the inside. The *istana* was so closely surrounded that I even heard the communication from Colonel Van Langen, who was in charge of storming the gates. He radioed his commanding general, "Sir, I am reporting we have captured Dr. Sukarno and are keeping him here."

I said to myself, "OK. If it occurs like this then it is the will of Allah. I need not fear."

At five P.M. the conquering heroes strutted through the *istana*, checked every room, window, door and exit, posted guards in front of each and requisitioned all the armament. The Colonel marched up to me smartly and announced, "You are under arrest." Turning to the servants, the rest of the palace staff, their families and the Cabinet, he made the pronouncement, "If in future any weapon is found on your persons every single one of you will be shot on the spot."

The Commanding General sent an armed party of six to fetch me to his headquarters by jeep. That is the small soul of the Dutch. Is a jeep what a President deserves? The Articles of War specifically mention that officers or persons of high station must be accorded courtesies commensurate with their rank. According to the military code, even if a major captures a colonel he is to salute his prisoner. But our conquerors did not treat me like a President because I was NOT a President in their eyes.

In a large office behind a large desk and in an even larger chair sat the General. His staff officers stood grouped behind him. On the other side of the desk, all alone, facing this battery of Dutch brass, was Sukarno.

The General demanded, "Mr. Sukarno, order your army to surrender. If you do not, your total force will be exterminated within one week's time. This I promise you."

Then he peered around smugly at his seconds and boasted, "It's all over for you and your country. You see, we already have your men pinpointed on the maps. We know your positions. You haven't a chance in the world. We'll use our air force, artillery, and infantry against you. We'll hit you with planes, tanks, guns. To avoid unnecessary bloodshed, I suggest you order your army to surrender."

Sitting there alone, facing my squadron of conquerors, I had been silent all this time. Now, slowly, in a very quiet voice, I made my simple reply. "General, is it that I am a prisoner or is it that I am a President? If I am a President I can negotiate. If I am a prisoner I cannot give that order."

There was no further talk. The General sent me back to the palace.

We were 150 internees in the *istana* under house arrest. At first we ate leftovers from our cupboard plus garden vegetables. Then the military supplied us with tins of corned beef and rice. We were allowed to walk around the *istana,* but were not permitted out. No outsider was permitted in.

It was nerve-wracking. The enemy didn't rough me up in any way other than talking disrespectfully. But, after all, I'm just a human being. Who knew what they were going to do with me? The feeling was they were going to kill me. I didn't know what to expect. The others gathered in the Great Hall to talk in low tones, but not I. I stayed mainly confined to my room. Every time I heard a strange sound I thought, "Uh-oh, here it comes. They're going to march me toward a firing squad." It was the first time I was a prisoner as a President. That somehow added burdens to me.

At seven A.M. on the 22nd, Colonel Van Langen, without any advance notice, gave me five minutes to pack two small cases and bid my family goodbye. Perhaps forever. I was bundled aboard a B-25 where elaborate security precautions were kept until the last. "Where are we headed?" I asked the officer in charge.

"I don't know," he grunted.

"Well, who knows this deep dark secret?"

"Perhaps the pilot."

"No, I don't know either," shrugged the pilot.

"Well, how are you going to fly this plane if you don't know where to?"

"After we're airborne, my orders are to take from my travelbag a leather-covered packet."

When we were thousands of feet in the air, the pilot broke the seal, unrolled his top-secret document, and then headed the bomber according to the confidential orders. He still would not reveal where we were going.

Sjahrir and a grand old freedom fighter, Pak Hadji Agus Salim, accompanied me. It was apparent old man Hadji wasn't feeling at all well. He had a blinding headache. The soldier assigned to watch Hadji was no officer or intellectual. Just a human with a heart who could not seem to understand why all this fighting. "What is this all about?" he kept asking. He had been told his army was LIBERATING us. A fair-minded enemy who felt sympathy for our cause, he cradled Hadji's head on his lap for the whole trip. When we landed in North Sumatra, I thanked him for his humanity. And I thanked him in good Dutch, too.

Berastagi was Bengkulu all over again. Only with a couple of differences. One—they didn't call it exile. Now it was termed being "in protective custody." Two—we weren't allowed our wives. And three—we were behind double rows of barbed wire, and between our house and the barbed wire six men with rifles patrolled in relays.

The lady who cooked for us liked me. Our second afternoon there, she slipped into my room trembling with fear. "Sir," she quaked, "I asked what I should cook for your supper tomorrow and the officer in charge said, 'Not a thing. Sukarno's going to be shot in the morning.' "

I was the most fearful I'd ever been in my life. I was in an icy sweat. I shut my eyes tightly and concentrated with all my soul. There is something about the stamina or faith of the Indonesians. They withstood, knowing that some day . . . somehow . . . *Inshallah*. . . . With me it was the same.

I prayed, "Dear God, I rely wholly on Your will. In everything I submit to You. Give me a sign. Show me You are with me."

I picked up my Koran, clasped it tightly to my breast and said, "No matter where I open this book, my sign will come from the first sentence on the left page." With trembling hands I opened the little green book at random. The top line on the left hand side read, "Do not believe what comes from the mouth of man. Only God Almighty knows the fate of His children."

That night our captors suddenly realized Berastagi was undefendable. There was a great flurry of plans and very early the next morning they moved us. They didn't even take time out to kill me.

Our band of exiles were driven a day's ride to Lake Toba in Prapat. The Dutch had taken this peninsula, which is filled with scented pine trees, in the first military action and they'd held it ever since. Before the war it had been used as an elegant resort. The homes were beautiful. Ours was set high up on the edge of a cliff overlooking the lake. Very picturesque. Also very inaccessible. We were surrounded on three sides by water. The rear of the house was on the mainland, reachable by means of a winding road.

One moonless night a group of young men tried to rescue Bung Karno. Unknown to me they rowed over the lake silently in a small boat. I was in my room, on the ground floor off the entrance hall. In the stillness I heard shots right next to my wall. They must have been very near. My windows fronted the lake, but the night was black. I saw nothing. And I was not permitted outside.

The next morning our servant whispered, "The boys were shot dead by the Dutch. Each one of them. But there isn't a sign of what happened." Today it's a government guesthouse and whoever sleeps in the "Sukarno Room" claims he feels ghosts walking around. The village is convinced the spirits of the heroes who tried to save Bung Karno are still present.

Our servant was Indonesian. One night he told me, "Not even

my son knows you are in our town. The Dutch made me swear I would tell nobody. They threatened to shoot not only me but my entire family if I passed the word."

"Do they watch you when you leave at night?"

"Yes, Pak," he answered. "My house is up on stilts and I know they're spying on me because the other morning I found Western cigarettes on the ground right under our floorboards."

This poverty-stricken servant, Ludin, used to bring food from his house—sometimes chicken, sometimes cake—because we didn't get enough to eat. After all, we were just prisoners. They figured why look after us too well. Wasn't important that we be cared for and well fed. Why waste money?

Ludin had contact with the guerrillas and one morning they sent word to him that "since you go to the market place every day there will be no suspicion attached to that area. That is where we will make contact from now on. Take your messages out rolled up in a leaf in your mouth or inserted in your trouser cuff. We will make the exchange when you pay for the foods. We will hand you a certain chicken. Look under the wings for your orders. Or we will hand you a fish. Cut open the belly for your orders."

Although the guards checked all incoming packages to make sure I had no radio or way of learning what was happening on the outside, they never noticed our food parcels from the *pasar* were carefully wrapped in the daily newspaper.

Kangkong is a reedy plant. The stem is thin and hollow like a hard piece of bamboo. From a stick of *kangkong* inserted in a fish's mouth came news that our guerrillas would stage a raid to rescue us. That night, a group tried to force their way through the barbed wire.

"Quick, go upstairs to the second landing and give the signal that it is too dangerous for them to come closer," I said to Pak Hadji. He lit a candle and put it in the window, but it was too late. The Dutch caught sight of the raiders and there was a gun battle. Only a few got away.

To be living together as exiles 24 hours a day does not make for harmony. And when two of the exiles are Sjahrir and Sukarno it is not harmonious at all. Whenever he had the opportunity, no matter who was around, Sjahrir cursed me. In front of anybody he would yell to my face, "You are stupid, Sukarno. You are a plain, bloody old fool, that's what."

He blamed the invasion on me. Nehru had invited me to India

to discuss our critical situation with other Asian leaders. My imminent departure was known to everyone because a President is not a private citizen who can leave his country at will, particularly a country in the throes of war. He has to tell his people. He cannot just take off without letting them know.

"You had to shoot your mouth off on radio and say, 'Look here, people, I, your President, am going to India,'" sneered Sjahrir to me. "Right after your big announcement, the Dutch invaded us. Why did you give them an opportunity to know you were leaving? I'll tell you why. Because you're stupid, that's why."

And this was after I'd risked my neck politically to save his. In 1946, he was kidnapped by a group violently opposed to his manner of giving in to the Dutch. I went on radio and broadcast an appeal to the kidnappers. "The Republic needs Sjahrir," I said. "Sukarno needs him." That's all it took. He was immediately released.

His gratitude showed in many ways, particularly this night when he was furious and raged at me at the top of his lungs. There were many people around. I answered very quietly, "Sjahrir, you are the stupid one. Don't you think the Dutch have their intelligence men around? They knew our every move even when it wasn't publicly announced."

In January, after we had been in Prapat a couple of weeks, the Prime Minister of the Netherlands, Dr. Drees, asked to speak to Sjahrir instead of Sukarno "because Sjahrir is more pro-Dutch."

Sjahrir jumped at the opportunity to go to Djakarta and be the big man of the Republic. "I am dead against this move," I warned. "Again it is negotiating from the standpoint of a prisoner."

We were sitting in the small living room onto which our three bedrooms opened. "I will only go," he swore, "to report back to you what is really in the minds of those Dutchmen. In one week I shall return and we shall discuss everything that happened."

The agreed-upon week went by. He did not come back. He never came back. He never reported. He went to Djakarta, had a talk with the Dutch Prime Minister, showed his willingness to cooperate and ended up a free man.

He told the Dutch I didn't mind exile because I had seven mirrors in my room. A lie. I had no mirrors in my room. Again a little thing but it hurts very much because it is so mean.

In late January I was transferred by Catalina to the island of Bangka, where Hatta, Air Marshal Suryadarma, my old PNI cohort

Ali Sastroamidjojo, and others were interned together. "Maybe this is a good sign," I remarked to Hadji. "Maybe they're putting the whole government of the Republic together because it's easier to negotiate."

"More likely it's because they hope we'll kill each other off," cracked Hadji.

In the beginning our Revolution had gone badly. Despite anguished diplomatic cries that they were in violation of the United Nations charter, the Dutch paid no mind. They took city after city. We were desperate. It looked as though we were all through. But on the first of March our guerrillas retook Jogja. They held it for six hours, long enough to show the world ours was a vital force that would never give up.

When the Security Council reported that Holland had invaded us while the *Renville* truce was still fully operative, the world called it a second Pearl Harbor. The British lion, with a paw on her juicy interests in Malaya, roared disapproval. Nineteen Asian nations convened in Delhi and the boycotting of Dutch goods began. American taxpayers screamed their protest upon learning that the millions Holland was receiving under the Marshall Plan coincided almost exactly with the amount it cost Holland to maintain her armies in the Indies. The arithmetic was embarrassing for the United States. Torn between loyalty to her European ally and responsibility to the spirit of '76, the U.S.A. finally hit postwar Holland where she was most vulnerable. Over and above the explosion of Dutch bombs and the cries of universal outrage, The Hague heard the sound of the American wallet snap shut.

While the courts of the world judged our fate, Indonesia took the law into her own hands. When General Sudirman issued the order to return to the lines, our "guerrillas" of 12, 13 and 14 years walked 300 miles—it took over a month—to reoccupy the pockets they'd held at the time of the *Renville*'s so-called cease fire. Dutch Imperialism would have to bow the knee because it was now all-out death, do or die.

If you tell me, as an engineer, "Hey, Sukarno, build a dam to kill the energies of the river so that it will no longer flow into the ocean," I must tell you it cannot be done. Every second more and more pressure will build up behind that dam. Every drop of water wants to reach the ocean. Finally the dam will break and the river will flow.

It is the same with freedom. From my Alcatraz on Bangka, I knew our 350-year sentence was at an end.

While the Netherlands held the cities, our soldiers took the highways leading to them, the towns surrounding them, the food coming into them. We had the villages, side roads, lakes, *kampongs,* the hills, the whole of what comprises Indonesia. Their cities were so cut off that several could only be supplied by airlifts. Come darkness our guerrillas infiltrated the cities, attacked the enemy positions, blew up their trains and convoys, set fire to their provisions. The enemy had to battle for survival just to live through the night. A road they'd repair by day would be destroyed at night. The Dutch became confused. They didn't know where we'd strike. They hadn't men enough to blanket the entire terrain. All their forces were walled up within metropolises. At night their cities were under siege. By day their cities fell under a subtler form of destruction.

Sabotage and obstruct, that was our slogan. Every child of six was a potential saboteur. Then, too, our tactic was 100 percent non-cooperation. No Indonesian civil servants would man Dutch offices or Dutch transport works. No Indonesian laborer would work their plantations. They could not even get their administrative bureaus functioning. To prevent anyone having to turn to the enemy for food, guerrilla "rice kitchens" were set up so our people could get the barest minimum to keep themselves alive.

The Republic, on the other hand, continued to operate. Local administrations met and transacted "business" under the open sky or crouched behind a bamboo tree. Guerrillas opened elementary schools and trading centers in the villages. Peta-trained officers conducted courses which every three months graduated more teen-aged soldiers. Our people are used to military authority. In some form they've lived under it all their lives. They were so attuned to respecting the man with the gun that one guerrilla put a civilian under arrest just by telephoning and ordering him confined to his hut. The civilian complied.

I had been in Bangka a few months when the situation worsened considerably for the Dutch. They sent word they wanted a *musjawarah.* They had to talk with me because they were losing battles everywhere. Their casualties and list of dead mounted nightly. It became obvious no matter how much money or how many troops poured in, it was utterly impossible for them to win the war. They hadn't a chance. This could drag on endlessly, for years and years, and their casualties were heavy, with no prospect in sight of their lessening. Holland faced the bitter fact she'd have to capitulate . . . and soon.

Much as Holland disliked the idea she realized she could *musjawarah* all she liked with the other leaders, but the men in the field— the generals, guerrillas, the masses—would make no move to stop if it didn't come directly from Sukarno. My answer was, "Restore the Republic. Restore Sukarno as President of the Republic and I will *musjawarah*. Not before."

Thus began a long procession of diplomats and couriers to the sleepy tin-mining town of Montok on Bangka. The final compromise of the Rum-Royen agreement was reached on my kitchen table in the miners' boarding house where I lived. Van Royen, representing Holland, agreed they'd restore the Republic's leaders. Dr. Mohammad Rum, representing Indonesia, agreed we'd recall the Republic's guerrillas. And both sides agreed to a Round Table Conference in The Hague to discuss the transfer of sovereignty to the Republic.

The Round Table Conference convened in August. Dutch stubbornness dies slowly. The *musjawarah* dragged on. However, time had run out for colonialism. We agreed to incur the debts of the former Netherlands East Indies regime amounting to 1,130,000,000 dollars. To saddle an underdeveloped colonized country which had suffered extensive devastation from three years of occupation and four years of revolution with a sum of such magnitude was unfair. But in turn they agreed to the irrevocable, unconditional and immediate recognition of our sovereignty over the whole of the former Netherlands East Indies, excepting West New Guinea.

The 28th of December, 1949, Bung Karno triumphantly came "home." Overnight two Royal Dutch KLM airplanes had been repainted with the sign of the Garuda, the Indonesian mythological eagle. At 11:40 A.M., the presidential vanguard, the sole plane of the day-old Garuda Indonesian Airways, taxied into Kemayoran Airport in Djakarta. First off was the honor guard bearing the sacred *Merah Putih*, which Mutahar had preserved with its original needleholes. With beating heart I stepped down into the sea of people.

We could not get through the crowds. Millions upon millions flooded the sidewalks, the roads. They were crying, cheering, screaming, "*Hidup* Bung Karno. . . . Long live Bung Karno. . . . *Hidup*. . . . *Merdeka*. . . ." Many were hurt. They ran in front of our car. Others were knocked down. Others were pushed. Some fainted. We were mobbed. I could not proceed forward even an inch at a time. They clung to the sides of the car, the hood, the running boards. They grabbed at me to kiss my fingers.

Soldiers beat a path for me to the topmost step of the big white palace. There I raised both hands high. A stillness swept over the millions. There wasn't a sound. Except for the silent tears nothing moved.

"*Alhamdulillah*—thank God," I cried. "We are free!"

⇥ 30. A Period of Survival

THUS ended our period of struggle. And thus began our struggle for survival. The deed to the house called Indonesia was now securely in our hands, but it was a badly damaged house. It leaked aplenty. Its windows, doors, roof, and walls were broken. Our economy, government administration, transportation systems, communications media, methods of production were all damaged. Even morally and mentally we needed repairs.

When I moved into the big white palace, it was completely empty. The building had been sacked of all treasures. It was par for the Dutch. Every carpet, including the small foot wipers, had been destroyed. The furniture had purposefully been carried off or ruined. Lamps, hinges, doorlocks had been shot at. Mirrors smashed. The front porch had been torn down.

The scene I surveyed from the front hall was typical of my whole country. Challenges overwhelmed us on all sides. With industry completely undeveloped, with insufficient foodstuffs and insufficient confidence, with a people scarred by feudalism, colonialism and Fascism, most of whom couldn't read or write—we still had to pick ourselves up and make order out of chaos. We very nearly sank. The reason was Holland's *denken*—Dutch ways of thinking—which were forced down our throats.

It began back in 1945. Our Constitution was based on a Presidential cabinet like the United States of America. But the Allies who landed on our soil were the British and Dutch and they were accustomed to titular chiefs of state like Queen Juliana, the King of England, or the President of the Republic of France, who had no responsibilities at all.

Their concepts of a society in which the President was liable for what went on had overtones of Nazi Germany or Imperial Japan. "If President Sukarno is Chief of the Government, Commander-in-Chief of the Army, and head of the Cabinet, it is Fascistic," thundered Sir Philip Christison and other British Generals.

264

"And no wonder, since his government is Japanese-influenced," cried The Hague.

"No," we exclaimed, "it is Indonesian-influenced. To us, a head of state is like a head of a family. In Moslem custom the father makes all decisions for his family. The elder or village chief shoulders all burdens for his village. This has been the Indonesian way through centuries." We strove desperately to garner the approval of the world. And so when friends and sympathizers overseas applied pressure to reshape our organs of state to fit Holland's pattern of democracy, our leadership, being mostly Dutch-educated, became unsure and yielded. On November 14, 1945, we changed to a Parliamentary Cabinet with a Prime Minister. In the Round Table Conference this conformity with Holland's *denken* became legal by means of a brand-new constitution. Well, so be it. We were beguiled. Even when they advocated a liberal, multiparty system, we nodded our heads.

In a nation previously denied political activities, the results were immediate. Over 40 dissimilar parties sprang up. So terrified were we of being labeled "a Japanese-sponsored Fascistic dictatorship" that single individuals forming splinter organizations were tolerated as "mouthpieces of democracy." Political parties grew like weeds with shallow roots and interests top-heavy with petty selfishness and vote-catching. Internal strife grew. We faced disaster, endless conflicts, hair-raising confusion. Indonesians previously pulling together now pulled apart. They were sectioned into religious and geographical boxes, just what I'd sweated all my life to get them out of. Each tried outdoing the other. Constant argument without results, mutual undermining, vying for position, slander, abuse, lethal criticism were the fruits. Every voice demanded to be heard.

I asked party chairmen, "What are your plans for our future if you get into power?" Very few had a concrete picture. Just as with my gutted palace, practically nobody offered constructive ideas outside of "Of course you need a bedroom and a dining room and you need chairs." That was all. Their exact blueprint was vague, undefined. The same with the politicians. Each had a mental "dream house," but how to build it—that they didn't know.

Frustrated energies were channeled into creating crises to topple whatever regime was in power. Almost every six months a cabinet fell and we'd have a brand-new government with new bosses and new resignations. Without real leadership at the helm and with obstacles to welfare and reconstruction monumental, how could a baby country hope to crawl forward and take its place among the adult nations of the world?

That's where the army came in. In 1952 they decided to settle the problem by training their guns on me. Our armed forces were not created by the State but were spontaneously born on a grassroots people-to-people level. Fifty percent of the soldiers today and 90 percent of all officers above the rank of major are ex-guerrillas. They're shareholders of the Revolution.

The habit of relying on the man with the gun carried over to peacetime. Where there was not yet stable civil administration rurally, villagers continued to look to the military for law enforcement. If they were sick it was the local platoon leader who supplied medicine. If they wanted a stepladder, the best-supplied outfit in the area was the army. Theirs is a trust given them by the citizenry. To this day the military feels duty bound to uphold it.

Early the morning of October 17, 1952, two tanks, four armored cars, and thousands of soldiers stormed the gates of *Merdeka* carrying "Dissolve Parliament" signs. An artillery battalion with four cannon rumbled into the surrounding square. British 25-pounders were wheeled up and leveled at me. The show of force reflected the hysteria of the times. It was scarcely intelligent, since the commanders who'd engineered it were inside the *istana* with me.

Colonel Abdul Haris Nasution, in charge of this attempted "half a coup," as he later termed it, pleaded their case. "This is not against you personally, Pak, but against the government system. You must abolish Parliament immediately."

My eyes blazed with anger. "You are right in what you want, but wrong in your method of bringing it about. Sukarno will never yield to pressure. Not for the whole Dutch army and not for one Indonesian battalion!"

"When there's trouble in the country, everybody looks to the army," countered Nasution. "It's the politicians who make the wars and the soldiers who do the dying. It is only right we should have a say in what's happening."

"Say what you like to Bung Karno—YES. But threaten the Father of the Indonesian Republic—NO! NEVER!"

I walked out quietly into the face of the mob who'd been verbally whipped into a frenzy. The entire district was under martial law. Instead of cowering under the power of the field guns, I looked straight into their mouths and fearlessly unleashed the full force of my fury on those who would try to assassinate democracy with a firing squad.

"Uh-oh," gasped one soldier, "what we're doing is wrong. Bapak doesn't want this."

"Yeah. . . ." "Bapak wants different. . . ," chimed in two more standing next to him.

Another shouted, "If Bapak doesn't want this, then . . ."

". . . we don't want it," finished another.

The "coup" failed dismally. The crowd dispersed, cheering *"Hidup* Bung Karno. . . . Long live Bung Karno." Nasution was dismissed. I did not wish to bring division between myself and our land forces so I later reinstated him, saying, "Sukarno is not a small boy and Nasution is not a small boy either. We will remain united because if our enemies succeed in dividing us the Republic will be destroyed."

Just as that hothead of 1945, His Excellency Chairul Saleh, is today my Third Deputy Prime Minister, so General Nasution is my Defense Minister. Many of those crazy young men of earlier days have proved themselves good and loyal assistants. It was not as though we were ever on opposite sides. It was just that we disagreed on tactics. That is the way with revolutionaries.

But the struggle for survival was just beginning. To the outsider there seemed nothing but turbulence in our nation. Our prestige abroad decreased until we became a laughing stock.

"Indonesia?" smirked the already established forces of the world. "She's not ripe enough for independence. . . ." "She can't stabilize herself. . . ." "Has no chance for survival. . . ." "Heading toward chaos. . . ." "Facing doom. . . ."

We understood that these instabilities were inherent in a multi-faceted revolution stemming from centuries of colonial insulation. Ours was an upheaval physically, economically, nationally, socially, and culturally. Time and again our Republic nearly fell and stood up, was hit and hit back. We were steadily attacked from within and without.

Before we could recover from our infections and stand up healthy and sound, economic miseries plus lack of representative leadership sowed seeds of discontent in Sumatra and Sulawesi, and the bosom of Mother Indonesia was ripped wide open with rebellion.

The beginning of 1958 I made a trip abroad. In Thailand, friends warned, "Pak, be watchful. Efforts are being made to break you.

A large-scale rebellion of the outer islands against the central government is in preparation and arms are coming from foreign governments. Do not return to Indonesia. Stay abroad."

Returning to Djakarta, my Cabinet informed me, "A few discon-
tented regional leaders claim three-fourths of all revenue comes
from Sumatra, but only a fraction returns there because most of the
money stays in Java. They complain the country suffers from Dja-
kartaism. They demand a greater division economically. And they
want to *musjawarah* with you. These rebels have already established
their own revolutionary government in Bukittinggi."

I cannot deny that some countrymen have gone against me, but
in every land troublemakers try to take the reins into their own hands
periodically. However, these dissidents were less than refuse. They
were the scum which floats atop the surging, agitated waters of a
revolution. All during our negotiations, they planned to hit the
Republic.

The first stage of our civil war was the cry from the outer islands,
"We want local representation and reconstruction funds for our territories." In stage two these words were discarded for the new words,
"The hell with the Republic's government. Hang Sukarno from the
highest tree. Djakarta is Communist. We are anti-Communist." Because they knew the West jumps at anything which smacks even
falsely of that word, our domestic revolt suddenly became an international affair and in today's cold war setup any involvement with
foreign elements must force you toward one of the two major powers.

When America was born in 1776, like us she had jungles, deserts,
prairies, but not our added burden of maturing in the mechanized
jet age between the power blocs. Still she had troubles. During the
latter half of the nineteenth century, when already many decades old,
she endured civil war. She was divided into two, with each part fighting the other. Negroes in her country are still in a revolution. How
could she then not understand how we, a child of 13 years with a
spirit not yet settled, would have growing pains?

It was no secret that U.S. sympathies lay solidly with the so-
called anti-Communist rebels. Heavy foreign arms entered their
area by ship. Tens of thousands of light, American-made weapons
were dropped by air. Non-Indonesian pilots were smuggled in.
Where did they come from? And where did the money come from
to purchase American Mustangs and bombers?

Often a third party intervenes to solve a conflict, but when they actually bombed us it was more than intervention. A Sunday morning in April, 1958, rebel planes staged a bloody raid on the Christian island of Ambon and they scored a direct hit on a church. The building was demolished. Everyone in it was killed. They sank a Republican vessel in the harbor and all hands went down. In that single run there were 700 casualties. The list of dead was incalculable.

Our boys with their poor ack-ack bit a B-52, and the pilot, with his leg and hip splintered, landed on a coconut tree. Our men brought him to a hospital before the bombs tore him apart. He has the Republic to thank for his life. And who was this paid murderer hired to kill my innocent women and children at worship? An American. The name is Allen Pope.

"The fact that your government is trying to pass him off as a 'Soldier of Fortune' is a ridiculous story," I lashed out to the American Ambassador. "It's childish. It is well known that America, Taiwan, and Britain are actively supporting the rebellion. I submit he is employed by the CIA. Draw a circle around my country and include airfields within refueling distance which can land and supply those planes that are dropping weapons to the rebels. You will find there are not many. These are either British airstrips in Singapore or the American field in the Philippines."

He was silent. "Is that correct?" I demanded.

"It would seem those are the nearest," he answered.

"Suppose Pope's jumping-off place is owned by either Britain or America, would I then not have reason to be angry and curse the imperialist powers who are trying to subvert my country?" I thundered.

I asked why this flier, who had killed so many of us and was to be sentenced to death and had no part in this quarrel to begin with, was making war on me. "Tell me why? Why did he do it?" I asked.

The answer came, "Because he heard you were a Communist and he wanted to contribute in the fight against Communism."

Before strangers signed on to kill Sukarno personally or politically, it seemed they should know something about him. Obviously nobody told Pope it was Sukarno who squashed the Communists in 1948. Indonesia's first Communist uprising was incited by my political teachers from Surabaya, Alimin and Muso, and the man whose life I saved during the occupation, Amir Sjarifuddin. I was not about to let them or anyone else throw God out of my beloved country. I went on radio to stop the bloody battle and, borrowing from Lincoln, pleaded, "The Republic cannot stand against itself. Choose between Sukarno-Hatta and the Communist party, which is forming a Soviet government under Alimin and Muso. With the Almighty's help, Sukarno will lead an independent Indonesia subject to no country whatsoever."

Within hours my people withdrew their support. I sent in our crack Siliwangi army division. They did the rest. Within days the back of the rebellion was broken. Let nobody say Sukarno flinched in crushing the Communist uprising. Let nobody say Sukarno is Communist. For a long while nobody did. Then, as American authorities subsequently admitted, the Dutch began spreading the virus. When calling me Japanese-influenced didn't work anymore, they called me Moscow-influenced. I scarcely believed, however, this was why Allen Pope bombed my people. I put it to his government straight.

"Pope's papers, found at the scene of the wreck, read he is a licensed plot for the Civil Air Transport, which, therefore, certifies his right to use the facilities at Clark. He refueled his American plane at an American base. He landed and received supplies at Clark Airfield near Manila. Now at what kind of U.S. base could a U.S. plane repeatedly load up with U.S. bombs and take off without anybody knowing it, eh? And what kind of officers would watch such proceedings without reporting to their superiors? The officers must know. The field must know. Consequently, the government must know, right? You can't land, arm, refuel, sleep, get supplies, clearance, weather reports, and the rest without permission. You and your government are playing with fire. Do you realize if one party aids the opposition, another can easily help me? It is so easy, with one blink of an eye, to summon assistance from volunteers of other countries who've already offered. But I don't want that. The outcome could be a third world war."

Let's say I'm 99.9 percent sure Pope was a CIA man. Of course I never had tangible proof. It's idiocy to imagine he'd carry incriminating evidence with him. But how about Powers a few years ago? What could you find on him? No papers. Nothing. Just a small needle with poison. But still the whole world knew the U-2 he was flying was for the CIA. In every new emerging country you'll find piles of America's agents around. We have tons in Djakarta. I know their faces. I know their names.

Current events so far have proved that all the trouble around the globe in places like Vietnam, Korea, and Guatemala was started by America's invisible government. Look how American intervention has improved conditions in Vietnam, for instance!

Pope's wife, a former stewardess with Pan American, asked to see me and I received her. She cried bitterly and begged me to pardon him. When it comes to women I am weak. I cannot stand even a strange woman's tears. Then his mother and sister visited me and those two sobbing was more than I could bear.

By now Pope had been released from the hospital where our doctors had saved him without amputating his leg and he was under house arrest pending removal to a military jail for execution. I sent word to him, "By the grace of the President you are pardoned. But I do so silently. I want no propaganda about it. Now go. Lose yourself in the U.S.A. secretly. Don't show yourself publicly. Don't give out news stories. Don't issue statements. Just go home, hide yourself, get lost, and we'll forget the whole thing." He obeyed. He hid in a small village in America until well after our three-year war was forgotten by everybody but us.

For a struggling nation there is no journey's end. When one confrontation is finished, another pounces upon us. If not confrontation with outside sources or problems of development, it's confrontation within ourselves. A revolution is a long chain linking one overturning to another. Day by day for these 20 years I have swung my sword around me defensively. These are not ordinary times. And I am not an ordinary man. I still lead a revolution even if it be just the Revolution of Rising Demands. This means living by the law of revolution: smash your enemies. Kill or be killed. Jail or be jailed.

I can understand when malcontents try to kill me. I also, therefore, understand I must retaliate and try to get them. A while back Sjahrir hatched a plot to overthrow me and grasp the government. Sjahrir is now in prison. I bear no malice. I am aware this is a two-sided, terrible game in which I'm involved. The game of survival.

When I am confronted with war or a difficult decision, I consult with myself, probing deeply into my soul. If prayer crystallizes the feeling that I must continue with the unpleasantness because at this stage it appears to be the best answer, then I just go ahead and do it the best I can. Suppose you're a criminal. My belief is until such time as prayer or progress convinces you to change your way, at least be a GREAT criminal.

It does not afford me pleasure to sign a death sentence. Nonetheless, a leader must lead regardless of what wrenches at his guts.

Take the man Kartosuwirio. In 1918 Kartosuwirio was a dear friend. We worked side by side with Tjokro for our country. In the '20's in Bandung we lived, ate, and dreamed together. However, as I progressed on nationalistic principles, he worked solely along Islamic principles.

There is always conflict between the force pushing toward progress and the force which retards. Darul Islam, the violent, limitedly religious fanatical right-wing terrorist group which demands an Islamic State, has waged war against me since 1948. In the '50's Kartosuwirio was the firespitter who preached, "Kill Sukarno. He is the obstacle keeping us from a Negara Islam. Sukarno says the Moslem God is not the only God. Sukarno works against us. Sukarno says Indonesia is based on *Pantja Sila,* not Islam. The answer to the problem is KILL SUKARNO!"

On the 30th of November, 1957, he nearly succeeded. I was leaving a fund-raising bazaar at the Tjikini School which was attended by my two eldest children. It had been a gala affair with balloons, confetti, music, songs, an auction, a playlet. Five hundred guests plus faculty, children, and thousands of spectators stood in the rain at 8:55 P.M. as our party came down the narrow little stairs from the second floor where the entertainment had been held.

In my gay mood I playfully touseled the hair of one child who trotted alongside me on my left and hugged another who clung to my right leg. I was covered with children. As we reached the outside, my limousine doors were flung open and, following the then official custom of signaling the President's departure, the Escort Commander called, "*Hormat*—Attention." This was a costly command. During that split second when everything and everybody stopped for a general salute, the first grenade was thrown.

From the left of the building another grenade. From the right another, followed by the beat of a heart. It became chillingly clear what was happening. My reflex action was to protect the babies. I stooped to shelter them when a guard pushed me down hard behind the car. I used that as a shield until a shell, thrown from about five meters off, went clean through the engine, blew out the windshield, ripped the interior apart and exploded two tires. The fourth, hurled from across the street, shattered the other side of the car. Children screamed and stampeded into the building. Guests rolled under cars or into ditches. Scores were hurt. Hundreds were dashed to the ground. I saw the force of the blast flatten one police inspector up against a pole. Blood was everywhere.

After the car was shelled, my aide, Major Sudarto, pulled me by the arm and we scrambled across the street. In the dark and in the panic we couldn't see our way and I fell flat out on the ground. He picked me up and clinging fast to each other we ran into a house. The fifth explosion caught him in the leg and opened the thigh of a second officer who was shielding me with his body.

The house we ran into belonged to a Dutchman. Lest the President of Indonesia meet his maker on Dutch territory, I scurried out and into another shelter. Within minutes nearby police and army garrisons were on the scene. An ambulance followed and an emergency hospital was set up in the school. Forty-eight children were critically wounded. Several were crippled for life. At 10 P.M. a reserve car brought me back to the *istana*. By 11 I was on the radio to calm the people and reassure them I was alive and unharmed. By midnight the religious fanatics who opposed my policy were rounded up. Within 24 hours our Intelligence Service had apprehended all four would-be assassins.

I thought of the innocent victims buried under the ground. I thought of the nine babies and the pregnant woman I saw fall dead at my feet. Because one fanatic wanted to kill me, many were killed. And so I affixed my signature to the order of Kartosuwirio's execution. In 1963 Kartosuwirio was shot before a firing squad. It was not an act of satisfaction. It was an act of justice.

On March 9, 1960, Darul Islam tried again. I was at home and, for some reason, sitting in a chair other than my usual one. A low-flying plane dropped its package of death squarely on the place in which, except for the hand of God, I would have been sitting.

Another time was the Idul Adha holy day. It was 1962. The faithful, including Sukarno, were on the grass in front of *Merdeka* bowed down in humble prayer. Suddenly shots rang out in rapid succession. It was one lone man with bad aim.

The government has demanded his death as due course of law and to show others that such deeds must meet with retribution, but I have not the heart to order him executed. The true murderers are those ultra-intellectual fanatics who plot these deeds. This particular youth was just a tool used by them. I think today he's sorry. If someone tries to harm me for whatever personal reasons, I am soft about forgiveness. It is when they maliciously try to harm the State that I am unforgiving. I cannot actually bring myself to sign this man's death warrant. I don't yet know what I shall do about him.

And what is my crime? Why are they trying to kill Sukarno? They claim I am a bad Moslem. Oddly enough, the motorcar they badly damaged in the Tjikini affair was mine because I'm such a GOOD Moslem. In 1955 I made a Friday pilgrimage to Mecca. To become Hadji on our holiest day makes you Hadji Akbar. Akbar means great. It signifies you have a religious soul seven times deeper than the average human being's. The custom is that the sandals, loincloth, and whatever you see on your week's Hadji in the desert is to be yours. When I left, the King of Arabia said, "President Sukarno, this Chrysler Crown Imperial motorcar has been your possession during your stay. I hereby offer it to you as a present." Naturally I wouldn't offend the custom. Besides, I'd had my eye on it since I arrived. That Chrysler was another of the victims of the Tjikini affair.

There have been two other attempts to assassinate me. Both were in Makassar. A sixth time, while driving in a procession, I spied a strange man looking furtive. As we rode abreast I saw he was about to throw a grenade. He caught my eye and something stopped him. In that pause for just a fraction of a hair's breath, I was out of range. To murder a guarded Head of State takes much nerve. The penalties are horrendous for the assailant; thus it is understandable one might hesitate when the moment arrives. But . . . and here's the big but . . . what, or rather, *who* made him hesitate?

All my life there's been a Supreme Power guarding, guiding, and protecting me. Perhaps some day one of these attempts will be successful and they will succeed in killing Sukarno. If that hour comes it will be because it is right in HIS eyes. I do not fear.

⇜ 31. A Period of Development

IN 1956, during my first trip abroad, I was still a hero to the West. One hundred ten correspondents interviewed me in the United States. They asked, "President Sukarno, what is the purpose of your trip to America?"

"My whole life I have been in love with your country," I answered. "In my mind I have seen all your buildings. I have traveled all your countryside. I know more about your geography than you do. I come here to appreciate you."

And they asked, "What do you consider the biggest difference between our countries?"

"The way politicians are elected to office," I answered. "Your American way of shaking hands with mothers and kissing babies is where we differ sharply. The Sukarno way is to shake hands with the babies and kiss the mothers."

America was kind to me my first trip there. She seemed to like me almost as much as I did her. I particularly liked very much the warm people. I have more friends in America than in any other foreign country. I find only one fault with Americans. They're too full of fear. Afraid of B.O. Afraid of bad breath. They're haunted by the fear they'll never get rid of dandruff. This state of mind I cannot understand.

Also I cannot understand the women. They're so aggressive. The American husband hands over the full pay envelope, does the dishes besides, and still shrinks in fear of his wife. I am not the type to marry such a strong-minded female. This may be fine in business, but not in a bedroom. I don't want a woman to instigate heated discussions with me at night. Give me the simple, unspoiled, open love of a peasant's daughter who pets, comforts, consoles, and massages my legs when I'm tired, and I'm happy. If I sign a decree into law, I want to come home and be praised and agreed with and given the adoration due either Supreme Emperor or tired husband. Who needs a wife to get into bed and tell you what you did wrong that day?

The expression for that is "Being under the *saya*." *Saya* means skirt. The phrase "Under *saya*" has been abbreviated to U.S.A. In our part of the world when a man is asked, "Hey, are you U.S.A.?" it means, "Are you henpecked?"

I liked very much America's department stores. It drove the security men crazy because, sans prearrangement or clearance or anything, I'd suddenly decide, "I'm going for a pair of shoes," and out I'd go. Mrs. Eric Johnson, widow of the motion picture czar, accompanied me to a large shop in California the day I remembered my wife wanted what we call in Dutch a "bustholder." "Let us go to the lingerie counter," I said to Mrs. Johnson. I saw the proper items lying there, but I didn't know the correct English term so I directed the salesgirl, who was very nervous at waiting on me, "Could I please see one of those meat cups in black satin?" Poor Mrs. Johnson! Her face colored. Meat cups, can you imagine?

The salesgirl brought some over but I'd forgotten the proper size. Finally Mrs. Johnson urged gently, "Please, Excellency, make your choice."

I explained my difficulty, then I asked, "Could they bring a whole group of shopgirls over so I can decide what size?"

Poor Mrs. Johnson! I think she feared the worst. However, over paraded the girls and, in my most reserved manner, I scrutinized each carefully, saying, "No, you are too small . . . oh, you are too large . . ." Then I pointed to one lady and declared, "Ah, you're perfect. I'll take a meat cup in your measurement, please."

It fitted my wife perfectly, too.

And I like very much Hollywood. Through my friend, the late Eric Johnson, I met many movie stars. I remember Jayne Mansfield wearing a tight velvet sheath with very, very obviously nothing on underneath. Later her strap broke. I'm told this happens to her frequently.

By far, that was the nicest so-called habit I found in America. American ways of showing hospitality are not particularly satisfying. In North Sumatra our Atjehnese welcome strangers by putting them through a ritual akin to a marriage ceremony. They provide a woman for a man and vice versa. This signifies they accept you into their family as a relative.

This happened to me. But afterwards, even before the guests filed out, security police whisked me outside fast and they removed my bride pretty quick, too. Later I went looking for my "wife," but she was gone. Unfortunately they just marry you there in name only!

In West Irian, a half-naked girl stands before the entrance to the village and visitors are expected to kiss her breast. Symbolically, they are feeding you with mother's milk and offering their purest form of love. A friend who was greeted in this manner joked to me, "Aaaahh, Bapak, now we know why you fought so hard to get back West Irian!"

But how does America welcome a visitor? With a drum majorette! Uggghhh! There is much that country could learn from Indonesia.

During my visit, I tried to explain our nation's political color to John Foster Dulles. "We have no desire to echo the Soviet Union nor to strictly follow the path America has laid out for us. We will never become a satellite of either bloc." But nonalignment can be easily misunderstood by America. America likes you only if you're on the side she selects. If you don't go along with her totally, you're automatically considered to have entered the Soviet bloc.

Mr. Dulles' retort was, "America's policy is global. You must be on one side or the other. Neutralism is immoral."

Later I conferred with President Eisenhower and we had an immediate nonmeeting of the minds. At the White House he could manage only to discuss our mutual love for motion pictures. After many lapses and lulls, his exact conversation went like this:

He: I hear you like movies, President Sukarno. Tell me, how often do you see them?

I: Three times a week in the palace.

He: Can you guess how many times I see them?

I: No. How many times do you see them, President Eisenhower?

He: Every single night. What kind of film is your favorite, President Sukarno?

I: Adventure stories, history, and biographies.

He: Is that so? Well, I like only Westerns. And I bet you'll never guess who my favorite star is.

I: No. Who?

He: Randolph Scott.

In between reels I told him, "Your government's present attitude fails to comprehend the Asian mind. Asia is in a euphoria of independence. The entire continent is in ecstasy about freedom. Please . . .

please . . . tell your America she must understand if all their lives a people have endured pain, curses, and threats for independence, they cannot give it up once they have attained it."

And I told him, "As a wise and older friend, America should counsel us, yes. But meddle in our affairs, no. We saw capitalism and Western democracy in action through the Dutch. We have no wish to maintain that system. Let us grow up with a new method that will fit our individual personality alone. It may not be an export commodity, but then neither are ivy-league doctrines import commodities for us."

From the United States of America, I visited Soviet Russia and the People's Republic of China. Returning home I expounded the Guided Democracy theory I've held since 1928. This had a bad reaction in Washington. To them, coming on the heels of visiting China and Russia, Guided Democracy smelled like another banner for Communism. First of all, Americans seem to consider every freedom movement Communist-inspired. They forget theirs was a freedom movement nearly 200 years ago. So, although they'd been nice to me during my trip, they were waiting . . . waiting for me to make what they considered the wrong move.

They decided Peking and Moscow was the wrong move. They didn't consider this the gentlemanly way to repay their hospitality. The American press immediately turned on me. That's when they began to label the great lover of God a fat Communist.

Indonesian democracy, much misunderstood outside our shores, works on a consensus, not a show of hands. We could no longer afford this Western democracy with its majority voting, where 51 percent wins and 49 percent ends up with a grudge. As we discovered with our 40 political parties, the dissatisfied segment retaliates by sucking the lifeblood of the other. It's a good way for a baby nation to stunt its growth.

To uphold Indonesia's democratic principles upon which our 1945 Constitution is clearly based, I suggested our tribes' indigenous *modus operandi* of *musjawarah* and *mufakat*—deliberations and agreement. For thousands of years village chieftains of our islands have governed by squatting around a council at which each tribesman presents his case by persuasive arguments. Afterwards, one may say, "My friends' reasoning is good, but I still think so and so." Another says, "I don't wholly agree but there's some merit on your side, too." Further *musjawarah* puts a little water in the wine and eventually it's a *mufakat*. Practically speaking, everybody gives a little.

In Guided Democracy the key ingredient is leadership. After hearing the general views and contra views, The Guider summarizes the points into a compromise palatable to each faction. No one side wins totally to the exclusion of the others. Only strong leadership is capable of synthesizing the final decision; otherwise the system will not work.

The Guider, whether he be village chief, Bung Karno, or any minister capable of commanding respect and confidence, incorporates a spoonful of so-and-so's opinions with a dash of such-and-such, always taking care to incorporate a *soupçon* of the opposition. Then he cooks it and serves his final summation with "OK, now my dear brothers, it is like this and I hope you agree. . . ." It's still democratic because everybody has given his comment. To call this Communistic is ridiculous.

In July, 1959, nationwide pressure decreed a return to the 1945 Constitution, which, like the American structure, provided for the Chief Executive to be head of his Cabinet, therefore his own Prime— or first—Minister. Throughout the years no Cabinet had been able to accomplish anything without Sukarno intervening. With every problem the Prime Minister came running to me. We no longer had to please the Dutch and it suddenly seemed pointless to play the figurehead role legally when I assumed the dominant one actually. Shortly thereafter a presidential edict limited the number of political parties to 10. And so, seven years after the army trained its guns on me, their wish for an abolition of the parliamentary system and a return to the 1945 Constitution was granted.

Indonesians breathed a sigh of relief. They had what they wanted: leadership. Westerners shivered in the moonlight. They had what they "feared": Sukarno.

Revolution needs leadership. Without it there is panic and fear. It is because we are still in an economic revolution that I shall not allow destructive criticism of my leadership nor do I permit freedom of the press. We are too young a country to encourage more confusion than we already have. What kind of army permits privates to publicly strip the general of his respect and confidence? And that's not because the general is vain but because such attitudes could undermine the psychological well-being of the entire army and cause doubt, lack of trust.

A foreign journalist asked, "But didn't you criticise the government when you were a young rebel?"

"Yes," I conceded. "I wrote blistering editorials against them. But they were the Dutch. That was not OUR government. However, I am now THEIR government."

"When the last remnant of the Revolution is some day over, will you then permit freedom of the press?" he asked me.

"I'll tolerate it only within certain limits. I think now that I shall never permit that free freedom which gives public prints the liberty to murder their Heads of State for the rest of the world to see. Japan, for instance, has headlined false and vicious things about Crown Princess Michiko which were so harmful they destroyed her self-confidence and faith in herself and she became ill. In a new baby country like ours it could destroy us. I give my newspapers freedom to write whatever they like provided it's not destructive to the safety of the State."

"And if they go too far?"

"I twist their ears. This means, I forbid the guilty papers to print for one week. Sometimes two. Should it occur again, I suspend them for three weeks. The next time I shut their doors indefinitely.

"Look here, at one point in our Malaysia dispute, we agreed to a cease fire. The temper of my people was for crushing Malaysia, but at that moment I'd pinned my hopes on peaceful negotiations. Utilizing all the sway and authority at my command, I laid my popularity on the line. Although the people were hostile to my decision, I ordered it nonetheless. But, while I was trying to effect something, suppose one hater should write against me, cause turmoil and churn public opinion against my project? I can't risk this!

"Two years ago a teacher insulted me publicly in his classroom. He said right out, 'Our Chief Executive is corrupt.' He said, 'Sukarno is stealing money.' Now, why should such smears be permitted? Isn't every citizen guaranteed protection from libel and slander? This kind of nonsense where youngsters are viciously told their President steals from the State is against the law of human dignity. And it is against the law of Indonesian justice which specifically states none may falsely accuse another."

When, without my knowing anything about it, the culprit was sentenced to six months in jail, American tabloids had a field day. Suppose a molder of public opinion in America told an eager, wide-eyed impressionable bunch of youngsters that President Johnson was a thief. Does anybody believe such malicious vilification of the Head of the United States would be tolerated? But because this happened to Sukarno, to the previous shouts of "Communist" and "Fascist" editorial writers added a third epithet. Me, the freedom-loving child of the smiling hills and the open seas, me they now called "dictator."

Western newspapers sneer at the Communist press. "They're forced to lie," sneer the Western papers. Well, what difference whether you're forced to lie or free to lie? Both are equally destructive.

I admit I never said, "Oh, no, I don't want to be President," but neither have I campaigned for the office. Even when I was elected President for life, it was by acclamation. I have a kindergarten which meets in a gazebo in the middle of my garden. There are two shifts of 40 children each, belonging to the servants of the palace. This particular morning in May, 1963, I was listening to the children screaming on my front lawn. It was 10 A.M. The first session had just let out. They were squealing and giggling and in between the duties of State I was enjoying their carefree youth and vitality when my Third Deputy Prime Minister, Chairul Saleh, called on me. Being Sumatran, Chairul came straight to the point. "Bung, there is a grassroots movement afoot to nominate you President for life. This has been growing for some time. I wish to know your opinion."

Despite my ego I became flustered. "The thought humbles me, Chairul," I said after a few moments. "I am very flattered, of course, but I fear it is too much pretension."

"Ninty-nine percent of our people would never want anybody but you for your whole life anyway and everybody knows you'll be re-elected as long as you live, so what difference?"

"To have it that way actually and to have it that way legally is different," I said worriedly. "A hard and fast law constitutionally is a little difficult for people to swallow. Even for me it is difficult. I cannot begin to imagine what the outside world would think. They would probably say I'm not democratic."

Chairul gestured toward the breakfast laid in front of us and laughed. "On this table you have British cigarettes, American marmalade, Arabian honey, Japanese medicine, and Dutch dry rusks. How can they call you not democratic?"

Without help on my part this became a groundswell. Many advisors championed it, pointing out it had nothing to do with personal feelings toward me but, rather, it was the only way to stem the dissident forces within the country. The West Irian confrontation had triggered a youth upsurge against all foreigners on our soil and caused the takeover of properties which required extra skills not yet possessed by us. This in turn set us further back economically.

The ensuing dissension accelerated the activities of the anti-Sukarnoists. Darul Islam unleashed a particularly vicious propaganda campaign against me and where there are ceaseless haters there is danger. The army feared the tensions were tailormade for the Communists. Each faction warred against the others, yet neither separately nor collectively could they produce one leader around whom the majority would rally. My counselors concluded the only way to show the Communists the extreme right wasn't going to take over the country and to show the Islamists that the extreme left wing wasn't going to take over the country and to prove to everybody the army wouldn't take over either was to see that Sukarno, the Human Balance, was sworn in for life.

"This is a political necessity," Chairul explained. "Otherwise we may be torn by civil war. The only way to strengthen against internal opposition and to unite the separatists against external subversion is to ensure for his lifetime the social cement that holds Indonesia together. Patriots worry that without Sukarno we're 10,000 islands again. Even those against your policies acknowledge that Sukarno alone is the saviour of Indonesia."

"I do not think it is a right action," I protested.

"Consider it not as a concession to your vanity, but as a solution to our unity," he argued.

Every year my strength decreases and my responsibilities increase. I have given the first 64 years of my life to my country. As of 1963 I pledged to it whatever I have left. *Inshallah.*

Am I a dictator? No. Five democratic bodies govern with me. The Madjelis Permusjawaratan Rakjat Sementara is like a Congress. It is comprised of all political parties, organizations, regional local bodies, leading figures in military, labor, peasant, and entrepreneur circles. They are not of coffeeshop calibre, but are the best sons and daughters of Indonesia. This consultative assembly which meets every five years to determine broad lines of State policy is higher than the President. The President is called the Mandatory of MPRS. His job is to implement their policies.

Dewan Perwakilan Rakjat or Parliament is the lawmaking body. The President and his Cabinet or Executive Branch are on one side, the DPR or legislative branch on the other. It is no menagerie of yes-men that Sukarno handpicked out of a garbage can either, but representatives of our eight political parties elected by their countrymen plus functional groups of workers, fishermen, farmers, artists, the veterans of 1945, the youth, those proficient in technical projects such as miners, architects, shipbuilders, industrialists, and irrigation experts, and it further includes ministers who have divorced themselves from political parties to be free of pressure or prejudice. Our Constitution calls for DPR, which is always in session, to pass everything before it becomes law. They modify, amend, and *musjawarah* with the Cabinet so that every final decision comes directly from the people, not Sukarno.

Another governing body is my 81-man Supreme Advisory Council. These experts in every department, free of ties, are my brain trust. If someone reports, "We're having a health problem in such-and-such a region," it is their task to straighten it out. The medical field is consulted, the economic field renders its opinion, housing authorities are polled, and when they've crystallized a plan they submit it to me.

Immediately underneath me is the presidium, a triumvirate of the Deputy Prime Ministers Subandrio, Lemeina, and Saleh. They're my assistants. When trouble hits, I first call the presidium for their comments. Then, ours being a great country for speeches, I summon the Supreme Advisory Council and throw it open to debate. "You . . . you . . . you . . . who wants to speak?" I ask. I do not dictate. I listen. I only do not listen if I have already heard it. Then I scold impatiently, "I know that. Tell me something else." The Supreme Advisory Council's final recommendations go to the DPR for ratification.

I shall remain to my dying day a democrat. The servant of my people. The executor of their will. I do not stuff commands down throats. I suggest and watch for reactions. My first mention of Guided Democracy was in 1956. The response was violent. I countered only, quietly, "But you know our brand of democracy isn't working." Still, because of the furor, I withdrew my idea. It was too early. They weren't ready. I brought it up again in 1959. Is that the way of a dictator? I think not. I think it is more the way of a patient man.

A dictator has a party behind him ready to grab the power. Sukarno has not. Sukarno has no one organization backing him. A dictator reigns from the throne. He is not among the people. Sukarno *is* the *people*.

No, my friends, I am no Hitler. If it's true that any leader gifted with the magnetism and authority to move multitudes must be a dictator, then let it be said I am a benevolent one.

To illustrate how I do not use my so-called despotic power, I'd best explain about my second wife, Hartini. In July, 1953, a group of emancipated minds were working to pass a bill on monogamous marriage. These Moslem ladies were trying to help the prophet Mohammed along and change his laws. Smack in the thick of things, their President married a second wife. There was excitement. These women, fearful that the dominant positions in their own households would now be shaky, even marched on the *istana* to protest. Their militant attitude distressed me, especially when the newspapers went to town on me.

If it had been demonstrations against the State I'd have taken action immediately. But, although the situation embarrassed and angered me painfully, it was directed against me personally. For this I take no action. Not only did I never order them to shut up, but I've tried, instead, to refrain from offending them further. For all these years I've gone out of my way to avoid protocol problems. A portion of the ladies refused to accord any but Fatmawati First Lady status. I do not command them to accept what they choose not to. So, to avoid controversy, she reigns in Djakarta and Hartini shares my little pavilion with me in Bogor. Even when I visit abroad, I still exercise prudence. I usually travel alone.

And why did I marry Hartini? A simple reason. The basic one that's gone on since the beginning of time and will long after Bapak is no longer around: I met her. I fell in love with her. And that was that. And it was not more than that.

Being the wife of a President is difficult. I once saw a cable I'd sent my wife. It was meant to be transmitted as a personal communication, but had been sent as an official one. It read: "My thoughts are always with you, my darling, and I send you ten thousand kisses." Instead of being signed "Mas," which means "Gold" and which is what she calls me, the signature on my love letter read "His Excellency, Dr. Ir. Sukarno, President of the Republic of Indonesia."

Fatmawati was bitterly angry about my second marriage. She should not have been so. My first and second wives are devout Moslems well aware of our holy laws. And they understand. Or should, anyway. However, Fatmawati stormed out of the *istana*. That was her individual choice. Not mine. I did not ask her to leave. For nearly a dozen years we have not lived together. She has her own house in a fashionable district in Djakarta. We see one another occasionally, but are today just close family friends—nothing more. Fatma is well taken care of. She wants for nothing. I am still her husband and she is supported by me, not the State.

I did not divorce Fatma because of our five children. To the West a second wife is uncivilized, indecent, and barbaric, but whatever the item that may be lacking in your homelife so you are perhaps drawn to another does not hurt the babies. In our way they still retain both parents. Our families are, therefore, not broken up.

I am keenly aware of my children's problems. When the mother lives away from the father it increases the hardship. Still it's better than if they had no father at all. I am very deeply devoted to my elder children and to my two youngsters by Hartini.

Of my two boys and three girls by Fatmawati, all but Guntur live in *Istana Merdeka* with me. Guntur is not as close as could be. He is a mother's child. I cannot blame him. I was myself. He attends the Bandung Institute, the same as his father did, where he studies electricity and a subject which was also my great love, city planning. I leave his future to destiny with only the passing prayer that he never becomes President. It is too hard a life.

All my children are talented. My second eldest daughter, Rachmawati, and Megawati, whom I call Ega, dance magnificently. Guntur sings and plays instruments well and has his own small band. Weekends he either travels about giving performances or stays with his mother. I cannot go to where his musical group is playing so unless he performs at the *istana* I see him seldom.

The others I see every morning before they go to school and it is my habit to lunch with them and try to help them with their homework at night. If they didn't live with me, I could never see them. I cannot go to little stores with them to buy shoelaces or hair ribbons. It is impossible. I cannot. In Indonesia, I cannot even shop for myself. There is no time. Besides, if I step one foot outside the gates, traffic snarls for miles, thousands rush us. We are not able to walk. That is not good for my children, either.

There is so little opportunity to attend to personal needs that friends shop for me. If someone is going to Tokyo I instruct him to get a dozen of those white cotton singlets I wear under my outerclothes. I never change my selections. I wear the same styles always. Another friend is off to Italy? Good. Don't dare come back without black silk to replace the one threadbare civilian suit I own. My good friends from New York keep me supplied with stretch socks from Saks Fifth Avenue.

I don't have lots of anything, but neither do I need lots. When I find a comfortable sportshirt I wear it for months. Every day it's laundered. Every day I put it on. The same with my one gray pair of slacks which are stained and shapeless. After seeing me in them day after day for six months, someone remarked they looked like they were painted on my legs.

And why do friends dress me and bring me things? Because I am a dictator? No. Because I joke with them. Laugh with them. Care about them. Because I'm just a human being. A Philippine friend visited the *istana* and saw I had the same plumbing fixtures that had been here since Dutch time. He shipped me a marvelous present from Manila. A toilet seat. That was really a fine present.

In 1963 the West Irian crisis added a few more names to those the West was already calling me. The additions were "warmonger" and "expansionist." In the 1949 Round Table Conference one matter remained unfinished. The western half of the huge island of New Guinea, which had formed part of the Netherlands East Indies territory, was not ceded to us. This is a great undeveloped, impenetrable area of towering mountains and vast swamps. The inhabitants are dark-skinned Papuans. Their tools are stone axes, shells, and sticks. Their weapons are bows and arrows. They exist in primitive Stone Age conditions.

Holland contended that ethnically and culturally the people were not Indonesian so there was no reason the land should be transferred from their jurisdiction. We asked, "Why? Are they closer to the pink-cheeked, blond-haired, freckle-faced Dutch?"

Nederlands Nieuw Guinea, or what we call Irian Barat—Barat means West—was valueless to Holland. The inhabitants migrate annually because the soil is poor. Oil profits are negligible compared to the cost of administering the area. Then why did Holland want it? To retain a toehold in Asia. To retain some vestige of her former greatness. It was psychological. Besides, Dutchmen are stubborn.

The outcome in the Round Table Conference was resolved by the well-known compromise. It was to remain in a position of status quo "with the stipulation that within a year from the date of transfer of sovereignty . . . the question of the political status of New Guinea would be determined through negotiations."

Well, we waited. Until perspiration broke out all over our bodies, we waited. Meanwhile, Dutch Armed Forces moved into the territory. Compared to our archipelago, West Irian is the size of a *kelor* leaf, yet West Irian is part of our body. Would anybody allow one of his limbs to be amputated without putting up a fight? Does not a man cry out in pain if even the tiniest finger of his hand is cut off?

As years rolled by, we understandably grew more bitter and less patient. Still we tried to negotiate, as they said. But whenever we depended on diplomacy and the game of words, they deceived and cheated us. At the United Nations we were continuously spat upon. When our sweet humble diplomats made a speech they first changed, retyped, corrected, and reread it for days so as not to hurt the feelings of the imperialists who kept laughing at us as they put us off.

In the General Assembly in 1960, about a dozen years since we were to have negotiated "within one year," Holland's foreign minister bleated, "Holland is willing to decolonize New Guinea, and transfer it to a United Nations Committee. Holland even offers to pay 30 million guilders yearly for this committee to administer Guinea and determine the true feelings of the inhabitants: Do they wish to remain under Holland's tricolor, do they wish to become independent, do they wish to join the Indonesian Republic? We, the Dutch, shan't interfere. We promise."

We were already familiar with Holland's promises. We knew all about that kind of talk. Sukarno, "the warmongering Fascist dictator," had already been exiled, bombed, and torn asunder by their promises. I turned that bid down firmly.

The then American Secretary of State, Herter, visited me when I made my speech at the U.N. He suggested more talks. "Sir," I said, "when we accused Holland of colonizing West Irian, she called us liars in front of the whole General Assembly. Yet yesterday Foreign Minister Luns forwarded the proposal that Holland would, indeed, 'be happy to decolonize West Irian.' First he denies it's colonized, then he shouts they'll decolonize it."

It was back then that I publicly announced the ineffectiveness of the U.N. To my thinking she was a worn-out old lady already who had outlived her usefulness. I addressed Christian Herter, "We instructed the Secretary General to inscribe this issue into the United Nations agenda in 1954. It was discussed. Nothing happened. This was repeated in 1955, 1956, 1957 . . . every year. Please explain to your government we've no intention of conquering part of the world which is not ours. I am no expansionist. But I must now begin a pressure policy. There's no other way to make the Old Established Forces of the world respect Indonesia. No more discussions. From now on we answer with guns."

Severing all negotiations, we placed the military in charge of the situation. Twice a U-2 plane flew over Irian, but my orders were, "Don't shoot it down. Always they sneer Sukarno is a big bluffer. Well, let them see the buildup of arms ringing Irian and the ships in the water ready to attack and the concentration of troops primed to move at my command. Let them report Sukarno doesn't just talk a good game, but that he's set to go to war."

It was like magic. Immediately the Dutch attitude changed. Even the United States of America began smiling our way.

Since we had no diplomatic relations with Holland, America interceded in February, 1962, and set up secret, informal talks in a private house outside Washington. Ambassador Ellsworth Bunker of the U.S. State Department acted as mediator. Dutch insistence on a plebiscite to determine the "self-determination" of the Irians caused a near stalemate. We felt we'd already established this in 1945 for the entire archipelago, so why again for one island?

America was helpful in solving this dispute. Realizing this meant war and fearful she'd have to become involved on the side of the Dutch, America applied pressure to the Netherlands. Holland reluctantly agreed to transfer Irian to us and we agreed to take over their commitments in the territory. In the last deadlock America's mediators managed to push up the transfer from a date two years off to one seven months away and we in turn gave in somewhat on the "self-determination" issue. Although the word "plebiscite" is strictly not mentioned, what we agreed to is that by December, 1969, we, not Holland, would conduct "an assessment of the people's wishes."

And so the first of May, 1963, West Irian was liberated and returned to the fold.

⇜ 32. Sukarno Answers Questions

PERSONALLY as well as politically, I am an enigma to people. Usually presidents sit back and wait to be catered to. Not Sukarno. I'm only happy if those surrounding me are happy. If I hear my aide came in at three the night before, I go over and ask, "Are you all right? Did you have enough sleep?" I also wouldn't mind learning what he did the night before but, really, I just want to start his day pleasantly.

On one plane trip it struck me the air conditioning was too high. I didn't wish to disturb the sleeping steward so I stood on the empty seats myself, dragged blankets off the shelves, and walked down the aisle covering my sleeping passengers. One foreigner nearly died of heart failure when she opened her eyes and found the President of Indonesia tucking her in. "My God," she gasped, staring at me in a state of shock, "I can just see De Gaulle tucking in the reporters!"

"Me, I'm the friendly Bung wherever I am," I grinned, "and that's one of my troubles. If I hug people on the streets or embrace a stewardess after a safe landing, I'm just being myself, but these so-called antics make unpleasant headlines around the world.

"When the Shah of Iran kissed girls in public, very friendly articles accompanied his printed photographs. 'Isn't His Majesty wonderful?' America's magazines purred. 'He kisses the common people.'

"Their attitude is different with Sukarno. When the University of Hawaii beauty queen placed a lei on me and kissed me, I asked, 'What have I to do now?' 'It's proper to kiss her back,' whispered my escort, Admiral Felt. 'You might offend otherwise.' 'I sure don't want to offend,' I said happily, and in a most presidential manner kissed both cheeks daintily as I do my friends. Following my speech she repeated the procedure. This time I did my part without coaching. Flashbulbs popped and so did the caption: 'There goes Sukarno the Connoisseur all over again.'"

There are still other things about me that do not fit with accepted routine, I think. For instance, is there another President who has 700 head of deer roaming untethered on his lawn? Originally, nine males and 48 females came with *Istana Bogor* and for a Moham-medan country that's about the right proportion because even the animals are polygamous. Whereas the Dutch kept the deer for slaughtering, I showed them I loved them. I fed them bananas from my hand and they procreated like they never had for the cold white man. They're part of my family now.

And is there another Chief Executive so poverty-stricken he must borrow from his aides? My salary is $220 a month and often I haven't enough to care for my family's needs. Financially, I haven't progressed much since Bandung!

And I'm certain no other Head of State conducts open house office hours as I do. From seven to nine every morning dozens of in-vited guests drop by informally for coffee. These can be ministers, advisors, high-level dignitaries, maybe the publisher whom I have just ordered to print The Holy Bible in Indonesian; or the sculptor recently commissioned to fashion a monument to our armed forces, the architect who wants approval on the plans for our new sky-scraper, representatives of some tribe who wish to award me an honor, or even my doctor, who, in the middle of everything, feeds his President a spoonful of tonic.

On my porch, unshaven, relaxed and often in pajamas, I make crucial decisions regarding life and death. I appoint ambassadors, pardon criminals, sign a law into effect, examine the latest figures on rice production, hold strategy meetings with my generals on our Malaysian confrontation, and curse those who deserve it. Yelling, incidentally, is good for me. I lose weight. I'm so busy working my mouth that I don't think about eating. Individually and collectively we discuss everything from the tensions in Southeast Asia to the new-est emergency in our country and each gets his turn to whisper his problems into Bapak's ear.

There are many demands on my time. I never talk on the tele-phone since it wearies me to the bone, and because I haven't the heart to refuse requests to see me, I inaugurated this system, which helps many a little instead of disappointing most every day.

It helps me, too, because in between the crises which day after day drain the marrow from my bones, coffeetime enables me to kid a bit. I perform best in front of an audience and often one visitor will share some gossip, or another offer the latest joke. The intoxicating sound of laughter takes a little sting out of making solemn decisions.

My capacity for joy is boundless. I can sing and dance until three A.M. and I can outplay anyone. But with so few opportunities to engage in frivolity, I must bring a little into my office hours or I will suffocate. Like Guided Democracy, this Sukarno method probably wouldn't fit anybody else, but it's custom-made for me.

Journalists, foreign and domestic, are invited to coffeetime. Sandwiched in between State business, I try to answer those questions the world keeps asking about Bapak. I would like now to comment on the subjects most often mentioned and for a change Sukarno will not be able to complain he's misquoted:

Regarding our economic plight, it is true we have difficulties. But it is also true that while in the same stage of growth as America was in 1796, we are compelled to take part in the international activities of the jet age. Although we've no wish to avoid our share of responsibility, sometimes we feel resentment at having to face this world we never made. In the 1900's, Holland had already labeled Java "a chronic distress area" suffering from centuries of "ingrained poverty," and the Minister of Colonies openly announced, "It is easier to demonstrate the presence of this disease than its cure."

It's useless to cite old wrongs that are not our fault, but the results for our present generation cannot be neglected in expounding these problems. Indonesia's riches were stripped for hundreds of years by private enterprise. None of the profits were put back into the soil. Unlike a patriot who loves his hallowed ground, the colonialists didn't nurture the land. They ravaged it. We played no part in this, yet we are the heirs.

Totally inexperienced Indonesia had to start from scratch. We still desperately need technical and managerial knowhow, but this takes generations to develop. Then, too, most of our peasantry lives in Java, the most densely populated area of the world with 70 million crowded into 48 thousand square miles. Lack of adequate farm land makes for poverty and hunger, but the plain fact is the Javanese want to live on Java. Transplanting them will also take time.

We are making strides, but there is no substitute for time. In the battle against hunger, our rice production has increased twice over, yet the government still imports more than a million tons at one million dollars a year. It's just that the population increases faster than the rice. Besides, under the Dutch the peasants only had rice once a day. Now they demand it three times a day. Every step of progress creates more headaches. Formerly our backwoodsmen used candles. Today it's hurricane lamps. This is progress, yes, but now we're behind in production of kerosene to service the hurricane lamps.

True, our exports fall below the level of the Dutch. That's because the Dutch produced ONLY for export. They didn't care about the natives. We, on the other hand, consume our sweet potatoes, soyabeans, and peanuts domestically, leaving little to export.

Since we don't earn adequate national capital, we must borrow. We recently counted 237 offers from countries and private enterprises eager to share in the profits that lie under the ground of Indonesia, but many other newly emerging forces boast "We are prosperous now" only to discover their prosperity hinges on foreign entrepreneurs. Indonesians are understandably touchy in that regard since they've had that stuffed down their throats since the 1500's!

There is still another factor. When a new country is born, and people who never had anything before are placed in positions of plenty, there is mismanagement and corruption even in high circles. I have recently had to threaten economic racketeering with the death penalty. One owner of a rice milling factory skyrocketed prices by hoarding six thousand tons. If he's found guilty I, myself, will sign his execution order.

Many of our enterpreneurs keep something very sweet tucked into foreign banks. I know that. But as long as they work with us, not against us, private ownership will not be abolished as in some Socialist systems. Sukarno happily allows his citizens wealth. Some of my personal friends are Capitalist Socialists. But it must be limited. Those who suck up the blood of our State and are patriots only when their pockets are filled will be shot. Our laws must now be drastic or our economy will never be put in order.

The West is very nice. One can buy sugar, good ties, luxury items like lipsticks and face cream. In the East there are serious shortages. In capitalist countries one can move about freely. In Socialist countries what is known as freedom doesn't exist. Even freedom from hunger doesn't always exist. There is restraint in every area. That isn't because our system is inferior, but because we are still in the process of realizing our dreams.

Suffering is strengthening. I do not wish it to my children, but if everything came easy, they'd think the Bung was Santa Claus. They'd sit back waiting for him to do all. Perhaps if it were in my power to only give joy I would not be a good father. I must feed my people's souls, not only their stomachs. Maybe if I put every cent into rice, I could stem their hunger. But if I have $5, I must put $2.50 into their backbone. The rearing of a nation is complex.

The spirit of a once-depressed person mustn't be neglected. In West Borneo, which we call Kalimantan, rivers are impassable, communications impossible. Most foodstuffs are imported. When I first visited there, you know what they wanted more than anything else? Not technical assistance. Not agricultural development. A faculty of law! And so today Daja Nasional University stands in the heart of the thick jungles of West Kalimantan.

Man does not live by bread alone. Although Djakarta's alleys are muddy and we lack roads, I have erected a brick-and-glass apartment building, a clover-leaf bridge, and our superhighway, the Djakarta Bypass, and I renamed the streets after our heroes: Djalan Diponegoro, Djalan Thamrin, Djalan Tjokroaminoto. I consider money for material symbols well spent. I must make Indonesians proud of themselves. They have cringed too long.

Many chicken-hearted souls with a grocer's mentality count rupiahs and accuse me of being a spendthrift. This is not for my glory, but to get my whole nation respected by the world. My country's spine stiffened when she heard the 1963 Asian Games would be held in her capital. We built a stadium with a circular roof like no other then on earth. Other cities have larger stadiums, but none then had a circular roof. Yes, eradicating hunger is important, but giving downtrodden souls something to be justifiably proud of—that, too, is important.

Indonesia must overcome self-consciousness and inferiority. She needs confidence. That I must give her before I'm taken away. Today Sukarno alone is the cohesive factor in Indonesia. After I'm gone the only cement to hold the islands together will be their national pride.

Another oft-asked question is, "Is Sukarno a Communist?" Sukarno is an individualist. A vain man with a burning ego who admits he loves himself could never be a satellite. Sukarno has never submitted to domination by any power. He could not be a puppet.

Communists want a one-nation world. They abolish nationalism in favor of internationalism. I am a revolutionary nationalist. An ultra-nationalist. A super nationalist. Does it not seem likely Communism and Sukarnoism would have ideological differences?

No good-thinking progressive can be against those Communistic ideals which include help in the social and economic fields. We're all for this. But I can never give up God. I can never renounce nationalism and I don't see how I can get rid of vanity so I can never be a Communist.

Nasakom is the title encompassing the three forces on which our country is balanced: *Nas* meaning the non-Communist Nationalists, A for *Agama* meaning the anti-Communist religionists, and *Kom* meaning the Communist Party. I even start *Nasakom* with *Nas,* not *Kom.* Many Communists whose bones fill the unmarked graves of Digul were great freedom fighters. They remain great patriots today. Always they have been behind Sukarno. Would the West suggest I kill them off while at the same time the fanatical right-wingers are trying to kill me?

When the other factions get off their seats and work hard for social and economic reforms and for what we are trying to protect instead of pulling against one another, nobody will ever overthrow them. Communism can be combated by commonsense instead of hysteria.

To me, both the Declaration of Independence and the Communist Manifesto contain undying truths, but the West doesn't permit a middle road. They manipulate you so you're no longer able to stay independent. To President Roosevelt's four freedoms I add a fifth: The freedom to be free! The West keeps threatening, "Do you want to be dominated by the Communists?" We answer, "No . . . but neither do we want to be dominated by you!" At least Russia and China didn't call us names when we smiled sweetly at America. A nation engaged in surviving must take help from all sides, accept whatever is useful and throw away the rest.

The West can be petty. For instance, take China's extermination of sparrows. Sparrows create famine because they devour the paddy immediately it ripens. Since they will die if they fly over four hours continuously, Mao Tse-tung ordered his six hundred million to sound bamboo bells, shake trees, yell or do anything to alarm their feathered enemies during one specific period from five to nine A.M. By nine-thirty all the birds had collapsed. They were caught, fried, and eaten, and the problem was over.

Not all China's accomplishments bear praise, but is this not an achievement, no matter what side of the political fence you're on? I publicly said so and was immediately branded by the Western press a Communist. I'll praise anything good whether it's from a Communist, a Moslem, or a two-headed Hopi Indian.

But, no matter how things look to the outside world, on the question of whether or not I shall ever become a Communist, the answer is no. N-O.

I am often asked about my alleged anti-Americanism. Over the years I have desperately wanted to be America's friend, but she wouldn't let me. She repeatedly mistakes foreign aid for friendship. America, I needed your acceptance. I was crying for it. And not because I wanted anything from you. Sure, I needed your help. Of course I needed help. I cannot afford to stand alone. I do not want to stand alone. I have repeatedly sought America's understanding, not her dollars, but I shall not, I cannot, I will not beg for it.

Wherever I visit I am surrounded by splendor, acclaimed, deluged with glittering receptions, and showered with praise. Not because it is Sukarno, but because these nations are showing respect for my country. In Sweden they were taking photographs and the King observed I was on his left. "Oh, no, Mr. President," he apologized, "it must be the right side for you." That is the honor due a chief of even a new nation.

In Moscow, 150 musicians playing "*Indonesia Raya*" greeted me at the airport although I arrived in an American plane. It brought tears of pride to my eyes that our land had come to this. Peking welcomes me with tremendous parades and gun salutes. The people with me are proud of me, proud that our downtrodden country has taken its place among the great nations.

And now, people of America, I ask you, why didn't Eisenhower accord me the same respect? Why did your President snub me, deliberately rebuff and insult me? I was invited to Washington in 1960. OK, Eisenhower didn't meet my plane—OK. He didn't greet me at the door of the White House—I guess that's still OK. But when he had me wait outside in the anteroom cooling my heels that is definitely not OK.

I waited and waited. Finally, when it was close to an hour, I spoke sharply to the Chief of Protocol, "Have I to wait any longer? Because if so, I am leaving right now." The man went pale. "Please, I beg of you . . . wait just a minute, Sir," he stammered and raced inside. Out came Eisenhower. He had no excuse. Didn't even bother to offer one when I ultimately was ushered in.

However, when Eisenhower wanted to win over Arabia, he greeted the King with all pomp even though the King wasn't even in America on an official visit, but was just hospitalizing his son. Eisenhower needed the King then. Me he didn't need. He thought he'd teach me a lesson because I was daring to act like an equal with my own thoughts and ideas.

Twice Eisenhower publicly humiliated me. When he was in Manila, practically on my doorstep, he refused to visit Indonesia. Let America never comment that Sukarno only plays host to Communist leaders. Not once has any American Chief of State set foot on our soil though I have repeatedly extended the invitation.

President Kennedy had promised to visit in the spring of 1964. I was so excited that I put a team of architects and engineers onto readying a special guest house for him on the grounds of the palace. I am very sorry that he never came.

President Kennedy understood me. He approached me directly and warmly. One day he took me by the arm and we enjoyed a short, private flight in his helicopter. I was so happy that the President of the United States of America and the President of the Republic of Indonesia were riding around together. Then he asked if I'd be interested in owning a helicopter like his. I still have it. I still have photographs of him and his family in my home.

Here was a man with a progressive mind. When I discussed my aid problems with him, he understood. He agreed. Perhaps if Mr. Kennedy were still here our countries might not have drifted so far apart.

Now about my saying to the United States of America, "Go to hell with your aid"—first let's explain this term "aid." I am very grateful for the six hundred million dollars with which America has helped me. However, American aid to Indonesia is NOT free. It is not a present from a rich father to a poor child. It is a system of borrowing and paying back.

Americans are under the impression they're saying to us, "Here, poor, dear, poverty-stricken brother . . . have some money . . . here, poor, little underdeveloped Indonesia, we are going to give you aid because we love Indonesia." This is hypocrisy. America tolerates underdeveloped Asian countries for two reasons. One, we're a good market. We pay back with interest. And, two, she worries we'll turn Communist. She tries to buy our loyalties. She gives bounty and plenty only because she's afraid. Then, if we don't act the way she wants, she yanks back her credit and warns, "No more unless you behave yourself!" Manuel Quezon of the Philippines once said, "It is better to go to hell without America than to go to heaven with her."

The U.S.A. does not give Indonesia free grant aid. Indeed we want to stand on our own feet and we don't want free grant aid, but for whatever Americans have done we are grateful. They helped eradicate malaria on Java and Bali. They sent young boys and girls from the Peace Corps. They sent the *Hope* ship although their doctors knew little about Indonesian diseases. They've offered technical assistance and small hardware such as jeeps, radios, and police equipment. They've given surplus agricultural produce which they no longer needed. While we were building the Gresik Cement Plant, they trained our personnel so that when the plant opened skilled Indonesians filled each job. We are appreciative of this help.

I am not asking America to give money. Let her remember we have begged all our lives. We can do it no longer. There's assistance other than financial. All I have really wanted from America was friendship. All right, maybe she didn't understand the struggles we were having. Maybe she couldn't see how our revolution paralleled hers. OK, America, don't help me again. Don't try to win my heart. But don't try to break it either. Don't embarrass me around the world. Instead of silently recalling this so-called aid, you did it in headlines. Have I not to save face in my own country? America, couldn't you have done it quietly? Why did your senators do it in open speeches killing me? Don't publicly treat Sukarno like a spoiled child by refusing him any more candy unless he's a good boy because then Sukarno has no choice but to say, "The hell with your aid."

If America could only understand our emotions and insecurities, she would realize a Niagara of dollars would never have won our hearts. If America dictates to me, "Sukarno, we will give you a thousand million dollars provided you say to hell with your foreign policy," then I must say, "To hell first with your dollars." But if America offered a loan on a reasonably low credit plan without strings attached, then, trembling with gratitude, I should have kissed her hand. China and Russia do not even use the erroneous term "aid."

Years ago I asked the U.S.A. for a loan. Not a gift. I felt like a hungry relation whimpering at the door of a rich uncle while negotiations took place over three years. All the time we were in desperate straits. China was offering. Other countries were offering. Still I waited. Still I hoped to spark the friendship from Columbia, that glamorous woman I've courted mentally since childhood. It never came.

Finally, I asked Khrushchev for the one hundred million. It was bitter cold, yet he came out of the Kremlin into the street to embrace me, welcome me with warm words and walk me inside personally There were no long, cold negotiations. His finance men deliberated just long enough to determine our rate of repayment and grace period. Two minutes later everybody said, *"Da,"* and that was it. Nor did they dictate my future behavior before giving me my crust of bread.

For two years I tried to buy a Ford at a discount. I was willing to accept one a year old. It was not forthcoming. Without my asking, Moscow sent me a Russian automobile free. Why shouldn't I be friendly with the Soviet Union? Russia's good to me. I would have to be stupid to look away when she gives me so much.

The Communist Bloc gave Indonesia a monument commemorating her struggles. The so-called free world didn't. Why not? We're a people who thrive on symbols. We'd love it. It would show we really meant something to the West on an emotional level. We're still waiting for any Western country to show some gesture of out-and-out kindness besides the sort only designed to guarantee we'd go their way, not "the other way." Please, Western World, why couldn't you have showed us your sympathies once? Showed you liked us a little? Patted us on the back instead of rapping our knuckles —once?!

I asked the late Eric Johnson, Chairman of the American Motion Pictures Corporation, about a United Artists film called, "Broken Arrow," the story of a great love betwen an Indian squaw and an American officer. "Why has this Indian girl to die in the end? Why can't you make them a happy couple? How do you think we feel at such obvious maneuvers on the screen? Your color barrier, which even in movies shows dark skin as plainly inferior, is a disgust to the Asian!"

Replied Johnson, "The film business is a business to make money. The South would boycott it if the white man and brown girl ended up living happily in society."

Films should be instruments to promote world solidarity, not kill it. Here's an inexpensive way to show us kindness. Never mind the dollars. Just make films showing you like us. Yet even in make-believe situations America tears us apart.

On the personal level, *humanly* I like America and her law-makers. I met the late Speaker Rayburn in his office and liked him. Also Fulbright is good. I would like them to like me, too, but Sukarno the politician is not Sukarno the human being. Once, in Flores, a scorpion crawled on me. I made no attempt to kill it. I prayed instead, "Dear God, let this animal who is the perfect reflection of Your creation not hurt me." But in politics I cannot pray away my enemies. When I know that America and England would like to overthrow me, then I must do what's best for myself and my country. And when Washington wags her purse at me and pouts that I am antagonizing her by being friendly with China, I have no choice but to roar back, "Am I not old enough to pick my own friends without your telling me? China and Indonesia have been friendly neighbors for centuries. Stop trying to run everybody's life!"

America's attitude is always connected with what course she must adopt toward Holland, Britain, or another imperialist power. She's like a tight-rope walker, always balancing. Soon the new countries won't be able to catch even a glimmer of that anticolonialist attitude which once symbolized the Stars and Stripes. The picture has become more and more blurred. Were I in the U.S.A.'s position now I would say, "Look here, world, as children of Washington and Lincoln we cannot support colonialism in any form." Just one brief, soothing statement and we'd be happy. It is America's policies, not ours, that over the years have nudged Indonesia and the rest of the Afro-Asian world in another direction.

Has America ever wondered why all the Afro-Asians are angry with her? Take Zanzibar. The U.S. meddled in its affairs, too, and made a mess. Zanzibar hates the U.S. What right had America to interfere there? It wasn't her territory. Take Cambodia. Sihanouk spits when he mentions America. One hundred thousand Cambodians show up at Sihanouk's speeches so he must have some influence on his people. The U.S.A. just can't discount leaders because they're Asians. And why do you figure this little man no longer trusts America, eh? Couldn't be that his nation felt the lash of CIA intervention and subversion, could it?

Why doesn't Washington stop scolding the world and instead look into her own policies and see why 61 nations consisting of two billion brown, black, and yellow people curse her? The superior white race ought not to discount us anymore. The nonaligned Asian and African states are the coming power. Individually we are not major powers, but united we constitute a powerful force.

The Afro-Asian countries look up to Indonesia. Many have adopted our *Pantja Sila*. They respect our tough stand. We've replaced our jelly-like insides with the spirit of a wounded bull and they see we fear not even a dry sea. When I first talked back to Washington, Zanzibar came to me. Guinea came to me. Their leaders said, "Always we feared we could do nothing without American help, but you have opened our eyes. Our self-confidence has returned. You've made us feel like men again. We, too, shall stand up for our rights."

International relationships are human relationships. I understand that America and Indonesia have become involved in a state of action, reaction, and counteraction and that emotions and tensions have plunged our relations to an all-time low. I must be honest. If there is an out-and-out question as to who began the name-calling between Sukarno and Washington, then I guess I have to admit it was Sukarno. But, look here, Sukarno is a shouter. He is emotional. If he is angry, he shoots thunderbolts. But he thunders only at those he loves. I would adore to make up with the United States of America. I once even made love with a girl who had hurt my feelings. To me there's nothing peculiar in that. And the situations seem identical in my mind.

If not for Sukarno, Indonesia would have broken diplomatic relations and lined up solidly against America long ago. My people partially temper their zeal only because Sukarno receives Americans warmly, because he has close, personal friends who are Americans, and because he still loves to travel to that country.

Oh, America, what is the matter with you? Why couldn't you have been my friend? I would love to have been yours.

Now about Malaysia. Three-quarters of Borneo or Kalimantan is Indonesian territory. The remainder constituted the British crown colonies of Sarawak and Sabah and the Protectorate of Brunei. We'd already heard Britain intended federating these territories with Malaya back in our Singapore smuggling days. I naturally welcome any form of decolonialization and when this new nation on my north border was launched in 1961 I gave it my blessings.

It was assumed the merger would proceed calmly. However, opposition against being pushed into a federation not of their choice became evident when an anti-Malaysia revolt erupted in Brunei in 1962. Indonesia always fights for the right of self-determination of all people and so my guerrillas backed up the rebellion. If Brunei wanted independence, I was determined she should have it. Brunei supported our Revolution with volunteers, supplies, money. Her men fought alongside ours. The Prime Minister of the rebel government, Azahari, was a captain in the Indonesian Army. He enlisted in Jogja. Have I not a moral obligation to him and his countrymen? And to anybody in any fight for independence? I even sent five million dollars to bolster Algeria's freedom struggle and she didn't share any land frontier with me.

In August, 1962, when the Chiefs of State of Malaysia, the Philippines, and Indonesia met in Manila to strengthen existing friendship among the Malay brothers, I agreed to accept Malaysia provided a U.N.-sponsored unbiased determination of the people's will in North Borneo was first undertaken.

From the start of the survey there were daily insults. Agreements were that the Philippines and Indonesia would send observers, but the British colonial government, unconcerned about preserving the good will of her big neighbor, delayed the visas, and the sounding of public opinion began before our observers arrived. Further, the areas were too vast for the limited personnel assigned to the mission, and technical facilities made available by colonial officials—plus their presence on the scene—resulted in unwarranted restrictions to the operation and adversely affected the true expression of the populace.

Meanwhile, a formal treaty drawn between Malaya, Singapore, Sarawak and Sabah—Brunei decided against joining—set the official establishment of the federation at August 31. The time allotted for the poll therefore was so embarrassingly short that U Thant even commented accordingly. To establish Malaysia before the U.N. report was completed would violate international agreement, so a formal announcement in the name of the Queen of England postponed the date of the transfer of sovereignty—but immediately named September 16 as the new one! Setting another arbitrary date two weeks later despite the fact that the poll was not completed showed Britain's utter disregard of the outcome of this puppet survey. Therefore, when the team found opinions FOR Malaysia and against the independence movement which had triggered the whole controversy, it caused storms in Manila and Djakarta.

I was infuriated. The Indonesian government had been tricked and made to look like a dummy. The subsequent demonstrations of enmity happened because of our bitter sense of betrayal. I told Howard Jones, the American Ambassador, "This high-handed announcement, made while the ascertainment of the people's wishes was only in the opening stages, is ludicrous. Britain never even awaited the outcome of the U.N. assessment. I state that under the nose of the

United Nations, internal conditions in Brunei were cleverly juggled by the colonialists who had considerable rubber, oil, and tin fortunes to lose. Indonesia has been duped and humiliated in the eyes of the whole world.

"This affront to my country is a personal hurt. But beyond that, as freedom fighters who continue to sympathize with any struggle for liberty, it is now a matter of principle."

And then I added, "I demand a new survey by the United Nations."

"You can't do that," protested Ambassador Jones. "U Thant undertook this because you requested it. He can't now make another and recertify it just to satisfy you a second time."

"But it is unfair," I stormed. "You know that it's an artificial unity. I will not accept it."

"Mr. President," said Mr. Jones, "refusal to abide by the decision will place you in an intolerable position. People will call you an expansionist all over again."

"I shall not accept it. I shall never accept it!"

We didn't fear the amalgamation of 10 million people, but it became obvious Malaysia was not to be a friendly neighbor. One article in the treaty of formation states the new country "will afford to the United Kingdom the right to continue to maintain military bases and permit that government to make such use of those bases as it may consider necessary . . . for the preservation of peace in Southeast Asia."

Fresh in our minds are those demonstrations of foreign pilots who operated from bases surrounding us—bases like that in Singapore; British territory; territory governed by Tunku Abdul Rahman, an avowed anti-Indonesian who protected, subsidized, and still shelters in Kuala Lumpur many rebels who revolted against me in 1958. Is that not ground for us to be on our guard, particularly when these colonies which ring us have been hastily and hostilely cemented together by steamroller tactics? Particularly when British military installations on that soil make it clear Malaysia isn't truly a sovereign, fully independent Asian nation but, in reality, the result of the brain of the British? Their "gift" of independence was wrapped in a form of new colonialism. Colonialism wasn't retreating in my backyard, just changing shape.

Without mutual understanding among neighbors, a change in

the status quo of a region could result in far-reaching consequences in the security and stability of that region. We cannot be willing spectators to this. Have we not to safeguard our borders?

I raised my voice in retaliation and the British cried, "The whole world knows how bad conditions are in Indonesia. This is only a tactic on Sukarno's part. Sukarno is playing with his personality again. Sukarno only focuses on this to divert the world's attention from the chaos in his nation." It is not true. Everything is not bad in Indonesia, except possibly from the non-Indonesian point of view.

Britain and Australia cursed us viciously. They cut us up every way they could. Their magazines called us a nation going down to rack, ruin, and collapse because of Sukarno's leadership. Have we to love such countries? After years of these tiresome propaganda smears, my people now curse back at England. And I am proud to see them do it. It proves we are not slaves anymore; that we are not subservient; that we are equal and can voice our own feelings in the world of nations. It is Britain's job to get our people NOT angry at her. It is not my business to stop them from disliking her.

Always they blame Sukarno. Sukarno can sway his millions, they say. Yes, if Sukarno personally requests *Sukarelawan-Sukarelawan* it is true these volunteers come running. Twenty-one million rich and poor, men and women, teen-agers and old men subscribed to my call for volunteer warfare in the jungles of Malaysia. No soldiers pulled them from their homes at bayonet points. They poured forth without a whip. You know why? Because Sukarno has his ear to the ground and listens to his people's cry. His talent lies in the fact that he uncannily interprets THEIR will and puts into words THEIR feelings.

I knew America was bound to protect her ancient alliance with Britain and that's why she rushed to the defense of Malaysia. I understood that in turn Britain was sworn to aid America in South Vietnam. I could even try to understand why America didn't see my side in the Malaysia issue. So, OK, don't help Indonesia. But don't hurt her. I can understand America couldn't help me. But let her not help my opponents openly. She pledges in headlines to defend my enemy and also pledges on radio, television, and the front pages of the world's newspapers to slap my wrists because I'm a troublemaker and then she throws up her hands in shock when I react. Hey, Washington, why must you always look down on us? OK, if you don't agree with us, I can't force you. But why couldn't you just shut up? Why couldn't you do whatever you felt right QUIETLY? I would have been happy if America had just said nothing. To me, just not hurting me is helpful.

If they publicly chastised Tunku, too, who was also much to blame, then I couldn't complain. But while they insulted me, they actively petted him. They invited him to Washington and wined and dined him while they shook their fist at Sukarno. The Tunku who announces one day he will talk with Sukarno and the next retracts his promise, the Tunku who deliberately helped the rebels against me, this is the man being helped loudly and vociferously by Johnson and Rusk. These cold war hostilities are dangerous. And where, in turn, Sukarno then accepts China's outstretched hand of friendship, the reactions from America are again loud and vociferous.

I do not wish to continue this confrontation. I realize we're now caught up in a vicious chain reaction and somewhere it must stop. All I want is to see that the liberty of my neighbors has been protected. At the June, 1964, Summit Meeting in Tokyo, I agreed unequivocally to leave Malaysia's fate in the hands of a four-party Afro-Asian Commission. In hopes of a settlement I suggested each Maphilindo partner select one Afro-Asian country and the combined three choose the fourth. "I go on record," I said, "that I not only agree in advance with whatever recommendations are made, but I shall abide fully by the Commission's decision." I went all the way. It still wasn't enough for the British.

As for the United Nations, I elucidated its shortcomings in my address before the General Assembly back in 1960. Number one: Its site is the territory of one of the Cold War protagonists and in this era of psychological warfare it should remove to Geneva, Asia, Africa, or any neutral ground outside the environs of either power bloc.

Two: Drawn when humanity was emerging from the horrors of war, its outmoded charter reflects the political and power constellation of the time of origin, not the realities of today. It is not the same body which was signed into existence on that June day in San Francisco twenty years ago nor is this the same world. Instead of dealing decisively with crises, its inflexibility and slow response to world conditions perverts the original purpose, which is to solve problems. Indonesia presented two burning issues before this body—West Irian and Malaysia. No solution was found in either case. The U.N. has become a mere debating platform.

I've regarded the United Nations with great hope and great fear. Hope because in its infancy it was useful to Indonesia's national struggle; fear because current inadequacies could crumble it, thus removing mankind's vision for a secure, united future.

Formed after World War Two to ensure peaceful coexistence, its basic principle is obsolete. Current global imbalance lies not between the major powers who keep one another checked by equaling each other off, but between developing nations and imperialist nations. As proved with the Southeast Asia and Congo tensions, newly emerging forces concern everybody. Therefore they should rightly be the concern of the U.N. But neither the Charter nor the preamble includes one word about colonialism.

During the 20-year revolution engulfing three-quarters of this planet, the West was spared hot war. Not so the East. After the European armistice, we endured atomic bombs, our own national revolutions, the torments of Vietnam, the bleeding of Korea, the agony of Algeria. And while Asia's wounds remain still unhealed, our African brothers are being tortured. Do you wonder that we demand respite from our pain?

Three: The Security Council reflects the economic, military, and power map of 1945, not the rise of the Socialist countries or the rocketing of Asian and African independence. The Great Powers alone decide the questions of war and peace. They have no right, singly or together, to settle the future of our world by themselves. Once voiceless, we are subjects of barter no more, but living, pulsating nations with a role to play, a contribution to make and the right to be heard.

Instead of preventing war, the Security Council will provoke it. Originally there were only a handful of Asian nations; thus there's no allowance for one of the newly emerging countries to be a permanent member of the Council. This can be revised. There exists procedure for doing so. There is even provision for the Charter to be reviewed after ten years and modernization is a matter of life and death for the United Nations. Nevertheless, since any of the five veto powers— America, England, Russia, France, Taiwan—can frustrate the possibility of change, no move was ever made.

Four: The Secretariat requires revision. The Chiefs of Staff favor America and play the game of power politics. I do not criticise the Secretary General, who does his best under outmoded conditions, but the organization is a product of a Western system which I cannot regard with reverence or affection although I respect it greatly and envy its achievements. Imperialism and colonialism were offspring of this system and, with the majority of the U.N. membership, I fear the consequences of their last stab at survival. Twice within my lifetime the Western system has ripped itself to shreds in bitter conflict and I am determined my nation shall not be the plaything of this small corner of the world.

Five: I find fault with an international body that rejects the earth's largest nation, China, while on the Security Council sits Taiwan, which my country does not recognize. Not because we have good relations with China, but because our position is guided by political realism we supported China's admission. By excluding a nation great and powerful in terms of numbers, culture, strength, economic power and vast attributes of an ancient civilization, a world court shortsightedly weakens its bargaining power.

Six: More equitable distribution among the U.N. Specialized Agencies' personnel. The late head of UNICEF was American. The Special Fund head is American. The United Nations Technical Assistance Board chief is British. There are several Easterners, true, but Westerners predominate. Even in an Asian dispute such as the formation of Malaysia, that abortive U.N.-sponsored plebiscite was headed by an American named Michelmore.

Indonesia had no intentions of leaving the organization, imperfect as it might be. More than one year ago I tried solving the Malaysian issue through United Nations channels until hope evaporated, patience dried up, tolerance reached an end, and we were left no alternative but to stiffen our attitude. Malaysia's admission as a nonpermanent member of the Security Council was further proof that the Council itself had become a tool of the big powers. Fully aware of the turbulence that would result from my decision, I prayed our walkout might be the catalyst to reform and retool the organization.

Malaysia was pushed into the U.N. by deliberate avoidance of any voting on September 17, 1963. Indonesia could have challenged the legality of the nonvoting procedure and also demanded a ballot. She did neither. Wishing to cooperate, Indonesia had no desire to obstruct the U.N., much less to wreck it. Despite our voiced disapproval, we remained patient until Malaysia's election into the Security Council made a mockery of that sacrosanct assemblage. Article 23 says the seating of a nonpermanent member is guided by the importance and contribution of the candidate country in the maintenance of peace and security in the world. What contribution had this controversial year-old state rendered? Rejected by two of the three signatories to the Manila agreement, its very birth caused insecurity in Southeast Asia. How can we entrust the security of our continent to a council which includes a country forcibly created by those colonialist powers from which our continent has just liberated itself?

Accusations that we withdrew in order to be free from reprisals against aggression are untrue. If attacked we will fight back, but Indonesia does not want war. We still welcome a U.N.-sponsored survey in Malaysia provided it's a genuinely democratic mission as originally guaranteed. Nonmembership in the U.N. is not an eternal condition. Someday, when conditions are changed, Indonesia may return. Meanwhile, my country will continue to uphold the lofty principles of international cooperation as enshrined in the United Nations Charter. Honor can be implemented outside as well as inside stone walls.

Perhaps this age does not agree with my decision to leave the United Nations. I pray only that they understand what prompted it.

ᕬ 33. Reflections

IT is 20 years since I moved into the bare bones of a dilapidated palace. There was precious little besides my own creativity to restore it with because we had no material means. Today, with its rolling gardens, majestic statuary, and handsomely appointed rooms, visitors assess Bogor as the most glittering palace in the East. Yet, despite Oriental carpets, French crystals, and priceless *objets d'art,* it is nothing measured by international standards.

It is the same with my beloved country. I have given my utmost but there is still a long way to go. Whether I am able to go that long way, I know not. We have now been two decades in a revolution. Doctors say it takes three to build a new generation. Whether Allah will grant me another 10 years is the secret of the Almighty alone. I am now 64 years of age. I am old. Tired. A thousand old men can but dream; one young man can change the world.

I still spend all my waking hours thinking of the future, but I've reached the age where, just before I drop off to sleep, my mind hearkens back to the past. And I think about our achievements. I lovingly roll my thoughts over such satisfying facts as the life expectancy of the Indonesian. Today it's 55. In Dutch time it was 35. Today we number 5,000 doctors, over 500 pharmacists and 4,000 mother-and-child health centers. Earlier, not one. Today 70 million are malaria-free, whereas once 30 million suffered yearly. We now produce 90 percent of the world's quinine, which is a 20 percent increase over 1950; cement, palm oil, fertilizer, rubber and oil products are also up since independence. Food production has doubled, we've ceased the import of fish, and there's a steady gain in wood and forestry exports. Additionally, our progress in human skill is phenomenal. During colonial times all interisland shipping was Dutch. Now we've developed our own merchant marine. Now, too, all tobacco, tea, and sugar estates plus enterprises such as copra and spices, which formerly were 100 percent Dutch-managed, are operated solely by Indonesians.

In terms of military accomplishments our armed forces are the largest in Southeast Asia. In educational progress we're number one. Take our high schools. In the beginning we had 32. Today we have 2,000. That's 60 times as many. Our program is so advanced that it's followed by other Asian countries. Socially, we've made enormous strides as well. In the emancipation of our Moslem women, we not only boast women ministers but well over 100 female judges. And there's our house-to-house program which has taught millions of ignorant peasants how to build stoves so the smoke drifts outside instead of accumulating indoors and causing eye disorders; how to build toilets so that even the humblest villager might learn about sanitation; and how to build bamboo huts with windows so that light and air and health flood the peasants' lives. And can I not justifiably express pride in the fact that whereas India is now battling over a unitary language and China has not yet a unitary language, my Marhaens, spread over 10,000 islands, all speak *Bahasa Indonesia?*

Yes, we have many achievements. But our greatest achievement is that we have survived!

Elaborate precautions are taken to see that Bapak, too, survives. My people know Allah will call me one day, but they go to great lengths to make certain nobody sends me to Him before He's ready. On my birthday in 1962, Tjakrabirawa was instituted. A special unit of 3,000, drawn from the four armed forces, Tjakrabirawa's job is to safeguard the President. Each man is an accomplished paratrooper. Each was an outstanding guerrilla fighter. Three hundred of my bloodtype act as bodyguards. Another detachment of specialists regulates my likes and dislikes. They know I enjoy entertainment so one special corps sings, dances, and doubles as musicians at every party. They know my habit of touching microphones before I speak so the regiment's electronic detail brings its own equipment. They know my favorite foods so at any outside buffet Tjakrabirawa technicians pretest each dish before it leaves the kitchen.

Although I have no fear for my safety, my people do. When I'm in a parade, my open convertible has a special runningboard so security agents, constantly bobbing forward and back, keep the President protected. When I'm on a State Visit, Tjakrabirawa drops a squad wherever my hotel window opens. Even when I'm in residence, two men are under my feet at all times, one company rings the palace, another stands watch outside the city.

I used to be able to slip out of the palace alone on occasion. Since Tjakrabirawa I no longer can. The morning after the last time

I tried a very polite but firm note was delivered to me. It read: "Dear Bapak. We are responsible for you. Please do not try to sneak away again. (Signed) Your Guards." The only thing Tjakrabirawa can't guard is my health. I have one kidney that's a stone factory and the other my doctors watch minutely as if it were under a microscope. Barring a glass of Arabian honey every day for *kraftwelle*—or strength —and some 10 vitamins which I down at one gulp every morning, I do with as little medication as possible. Week after week my physicians solemnly tell me, "If you just keep calm and don't shout you won't have ulcers." And I get so annoyed that I shout, "How can I keep calm when I get bad news every five minutes?" My remedy is to shriek and scream and get rid of the tension. Maybe somebody else winds up getting the ulcer, but not I.

They also urge a nap mid-day, but my mind is a-whirl. I sometimes relax and read, but I cannot sleep. My room is so full of books on the dresser, chair, floor, even the sink, that in this glorious chamber of this glamorous, high-living potentate, my servants just found *tinggi* bedbugs from all the books. They don't let me keep them on the bed anymore.

For one who is pressured and burdened, I am reasonably healthy and I suppose as happy as can be in an abnormal existence fraught with hourly anxieties. However, I would be even less happy away from my calling. When friends caution me to rest or retire to preserve myself, I say, "Retire? I could not. I could not live out my last years in peace and freed from fear of assassination—no. I must work for my nation with whatever breath I have left."

Besides, where would I go? I have no home of my own. No land. No savings. It has happened more than once that I was without a rupiah left for my household expenses. In one country my Ambassador had to buy pajamas for me. The President's only pair had ripped. The State provides free house, free light, four official limousines and three in a motorpool for State Guests—NOT 15 personal motorcars for me, as one magazine said—and they pay for my uniforms. But I am the only President in the world without a house of his own. Not long back my Marhaens raised funds to build such an edifice and the next day I forbade it. It is against my principles. I don't wish to take from my people. I wish to give to them.

Friends complain that my speeches lately are peppered with references to the time when I shall eventually leave them. Consciously or unconsciously I am readying them and myself for that certain moment when every human being will be called into the presence of the Almighty. I believe strongly in the hereafter. I also believe there are invisible angels near me at all times. The angel at my right does the good deeds. When comes the Day of Reckoning, he'll brag, "Here, Sukarno, are all your good deeds. Look at them." Then the angel on the left will gloat, "Aaaahhh, Pak, but your vices and dread sins you will note make it a much longer list. That being the case I'm afraid we have no choice but to send you to Hell."

This reminds me of a story the Bishop of West Irian told me: One day Sophia Loren, my favorite movie actress, knocked on the Golden Gates and cooed to St. Peter, "I am Sophia Loren, sir. Would you please admit me to Heaven?" Knitting his brows in puzzlement, St. Peter cogitated, "Now just wait a minute while I check the schedule." He scanned the roll, muttering, "Loren . . . Loren . . . S-O-P . . . . No, don't see your name on my records. Sorry, Miss, but you can't come in."

Pouting sadly she pleaded, "Oh, please, dear St. Peter, you must admit me."

Consoled St. Peter, "Well, I'm a fair man. Tell you what I'll do. If you pass the test, we'll take you. Now, over there is a lake with a very narrow bridge spanning it. You go over safely and I guarantee I'll admit you."

Inquired Sophia, "But what is the difficulty about crossing?"

Sighed St. Peter, "Somehow, blackhearted sinners never make it. They always fall into the water."

Off they went to the bridge and, as St. Peter had promised, it was terribly narrow. They had to inch across single file. St. Peter followed behind his visitor. Gorgeous, voluptuous Sophia wore a tight skirt and as she snaked along she wriggled and waggled her sexy backside very appetizingly. St. Peter watched her from the rear and all of a sudden just as Sophia crossed to safety, there was a big splash behind her.

So, if St. Peter was dunked, what would happen to Sukarno? He'd be drowned! I very much fear that if there really is a Doorkeeper in The House of The Lord and he's going to have the say where I go, then . . . alas . . . I shall probably plunge straight to Hell.

I don't dare hope where He will send me. I hope only that when my time comes it will be over quickly. In Flores I watched my mother-in-law linger five days. To be unconscious for so long is not good, I think. It is not a nice death. We have a magic tree in the world of Indonesian mythology. The story goes that whoever stands in the shade of this *Calpataru* will have his wish fulfilled. If this moment an angel deposited me under the *Calpataru* branches and asked, "President Sukarno, please express a wish," I would wish to die quickly and quietly in my bed. When the moment comes for me to go, I wish to merely close my eyes and be gathered into the arms of the Lord.

I've cautioned friends not to bury me à la Gandhi. My good friend, Nehru, enriched Gandhi's tomb with all kinds of decorations. It is too fancy. I'd have fashioned for Gandhi a place with trees, birds, a garden. Back to simplicity, nature, the basic qualities of the man. True, he was a world leader and should be accorded such honors as befit his station, but I can't help thinking he would not have wished it so.

I know I do not. I yearn to rest under a leafy tree, surrounded by beautiful landscape, beside a river with fresh air and a lovely view. I want to lie among rolling hills and serenity. Just the beauty of my beloved country and the simplicity from which I come. And I wish my final home to be the cool, mountainous, fertile Priangan area of Bandung where I first met Farmer Marhaen. It was always my desire to have my casket wrapped with the flag of the Islamic order, Mohammadiyah. Friends complain this will create great difficulties because others will insist on burying me with their special symbols, while others will say why not the flag of the Republic? Oh, it will be very troublesome. I don't wish to unite my brethren in life and divide them in death, so let the flags of all the parties be placed on me.

On one point I remain adamant. I do not wish all my titles on my tombstone so that it reads, "Here lies His Most Exalted Excellency, the Honorable Doctor Ingenieur Hadji Raden Sukarno, the First President of the Republic of Indonesia, Commander-in-Chief of the Armed Forces, Great Leader of the Revolution, Prime Minister, Mandatory of MPRS, Chairman of the Supreme Advisory Council, Peperti Chief War Administrator, Highest Leader of the National Front, Commander of the State Police" and so on. . . . If that happened my spirit would return to walk the earth, for it could surely never rest quietly under all that. Please, no big imposing monument for me.

If I have accomplished something in this world, it is because of my people. Without them I am nothing. When I die, bury Bapak in accordance with the Islam religion, and on a plain little stone write simply: Here lies Bung Karno, the mouthpiece of the Indonesian people.

Glossary

ajat—prayer

Bapak—affectionate term for father

betjak driver—taxi driver

Bhinneka Tunggal Ika—Unity in Diversity

buka—meal breaking the fast of Ramadan

dalang—professional storyteller

djambu—a native tree

Dwi Tunggal—two-in-one

fatma—lotus flower

gado-gado—vegetable salad with a peanut sauce

gamelan—Indonesian native orchestra

gang—alley

golok—cleaver

gotong royong—cooperation; mutual assistance

guling—hugging pillow

Istana Merdeka—Freedom Palace

Kadi—Moslem religious judge

kampong—neighborhood

Kawin Gantung—a "hanging marriage," a marriage not to be consummated until either or both partners are of age

kebaya—low-necked, long-sleeved blouse, commonly worn over a sarong

Kempeitai—Japanese secret police

Kerontjongs—happy songs

ketongan—hollow wood pipe

kiayi—religious leader

klambu—mosquito netting

klavih—a native tree

kopi tubruk—strong black Javanese coffee

kraton—a Sultan's palace

kris—a short ceremonial dagger

Mahaputera—literally, "great son of the Indonesian people"

Mantri guru—outstanding or distinguished teacher

mufakat—an agreement

musjawarah—deliberation

nasi goreng—chicken-fried rice

ontjom—soyabean cake

Oom—uncle (Dutch)

Pak—an affectionate term for father

Pantja Sila—The five principles upon which the Indonesian State is formed

pasar—market place

patih—county chief

pemuda—young man

pepetek—slang expression for peasants

pitji—a black velveteen cap

puluk—eating with one's fingers

raden—lord

rakjat—people

romusha—male laborers

runtjing—a bamboo spear

sahur—the last meal before sundown during the Moslem fasting season

sarekat—union

sate—meat barbecued on a skewer

Saudara-Saudara—"Ladies and Gentlemen," as in beginning a speech

Selametan—a feast

sukarelawan-sukarelawan — volunteers

313

sukun—an avocado-like fruit

talak—a legal term describing a stage in Moslem divorce proceedings

tarum—indigo

tempe—a soft cake of fermented soyabean; also, a weak or cowardly nation

terima kasih—thank you

Tjakrabirawa—the president's personal guard regiment; literally, "powerful weapon"

tjitjuks—lizards

ubi bolet—corn chopped with other vegetables

wati—in possession of

Wayang—shadow play

Index

315